MW01256902

THE PAULINE CHURCH AND THE CORINTHIAN *EKKLĒSIA*

Greco-Roman Associations in Comparative Context

Volume 164

Moving past earlier descriptions of first-century Christ groups that were based on examining the New Testament in isolation from extant sources produced by analogous cult groups throughout Mediterranean antiquity, this book engages with underexplored epigraphic and papyrological records and situates the behaviour of Paul's Corinthian *ekklēsia* within broader patterns of behaviour practised by Greco-Roman associations. Richard Last's comparative analysis generates highly original contributions to our understanding of the social history of the Jesus movement: he shows that the Corinthians were a small group who had no fixed meeting place, who depended on financial contributions from all ten members in order to survive, and who attracted recruits by offering social benefits such as crowns and office-holding that made other ancient cult groups successful. This volume provides a much-needed robust alternative to the traditional portrayal of Pauline Christ groups as ecclesiastically egalitarian, devoid of normative honorific practices, and free for the poor.

RICHARD LAST is a Banting Postdoctoral Fellow in the Department of Humanities at York University. His articles have appeared in journals such as *Harvard Theological Review*, *New Testament Studies*, and the *Journal for the Study of Judaism*.

SOCIETY FOR NEW TESTAMENT STUDIES

MONOGRAPH SERIES

General Editor: Paul Trebilco

164

THE PAULINE CHURCH AND THE CORINTHIAN EKKLESIA

SOCIETY FOR NEW TESTAMENT STUDIES

MONOGRAPH SERIES

Recent titles in the series:

The Pauline Church
and the Corinthian *Ekklēsia*

*Greco-Roman Associations
in Comparative Context*

Volume 164

RICHARD LAST

CAMBRIDGE
UNIVERSITY PRESS

CAMBRIDGE
UNIVERSITY PRESS

32 Avenue of the Americas, New York NY 10013-2473, USA

Cambridge University Press is part of the University of Cambridge.

It furthers the University's mission by disseminating knowledge in the pursuit of education, learning and research at the highest international levels of excellence.

www.cambridge.org
Information on this title: www.cambridge.org/9781107100633

© Richard Last 2016

This publication is in copyright. Subject to statutory exception and to the provisions of relevant collective licensing agreements, no reproduction of any part may take place without the written permission of Cambridge University Press.

First published 2016

A catalogue record for this publication is available from the British Library

ISBN 978-1-107-10063-3 Hardback

Cambridge University Press has no responsibility for the persistence or accuracy of URLs for external or third-party internet websites referred to in this publication, and does not guarantee that any content on such websites is, or will remain, accurate or appropriate.

CONTENTS

vii

Contents

TABLES

PREFACE

Gerd Theissen's and Wayne Meeks's groundbreaking studies on the social world of Pauline groups still provide starting points for social descriptions of the earliest *ekklēsiai's* practices. Both researchers made positive contributions particularly in clarifying the social standing of members in Christ groups and in illuminating Pauline strategies of conflict management. The present volume builds from their work in these areas. Yet Theissen's and Meeks's foundational works paid little attention to the thousands of inscriptions and papyri produced by Greco-Roman associations. As a result, Paul's Corinthian group often came off looking quite distinct from other ancient private cult groups, which is remarkable given how diverse associations were in their behaviours. In more recent publications, both Theissen and Meeks express enthusiasm for new research that situates Christ groups within the context of ancient associative practices, and both have contributed valuable new insights gained from employing this comparative project.

As a private cult group, the Corinthian *ekklēsia* should be studied comparatively with associations, including Judean synagogues (which I call Yahweh groups) and philosophical cults. The outcome of this comparative methodology is rather sweeping: when Paul's information about Corinthian behaviour is interpreted in light of the spectrums of activities practised by other Greco-Roman associations, the Corinthians will emerge as almost unrecognisable to the researcher familiar with traditional portrayals of the group. Yet, I will argue, this book's re-description of the Corinthian *ekklēsia* is more plausible in the context of first-century Roman Corinth.

This monograph is a revised version of my dissertation, written under the supervision of John Kloppenborg at the University of Toronto's Department for the Study of Religion, and defended on September 17, 2013. The Introduction, Chapters 1–2, Conclusion, and Appendix were written when I was an SSHRC and SARC Postdoctoral Fellow at Queen's University in Kingston (2013–2015).

While at the University of Toronto, John Kloppenborg was an ideal scholarly role model who encouraged me to ask new questions about Paul's groups and introduced me to epigraphic, papyrological, and theoretical material that challenged my prior assumptions about the character of the Jesus movement. I am especially thankful that John invited me to be one of his research assistants from September 2012 to April 2013, along with Sarah E. Rollens and Callie Callon. My task as a research assistant was to select some papyri from John's database of Egyptian associations that I would like to translate and possibly contribute to a forthcoming volume. I chose to research papyri that dealt with the spending activity of associations (e.g., club accounts, price declarations, and collections), and it was from this research that Chapters 3 and 4 emerged. Throughout my time at Toronto, John was generous in sharing his vast resources on associations, as well as in advancing copies of his new research to me. John's leadership in research on associations and Christ groups has created exciting new possibilities for understanding the social history of the earliest Christ-believers, and I am fortunate to have studied under his supervision.

Queen's University was an excellent location to complete this monograph as it allowed me to work closely on association sources with Richard Ascough, from whom I learnt much. During my time there, I had begun new projects that took me away from the Corinthians but my discussions with Richard about his exciting new findings on association taxonomy, membership size in Pauline groups, and Christ groups' meeting space kept me returning to and updating this manuscript in order to engage with the research Richard has presented in his recent publications. I am thankful for the hospitality shown to me by Richard and the School of Religion at Queen's.

I would like to express my gratitude to John Marshall for reading and providing feedback on previous versions of these chapters. John challenged me to clarify sections and terms in this book that were formerly obscure, asked difficult and honest questions, and helped me gain a clearer sense of how to frame and connect the research that went into each chapter.

I thank, as well, Andreas Bendlin, who read a previous version of the manuscript and was particularly helpful in conversations and literature recommendations concerning the legal dimensions of ancient clubs and synagogues. I also owe a debt of gratitude to Dennis Smith and Bradley McLean, who offered valuable ideas that helped to strengthen this study.

Many others have read, or heard, earlier versions of chapters, and I have benefitted from their feedback. I extend special thanks to Edward

Adams, William Arnal, John Barclay, Brigidda Bell, Ian Brown, Terence Donaldson, Phil Harland, David Kaden, Markus Öhler, Ryan Olfert, Sarah Rollens, Anders Runesson, and Paul Trebilco. I would like to thank Laura Morris and Alexandra Poreda of Cambridge University Press, and Paul Trebilco, the general editor of SNTSMS, for accepting this book for publication. I am also grateful for the work of Sathishkumar Rajendran, the Senior Project Manager with Integra Software Services, and the copy editors who worked on this volume.

I gratefully acknowledge *New Testament Studies* for its permission to include 'The Election of Officers in the Corinthian Christ-Group'. I am very appreciative of the financial support I received for writing this book from the Social Sciences and Humanities Research Council of Canada, the Government of Ontario, the Senate Advisory Research Committee at Queen's University, the Faculty of Arts and Science at the University of Toronto, the Department for the Study of Religion at the University of Toronto, and the School of Religion at Queen's University.

I thank my family, Rob, Debbie, Jason, Derek, and Wally, for their love and support. I am especially grateful for the love and support of my wife, Vanessa Kehoe-Last, who shares with me a passion for the pursuit of knowledge; and we are both thankful for our daughter, Sophia Last, who mostly lets us sleep at night and always makes us extra happy when we are awake.

ABBREVIATIONS AND TRANSLATIONS

Abbreviations follow *The SBL Handbook of Style* (Peabody, MA: Hendrickson, 1999). Many abbreviated papyrological and epigraphic sources can be found in one of the following three recent collections:

AGRW   Ascough, Richard S., Philip A. Harland, and John S. Kloppenborg. *Associations in the Greco-Roman World. A Sourcebook.* Waco, TX: Baylor University Press, 2012.

GRA I   Kloppenborg, John S., and Richard S. Ascough. *Attica, Central Greece, Macedonia, Thrace.* Volume 1 of *Greco-Roman Associations: Texts, Translations, and Commentary.* BZNW 181. Berlin: Walter de Gruyter, 2011.

GRA II   Philip A. Harland. *North Coast of the Black Sea, Asia Minor.* Volume 2 of *Greco-Roman Associations: Texts, Translations, and Commentary.* BZNT 204. Berlin: Walter de Gruyter, 2014.

The papyri and epigraphy cited in this book that are from outside of those sources that appear in *GRA I*, *GRA II*, and *AGRW* can be located in the following volumes.

AM   *Mitteilungen des Deutschen Archäologischen Instituts.* Athenische Abteilung. Berlin: Deutsches Archäologisches Institut, 1896– .

ASSB   Runesson, Anders, Donald D. Binder, and Birger Olsson. *The Ancient Synagogue from Its Origins to 200 C.E. A Source Book.* AJEC 72. Leiden and Boston: Brill, 2008.

BGU   *Aegyptische Urkunden aus den Königlichen* (later *Staatlichen*) *Museen zu Berlin, Griechische Urkunden.* Berlin: Weidmann, 1895–.

CIG   Boeckh, A., ed. *Corpus inscriptionum graecarum.* 4 vols. Berlin: Georg Reimer, 1828–1877.

CIJ	Frey, J. B., ed. *Corpus inscriptionum iudaicarum: Recueil des inscriptions juives qui vont du IIIe siècle avant J.-C.* 2 vols. Roma: Pontificio istituto di archeologia cristiana, 1936–1952. I. Europe (1936); II. Asia-Africa (1952).
CIL	*Corpus inscriptionum latinarum.* Consilio et Auctoritate Academiae Litterarum Regiae Borussicae editum. Berlin: Georg Reimer, 1863–1974.
CJZ	Lüderitz, Gert, and Joyce Maire Reynolds, eds. *Corpus jüdischer Zeugnisse aus der Cyrenaika.* Wiesbaden: L. Reichert, 1983.
CPJ	Tcherikover, Avigdor, Alexander Fuks, and Menahem Stern, eds. *Corpus papyrorum Judaicarum.*
DFSJ	Lifshitz, B. *Donateurs et fondateurs dans les synagogues juives.* Cahiers de la Revue Biblique 7. Paris, 1967.
GCRE	Oliver, James H. *Greek Constitutions of Early Roman Emperors from Inscriptions and Papyri.* Memoirs of the American Philosophical Society 178. Philadelphia: American Philosophical Society, 1989.
IAlexandriaK	Kayser, François. *Recueil des inscriptions grecques et latines, non funéraires, d'Alexandrie imperial: Ier-IIIe s, apr. J.-C.* Cairo: Institut français d'archéologie orientale du Caire, 1994.
IApamBith	Corsten, Thomas. *Die Inschriften von Apameia (Bithynien) und Pylai.* IGSK 32. Bonn: Rudolf Habelt, 1987.
IAsMinVers	Peek, Werner. *Griechische Versinschriften aus Kleinasien.* Denkschriften der Österreichischen Akademie der Wissenschaften in Wien, Philosophisch-historische Klasse 143. Vienna: Verlag der Österreichischen Akademie der Wissenschaften, 1980.
IChios	McCabe, D., and J. V. Brownson. *Chios Inscriptions. Texts and List.* Princeton: Institute for Advanced Study, 1986.
ICorinth I	Meritt, Benjamin Dean. *Corinth: Results of Excavations. Greek Inscriptions 1896–1927.*

Vol. 8/1. American School of Classical Studies at Athens. Cambridge, MA: Harvard University Press, 1931.

ICorinth III   Kent, John Harvey. *Corinth: Results of Excavations. The Inscriptions 1926–1950.* Vol. 8/3. American School of Classical Studies at Athens. Cambridge, MA: Harvard University Press, 1966.

IDelta   Bernand, A., ed. *Le delta égyptien d'après les texts grecs 1: Les confines libyques.* 3 vols. Mémoires publies par les membres de l'Institut français d'archéologie orientale du Caire 91. Cairo: Institut français d'archéologie orientale, 1970.

IEph   Engelmann, H., H. Wankel, and R. Merkelbach. *Die Inschriften von Ephesos.* IGSK 11–17. Bonn: Rudolf Habelt, 1979–1984.

IErythrai   Engelmann, H., and R. Merkelbach. *Die Inschriften von Erythrai und Klazomenai.* Bonn: R. Habelt, 1972–1974.

IG II^2 Kirchner, Johannes, ed. *Inscriptiones Atticae Euclidis anno anteriores.* 4 vols. Berlin: Walter de Gruyter, 1913–1940.

IG V/1   Kolbe, W., ed. *Inscriptiones Laconiae et Messeniae,* part 1. Berlin: Georg Reimer, 1913.

IG XII/1   Hiller von Gaertringen, Friedrich F., ed. *Inscriptiones Rhodi, Chalces, Carpathi cum Saro, Casi.* Berlin: Georg Reimer, 1895.

IG XII/5   Hiller von Gaertringen, Friedrich F., ed. *Inscriptiones Cycladu.* 2 vols. Berlin: Georg Reimer, 1903–1909. I: *Inscriptiones Cycladum praeter Tenum* (1903); II: *Inscriptiones Teni insulae* (1909).

IG XII/7   Delamarre, J., ed. *Inscriptiones Amorgi et insularum vicinarum.* Berlin: Georg Reimer, 1908.

IGRR   Cagnat, R. L., J. F. Toutain, V. Henry, and G. L. Lafaye, eds. *Inscriptiones graecae ad res romanas pertinentes.* 4 vols. Paris: E. Leroux, 1911–1927. Vol. 1: (nos. 1–1518) ed. R. L. Cagnat, J. F. Toutain, and P. Jouguet (1911); Vol. 2: never published; Vol. 3: R. Cagnat and G. Lafaye (1906); Vol. 4: Asia (nos. 1–1764) ed. G. L. Lafaye (1927).

IGUR	Moretti, Luigi. *Inscriptiones graecae urbis Romae.* 4 vols. in 5 parts. Rome, 1968–1990.
IJO	*Inscriptiones Judaicae Orientis.* Tübingen: Mohr Siebeck, 2004. Vol. I: David Noy, Alexander Panayotov, and Hanswulf Bloedhorn, *Eastern Europe.* TSAJ 101 (2004); Vol. II: Walter Ameling, *Kleinasien.* TSAJ 99 (2004); Vol. III: David Noy and Hanswulf Bloedhorn, *Syria and Cyprus.* TSAJ 102 (2004).
IMagnesia	Kern, Otto. *Die Inschriften von Magnesia am Maeander.* Königliche Museen zu Berlin. Berlin: W. Spemann, 1900.
IMT	Barth, Matthias and Josef Stauber. *Inschriften Mysia und Troas.* Munich: Leopold Wenger-Institut, 1993.
IPerinthos	Sayar, Mustafa Hamdi, ed. *Perinthos-Herakleia (Marmara Ereğlisi) und Umgebung. Geschichte, Testimonien, griechische und lateinische Inschriften.* Österreichische Akademie der Wissenschaften. Philosophisch-historische Klasse. Denkschriften, 269 = Veröffentlichungen der kleinasiatischen Kommission 9. Vienna: Österreichischen Akademie der Wissenschaften, 1998.
IPrusa	Corsten, T., ed. *Die Inschriften von Prusa ad Olympum.* IGSK 39–40. Bonn: Rudolf Habelt, 1991–1993.
JIWE	Noy, David. *Jewish Inscriptions of Western Europe.* Cambridge: Cambridge University Press, 1993–1995. I: *Italy (excluding the City of Rome)* (1993); II: *The City of Rome* (1995).
LSAM	Sokolowski, Franciszek. *Lois sacrées de l'Asie Mineure. Ecole française d'Athènes.* Travaux et mémoires 9. Paris: E. de Boccard, 1955.
LSS	Sokolowski, F. *Lois Sacrées des Cités Grecques.* Paris, E. de Boccard, 1969.
MAMA	Calder, W. M., E. Herzfeld, S. Guyer and C. W. M. Cox, eds. *Monumenta Asiae Minoris antiqua.* 10 vols. American Society for Archaeological Research in Asia Minor. Publications 1–10. London: Manchester University Press, 1928–1993.

NewDocs I–V	Horsley, G. H. R. *New Documents Illustrating Early Christianity*. North Ryde, Australia: Ancient History Documentary Research Centre, Macquarie University, 1981–1989.
NewDocs VI–IX	Llewelyn, S. R. *New Documents Illustrating Early Christianity*. North Ryde, Australia: Ancient History Documentary Research Centre, Macquarie University, 1992–2002.
NGSL	Lupu, Eran. *Greek Sacred Law: A Collection of New Documents (NGSL)*. Religions in the Graeco-Roman World 152. Leiden: Brill, 2005.
O.Edfou	*Tell Edfou*. Cairo: Institut Français d'Archéologie Orientale, 1937–1950.
OGIS	Dittenberger, Wilhelm, ed. *Orientis graeci inscriptiones selectae. Supplementum Sylloge inscriptionum graecarum*. 2 vols. Leipzig: S. Hirzel, 1903–1905. Repr. Hildesheim: G. Olms, 1970.
O.Mich	Amundsen, L., ed. *Greek Ostraca in the University of Michigan Collection*. Ann Arbor: University of Michigan Studies, Humanistic Series 34. 1935.
O.Narm.	Pintaudi, R., and P. J. Sijpesteijn, eds. *Ostraka greci da Narmuthis (OGN I)*. Pisa, 1993.
O.Wilck	Wilcken, U., ed. *Griechische Ostraka aus Aegypten und Nubien*. 2 vols. Leipzig-Berlin, 1899.
P.Ant.	*The Antinoopolis Papyri*. London: Egypt Exploration Society, 1950–.
P.Athen.	Petropoulos, G. A., ed. *Papyri Societatis Archaeologicae Atheniensis*. Athens, 1939.
P.Cair.Zen.	Edgar, C. C., ed. *Zenon Papyri, Catalogue général des antiquités égyptiennes du Musée du Caire*. Cairo, 1925–1940.
P.Coll.Youtie	*Collectanea Papyrologica: Texts Published in Honor of H.C. Youtie*, ed. by numerous contributors under the direction of A. E. Hanson. Bonn, 1976.
P.Corn.	Westermann, W. L., and C. J. Kraemer, Jr., eds. *Greek Papyri in the Library of Cornell University*. New York, 1926.
P.Enteux.	Guéraud, O., ed. ΕΝΤΕΥΞΕΙΣ: *Requêtes et plaintes adressées au Roi d'Égypte au IIIe siècle avant J.-C.* Cairo, 1931–1932.

P.Fay.	Hunt, A. S., and D. G. Hogarth, eds. *Fayum Towns and Their Papyri*. London: Egypt Exploration Society, Graeco-Roman Memoirs 3, 1900.
P.Fouad	*Les Papyrus Fouad I.* ed. A. Bataille, O. Guéraud, P. Jouguet, N. Lewis, H. Marrou, J. Scherer, and W. G. Waddell. Cairo, 1939. (Publ. Soc. Fouad III). Nos. 1–89.
P.Giss.	Eger, O., E. Kornemann, and P. M. Meyer, eds. *Griechische Papyri im Museum des oberhessischen Geschichtsvereins zu Giessen.* Leipzig-Berlin, 1910–1912.
P.Hibeh I	Grenfell, B. P., and A. S. Hunt. *The Hibeh Papyri.* London: Egypt Exploration Society. Graeco-Roman Memoirs 7, 1906.
P.Lille dem.	Sottas, H., ed. *Papyrus démotiques de Lille.* Paris, 1927.
P.Lond.	*Greek Papyri in the British Museum.* London: British Museum, 1893–1974. I: ed. F. G. Kenyon, 1893; II: ed. F. G. Kenyon, 1898; III: ed. F. G. Kenyon and H. I. Bell, 1907; IV: *The Aphrodito Papyri*, ed. H. I. Bell, with appendix of Coptic papyri, ed. W. E. Crum, 1910; V: ed. H. I. Bell, 1917; VI: *Jews and Christians in Egypt; The Jewish Troubles in Alexandria and the Athanasian Controversy*, ed. H. I. Bell, 1924; VII: *The Zenon Archive*, ed. T. C. Skeat, 1974.
P.Lund.	Knudtzon, E. J., ed. *Bakchiastexte und andere Papyri*. 1945–1946.
P.Mich.	*Michigan Papyri*, 1931–.
P.Mil. Vogl. III	*Papiri della Università degli Studi di Milano*. Milan, 1965.
P.Oslo	Eitrem, S., and L. Amundsen, eds. *Papyri Osloenses*, 1925–.
P.Oxy.	Grenfell, B. P., et al. *The Oxyrhynchus Papyri*. 1898–.
P.Ryl.	Johnson, J. M., V. Martin, A. S. Hunt, C. H. Roberts, and E. G. Turner. *Catalogue of the Greek Papyri in the John Rylands Library, Manchester.* Manchester: Manchester University Press, 1911–1952.

PSI III	*Papiri greci e latini.* Pubblicazioni della Società Italiana per la ricerca dei papiri greci e latini in Egitto. Vol. 3 = 1914.
P.Tebt.	Grenfall, B. P., A. S. Hunt, and J. Gilbart Smyly, eds. *Tebtunis Papyri.* Cambridge: Cambridge University Press, 1902–.
RIChrM	Feissel, Denis. *Recueil des inscriptions chrétiennes de Macédoine du IIIe au VIe siècle.* Bulletin de correspondance hellénique. Supplément 8. Paris, 1983.
SB	Preisigke, F., F. Bilabel, et al., eds. *Sammelbuch griechischer Urkunden aus Ägypten.* Strassburg: K. J. Trubner; Wiesbanden: Otto Harrassowitz, 1915–.
SEG	*Supplementum epigraphicum graecum.* Leiden: Brill, 1923–.
Syll³	Dittenberger, Wilhelm. *Sylloge inscriptionum graecarum.* 3rd ed. 4 vols. Leizpig: S. Hirzel, 1915–1924.
UPZ	Wilcken, U., ed. *Urkunden der Ptolemäerzeit (ältere Funde).* 2 vols. Berlin: Leipzig, 1927–1957.

INTRODUCTION

The Corinthian *Ekklēsia* and Greco-Roman Associations

In approximately 42 BCE, eighty-six kilometres west of ancient Corinth, a certain Diodoros founded an association (κοινόν) in Athens that was devoted to Artemis the Saviour (σώτειρα). Diodoros's service as the association's priest in 38/37 BCE, during which time he functioned as a host of the club's common meals, indicates that he continued, here and there, to take on leadership roles in the group that he founded. In honour of Diodoros, the association voted in 36 BCE to give commendatory awards to their founder: yearly crownings, proclamations, and an honorific inscription (*IG* II² 1343.32–40 = *GRA* I 48). The inscription does not state how the honours were funded; however, the presence of common funds (τὰ κοινά, l.18) in this group suggests that the Athenian κοινόν collected subscription dues regularly from all members, and used these to help cover expenses such as honorifics.

The three associative behaviours described here (i.e., selection of officers, commendation of service providers, and collection of subscription dues) were so typical for the thousands of associations throughout the ancient Mediterranean that they now form part of the very definition of an ancient association for Jinyu Liu.[1] Curiously, given the ubiquity of these three practices in ancient associations, there stands an impressive consensus *against* the presence of these organisational features in Paul's Corinthian group.[2]

---

[1] Jinyu Liu, 'Pompeii and *collegia*: A New Appraisal of the Evidence', *AHB* 22 (2008), 53–69 (54).

[2] Three recent articulations of the position will suffice for now. Gerd Theissen, while commenting on the Corinthians' hierarchical organisation, states that 'it is obvious' that the Corinthians did not elect or appoint temporary officers. Eva Ebel, in her analysis of the *ekklēsia*'s usage of money, suggests it is 'unübersehbar' that the Christ group would not have collected subscription fees. And Wayne Meeks contends that the *ekklēsia* was 'quite different' from associations, in that it did not 'reward its patron[s] with encomiastic inscriptions, honorary titles, [and] wreaths'. See Gerd Theissen, 'The Social Structure of

2   *Introduction*

The majority position that 'There [was] no organization ... no hierarchy of ministries, no priestly state ... no firm regulating of the cult, but only the occasional instruction when the "management" threatens to get out of control'[3] affects more than just scholarship on the Corinthians. The Corinthian *ekklēsia* often serves as the model for understanding the organisational and financial structure of first-century *ekklēsiai* more generally.[4] Specifically, the Corinthian group's supposed absence of officers, crowns, and fees is typically taken to mean that these structural features of Greco-Roman associations were comprehensively absent from cult groups who took Christ as their patron hero/deity, at least until later periods when the Jesus movement had become institutionalised and lost its special prior pneumatic substance (variously understood) in the process.[5] This volume highlights evidence from the Corinthian correspondence and wider Mediterranean antiquity that casts doubt on the traditional portrayal of the Corinthian group's organisational structure as underdeveloped in comparison with other associations. In doing so, this book provides the framework for a new social history of the Corinthian group's formative years, and it lays the groundwork for alternative ways to understand the founding and growth of Christ groups more generally in pre-Constantine periods.

Pauline Communities: Some Critical Remarks on J. J. Meggitt, *Paul, Poverty and Survival*', *JSNT* 84 (2001), 65–84 (78); Eva Ebel, *Die Attraktivität früher christlicher Gemeinden: Die Gemeinde von Korinth im Spiegel grichisch-römischer Vereine* (WUNT II/178; Tübingen: J. C. B. Mohr Siebeck, 2004), 217; and Wayne A. Meeks, *The First Urban Christians: The Social World of the Apostle Paul*, 2nd ed. (New Haven: Yale University Press, 2003 [1983]), 78.

[3] Hans Conzelmann, *An Outline of the Theology of the New Testament*, 2nd ed. (New York: Harper & Row, 1969), 267–8.

[4] Richard S. Ascough recently commented on the 'assumption, explicit or implicit, that Corinth is the paradigm for other Pauline communities'. See Richard Ascough, 'Of Memories and Meals: Greco-Roman Associations and the Early Jesus-Group at Thessalonikē', in *From Roman to Early Christian Thessalonikē. Studies in Religion and Archaeology*, ed. Laura Nasrallah, Charalambos Bakirtzis, and Steven J. Friesen (HTS 64; Cambridge, MA: Harvard University Press, 2010), 49–72 (58).

[5] This narrative is so pervasive in scholarship that it has been the subject of critical reflection in two paramount methodological studies. See Jonathan Z. Smith, *Drudgery Divine: On the Comparison of Early Christianities and the Religions of Late Antiquity* (Jordan Lectures in Comparative Religion 14; London: The School of Oriental and African Studies; Chicago: University of Chicago Press, 1990), 19–25, 34, 45, 143; and John S. Kloppenborg, 'Egalitarianism in the Myth and Rhetoric of Pauline Churches', in *Reimagining Christian Origins: A Colloquium Honouring Burton L. Mack*, ed. Elizabeth A. Castelli and Hal Taussig (Valley Forge, PA: Trinity Press International, 1996), 247–63.

What difference will the placement of fees, officers, and crowns in Paul's Corinthian group make for our understanding of the social history of the Jesus movement? Let us first consider subscription dues and look at how the Corinthian group's collection of them changes our image of Pauline *ekklēsiai*. By requiring payment of membership fees at each banquet from each participant, as this book suggests the Corinthians did, the *ekklēsia* would have shut its doors to the poorest small artisans and merchants in the city who lived dangerously close to, or below, the level of subsistence – and the scores of others who could not have afforded the luxury of membership in a Christ group. This scenario is incompatible with aspects of the charitable ethic that supposedly shaped the ethos of Pauline groups.[6] No longer can it be assumed that the Corinthians handed out free meals to their destitute recruits out of 'brotherly love', or that they were interested enough in 'desiring the well-being of the other' (1 Cor 10:24) to count the destitute among their ranks.[7]

On a related point, if the Corinthians collected subscription dues, this would raise new questions about the economic status of the group's members – and it would caution, particularly, against the notion that there was a 'nearly complete absence of wealth' among Pauline Christ believers.[8] Unless Paul's groups offered free membership, the economic

[6] Gerd Theissen understands Pauline groups' brand of care for the poor as distinctive, and calls it 'love patriarchalism', while Justin Meggitt labels it with the phrase, 'economic mutualism'. See Gerd Theissen, *The Social Setting of Pauline Christianity* (Philadelphia: Fortress, 1982), 107; and Justin J. Meggitt, *Paul, Poverty and Survival* (Edinburgh: T&T Clark, 1998), 155–64. The Thessalonian group in particular has been described as 'remarkable for its love' in Abraham J. Malherbe, *The Letters to the Thessalonians* (New York, Doubleday, 2000), 256; cf. Bruce Longenecker, *Remember the Poor: Paul, Poverty, and the Greco-Roman World* (Grand Rapids, MI and Cambridge: Eerdmans, 2010), 148–9.

[7] Recently, Bruce Longenecker proposed that Paul's care for the poor 'must have been shared by the communities he had founded and that their practices were not (usually) negligible in that regard' (*Remember the Poor*, 156). Longenecker is unable to find any evidence from the Corinthian correspondence to support this claim. For the secondary literature that supposes charitable practices among *ekklēsiai*, see Longenecker, *Remember the Poor*, 140–55; and Judith Lieu, 'Charity in Early Christian Thought and Practice', in *The Kindness of Strangers: Charity in the Pre-Modern Mediterranean*, ed. Dionysios Stathakopoulos (CHS Occasional Publications; London: King's College London, 2007), 13–20.

[8] The quote is from Steven J. Friesen, 'The Wrong Erastus: Ideology, Archaeology, and Exegesis', in *Corinth in Context: Comparative Studies on Religion and Society*, ed. Steven J. Friesen, Daniel N. Schowalter, and James C. Walters (Leiden and Boston: Brill, 2010), 231–56 (256); cf. Steven J. Friesen, 'Poverty in Pauline Studies: Beyond the So-called New Consensus', *JSNT* 26 (2004): 323–61; and Meggitt, *Paul* (throughout).

profile of Pauline Christ believers needs to be situated within the range
of economic levels held by members of other associations, individuals
who were typically expected to provide subscription dues regularly to
their club. In these ways and others, this volume's new position concerning the requirement of fee payment in the Corinthian *ekklēsia* requires
an alternative to older models of finances and morality in the Corinthian
ekklēsia.
    The implications of this book's description of leadership in the
Corinthian *ekklēsia* also reach beyond the Corinthians themselves.
The evidence from Paul suggests that Corinth's Christ group selected
administrative officials and rewarded magistrates with typical forms of
symbolic capital (e.g., proclamations, crowns, honorific inscriptions, and
exemptions from liturgies and fees). The presence of these structures in
the 50s CE is incompatible with the more pervasive narrative that early
Christ groups evolved slowly from charismatic and pneumatic organisation in the first-century to structurally organised churches under the
authority of regional bishops and various subservient clerics in the fourth
century.[9] That old framework fails to account for crucial details in the
Corinthian correspondence relating to organisational structure in the
early Corinthian *ekklēsia*; in fact, its assumptions about the organisational structure of first-century Christ groups are disturbingly identical
with Paul's own ideals (1 Cor 12) and, overall, are inattentive to problems on the ground level that would be created by 1 Cor 12 if an
association were to put it to action. Since institutional features such as
officers, formal commendation, and collections can be demonstrated in
the Corinthian group in the 50s CE, the present model for understanding
the evolution of institutional forms in Christ groups during the first four
centuries requires nuancing and revision.
    While these broader implications are addressed here and there, the
book focuses primarily on the narrower outcomes of a Corinthian group
re-described with officers, crowns, and fees – namely, the book under-
scores how this new description of the Corinthians' financial and leadership practices changes the social setting of the *ekklēsia*. In this respect,
I make two contributions. First, the Corinthians are stripped of their

---

[9] The modern narrative of Christ groups beginning in a charismatic mode of leadership
is rooted in late nineteenth-century and early twentieth-century works, such as
Adolf Harnack, *The Mission and Expansion of Christianity*, 2 vols. (Theological
Translation Library 19. Rev. and enl. ed.; New York: Putnam's Sons, 1908), 202–15.
James Tunstead Burtchaell traces it as far back as the fourteenth century in his *From
Synagogue to Church: Public Services and Offices in the Earliest Christian Communities*
(Cambridge and New York: Cambridge University Press, 1992), 1–190.

special financial status: the prevalent notion that they could survive even if 90 per cent of members failed to pay for food, wine, and a host of other expenditures is untenable.[10] As a new group devoted to a Galilean hero otherwise unknown in Corinth, the Christ group would have struggled to compete with local associations for recruits and benefactions. Income needed to be collected from all of the few recruits they managed to secure in order to avoid debt and promises of formal commendation for service providers needed to be issued and even advertised to the public in order to keep up with the θιασῶται, so to speak. Second, the so-called weak (ἀσθενεῖς; e.g., 1 Cor 8:8–12) will be strengthened. Since the 1970s, it has been commonplace to imagine factions, hostilities, theologies, and leadership in the Corinthian *ekklēsia* according to the hypothesis that the group was divided between fixed economically strong and economically weak factions. But social–hierarchical rankings in the group would have been more fluid than this, and would have been constantly subject to change based on individual efforts of zeal. All members would have had opportunities to generate status, show generosity, hold offices, and enhance their honour in the *ekklēsia* by showing more zeal for their Christ group than what other members provided recently. The modest symbolic capital they earned from the *ekklēsia* would eventually be superseded by the outcomes of more recent competitions for honour, though, and so the current placement of any member in the group's social hierarchy was fragile. Evidence in support of these two contributions comes from both association inscriptions and papyri, as well as from Paul's description of Corinthian behaviour and *ekklēsia* practices.

A Pneumatic Consensus

The contemporary conviction that the Corinthians lacked organisational features that were ubiquitous in Greco-Roman associations (i.e., officers, membership fees, and crowns) is indebted to a long trajectory of principally Protestant scholarship, tracing back to the fourteenth century according to James Burtchaell.[11] Rudolf Sohm's and Adolf Harnack's important contributions from the late nineteenth century and early twentieth century have particularly shaped the current discussion. Sohm and Harnack described ancient Christ groups as endowed with a special

[10] Peter Lampe, 'Das korinthinische Herrenmahl im Schnittpunkt hellenistisch-römischer Mahlpraxis und paulinischer Theologia Crucis (1 Kor 11, 17–34)', *ZNW* 82 (1991), 183–212 (191–3); and Theissen, *Social Setting*, 148–56.

[11] Burtchaell, *From Synagogue*, 1–190.

religious character (the divine pneuma) that made them 'better'[12] than the 'second-class religion' and 'rudimentary' cults known to Greeks and Romans.[13] In Harnack's words,

> Other religions and cults could doubtless point to some of these actions of the Spirit [so common in the churches], such as ecstasy, vision, demonic and anti-demonic manifestations, but nowhere do we find such a wealth of these phenomena presented to us as in Christianity.[14]

For Harnack and Sohm, the religious superiority of early Christianity generated Christ groups that lacked ecclesiastical organisation (especially in the Corinthian *ekklēsia*). The divine pneuma, it was supposed, empowered all Christ adherents to contribute to the good of their *ekklēsia* according to their God-given gifts (χαρίσματα), such as wisdom, prophetic abilities, and miracle-working (1 Cor 12:8–10). Since the pneuma was available to all, the result was status equity, where no member was ranked higher than any other. Rudolf Sohm described this leadership model in early Christ groups as follows:

> The Church has no absolute need of any class of officials. They are all born ministers of the Word and ministers they ought to be. They all, by the Holy Spirit living within them, are bearers of the keys of heaven, and of the royal power which in the House of God is given to the Word of God.[15]

The possession of divine pneuma by all members of the Corinthian Christ group (1 Cor 12:1–31), and the resultant needlessness to select guild officers in this group, was reiterated by Adolf Harnack. Harnack received positively Edwin Hatch's groundbreaking work on economic and administrative structure in early Christ groups,[16] but he believed that the first-century Corinthian group, unlike the Macedonian *ekklēsiai* that were equipped with financial administrators, had 'no organization

---

[12] Rudolf Sohm, *Outlines of Church History* (London and New York: MacMillan and Co., 1895), 11.

[13] Harnack, *Mission and Expansion*, 291, 432; cf. Sohm, *Outlines*, 31–40.

[14] Harnack, *Mission and Expansion*, 202.

[15] Sohm, *Outlines*, 34.

[16] Edwin Hatch, *The Organization of the Early Christian Churches: Eight Lectures Delivered before the University of Oxford in the Year 1880 on the Foundation of the Late John Bampton* (London: Rivingtons, 1881).

whatsoever ... for a decade, or even longer. The brethren submitted to a control of "the Spirit".[17] What emerges from Sohm and Harnack is a model where 'guild-life may have paved the way' for social formations in the Jesus movement, but remained 'rudimentary' and lacked the 'spiritual benefits' of Christ groups.[18]

Sohm's and Harnack's description of the Corinthians' pneumatic organisation was rooted in a peculiar reading of 1 Cor 12–14, a sequence of chapters that, ironically, illuminates little about *ekklēsia* leadership other than Paul's ecclesiastic idealisations that revolve around his supposition that the Corinthians enjoyed the presence of the divine pneuma. In other words, 1 Cor 12–14 primarily tells us about the Pauline Church – a fictive, apologetic, construction that is present nowhere in antiquity outside of Paul's own mind. Paul's prescriptions in 1 Cor 12–14 bear no resemblance to any social practice in this *ekklēsia*. As this book shows, Pauline description of actual Corinthian activities can be located mostly outside of these chapters.

The legacy of Sohm and Harnack on scholarship until the sociological turn in the 1960s and 1970s need not be reviewed in full here[19] – it is enough to say that it was pervasive. For example, Eduard Schweizer's position on the group's polity is very similar to what Sohm and Harnack already established. For Schweizer, there existed 'no fundamental organization of superior or subordinate ranks, because the gift of the Spirit is adapted to every Church member ... the enumerations of the different kinds of gifts are quite unsystematic, with no sort of hierarchical character'.[20] Even well into the 1960s, Hans von Campenhausen imagined the impact of pneumatism on early Christ group organisational structure as equally idyllic: 'love [was] the true organising and unifying force within the Church, and [it] creates ... a paradoxical form of order diametrically opposed to all natural systems of organization'.[21]

---

[17] This quotation is from a later printing of Harnack's, *The Expansion of Christianity in the First Three Centuries* (2 vols.; Eugene, OR: Wipf and Stock, 1998), 1.51 n.1.

[18] Harnack, *Mission and Expansion*, 1.432–3; cf. Sohm, *Outlines*, 4–5.

[19] For reviews, see Burtchaell, *Synagogue to Church*, 1–190; Kloppenborg, 'Egalitarianism', 247–63; and John S. Kloppenborg, 'Pneumatic Democracy and the Conflict in *1 Clement*', in *Early Christian Communities Between Ideal and Reality*, ed. Mark Grundeken and Joseph Verheyden (WUNT I/342; Tübingen: Mohr Siebeck, 2015), 61–81.

[20] Schweizer, *Church Order*, 99–100.

[21] Hans von Campenhausen, *Ecclesiastical Authority and Spiritual Power in the Church of the First Three Centuries* (London: Adam and Charles Black, 1969), 46.

The Pneumatic Consensus in Current Scholarship
on the Corinthians

The misrecognition of Pauline idealisation for Corinthian social reality in some recent scholarship is fostered by Paul's rhetorical strategy for creating 'alternative communities'.[22] As Stanley Stowers observes,

> Paul did not merely try to persuade those whom he wanted as followers that they ought to become a very special kind of community. He told them that they had in their essence already become such a community. This was a brilliant strategy. Instead of putting an impossible ideal before them and saying, 'try to reach this goal', he said 'you are this community of transformed people so live up to what you are.'[23]

Recent social historians of the Jesus movement, including Stowers, have detected vestiges of Harnack's and Sohm's model of Corinthian organisation in contemporary scholarship. It was the observation of this that led Stowers to label some contemporary traditional scholarship on the Corinthians as 'academic Christian theological modernism'.[24] Stowers's critique builds from the works of Burton Mack and Jonathan Z. Smith

---

[22] Richard Horsley famously used this descriptor for Paul's vision of the *ekklēsiai* in his '1 Corinthians: A Case Study of Paul's Assembly as an Alternative Society', in *Paul and Empire. Religion and Power in Roman Imperial Society*, ed. Richard Horsley (Harrisburg, PA: Trinity Press International, 1997), 242–52. Horsley also imagines the groups themselves as alternative communities: 'Nor ... were Paul's communities modeled on the associations or guilds ... Paul's communities were both far more comprehensive (even totalistic) in their common purpose, exclusive over against dominant society, and parts of an intercity, international movement ... Paul's *ekklēsiai* are ... local communities of an alternative society to the Roman imperial order ... It has often been observed that Paul's communities were exclusive, separated from "the world." More than that, however, Paul's alternative society stood sharply against the Roman imperial order' (Richard Horsley, 'Building an Alternative Society: Introduction', in *Paul and Empire*, 206–14 [208–10]).

[23] Stanley K. Stowers, 'The Concept of "Community" in the History of Early Christianity', *MTSR* 23 (2011), 238–56 (242).

[24] Stanley Stowers, 'Kinds of Myth, Meals, and Power: Paul and the Corinthians', in *Redescribing Paul and the Corinthians* (Early Christianity and Its Literature 5; Atlanta: Society of Biblical Literature, 2011), 105–49 (106–9). Examples of this tradition, according to Stowers, include 'the scholarship documented by Werner Georg Kümmel in *The New Testament: The History of the Investigation of Its Problems*, trans. S. Michael Gilmour and Howard C. Kee (Nashville: Abingdon, 1972)'. As well, Stowers continues, 'A very important spinoff from this tradition, but remaining within it, in my view, is the movement to do social history and work inspired by the social sciences pioneered by such figures as John Gager, Wayne A. Meeks, Gerd Theissen, and Bruce Malina.' See 'Kinds of Myth', 106 n.7 and 107 n.8.

from the 1990s. Particularly relevant for this volume is Mack's observation that much scholarship tends to assume that the Corinthians were destined to succeed – and it overlooks how real the possibility was for an early Christ group to disband in the face of economic and recruitment challenges.[25] An equally crucial insight by Stowers is that many post-1970 descriptions of the earliest Christ groups include statements concerning their moral superiority to Greek and Latin associations, which we have seen to be central already in Sohm's and Harnack's programme.[26]

For present purposes, the most significant agreement between Sohm/Harnack and most contemporary scholarship is the supposed impact of a pneumatic presence on the ecclesiastic structure of the Corinthian *ekklēsia*. It will be recalled that pneumatic presence was the basis for Sohm's and Harnack's argument concerning the lack of organisational sophistication in the Corinthian group. While this notion continues to shape contemporary sociological analysis of organisational structure in Pauline groups, one difference is that modern social historians now describe the pneuma as a construct of *ekklēsia* members rather than an objective presence of divinity in the *ekklēsia*,[27] but little else has changed: 1 Cor 12–14 continues to be wheeled out in defence of Corinthian organisational uniqueness, the divine pneuma still equalises members socially and ecclesiastically, and pneuma still directs the Christ group away from economic and hierarchical practices generalised in the associations and necessary for their survival.

The now classic articulation of Sohm's and Harnack's position from a sociological perspective is Wayne Meeks's 1983 monograph, *The First*

---

[25] Burton L. Mack observes that in previous scholarship the successes of Christ groups have been imagined as 'the overwhelming activity of a god' in his 'On Redescribing Christian origins', *MTSR* 8 (1996), 247–69 (254). While there is no direct evidence of this position in the sociological contributions to the study of the Corinthians by Meeks or Theissen (comparable to, say, Sohm, *Outlines*, 6: 'By virtue of the spirit which is alive within her, the Christian Church in its slow upward growth had power to outlast the great Roman Empire, to join the ancient to the modern world, and to be the educator of the race of men that was to come'), there are hints in post-1970 research in general. Most obvious is the entirely undocumented thesis that the Corinthian group – a still new cult at the time of the Corinthian correspondence – had large membership numbers, somewhere between 40 and 100 (see Chapter 2 for bibliography and an alternative proposal).
[26] Stowers, 'Kinds of Myths', 107–9.
[27] Meeks (*First Urban*, 120) speaks of the 'general framework of interpretation' held by the Corinthians. An example of this is the notion that 'God's spirit ... is at work in glossolalia'.

Urban Christians. In terms of methodology, Meeks – like Sohm and Harnack – finds association data ultimately of little value for understanding the ethos of the Corinthians.[28] He evaluates 1 Cor 12–14, wherein Paul instructs the Corinthians to organise their group pneumatically, to be crucial for understanding the structure of the *ekklēsia*. For Meeks, it is texts such as 1 Cor 12–14 that were causative factors in the creation of 'a unique culture' among Pauline groups.[29] The following quote is illustrative:

> Paul and the other founders and leaders of those [Christ] groups engaged aggressively in the business of creating a new social reality. They held and elaborated a distinctive set of beliefs . . . They developed norms and patterns of moral admonition and social control that, however many commonplaces from the moral discourse of the larger culture they might contain, still in ensemble constituted a distinctive ethos. They received, practiced, and explicated distinctive ritual actions. None of these was made *ex nihilo* . . . *The resultant, nevertheless, was an evolving definition of a new, visibly different subculture.*[30]

Meeks's notion that the Corinthians' 'visibly different subculture' was distinct from, yet to a lesser extent similar to, the ethos of associations is continuous with Harnack's perspective that 'guild-life may have paved the way' for Christ groups; however, ultimately, the Christ groups were 'novel and unheard-of' social formations;[31] and it is also consistent with Sohm's notion that 'Seen from the outside, the Christian community seemed to be only one more newly formed club' but that ultimately was distinct 'By virtue of the spirit'.[32] In other words, there were some similarities between Christ groups and associations, but these were two distinct categories of social formation due to the presence of the pneuma within *ekklēsiai*.

In terms of the Corinthians' organisational structure, for Meeks it is still 'The Spirit [which] counted as authority par excellence in the

---

[28] See Meeks, *First Urban*, 75–84. See now Meeks's revised assessment of the association model: Wayne A. Meeks, 'Taking Stock and Moving On', in *After the First Urban Christians. The Social-Scientific Study of Pauline Christianity Twenty-Five Years Later*, ed. Todd D. Still and David G. Horrell (London: T&T Clark, 2009), 134–46, (140–1).

[29] For this phrase, see Meeks, *First Urban*, 85.

[30] Meeks, *Frist Urban*, 104–5 (emphasis added).

[31] Harnack, *Mission and Expansion*, 432–3.

[32] Sohm, *Outlines*, 5–6.

Pauline communities'.[33] But, now, for a different reason than what was proposed by Sohm and Harnack: it is the persuasiveness of Paul as a missionary, not the 'truth' of the Christian tradition (as it is in Sohm and Harnack), that generates the 'common ethos of the Pauline group'.[34] This new subculture that Meeks describes finds its most complete attestation in 1 Cor 12. For his overall description of *ekklēsia* organisation, Meeks relies heavily on Paul's list of functionaries in 1 Cor 12:8–10, 28–30[35] and makes much out of the fact that Paul provides 'no mention of formal offices'. Meeks argues that 'This fact is striking when we compare [Pauline] groups with the typical Greek or Roman private association.'[36]

To be sure, Meeks's description of organisational structure in Corinth is not identical to Sohm's or Harnack's. One of the lasting contributions of Meeks's important book is his nuancing of Sohm's charismatic/institutional binary.[37] Nonetheless, he reaffirms Sohm's other distinction between Christ group/association with respect to organisational structure, and this is because of an over-reliance on Paul's own categories of functionaries and leaders in Corinth.[38]

In German scholarship, one of the most interesting social–historical defences of the Sohm/Harnack description of Corinthian organisational structure is Schmeller's 1995 monograph, *Hierarchie und Egalität*.[39] This volume compares early Christ groups and Greco-Roman associations, asking 'Gibt es nur hier (auf der christlichen Seite) Egalität und nur dort (auf der nichtchristlichen Seite) Hierarchie?'[40] Schmeller finds that both the associations and the Corinthians had a bit of egalitarianism and hierarchy, but he underestimates the level of organisational structure in *ekklēsiai*. Regarding hierarchy in the Corinthian group, he contends that

[33] Meeks, *First Urban*, 138.

[34] Meeks, *First Urban*, 136.

[35] Meeks, *First Urban*, 134–6; cf. 111–39.

[36] Meeks, *First Urban*, 134.

[37] Meeks, *First Urban*, 120–1; cf. Bengt Holmberg, *Paul and Power: The Structure of Authority in the Primitive Church as Reflected in the Pauline Epistles* (Philadelphia: Fortress, 1980), 198–9, and throughout; Margaret Y. MacDonald, *The Pauline Churches: A Socio-Historical Study of Institutionalization in the Pauline and Deutero-Pauline Writings* (SNTSMS 60; Cambridge and New York: Cambridge University Press, 1988), 15–16, and throughout.

[38] This is especially striking since Meeks acknowledges that in 1 Cor 12:1–31 Paul 'is trying to play down differences of status and to stress cohesion of the group' (*First Urban*, 135).

[39] Thomas Schmeller, *Hierarchie und Egalität: eine sozialgeschichtliche Untersuchung paulinischer Gemeinden und griechisch-römischer Vereine* (Stuttgart: Verlag Katholisches Bibelwerk, 1995).

[40] Schmeller, *Hierarchie und Egalität*, 9–10.

it existed in the form of patrons, but that a leadership structure between patrons and general membership was absent. He ultimately opines that 'Alles in allem war die Struktur paulinischer Gemeinden vage'[41] and draws Sohm's and Harnack's conclusion from a century earlier: 'Es existierte in den Paulusgemeinden zwischen Patronen und einfachen Mitgliedern keine klar definierte Schicht von Amtsträgern ... die den Gegebenheiten in Vereinen auch nur in etwa entsprach'.[42] For Schmeller, this lack of local structure is due to Paul's dominant role as the founder, the first teacher of Christ to the Corinthians, and the group's disciplinarian.[43] In other words, it is based on Pauline idealisations such as those found in 1 Cor 12–14.

Despite Schmeller's methodology, which sets him apart from the treatment of associations by Meeks, he strikingly fails to move forward the discussion about Christ groups' organisational structure in the earliest period. His interest in associations was to locate some peculiar aspects of Christ groups (i.e., so-called egalitarianism) in them rather than to challenge the basis for assertions that Christ groups were peculiar. Unfortunately, Schmeller's findings of 'egalitarianism' in associations actually amount to democratic features of association *hierarchies* (e.g., rotating officers, democratic mechanisms for deciding whether or not to honour magistrates), and these findings fail to affirm the plausibility of pneumatic egalitarianism that previous scholarship imagines in Pauline groups. Since Schmeller equates Corinthian social structure with Paul's doctrine of social egalitarianism (Gal 3:27–8; 1 Cor 12:12–13) as well as with Paul's body metaphor (1 Cor 12:22–5),[44] he is unable to find much *Hierarchie* in the Corinthian group outside of patronage relationships. On top of that, because the Corinthian patrons attributed greater honour to social inferiors (1 Cor 12:22–5), Schmeller actually reproduces the egalitarian theory familiar from Sohm, Harnack, and more recent scholarship that rejects the associations as proper analogies to Christ groups.

First Corinthians 12 as Evidence for *Ekklēsia* Organisation

The most obvious problem in equating 1 Cor 12 with the full range of Corinthian organisational structure is Paul's unimpressive influence over Corinthian behaviour. To be sure, some Corinthians' practices

---

[41] Schmeller, *Hierarchie*, 77.
[42] Schmeller, *Hierarchie*, 78.
[43] Schmeller, *Hierarchie*, 77.
[44] Schmeller, *Hierarchie*, 92.

presuppose a certain level of social obligation to Paul – for example, Chloe's people and Stephanas's household keep Paul informed on group disputes and administrative matters (1 Cor 1:11, 16:15–18)– but this is a Christ group that disagreed with Paul concerning customs at the weekly club meal (1 Cor 11:17–34), cult practices at their most basic level (10:14), benefactions for Jerusalem (1 Cor 16:1–3; 2 Cor 8–9), proper conduct at symposium sections of *ekklēsia* meetings (1 Cor 14: 1–40), resurrection doctrines (15:1–58), Jesus traditions (2 Cor 11:4), and more.

Even if we accept that the Christ group's practices should be understood outside of the spectrum of activities practised in ancient associations, there is little merit to suppose that the Corinthians organised themselves based on Paul's rather problematic suggestions in 1 Cor 12. In reality, if the Corinthians adhered to Pauline directives on money and leadership, the outcome would have been bankruptcy and disbandment more likely than the creation of an 'alternative society'.[45]

At this point, an objection might be raised: some Corinthians actually did practice πνευματικά ('pneumatic activities'; 1 Cor 12.1[46]) such as those individuals whom Paul describes in 12:8–10. Specifically, it appears that many or all Corinthians had the ability to speak in tongues (14:23, 27), all members vied for status through hymns, revelations and other verbal acts (14:26), and some prophesised and claimed to be πνευματικοί (14:37). Does this give credence to imagining the Corinthian *ekklēsia* as a physical manifestation of Paul's idealised church?

The problem with this line of reasoning is its basis in a crude Weberian sociology of authority, wherein one type of authority, namely, charismatic, precedes and gradually gives way to traditional, legal forms of authority. It is true that Paul describes some Corinthians as 'experts of medicine' (χαρίσματα ἰαμάτων, 12:9), capable in 'works of magic' (ἐνεργήματα δυνάμεων, v.10), prophecy (προφητεία, v.10), and glosso-lalia (γένη γλωσσῶν, v.10). These individuals have in the past been profitably described as 'charismatics', but they now need to be situated within the broader category of ancient self-legitimating individuals who created their own authority by means of providing cultural products such as knowledge and other services (e.g., astrologers, magicians, and diviners). Stanley Stowers designates these individuals as 'religious

---

[45] Richard Horsley, '1 Corinthians: A Case Study', 242–52.

[46] I take the adjective in the neuter here as it appears elsewhere (1 Cor 9:11; 14:1; 15:46) but it could be masculine ('pneumatic persons'). The latter reading would not impact my discussion – as Barrett puts it, there is 'little difference' between these options; 'spiritual persons are those who have spiritual gifts' (Charles Kingsley Barrett, *The First Epistle to the Corinthians* [Black's; London: Hendrickson, 1968], 278).

experts'.[47] Interestingly, we find individuals who fall within Stowers's category of religious expertise regularly in Greco-Roman associations alongside elected or appointed magistrates, thus merging Weber's various ideal types of authority and reaffirming that in practice, 'charisma' coexisted with 'law' (to employ Weberian terminology).[48] In other words, the presence of religious expertise in the Corinthian *ekklēsia* has no bearing on the question of the Christ group's overall organisational structure.

Paul describes pneumatic practices as patterns of discourse during the symposium section of *ekklēsia* meetings, not as the group's full organisational structure.[49] Not even the reference to ἀντιλήμψεις and κυβερνήσεις (12:28) – which seemingly affirms the presence of administrative magistrates in the group[50] – tells us much about how the group chose their leaders or rewarded them for providing services to the *ekklēsia*, or, moreover, how the Christ group funded its banquets and other activities.

In summary of scholarship on the lack of organisational structure in the Corinthian *ekklēsia*, 1 Cor 12–14 says little about routine, everyday,

---

[47] For this category, see Stanley Stowers, 'Kinds of Myth', 115–17; Daniel Ullucci, 'Towards a Typology of Religious Experts in the Ancient Mediterranean', in *'The One Who Sows Bountifully': Essays in Honor of Stanley K. Stowers*, ed. Caroline Johnson Hodge, Saul M. Olyan Daniel Ullucci, and Emma Wasserman (Brown Judaic Studies Press, 2013), 89–103; Heidi Wendt, 'At the Temple Gates: The Religion of Freelance Experts in Early Imperial Rome (PhD Diss.; Brown University, 2013); Heidi Wendt, '*Iudaica Romana*: A Rereading of Evidence for Judean Expulsions from Rome', *Journal of Ancient Judaism* 6 (forthcoming).

[48] A prophet (προφήτης) associated with guilds of sacred victors: *IDidyma* 272 (Miletos; 25/26 CE); theologians (θεολόγοι) in an association with a treasury office: *ISmyrna* 653 = *GRA* II 138 (Smyrna, Ionia; I–II CE), see also the comments in Philip A. Harland, *North Coast of the Black Sea, Asia Minor*. Volume 2 of *Greco-Roman Associations: Texts, Translations and Commentary* (BZNW 204; Berlin and Boston: Walter de Gruyter, 2014), 310–11. Association founders also fit within the category of expertise, and these individuals created associations that were not exclusively 'charismatic' in organisation: *IG* II² 1343 = *GRA* I 48 (Athens, Attica; 37/6 or 36/5 BCE); *IG* II² 1365 + 1366 = *GRA* I 53 (Laurion, Attica; late II/early III CE); *IG* XI/4 1299 (Delos; 166 BCE); *SIG*³ 985 = *AGRW* 121 (Philadelphia, Lydia; late II–early I BCE); *IG* X/2 255 = *GRA* I 77 (Thessalonica, Macedonia; I–II CE).

[49] For the occurrence of these activities after the meal, during the drinking party of the banquet, see Dennis Smith, *From Symposium to Eucharist: The Banquet in the Early Christian World* (Minneapolis, MN: Fortress Press, 2003), 201.

[50] See Bradley H. MacLean, 'The Agrippinilla Inscription: Religious Associations and Early Church Formation', in *Origins and Method: Towards a New Understanding of Judaism and Christianity. Essays in Honour of John C. Hurd*, ed. Bradley H. McLean (JSNTSup 86; Sheffield: JSOT Press, 1993), 239–70 (259).

practices of economic and leadership organisation and, unfortunately, so has traditional scholarship on the Corinthians since its portrayals of Corinthian organisation stem from 1 Cor 12–14. Much more needs to be said about financial and leadership organisation in the Corinthian group from texts falling outside of these three chapters of First Corinthians.

The Thesis of This Book

This book offers a new perspective of the organisational structure in the Corinthian group. Working within an analogical comparative methodology established by Jonathan Z. Smith, and introduced to the study of ancient cult groups by John Kloppenborg, I propose that the Corinthian *ekklēsia* organised its finances and honorifics in ways that fit within the range of economic and honorific practices attested by economically modest[51] and middling Greco-Roman association. These data show that Paul's Corinthian *ekklēsia* would have incurred debt and, moreover, would have appeared unattractive to potential recruits in Roman Corinth's honour–shame culture unless it adopted three generalised organisational features: collection of subscription fees at every δεῖπνον, a hierarchical system of group magistrates, and delivery of normative forms of symbolic capital to responsible leaders. Strikingly, most researchers agree that the Corinthians lacked all three.[52]

To be sure, individual associations, depending on their members' socio-economic status, collected different amounts of fees at their banquets, required varying financial commitments from magistrates, and delivered different types of rewards to their service providers. Nonetheless, these three organisational features – collection of subscription fees, temporary offices, and delivery of honorific prizes – were rather ubiquitous and, indeed, necessary for most associations' ability to function for reasons that will be explored throughout this book.

Comparing the Corinthians

Our quick review of Sohm and Harnack revealed a system of comparison that Sheldon Pollock calls, in a different context, 'comparison with

---

[51] Throughout this study, I refer to associations as modest if their members lived below middling economic categories and above the subsistence level.

[52] See n.2 in this chapter.

hegemony'.[53] For Sohm and Harnack, any manner in which the Greek and Roman cults differed from *ekklēsiai* represented data concerning the Greek and Roman cult groups' moral and religious deficiency. For example, the dissimilarity in levels of organisational structure within the associations and Christ groups was interpreted as a result of associations' deficiency in the presence of the pneuma.

The comparative methodology employed in this book is sensitive to the 'will to domination' that has been 'built into the comparative method' in some previous scholarship on ancient Christ groups and Greco-Roman associations.[54] It attempts to offer comparison without hegemony by framing the comparison as one of Greco-Roman associations in comparative context, rather than between 'churches' and associations, which privileges ancient cult groups devoted to the hero, Christ, by giving them a special name ('churches'), and which carries the implication (intentional or not) articulated explicitly by Sohm that since early 'churches' – supposedly different from associations – gradually dominated and survived associations, this historical accident must have been part of a divine plan for them to do so.[55] This leads to a second aspect of this book's comparative methodology.

Bruce Lincoln, in his 'Theses on Comparison', has called for the granting of 'equal dignity and intelligence to all parties considered'.[56] The very idea that a single Christ group could be different or similar to ancient associations (of which there were thousands) with respect to any single practice involves an overgeneralisation about the static nature of associations and, thereby, fails to treat associations with intellectual dignity. The hypothesis with which I approach the association data is that the Corinthian group was likely different from hundreds of ancient associations and similar to hundreds more with respect to the precise way in which they practised each of their associative activities (i.e., selecting leaders, collecting income, and rewarding service providers). Granting equal dignity to associations means avoiding the assumption that the

---

[53] Sheldon Pollock, 'Comparison without Hegemony', in *The Benefit of Broad Horizons. Intellectual and Institutional Preconditions for a Global Social Science. Festschrift for Björn Wittrock on the Occasion of his 65th Birthday*, ed. Hans Joas and Barbro Klein (Leiden and Boston: Brill, 2010), 185–204.

[54] Pollock, 'Comparison without Hegemony', 202.

[55] Sohm contended that ancient Christ groups survived, unlike ancient associations devoted to Greek and Latin deities and heroes, because of the 'living power' of the Christian religion (*Outlines*, 4–5).

[56] Bruce Lincoln, *Gods and Demons, Priests and Scholars: Critical Explorations in the History of Religions* (Chicago: University of Chicago Press, 2012), 122.

most famous association sources (e.g., the Lanuvium inscription, the Philadelphia inscription, and the Iobacchoi inscription) adequately represent the language and practices of all ancient associations from IV BCE to IV CE. At several points in this book, I am concerned with outlining differences in the way that associations do similar things (e.g., choosing officers, funding their activities), which takes me well beyond these famous inscriptions.

True, this book suggests that associations were universally required to stay out of debt and needed to devise attractors to recruit members who lived in honour–shame cultures. Often, this led to the collection of membership fees and to the offering of opportunities for generating and affirming status to members. But within these basic practices there were a number of differences and varieties: rules regulating collections of fees were established differently by different cult groups; the amount of fees owed varied based on the group's membership profile; the methods for selecting magistrates varied; the types of symbolic capital rewarded to service providers also varied. By granting 'equal dignity and intelligence' to Pauline data about the Corinthians, on the one hand, and epigraphic and papyrological data on the association, on the other, my main concern is to locate the practices of the Corinthians within spectrums of diverse behaviours practised by other associations, not to make arguments for why the Corinthians belong or do not belong in the association *genus* (though, see Chapter 1).[57]

Pollock suggested that comparison can be done without hegemony only if we 'explain what role [our comparisons] are playing in the interpretation of our primary object'.[58] In the interest of disclosing my

---

[57] Although I find the recent edited volumes on Corinth to be highly informative, the present study on associations in the ancient Mediterranean necessarily takes us beyond analysis of the few extant association inscriptions from Hellenistic and Roman Corinth. Associative behaviour cut through Roman Corinth; there was nothing uniquely Corinthian about establishing a cult devoted to a hero. To be sure, the database of association sources reveals some regional differentiation: for example, the earliest attested Athenian associations tend to have consisted primarily of citizens, and membership in an occupational guild in IV CE Egypt seems to have been required (not voluntary) for artisans and merchants. Variation in nomenclature also occurred on geographical lines as we will see later. But the basic presence of subscription dues, officers, and honorific prizes – and the economic and recruitment pressures that made them staple features in associations – goes well beyond Corinth and requires consideration of our full database of ancient clubs. I follow Richard Ascough in referring to the association category as a 'genus'. See Richard S. Ascough, 'Apples-to-Apples: Reframing the Question of Models for Pauline Christ Groups' (paper presented at the annual meeting of the SBL, San Diego, CA, November 24, 2014).

[58] Pollock, 'Comparison without Hegemony', 202.

reason for researching the Corinthian group in comparison with associations, this book analyses association data because clubs encountered many of the challenges, and experienced several of the concerns and practices, that we know to have been faced and experienced by the Corinthians. Paul alludes to Corinthian financial and leadership practices but since they are mundane, routine, everyday behaviours, he fails to provide description of them in his letters to the group that is performing them every week when they assemble. Fortunately, these are the kinds of mundane behaviours that are illustrated time and again in honorific inscriptions, bylaws, financial accounts, and contracts produced by associations. The association data reveal the ways in which private cult groups organised meals, resolved conflicts, selected leaders, managed finances, and established group regulations – all of which are activities mentioned in passing in Paul's epistles to the Corinthians. Comparison – as long as it is analogical rather than genealogical,[59] – of the Corinthians with the varieties of ways associations responded to the challenges faced by the Corinthians is heuristically useful for allowing us to generate new questions about finances and leadership in the Corinthian group.[60] This is the role that associations play in my description of the Corinthian group.

My interest in the new questions that associations can raise about Christ groups leads to an approach that differs from some older comparisons between the Corinthians and associations, where the objective was to show the superiority of Christ groups (e.g., Sohm, Harnack). This book's approach to comparison also differs from some more recent comparisons where the objective was seemingly to locate supposed peculiarities of the Corinthian group (e.g., egalitarianism and free

---

[59] Genealogical concerns were foundational for earlier comparisons of Christ groups and associations. See, e.g., the argument that the Corinthian group was a cultic association in Georg Heinrici, 'Die Christengemeinden Korinths und die religiösen Genossenschaften der Griechen', *ZWT* 19 (1876), 465–526; and the argument that it was not an association in Edwin A. Judge, 'Did the Churches Compete with Cult Groups?', in *Early Christianity and Classical Culture: Comparative Studies in Honor of Abraham J. Malherbe*, ed. John T. Fitzgerald, Thomas H. Olbricht, and L. Michael White (NovTSup 110; Leiden: Brill, 2003), 501–24. In contrast to the genealogical approach, Richard Ascough explains that analogical comparisons do not look 'for the "earlier" exemplar, nor . . . [try] to determine the direction of borrowing. Rather, one type of association is compared to another in order to highlight both similarities *and* differences' (*Paul's Macedonian Associations: The Social Context of Philippians and 1 Thessalonians* [WUNT II/161; Tübingen: Mohr Siebeck, 2003], 2 [emphasis in original]).

[60] On this point, see John S. Kloppenborg, 'Membership Practices in Pauline Christ Groups', *Early Christianity* 2 (2013), 183–215 (187–9).

membership) within the association data.[61] Both previous comparative methodologies reached limited success.

An objection to the association model might be that Christ groups were categorically different from associations and, therefore, that they probably practised finances and leadership in ways that fall outside of the spectrum of practices attested in association sources. How can associations be heuristically useful for us if Christ groups fell into a different classification of group formation than them? Would it not be better to situate the financial and leadership practices of the Corinthians within the financial and leadership customs of synagogues, philosophical cults, or houses instead? This objection is addressed in Chapters 1 and 2.

As a preliminary response, it should be clarified that whatever dissimilarities may have existed between Christ groups and associations, they were not so great to dissuade Eusebius and Celsus from referring to Christ followers as θιασῶται (Origen, Cels. 3.23), or Pliny from calling them hetaeria (Ep. 10.96), both designators for collegiati and collegia;[62] or for Paul to use a term from civic discourse, ekklēsia, as a designation for Christ groups.[63] More crucially, to say that a single Christ group was somehow different from the thousands of ancient associations attested in inscriptions and papyri is no easy task. It is especially difficult today when we have the benefit of several volumes of now easily accessible association sources published by John Kloppenborg, Richard Ascough, and Philip Harland.[64] These volumes clarify that each association behaved a little differently despite many broad similarities. Arguing that a single Pauline ekklēsia was categorically different from each of the thousands of Greco-Roman associations will involve

---

[61] See especially, Schmeller, Hierarchie; and Ebel, Attraktivität, both of which are overviewed later.

[62] Kloppenborg, 'Greco-Roman Thiasoi', 195 n.25.

[63] The association database is filled with mimicry of civic discourse: from self-designators (συναγωγή, σύνοδος, κοινόν), to office titles (e.g., ἄρχοντες, γραμματεῖς), to designations of meetings (ἀγορά, ἐκκλησία), to elections (αἱρέσεις, χειροτονεῖν). To suggest, as some critics of the association model have, that the Corinthians' self-designator (e.g., ekklēsia) is fundamentally unique from the ubiquity with which civic terminology is employed by other private cultic groups is untenable: the spectrum of discourse and practices in private cultic groups is broad enough to account for common self-designators (θίασος, συναγωγή, σύνοδος) as well as less-common ones (στέμμα, συνέδριον, συντεχνια). For a sample of the wide range of Greek associations' self-designators, see Franz Poland, Geschichte des griechischen Vereinswesens (Leipzig: Teubner. Repr. Leipzig: Zentral-Antiquariat der Deutschen Demokratischen Republik, 1967 [1909]), 153–68.

[64] I refer here to GRA I, GRA II, and AGRW.

overgeneralisations concerning the uniformity of ancient clubs that are now obvious in light of the work of Kloppenborg, Ascough, and Harland. Already in 1993 Kloppenborg observed that 'there was a broad spectrum of forms of *collegia*, broad enough that most of the particularities seen in Pauline churches could fit comfortably within that spectrum'.[65]

Overview of Chapters

The first chapter provides a fresh consideration of the relationship between associations, synagogues, philosophical cults, and Christ groups. It proposes that these groups all belong under the association *genus*,[66] and that each individual group should be classified into one of five species of associations, based on membership profile (e.g., ethnic coherence, occupational coherence, cultic coherence). The designator, synagogue, carries special problems, and much of the chapter defends a decision to use the new term, Yahweh groups, to designate associations devoted to the Judean deity.

Chapter 2 responds to recent suggestions that the Corinthian *ekklēsia* operated according to household customs rather than in accordance with association practices. Support for this hypothesis tends to consist of the theory that several baptised families joined the Christ group, bringing with them their household organisational practices. Additional evidence is imagined from the supposed reality that the Corinthians assembled exclusively in domestic architecture. Both of these proposals are less obvious than researchers typically acknowledge. The only known host of the Christ group, Gaius, was an occasional guest of the group, not a host; and Paul's references to *ekklēsia* members who were married does not indicate that these members' entire families gained automatic admittance into the group. The household model tends to function as an apologetic strategy of establishing the moral and religious superiority of ancient Christ groups over associations. The evidence suggests to me that the group consisted of ten members rather than scores of families.

---

[65] John S. Kloppenborg, 'Edwin Hatch, Churches and *Collegia*', in *Origins and Method: Towards a New Understanding of Judaism and Christianity. Essays in Honour of John C. Hurd*, ed. Bradley H. McLean (JSNTSup 86; Sheffield: JSOT Press, 1993), 212–38 (231).

[66] For usage of this phrase, see Richard S. Ascough, 'Apples-to-Apples: Reframing the Question of Models for Pauline Christ Groups' (paper presented at the annual meeting of the SBL, San Diego, CA, November 24, 2014).

Recent economic descriptions of Pauline Christ believers by Justin Meggitt,[67] Steven Friesen,[68] and Bruce Longenecker[69] portray the Corinthians as too poor to participate in the activities of middling associations (i.e., collecting membership fees from all members, purchasing honorifics for magistrates, selecting officers, and thereby expecting financial services from members). To test this assumption, in Chapter 3, I analyse two economically modest associations from below the middling socio-economic category(ies): a small slave association, and a club whose assemblies rotated between rented space and the houses of members. These associations show us how economically modest individuals used their surplus economic resources on club membership. Instructively, both associations collected modest subscription dues, purchased cheap honorifics for their service providers, and some of their members were even able to commit additional financial resources towards club activities resembling the Jerusalem collection. The data from this chapter illustrate that even on Meggitt's, Friesen's, and Longenecker's low assessment of Corinthian socio-economic status, the presence of a typical organisational structure would have been manageable for the *ekklēsia* in Corinth.

Chapter 4 argues that the Christ group needed to collect subscription fees from all members in order to survive. Gerd Theissen's[70] and Peter Lampe's[71] oft-followed proposals concerning mechanisms by which the Corinthians obtained their banquet menu items are not persuasive when scrutinised and, in any case, would not free the Christ group from the necessity of collecting subscription dues: the *ekklēsia*'s financial pressures went well beyond banquet expenses, and it is unlikely that two or three members covered all necessary expenditures while the majority freeloaded. After exploring the financial challenges of club membership, Pauline evidence for the presence of a Corinthian *ekklēsia* common fund is provided.

Chapter 5 marks a shift in this book's focus from economic matters to issues of social hierarchy and leadership. The combined outcome of Chapters 5–7 is a strengthening of the Christ group's so-called weak members, and a re-description of *ekklēsia* social hierarchy as fluid and constantly in flux based on the recent activity of members. Chapter 5 clarifies what would have been at stake if an association decided to do

---

[67] Meggitt, *Paul*.
[68] Friesen, 'Poverty', 323–61.
[69] Longenecker, *Remember*.
[70] Theissen, *Social Setting*, 145–74.
[71] Lampe, 'Das korinthinische Herrenmahl', 183–212.

what researchers nearly unanimously claim the Corinthians did: fail to deliver formal commendation to officers and benefactors. A precondition for being able to successfully recruit members to an association in honour–shame cultures, such as Roman Corinth, was the provision of opportunities to earn symbolic capital in the form of office-holding and to win commendatory prizes. These opportunities needed to be accessible to all members, not just the wealthiest ten per cent of members. Complacency on the part of the wealthiest ten per cent, coupled with zeal for the Christ group among some members of lower ranks, would result in honorific rewards for the generous members, and would strengthen the weak in the context of the group's social hierarchy.

Chapter 6 explores two specific instances where opportunities arose for all members, including the weak, to generate status in the context of the *ekklēsia*: the Jerusalem collection and travelling services. These activities represent a broader culture of opportunity that *ekklēsia* membership would have offered to prospective recruits.

Paul alludes to this culture of opportunity most clearly in 1 Cor 11:17–34, which is the focus of Chapter 7. I locate in this passage overlooked references, but explicit nonetheless, to elected *ekklēsia* officers. Paul's recommendation that the current officers do not deserve ἔπαινός, a formulaic word that appears in numerous Attic honorific inscriptions, indicates that ἔπαινός (i.e., crowns, inscriptions, proclamations, and exemptions) was normally available at the end of a magistrate's tenure. With elections of temporary officers, the group's social relationships emerge once again as fluid. Not only were opportunities available for members to generate status by showing generosity voluntary at any time (i.e., contributing to financial projects, agreeing to provide space for the group's banquet), but members also had opportunities to be elected as officials in the Christ group. The status of members in relation to each other in outside society (i.e., strong or weak) had little impact on social–hierarchical relations in the *ekklēsia*; showing generosity and providing service to the *ekklēsia* was the route to recognition and status affirmation in the Christ group. The outcome is that the group's social hierarchy, and its calculation of each member's acquired honour, was never settled. Social–hierarchical relationships in the *ekklēsia* were constantly being reinscribed according to members' most recent acts of generosity and service.

1

GRECO-ROMAN ASSOCIATIONS
AS AN ANALYTIC CATEGORY

Defining and Classifying Associations

Before proceeding any further, the association concept requires elaboration. John Kloppenborg and Richard Ascough provide the following description:

> Between poles of the family and the *polis* there existed a large number of more or less permanent private associations, guilds, or clubs, organized around an extended family, the cult of a deity or hero, an ethnic group in diaspora, a neighbourhood, or a common trade or profession. Most of these associations had cultic aspects and most served broadly social goals.[1]

Jinyu Liu offers a substantive definition:

> A *collegium* should have had at least the following stock features: the minimum size was three; it had structural features such as magistrates, a name, by-laws, membership requirements, and some sort of common treasury (*pecuniae communes*); and a *collegium* could formally take a patron or patrons.[2]

Liu's definition finds affirmation in many association documents, but the project of constructing a substantive definition of ancient associations results in confusion more than clarity since it smooths over the variety of forms that associations took, and it generates the impression that clubs practised common activities in generalised manners. Unfortunately, researchers of Pauline groups who are intent on debating the differing essential features of associations, synagogues, and philosophical cults

---

[1] John S. Kloppenborg and Richard S. Ascough, *Attica, Central Greece, Macedonia, Thrace*. Volume 1 of *Greco-Roman Associations: Texts, Translations, and Commentary* (Berlin and New York: W. de Gruyter, 2011), 1.

[2] Jinyu Liu, 'Pompeii and Collegia: A New Appraisal of the Evidence', *AHB* 22 (2008), 53–69 (54).

necessarily work with substantive definitions of each aforementioned model. The objective of those endeavours has been to find a proper model for Christ groups or, alternatively, to conclude that Christ groups were unique and exempt from all possible analogies.[3]

This book will not distinguish between Judean groups, philosophical cults, and associations because there was too much diversity within these models to speak of universal points of difference.[4] Rather, it will work with a fivefold membership-based taxonomy of Greco-Roman associations. Philip Harland, following an earlier article by John Kloppenborg, typologised associations on the basis of primary membership linkages. These linkages were fivefold: (1) household or family networks, (2) shared ethnicity, (3) residence in the same neighbourhood, (4) occupational networks, and (5) linkages based on participation in a particular deity's cult.[5] As Harland observes, associations often brought together members *primarily* according to one of these social linkages even though multiple types of linkages contributed to many groups' membership profiles.[6] When I refer to, say, an 'occupational guild' in this book, I am not denying the very real likelihood that some members would have joined who were linked to the other members on the basis of different types of social connection – for example, some members of a purple-dyers association could have been from the same neighbourhood in which most of the group members worked their common trade even

---

[3] Meeks famously concluded that 'the structures worked out by the Pauline movement itself ... may after all have been unique' (*First Urban*, 84). Richard Horsley's striking response to Meeks was that associations 'offer far less by way of "significant analogies" than Meeks thought. Indeed ... we must look for the distinctive features of the *ekklēsiai* that Paul advocated within his letters themselves' in '1 Corinthians: A Case Study of Paul's Assembly as an Alternative Society', in *Urban Religion in Roman Corinth. Interdisciplinary Approaches*, ed. Daniel N. Schowalter and Steven J. Friesen, Harvard Theological Studies 53 (Cambridge: Harvard University Press, 2005), 371–95 (381).

[4] Recently, John M. G. Barclay stated that 'To ask ... in what respects the Diaspora synagogues or early churches were like "associations" is akin to asking whether churches today are like clubs: there are too many different kinds of church, and too many different kinds of club to make this vague and over-generalised comparison of much heuristic value.' See 'Money and Meetings: Group Formation among Diaspora Jews and Early Christians', in *Vereine, Synagogen und Gemeinden in kaiserzeitlichen Kleinasien*, ed. Andreas Gutsfeld and Dietrich-Alex Koch (STAC 25; Tübingen: Mohr Siebeck, 2006), 113–27 (114–15).

[5] Philip A. Harland, *Associations, Synagogues, and Congregations. Claiming a Place in Ancient Mediterranean Society* (Minnesota: Augsburg Fortress, 2003), 28–9; John S. Kloppenborg, 'Collegia and *Thiasoi*: Issues in Function, Taxonomy and Membership', in *Voluntary Associations in the Graeco-Roman World*, ed. John S. Kloppenborg and Stephen G. Wilson (London: Routledge, 1996), 16–30 (23).

[6] Harland, *Associations*, 29.

though they did not work as purple-dyers themselves. Members in such a group would have occupational linkages primarily, but also other types of social connections among its affiliates, such as residence in a common neighbourhood. Judean groups and Christ groups could be understood according to any of the five membership types and need to be classified on an individual basis, while social connections among members of philosophical cults generally can be understood in occupational terms (see the following paragraphs).

Phenomena formerly labelled 'synagogues' will be called 'Yahweh associations/groups' in this book in order to maintain consistency with my designations for associations that took on other patron deities/heroes: 'Herakles associations', 'Christ groups', and 'Zeus associations'. This allows for the avoidance of two problematic assumptions that will be explored now. The first problem is the ethnic connotation inherent in the designator 'synagogue'. The Judean deity, like the gods of Egypt, Attica, and other territories, served as the patron deity of associations throughout the ancient Mediterranean. Members of these associations were from multiple ethnicities, not just from the ethnic origins of the deity's original worshippers. Understanding Yahweh groups as synagogues – a modern term that carries ethnic connotations – conflates the geographical setting of the myths of the deity with the ethnicities of members who joined Yahweh associations and assumes an ethnic coherence among devotees of Yahweh that we do not find in the membership profiles of associations devoted to other deities and heroes.

A second problem with designating Yahweh groups as synagogues is that the English designator derives from the Greek συναγωγή, which was one of many words that simply meant 'association', without any Judean connotation.[7] So when researchers speak of 'ancient synagogues', typically they do not mean to signify the συναγωγή of non-Judean barbers in Thrace (*IPerinthos* 49 = *GRA* I 86; Perinthos-Herakleia, I–II CE), but as this Thracian group and several other non-Judean associations used συναγωγή as their self-designator, the utility of the modern category disappears for researchers of associations. A related problem emerges when Yahweh groups began (at a very early date) to call themselves by other association designators (e.g., σύνοδος, θίασος).[8] When the modern

---

[7] It could denote any gathering whatsoever, but given this book's subject, my principal concern is with its usage by associations of all types.

[8] Designators other than συναγωγή that appear in association sources include θίασος: *IJO* I Ach. 41 (Piraeus, Attica; III/IV BCE), and Josephus, *Ant.* 14.216; and ἐκκλησία and σύλλογος: Philo, *Spec.* 1.324–5; *Deus* 111. For the Philo, *Spec.* 1.324–5 references, see the comments in Anders Runesson, Donald D. Binder, and Birger Olsson, *The Ancient*

designator, ancient synagogue, is employed in current scholarship, do Yahweh groups such as these count among the referents even though they did not self-identify as συναγωγαί?

For these two reasons, 'Yahweh groups' becomes preferable to '(Judean) synagogues'. Not all associations devoted to the Judean God called their deity 'Yahweh' (e.g., *IJO* I, BS7.8; Panticapaion, Bosporan region; I CE). There were also multiple names used by groups devoted to other deities and heroes, and so the designator, Yahweh groups, is no more problematic than referring to a Theos Hypsistos association (where the deity is Zeus) as a Zeus group, for example (e.g., *IG* X.2,1 68; Thessalonica, Macedonia; I CE). Usage of the old designator, synagogue, by comparison, generates avoidable inaccuracies.

As with 'synagogue', the designator 'philosophical cult' emerges as unnecessary in light of new research on the activities of these groups. Philip Harland in particular has demonstrated that these cults are better understood as associations of individuals with occupational social connections rather than as a separate category of social formation (see the section 'Financial and Honorific Practices'). In the following subsections, a case will be made for understanding Yahweh groups and philosophical cults within Harland's fivefold membership-based taxonomy of associations rather than as *genuses* of their own.

Yahweh Groups

Some scholars of the Jesus movement propose that Pauline groups are better understood as synagogues than as associations.[9] However, most researchers (especially those of ancient Judean religion) now recognise that Yahweh groups' activities fit within the spectrum of practices of Greco-Roman associations.[10] For the latter group of scholars, synagogues

---

Synagogue from Its Origins to 200 C.E. A Source Book (Arbeiten zur Geschichte des antiken Judentums und des Urchristentums 72; Leiden and Boston: Brill, 2008), 259–62.

[9] Hans-Josef Klauck, *Hausgemeinde und Hauskirche im frühen Christentum*, SBS 103 (Stuttgart: Katholisches Bibelwerk, 1981), 99; James Tunstead Burtchaell, *From Synagogue to Church: Public Services and Offices in the Earliest Christian Communities* (Cambridge and New York: Cambridge University Press, 1992), 339–57; Roger W. Gehring, *House Church and Mission: The Importance of Household Structures in Early Christianity* (Peabody, MA: Hendrickson, 2004), 21–2.

[10] See, e.g., Peter Richardson, 'Early Synagogues as Collegia in the Diaspora and Palestine', in *Voluntary Associations in the Graeco-Roman World*, ed. John S. Kloppenborg and Stephen G. Wilson (London and New York: Routledge, 1996), 90–109; Anders Runesson, *The Origins of the Synagogue: A Socio-Historical Study* (Coniectanea Biblica/New Testament Series 37; Stockholm: Almqvist and Wiksell

were mostly ethnic associations of Judeans. In a later section, I will take the valuable move of situating Yahweh groups within the association model one step further: Yahweh groups should be typologised on an individual basis according to how each group's members are connected primarily. Five possibilities exist: workers of the same occupation, members of the same household network, workers or dwellers in the same neighbourhood or street, members of the same ethnicity/homeland living in a diasporic setting, and practitioners of the cult of the same deity/hero.[11] Supposing that Yahweh groups were all primarily ethnic associations carries no more plausibility than would the claim that all associations devoted to Sarapis were comprised of Egyptians exclusively, or that all associations devoted to Herakles were cult groups of Achaeans.

My immediate concern, though, is with the primary reasons why many researchers now classify Yahweh groups within the association category. These reasons include the self-designators chosen by members of Yahweh groups, which reflect emic perspectives on Yahweh group identity, the activities practised, and the functions served by Yahweh clubs. The following sections review some of the association data concerning the self-designators and behaviours of Yahweh groups.

Self-Designators of Yahweh Groups

When Josephus described Julius Caesar's ban of θίασοι banquets in Rome, he quoted a Roman decree that clarified that Yahweh associations were exempted from this law against θίασοι (*Ant.* 14.213–16).[12] The

International, 2001), 467–86; Tessa Rajak, 'Synagogue and Community in the Graeco-Roman Diaspora', in *Jews in the Hellenistic and Roman Cities*, ed. John R. Bartlett (London and New York: Routledge, 2002), 22–39; Richard S. Ascough, 'Apples-to-Apples: Reframing the Question of Models for Pauline Christ Groups' (paper presented at the annual meeting of the SBL, San Diego, CA, November 24, 2014).

[11] See n.5 in this chapter.

[12] Presumably, the decree pertained to ethnic associations of Judeans rather than to, trade associations of Greeks who happened to offer cult to Yahweh. Any inaccuracies in Josephus's passage concerning the Caesarian decree were likely introduced during later transmissions of the text. For discussions of this issue, see Miriam Pucci Ben Zeev, *Jewish Rights in the Roman World: The Greek and Roman Documents Quoted by Josephus Flavius* (TSAJ 74; Tübingen: Mohr Siebeck, 1998), 107–18; Zvi Yavetz, *Julius Caesar and His Public Image* (Ithaca, NY: Cornell University Press, 1983), 85–93; and Tessa Rajak, 'Was There a Roman Charter for the Jews?' *JRS* 74 (1984): 107–23. Despite the text's possible inaccuracies, Barclay finds it useful since it 'suggests that [Josephus] did not consider this categorisation of Diaspora communities to be implausible' ('Money and Meetings', 113, n.1).

implication from this passage is that for some ancient observers, ethnic
Judean groups belonged within the broader Greek category of the θίασος,
so much so that it was necessary to specify that Judean (θίασοι) gatherings were the only ones (i.e., the only θίασοι) that Caesar's law did not
hinder (μόνους τούτους οὐκ ἐκώλυσεν) in this respect. The designator
θίασος was widely employed by associations in Greece and throughout
the Eastern Mediterranean.[13] Josephus also mentions that the Judeans in early Roman Sardis
had established 'their own association' (σύνοδος ... ἰδίᾳ; *Ant.*
14.235). The term σύνοδος represents another designator often
preferred by associations throughout the ancient Mediterranean,
not least for Greco-Egyptian clubs.[14] This designation was
employed as late as III or IV CE by other Yahweh groups
such as the one[15] in the following inscription from Nysa (Asia
Minor):

> Μένανδρος ᾿Απολλωνίδου ἐποίησεν
> οἰκοδομήσας τὸν τόπον ἀπὸ τῆς
> ἐπιγραφῆς τὸν πρὸς ἀνατολὴν
> τῶι λαῶι καὶ τῇ συνόδωι τῇι περὶ
> Δωσίθεον Θεογένου (*IJO* II Nysa 26, III–IV CE)   5

> Menandros son of Apollonides made (this), having built the
> place to the East of the inscription for the people and the
> σύνοδος of Dositheos son of Theogenes.

Walter Ameling argues that the building 'made' by Menandros could not
have been a 'synagogue' structure since it was to be shared by 'the Jewish
people' and a (Yahweh) association.[16] Be this as it may, the more
important feature of the inscription for present purposes is its seeming

---

[13] See Franz Poland, *Geschichte des griechischen Vereinswesens* (Leipzig: Teubner,
1909), 16–28; and, now, the index in Philip A. Harland, *North Coast of the Black Sea, Asia
Minor*, Volume 2 of *Greco-Roman Associations: Texts, Translations and Commentary*,
BZNW 204 (Berlin and Boston: Walter de Gruyter, 2014), 469.

[14] See, e.g., *P.Oslo* III 143.1 (Oxyrhynchos, Egypt; I CE); *P.Ryl.* IV 590.4,8 (Unknown
provenance, Egypt; 51–30 BCE); and *IAlexandriaK* 65.5 (Alexandria, Egypt; I CE). See
also Poland, *Geschichte*, 159–63; and Harland, *North Coast*, 474.

[15] This dating follows Baruch Lifshitz, *Donateurs et fondateurs dans les synagogues
juives: répertoire des dédicaces grecques relatives à la construction et à la réfection des
synagogues* (Paris: J. Gabalda, 1967), 33–4.

[16] Walter Ameling, ed., *Kleinasien*, Volume 2 of *Inscriptiones Judaicae Orientis* (TSAJ
99; Tübingen: Mohr Siebeck, 2004), 139.

reference to a private σύνοδος founded by an individual who holds a Judean name (Dositheos).[17] Just as the terms θίασος and σύνοδος could refer to associations devoted to Greek gods *as well as* to associations of the Judean deity, the word συναγωγή could designate clubs who revered various deities, including Yahweh.

Nonetheless, some scholars have made the case that συναγωγή was particularly reserved for ethnic Judean groups, despite its analogous employment by Greeks, Egyptians, and West Asians. One example is Tessa Rajak's claim that evidence for non-Judean συναγωγαί is 'strikingly localized in northern Greece'.[18] This is broadly accurate, but it fails to properly articulate the range of local cultures in which the term described an association devoted to non-Judean deities. As evidence of non-Judean groups who called themselves συναγωγαί in the rather large territory designated by Rajak as 'Northern Greece', I list in the following paragraphs associations from Thrace, Bithynia, and Ionia. At Perinthos, in northeastern Thrace, there were at least two συναγωγαί in the Roman period, and both were occupational guilds. One was an association of barbers (*IPerinthos* 49A = *GRA* I 86; Perinthos, Thrace, I CE and II CE):

> [N.N.] the administrator and Marcus Pompeius Komikos, son of Komikos, restored the altar to the association (συναγωγή) of barbers, those around the chief-convener (ἀρχισυναγωγός) Gaius Iulius Valens, and provided the location.
> (Kloppenborg and Ascough, 2011)

The other was a group of non-Judean oar sellers (*IPerinthos* 59; I–II CE). In the city of Apamea Myrlea (Bithynia), we hear of a cultic association (συναγωγή) devoted to Zeus (*IApamBith* 35 = *GRA* II 99; 119 or 104 BCE), and in Teos a συναγωγή of loyalists to the Attalid rulers (*OGIS* 326 = *GRA* II 141; Ionia, Asia Minor; 146–133 BCE), who use συναγωγή (l.12) nearly interchangeably with σύνοδος (l.3).

Moving beyond Northern Greece, a very fragmentary dedication, made by a certain Artemon son of Nikon, comes from an association with a προστάτης officer. This group called itself a συναγωγή (*IAlexandriaK* 92 = *AGRW* 283; Alexandria, Egypt; imperial period). The word συναγωγή was frequently employed by Egyptian associations

---

[17] Ameling, *Kleinasien*, 139.
[18] Rajak proposes that συναγωγή 'comes in the Roman period to be largely associated with Jews and with the practice of Judaism. Unequivocal pagan occurrences in the sense of "association" are at any time few and far between' ('Synagogue and Community', 26).

to describe the act of coming together for a meeting in the formulaic phrase ἐπὶ τῆς γενηθείσης συναγωγῆς ('having come together in the assembly').[19] Moreover, associations in Egypt and elsewhere often referred to their leaders as συναγωγοί (and cognates) even when using other terminology for their self-designation, which further attests to the connection between synagogue terminology and non-Judean associative practices.[20] We could split hairs and argue that Yahweh groups employed the term συναγωγή in a special way.

But this still would not permit Yahweh groups to be classified differently than associations: the more telling observation is that synagogue terminology was employed rather extensively by associations of various ethnicities. Whether these groups used the word to designate the association itself, the building in which the club met, or the act of coming together is irrelevant for taxonomical purposes. Nonetheless, Lee Levine has observed that by II CE Judeans uniformly preferred the term συναγωγή for 'the building in which communal activities were held'.[21] While this claim holds questionable relevance for my present discussion, it is worth pointing out that an Augustan decree speaks of 'Sabbath houses' (σαββατεῖον) and banquet halls (ἀνδρών) equipped with holy books and sacred money in West Asia (Josephus, *Ant.* 16.164). It is unclear what locals called these buildings but the structures likely survived into the second century and, therefore, their existence pose a challenge for Levine's argument unless it is assumed that Judeans did not call them the names used in the Augustan decree.

By the second or third century, there was also a Σαμβαθεῖον in Thyateira (Lydia), but there is much we do not know about it (*IJO* II 146 = *TAM* V 1142; c.120–220 CE). Unfortunately, we cannot be sure if this structure was a meeting place for devotion to the Judean God, or the sibyl Sambathe – who was of either Chaldean origins (Pausanias, *Description* 10.12.9) or Hebrew origins (*In Phaedrum* 244) – or the Lydian/Anatolian god Sabathikos/Sambathikos (e.g., *IAsMinVers* 8; Kastolupedion; I BCE), whose relationship to the Judean deity is

---

[19] See, e.g., *BGU* IV 1137.2 (Alexandria, Egypt; 6 BCE); *IAlexandriaK* 91.3 (Alexandria, Egypt; 3/4 CE); *IDelta* I 446 = *AGRW* 287 (Psenamosis; Delta Region, Egypt; 67, 64 BCE).

[20] For example, *IGRR* I 1106 = *AGRW* 286 (Naucratis, Egypt; 30 BCE–14 CE); *SB* XXII 15460 = *AGRW* 280 (Alexandria; 5 BCE); and *IBosp* 75 = *GRA* II 94 (Panticapaion, Bosporan region; 150–125 BCE).

[21] Lee I. Levine, *The Ancient Synagogue: The First Thousand Years*, 2nd ed. (New Haven: Yale University Press, 2005), 1.

unresolved.[22] In addition to Sabbath houses in Asia, it is noteworthy that terms such as εὐχεῖον (*CPJ* II 432, col. II, ll.57, 60 = *P.Lond.* III 1177; Arsinoe, Egypt; 113 CE) and προσευχή (*IJO* I, BS1 = *ASSB* 123; Olbia, Bosporan region; II–III CE) were still in usage at this time to refer to the buildings of Yahweh groups.

In summary of the evidence outlined in this section, the classification of Yahweh groups within the association category is consistent with the ancients' own identification of Yahweh groups as associations.

Financial and Honorific Practices

Yahweh groups not only called themselves Greco-Roman associations (i.e., θίασοι, σύνοδοι, συναγωγή) but also behaved much like associations in terms of finances and honour, the two aspects of associative life that this book explores. This is an important observation since I will argue that membership dues, magistrates, and the delivery of symbolic capital were rather ubiquitous among associations, regardless of the deity/hero to which they devoted themselves. The contention that Yahweh groups had their own way of working with money and honour – and therefore that the Corinthians likely did, too, as they were modelled after Yahweh groups – cannot be accepted.

With respect to membership dues, a crucial piece of evidence comes from the Roman decree quoted by Josephus, wherein the consul, Julius Gaius, affirms that Yahweh groups (θίασοι) are able to assemble 'to collect money for common meals and the sacred rituals' [χρήματα εἰς σύνδειπνα καὶ τὰ ἱερὰ εἰσφέρειν] (*Ant.* 14.214–15; cf. *ASSB* 180). This is the practice attested in a fragmentary list of Judean contributors to a meal in *CPJ* I 139 (Apollinopolis Magna, Egypt; I BCE). Several other sources suggest a similar method of funding communal meals in Yahweh groups: the reference to a 'contributory feast' (συνβολή, l.13) in *CPJ* III 456 (provenance unknown, Egypt; II CE); mention of a 'common fund' (οἵ συνκαταθεμένοι) in *IJO* II 168.6–7 = *AGRW* 145 (Phrygia, Asia Minor; I–II CE); and a reference to 'contributions to the god' (τά ἰσφερόμενα) in *OGIS* 573.25 = *AGRW* 213 (Cilicia, Asia Minor; I BCE–I CE) are examples from around the time of the Corinthian correspondence.[23]

---

[22] For a recent review of the primary data, see Harland, *North Coast*, 427–34.

[23] See also the earlier inscriptions, *IJO* 1, Ach66 = *ASSB* 100 (Delos, Asia Minor; 250–175 BCE) and *IJO* 1, Ach67 = *ASSB* 101 (Delos, Asia Minor; 150–50 BCE). Here, an ethnic association of Samaritans paid contributions (ἀπάρχεσθαι) towards the Samaritan temple at Mount Gerizim.

Even when we do not have direct evidence for membership fees collected in Yahweh groups, the practice can be inferred from their inscriptions. In Hierapolis in Phrygia, fines for breaches were to be deposited in the common fund of the λαός τῶν Ἰουδαίων (*IJO* II 206.5–6 = *CIJ* 776; II/III CE).[24] The same practice was followed in other associations devoted to the Judean deity.[25] Another Yahweh group from Aegina was equipped with 'a standing fund, as well as *ad hoc* collections'.[26] Mention is made of 'sacred funds' in the Yahweh group at Stobi (*IJO* I Mac1.10–16 = *GRA* I 73; Stobi, Macedonia; II–III CE). And when architectural repairs needed to be made by a Yahweh group that had no patron to cover them 'from his/her own resources', contributions were made by various affiliates to cover the cost of the repairs (*CJZ* 72 = *ASSB* 133; Berenice, Cyrenaica; 55 CE). These sources show Yahweh associations engaging in practices that fit squarely within the range of associative financial behaviour, such as establishing common funds and collecting fees from group affiliates.

The honorific behaviours of many Yahweh groups also resembled those of Zeus groups, Dionysos groups, Herakles groups, and associations more broadly. Rajak observes that synagogues are concerned, 'like so many other ancient associations, with the standing of their members and are seen busily reinforcing their own internal hierarchies by publicly acknowledging patrons with expressions of esteem encompassing both insiders and outsiders'.[27] One of the fourteen Yahweh groups in ancient Rome honoured a certain Gaudentius at his death, noting that he was 'twice archon' in the group (*CIJ* I 316; Rome, III–IV CE). The archon position in this club must have been temporary, as was common in clubs devoted to non-Judean deities and heroes.[28] In Egypt, an association (σύνοδος) that assembled in a prayer hall (προσευχή) was equipped with a variety of officers: doorkeepers (θυρωροί), ushers (εἰσαγγελέων), chief attendants (ἀρχυπηρετῶν), and scribes

[24] For λαός as a 'synagogue' designator, see n.35 below.
[25] *IJO* II 43 = *AGRW* 196 (Smyrna, Asia Minor; II–III CE); *IJO* II 205 = *CIJ* 775 (Hierapolis, Asia Minor; II CE); *IJO* II 196 = *CIJ* 777 (Hierapolis, Asia Minor; III CE); *IJO* II 208 = *CIJ* 778 (Hierapolis, Asia Minor; III CE); and *IJO* II 233 = *CIJ* 786 (Corycus, Cilicia, Asia Minor; II–III CE).
[26] Quote from Rajak, 'Synagogue and Community', 36. Rajak refers to *IJO* I Ach 58 = *CIJ* 722 (300–350 CE) and *IJO* I Ach 59 = *CIJ* 723 (300–350 CE).
[27] Rajak, 'Synagogue and Community', 36.
[28] See also *CIJ* I 505 (unknown provenance, III–IV CE). Some scholars maintain that the organisation of Yahweh groups in Rome differed from that of Yahweh groups in other cities such as Alexandria and Berenice. For a review of this issue, see Levine, *Ancient Synagogue*, 413–14.

(γραμματεῖς) (*CPJ* I 138 = *ASSB* 170; unknown location, Egypt; second half of I BCE), who may well have been honoured with crowns and honorific inscriptions at the conclusion of their terms (see *OGIS* 573 = *AGRW* 213; Cilicia, Asia Minor; late I BCE–I CE).[29]

Typologising Yahweh Groups

Many researchers now follow Josephus in categorising Yahweh groups as associations.[30] For example, Philip Harland recently identified Yahweh groups in Asia Minor as associations whose membership profiles were based on ethnic or geographic connections primarily. He observes, 'In light of the tendency of Italians, Pergaians, Alexandrians, and others to congregate together [in Asia Minor], it is not surprising to find Judeans (*Ioudaioi*) in the cities of Asia (and "Israelites" or Samaritans on the island of Delos, for instance) forming similar groups, sometimes using terminology common to other associations.'[31] Rajak arrives at a similar conclusion: Yahweh groups fit '*within* the broad framework of a spectrum of types of Graeco-Roman associations. The Jewish heritage and the people's needs were expressed within the available models, whether primarily pious associations, trade guilds, emigrant ethnic groups or philosophical schools'.[32] More recently, Richard Ascough has helpfully classified synagogues as species of the association *genus*.[33]

Rajak's, Harland's, and Ascough's placement of Yahweh groups within broader ancient associative behaviour seems more sustainable than positing a separate category altogether for them. But the data allow us to build further from the foundations they laid. Since the

---

[29] Several other Judean inscriptions also attest to strategies implemented to meet honorific concerns. See, e.g., *IJO* I Mac1 = *GRA* I 73 (Stobi, Macedonia; II–III CE) and *IJO* II 36 = *AGRW* 105 (Kyme or Phocaea, Asia Minor; III CE).

[30] See, e.g., Runesson, *Origins of the Synagogue*, 467–86; Kloppenborg and Ascough, *Attica*, 340–5; Richardson, 'Early Synagogues as Collegia', 90–109; Peter G. Richardson, 'An Architectural Case for Synagogues as Associations', in *The Ancient Synagogue from Its Origins Until 200 C.E.: Papers Presented at an International Conference at Lund University October 14–17, 2001*, ed. Birger Olson and Magnus Zetterholm (CBNT 39; Stockholm: Almqvist and Wiksell, 2003), 90–117; and Matthias Klinghardt, 'The Manual of Discipline in the Light of Statues of Hellenistic Associations', in *Methods of Investigation of the Dead Sea Scrolls and the Khirbet Qumran Site: Present Realities and Future Prospects*, ed. Michael O. Wise, Norman Golb, John J. Colllins, and Dennis G. Pardee (Annals of the New York Academy of Sciences 722; New York: New York Academy of Sciences, 1994), 251–70.

[31] Harland, *Associations*, 34.

[32] Rajak, 'Synagogue and Community', 37 (emphasis added).

[33] Ascough, 'Apples-to-Apples'.

membership profiles of Zeus groups, Herakles groups, Christ groups, and so on cannot be understood as primarily ethnic or cultic networks, the possibility that the same is true of Yahweh groups deserves attention.[34] Yahweh groups, I suggest, are subject to the same fivefold typology with which other associations are now understood. This means that the membership profiles of Yahweh groups require scrutiny on a case-by-case basis.

Yahweh Groups without Ethnic Coherence

Ethnic uniformity is discernible in some membership profiles of Yahweh groups. However, it is misleading to think that Yahweh groups attracted only Judeans or an inordinately high percentage of Judeans. In diasporic settings, some ethnic associations of Judeans emerged,[35] but other types of Yahweh groups existed alongside them. For example, the

[34] Anders Runesson has drawn attention to this, and his research generates a twofold typology of Yahweh groups: public village assemblies (e.g., Luke 4:16–30) and mostly private associations (e.g., Acts 6:9). For a summary of this model, see Anders Runesson, 'The Origins of the Synagogue in Past and Present Research – Some Comments on Definitions, Theories, and Sources', *Studia Theologica* 57 (2003), 60–76 (68–73).

[35] Ethnic associations devoted to the Judean deity were taxonomically similar, in terms of membership profile and function, to ethnic associations of other immigrant communities in Greek and Roman cities. Delos, for example, was home to multiple immigrant communities who formed ethnic associations in Hellenistic and Roman eras. One of these groups was Samaritan. Two inscriptions from the Hellenistic era attest to an association of Samaritans who identified themselves as οἱ ἐν Δήλῳ Ἰσραηλῖται (*IJO* I Ach 66 = *AGRW* 222a [250–175 BCE]; *IJO* I Ach 67 = *AGRW* 222b [150–50 BCE]). A second group was Judean. Josephus preserves a Roman decree attesting to the practices of an ethnic Judean association in Delos, as well as affirming its right to assemble (*Ant.* 14.213–16). A third group was Tyrian. Tyrian immigrants living in Delos constructed a temple devoted to Herakles (*IDelos* 1519 = *AGRW* 223; 153/152 BCE), whom they identified with the divine founder of Tyre, the deity Melqart (l.15). A fourth group was Berytian. We have epigraphic evidence for this association (*IDelos* 1520; 1772–1796; 2325). At one of their meetings, they decided that the Berytian community at Delos would hold a celebratory banquet each year in honour of their patron, Marcus Minatius, who assisted in the financing of the association's clubhouse, as well as contributed funds to the association for various other purposes (*IDelos* 1520.34–6 = *AGRW* 224; Delos, after 153/152 BCE). Venturing beyond Delos would bring our attention to further ethnic associations. For some of these data, see Philip A. Harland, *Dynamics of Identity in the World of the Early Christians. Associations, Judeans, and Cultural Minorities* (New York and London: T&T Clark, 2009), 99–122; Harland, *Associations*, 33–6; George La Pina, 'Foreign Groups in Rome during the First Centuries of the Empire', *HTR* 20 (1927): 183–403; Lelia Ruggini, 'Ebrei e orientali nell'Italia settentrionale fra il IV e il VI secolo', *Studia et documenta historiae et iuris* 25 (1959): 186–308; and David Noy, *Foreigners at Rome: Citizens and Strangers* (London: Gerald Duckworth, 2000).

Nysa inscription quoted earlier (*IJO* II Nysa 26) mentions both the ethnic Judean community called the λαός (1.4)[36] and a private association (σύνοδος) established by a certain Dositheos (1.5). This individual's association could have very well consisted of an ethnically diverse membership profile and, therefore, could have been representative of a different type of association than the former ethnic group who also met in the building.

In Rome, we have five inscriptions attesting to a Yahweh group that seemingly comprised of lime workers (*calcarenses*).[37] If this group's members were all Judeans, that might have been an arbitrary result of forming an occupational guild of *calcarenses* in the Trastevere area of Rome, where there was a strong Judean presence (Philo, *Leg. Ad Gaium* 155, 157).[38] The 'synagogue of freedmen' in Jerusalem (ἡ συναγωγὴ ἡ λεγομένη λιβερτίνων, Acts 6:9) apparently banded together foreigners from Cyrene, Alexandria, Cilicia, and Asia. Membership in this group was limited to those interested in devotion to Yahweh, and who, additionally, were of the appropriate free status and homelands. Crucially, a common ethnicity did not necessarily bind together the members of this Yahweh group.[39] Other Yahweh groups are best categorised as neighbourhood associations.[40]

These examples of non-ethnic Yahweh groups might have *arbitrarily* comprised exclusively of Judeans, but the possibility that they were ethnically diverse needs to be considered. There is a wealth of data indicating that non-Judeans clubbed together with Judeans to worship Yahweh. Josephus provides a starting point for investigating this practice:

> But no one need wonder that there was so much wealth in our temple, all the Jews throughout the habitable world, and those

---

[36] For λαός as a synagogue term, see Runesson, *Origins*, 171–2, esp. 172, n.10.

[37] *JIWE* II 69 (Rome; III/IV CE?), 98 (Rome; III/IV CE?), 165 (Rome; III–IV CE?), 558 (Rome; III–IV CE?), 584 (Rome; III/IV CE?).

[38] For other occupational Yahweh groups, see t. *Suk.* 4:6 and *y. Sheq.* 2:47a. For secondary literature on this phenomenon, see Samuel Krauss, *Synagogale Altertümer* (Berlin: B. Harz, 1922), 201–6, 261–3; and Shimon Applebaum, "The Organization of the Jewish Communities in the Diaspora," in *The Jewish People in the First Century: Historical Geography, Political History, Social, Cultural and Religious Life and Institutions*, ed. Shemuel Safrai and Menahem Stern (CRINT 1/1; Assen: Van Gorcum; Philadelphia: Fortress, 1974), 464–503 (476–81).

[39] Luke's description of this group is ambiguous; he could have in mind five different Yahweh groups rather than just one group. For analogies to the immigrant type of Yahweh group that I understand to be denoted in Acts 6:9, see t. *Meg.* 3:6; and y. *Ber.* 3:6a.

[40] For neighbourhood Yahweh groups in Rome, see Levine, *Ancient Synagogue*, 284.

who worshipped God (Ἰουδαῖοι καὶ σεβόμενοι τὸν θεόν), even those from Asia and Europe, had been contributing to it for a very long time. (*Ant.* 14.110 [LCL])

[The Judeans in Antioch] were constantly attracting to their religious ceremonies multitudes of Greeks, and these they had in some measure incorporated with themselves'. (*War* 7.45 [LCL])

Josephus might have exaggerated the number of non-Judeans who became members of various Yahweh groups in the diaspora, but Luke and epigraphic data affirm (or, at least provide additional attestation to) the presence of Greeks in Yahweh groups. Luke not only mentions σεβόμενοι and φοβούμενοι τὸν θεόν, whose identities continue to be disputed, but also ιουδαῖοι and ἕλληνες in synagogues (Acts 14:1; 17:1–4; 18:4). The ἕλληνες could be proselytes but elsewhere Luke's word for converts is προσήλυτοι (e.g., Acts 2:11). The epigraphy confirms the presence of Greeks in Yahweh groups. Documentation of θεοσεβεῖς in Yahweh groups represents the best evidence for this, even though the word carried a rather wide semantic range in the epigraphy. We begin in the first or second century, where we have a fragmentary inscription documenting the manumission of a house-bred slave, Elpias or Elpis, in a συναγωγή:

[— — — — — —]κα-
κου ἀφίημι ἐπὶ τῆς προσευ-
χῆς Ἐλπία[ν — —]α[.]της θρεπτῆ[ς]
ὅπως ἐστὶν ἀπαρενόχλητος
καὶ ἀνεπίληπτος ἀπὸ παντὸς   5
κληρονόμου χωρὶς τοῦ προσ-
καρτερεῖν τῇ προσευχῇ ἐπι-
τροπευούσης τῆς συναγω-
γῆς τῶν Ἰουδαίων καὶ θεὸν
σέβων (*IJO* I BS7; Panticapaion, Bosporan region; I–II CE).10

Unfortunately, it is unclear whether καὶ θεὸν σέβων (ll.9–10) should be taken as a requirement placed upon the freed slave, along with attendance at the prayer house (ll.6–7). If so, the sentence structure is odd.[41] The alternative is that θεὸν σέβων is a category of non-Judean membership in the association, in which case the spelling is odd (it should be a genitive

[41] Though, see Irina Levinskaya, *The Book of Acts in Its Diaspora Setting*, Volume 5 of *The Book of Acts in Its First Century Setting* (Grand Rapids: Eerdmans, 1996), 74–6, 232–4.

plural, θεοσεβῶν).[42] This specific issue cannot be resolved perfectly, but both possibilities point towards the presence of non-Judeans in this association. In the second possibility, the presence of non-Judeans is obvious. In the first option, Elpias/Elpis, a non-Judean,[43] was required to attend this association's activities. She/he is an example of a non-Judean in an ethnically diverse Yahweh group. There are many other instances of θεοσεβεῖς as members in Yahweh groups, from the first century to the fifth, but each is disputed.[44] The Aphrodisiac inscription (III–V CE) is worth mentioning only because in this specific instance the θεοσεβεῖς are rather clearly a category of affiliates differentiated from proselytes and Judeans.[45] There remains dispute, however, concerning whether these individuals were Greek benefactors who were being called 'pious', or actual members who participated in the group's activities with the Judeans and proselytes.[46]

Further evidence of non-ethnic associations devoted to Yahweh may exist in some instances of θεός ὕψιστος associations,[47] some manifestations of the Sabazios cult,[48] and in the Sabbatists' association.[49] Lee

---

[42] If θεοσεβῶν was meant, then an additional possibility is that it should read, 'the synagogue of Judeans who are also pious'. For refutation of this possibility, see Paul R. Trebilco, *Jewish Communities in Asia Minor* (SNTSMS 69; Cambridge: Cambridge University Press, 1991), 156.

[43] For three analogous inscriptions, see *IJO* I BS5 = *AGRW* 86 (Panticapaion, Bosporan region; 81 CE); *IJO* I BS6 (Panticapaion, Bosporan region; 90–150 CE); and *IJO* I BS9 = *ASSB* 127 (Panticapaion, Bosporan region; I–II CE).

[44] For a review of the relevant data, see Joyce Maire Reynolds and Robert Tannenbaum, *Jews and Godfearers at Aphrodisias. Greek Inscriptions with Commentary: Texts from the Excavations at Aphrodisas* (Cambridge: Cambridge Philological Society, 1987), 46–67; Trebilco, *Jewish Communities*, 152–64.

[45] For this text, see Reynolds and Tannenbaum, *Jews and Godfearers*, 5–7.

[46] Jerome Murphy-O'Connor, 'Lots of God-Fearers? Theosebeis in the Aphrodisias Inscription', *RB* 99 (1992), 418–24.

[47] Philippe Bruneau, *Recherches sur les cultes de Délos à l'époque hellénistique et à l'époque impériale* (BEFAR 217; Paris: de Boccard, 1970), 480–93; Trebilco, *Jewish Communities*, 133–40.

[48] See, e.g., Franz Cumont, *Hypsistos,* Supplément à la *Revue de l'instruction publique en Belgique* (Brussels: Polleunis & Ceuterik, 1897), 5–7; Rudolf Fellmann, 'Der Sabazios-Kult', in *Die orientalischen Religionen im Römerreich*, ed. Maarten J. Vermaseren (EPRO 93; Leiden: Brill, 1981), 316–40 (318). This is now disputed on good grounds. See A. Thomas Kraabel, 'Paganism and Judaism: The Sardis Evidence', in *Paganisme, Judaïsme, Christianisme. Influences et affrontements dans le monde antique. Mélanges offerts à Marcel Simon*, ed. André Benoit, Marc Philonenko, and Cyrille Vogel (Paris: Boccard, 1978), 13–33 (29–33); Eugene N. Lane, 'Sabazius and the Jews in Valerius Maximus: A Re-examination', *JRS* 69 (1979), 35–8; Trebilco, *Jewish Communities*, 140–2.

[49] See, now, Harland, *North Coast*, 426–34.

38   *Greco-Roman Associations as an Analytic Category*

Levine's summary of the scholarly opinion concerning the θεός ὕψιστος evidence reflects the discussion surrounding all three of the above-mentioned datasets: 'Whether these were Jewish or pagan groups, or perhaps Jewishly inspired associations ... consisting mainly, if not exclusively, of God-fearers, has been a matter of dispute.'[50] Since the research on these groups is vast, and the primary data ultimately inconclusive, it is not necessary to review all of it here for present purposes. The point in mentioning it is to offer some examples of what Josephus and Luke might be talking about when they speak about non-Judeans interested in Yahweh.

Rajak has suggested that Yahweh groups held commonalities with ethnic, cultic, and professional types of associations.[51] I would tweak that proposal. The evidence seems to suggest that the membership profiles of individual Yahweh groups differed from group to group – some Yahweh groups were formed primarily from immigrant populations in a locality, some were coherent primarily in terms of occupational status, others pulled members of different ethnicities who were interested in providing cult to Yahweh (i.e., Acts 6:9). In this way, the diversity of membership profiles in Yahweh groups matched the assortment of membership profiles in Zeus groups, Herakles groups, Christ groups, and ancient associations more broadly. In summary, there was no uniform social formation in antiquity that the modern word 'synagogue' can adequately signify. As in the case of associations devoted to other deities and heroes, Yahweh groups' membership profiles varied, their primary functions varied, and their classification also varied on an individual basis.

Philosophical Groups

Some researchers have argued that the Christ groups are better understood as bands of philosophers than as associations.[52] Arthur Darby Nock provided the contemporary basis for distinguishing between ancient

---

[50] Levine, *Ancient Synagogue*, 293, n.122.

[51] Rajak, 'Synagogue and Community', 37.

[52] Edwin A. Judge, *The Social Pattern of Christian Groups in the First Century: Some Prolegomena to the Study of New Testament Ideas of Social Obligation* (London: Tyndale: 1960), 45; Edwin A. Judge, 'Did the Churches Compete with Cult- Groups?', in *Early Christianity and Classical Culture: Comparative Studies in Honor of Abraham J. Malherbe*, ed. John T. Fitzgerald, Thomas H. Olbricht, and L. Michael White (NovTSup 110; Leiden: Brill, 2003), 501–24; Stanley K. Stowers, 'Does Pauline Christainity Resemble a Hellenistic Philosophy?', in *Redescribing Paul and the Corinthians*, ed. Ron Cameron and Merrill P. Miller (Early Christianity and Its Literature 5; Atlanta, GA: Society of Biblical Literature, 2011), 219–43.

associations and philosophical groups in his book from the early twentieth century. Nock argued that associations primarily took part in temporary ritual practices, whereas philosophical schools mostly showed concern for ongoing moral exhortation.[53] Unfortunately, we do not know enough about the philosophical groups to identify their main function, but already in 1873 Paul Foucart found that groups of philosophers, such as Plato's Academy in Athens, had cultic dimensions, and he discussed these groups in the context of *associations religieuses*.[54] Plato's Academy was equipped with a shrine honouring their patron deities, the Muses. Groups of later Platonists, Pythagorean groups, as well as Peripatetic philosophers also provided cult for the Muses, or self-identified in part as cult groups.[55] Even the Epicureans, who did not offer cult to the Muses, provided honours to their founding heroes, Epicurus and Metrodoros (Athenaeus, *Deipnosophists* 298d), and this has led scholars to identify them as θίασοι.[56] Philip Harland contends that 'the philosophers [who] gathered together around the teaching of Plato or others were more or less voluntary groups that sometimes chose the Muses as patron deities and engaged in communal rituals and meals within this context'.[57]

[53] Arthur Darby Nock, *Conversion. The Old and the New in Religion from Alexander the Great to Augustine of Hippo* (Oxford: Clarendon Press, 1993), 1–14. See also Robert L. Wilcken, 'Collegia, Philosophical Schools, and Theology', in *The Catacombs and the Colosseum: The Roman Empire as the Setting of Primitive Christianity*, ed. Stephen Benko and John J. O'Rourke (Valley Forge: Judson, 1971), 268–91. Re-assessments include: Steve N. Mason, '*Philosophiai*: Greco-Roman, Jewish, and Christian', in *Voluntary Associations*, ed. Kloppenborg and Wilson, 31–58 (38–41); and John S. Kloppenborg, 'The Moralizing of Discourse in Graeco-Roman Associations', in *'The One Who Sows Bountifully': Essays in Honor of Stanley K. Stowers*, ed. Caroline Johnson Hodge, Saul M. Olyan, Daniel Ullucci, and Emma Wasserman (Brown Judaic Studies 356; Providence, Rhode Island: Brown Judaic Studies, 2014), 215–28.

[54] Paul Foucart, *Des associations religieuses chez les Grecs: Thiases, èranes, orgéones, avec le texte des inscriptions relatives à ces associations* (Paris: Klincksieck, 1873), 177–87; cf. Harland, *North Coast*, 373.

[55] For the cultic practices of the Peripatetics, see Diogenes Laertius, *Lives of Eminent Philosophers* 5.51; for the cultic aspect of the Pythagorean's group self-identification, see Philo, *Every Good Man is Free*, 2.13–15; for the cultic dimensions of Platonists and Pythagoreans, see Strabo, *Geography* 10.3.10; cf. Harland, *North Coast*, 374–6.

[56] Ulrich von Wilamowitz-Moellendorff, 'Excurs 2: Die rechtiliche Stellung der Philosophenschulen', in *Antigonos von Karystos* (Philologische Untersuchungen 4; Berlin: Weidmann, 1881), 263–91 (275); Diskin Clay, *Paradosis and Survival: Three Chapters in the History of Epicurean Philosophy* (Ann Arbor, MI: University of Michigan Press, 1998), 74; cf. Harland, *North Coast*, 376.

[57] Harland, *North Coast*, 374.

More recently, John Kloppenborg has demonstrated that the second part of Nock's distinction also fails to represent the data. Associations, Kloppenborg shows, engaged in moralising discourse resembling the intellectual practices of philosophies to a greater extent than had been recognised previously.[58] Thus, the functional distinction between associations and philosophical cults established by Nock can no longer be maintained.

Analysis of philosophical groups' other practices reveals similarities to those of cultic associations with respect to common meals and honorifics. One example is the philosophical group that assembled in the Alexandrian Mouseion (*IAlexandriaK* 98, Alexandria, Egypt; 3/4 CE):

> Ἄϊλιον Δημήτριο[ν]
> τὸν ῥήτορα
> [ο]ἱ φιλόσοφοι,
> [Φλα]ουΐου Ἱέρακος
> [τοῦ] συσσίτου ἀναθέντος,   5
> [— —ca.13— —] καὶ πατέρα.

The philosophers (honour) Aelios Demetrios, the orator. Flavios Hierax, member of the banqueters (at the Alexandrian Museum), dedicated (the statue) . . . and father.

Strabo provides additional information about this association (17.1.8):

> [t]he Museum is also a part of the royal palaces; it has a public walk, an *Exedra* with seats, and a large house, in which is the common mess-hall (συσσίτιον) of the men of learning (φιλολόγων ἀνδρῶν) who share the Museum. This group of men not only hold property in common, but also have a priest in charge of the Museum, who formerly was appointed by the kings, but is now appointed by Caesar (Horace Leonard Jones, LCL).

This group of philosophers dined in a banquet room at the Alexandrian Mouseion[59] and identified themselves by the name of the room: the συσσίτιον.[60] Their common meal needed funding – which, unlike

---

[58]   Kloppenborg, 'Moralizing of Discourse', 215–28.

[59]   Mariano San Nicolò argues that this association of philosophers was independent from the Alexandrian Museum. See his book, *Ägyptisches Vereinswesen zur Zeit der Ptolemäer und Römer* (2 vols, Münchener Beiträge zur Papyrusforschung und antiken Rechtsgeschichte 2; Munich: Berk, 1972), I, 196–8.

[60]   François Kayser, *Recueil des inscriptions grecques et latines, non funéraires, d'Alexandrie imperial: Ier-IIIe s, apr. J.-C.* (Cairo: Institut français d'archéologie orientale du Caire, 1994), 290, n.2.

the meals of other philosophical cults, may have been provided by the emperor (Philostratus, *Lives of the Sophists* 524, 533).[61] Their honorific activity required further income. The remaining epigraphic attestation to philosophical groups[62] need not be described individually here since little more can be done outside of repeating insights recently put forward by Philip Harland on the matter after his thorough investigation of associative behaviour among ancient philosophers. Harland summarises his findings as follows: 'philosophers could . . . function in a manner similar to other occupational associations in corporately engaging in honours for benefactors and banqueting together'.[63] In light of these data, the association model includes, not excludes, data from our inscriptions, papyri, and literary evidence of associative behaviour among philosophers.

Conclusions: Abandoning the Old Categories

It is no longer possible to differentiate between synagogues, philosophical groups, and associations on the basis of differing primary features/ functions. That old typology erroneously assigns a uniform character to associations and attributes different uniform features to other supposedly homogeneous social groups (e.g., synagogues and philosophical groups). It then proceeds to place all ancient Christ groups into one of the homogeneous categories or to argue that Christ groups represent a fourth homogeneous category. Each of these assumptions is now untenable, which has caused the breakdown of the old typology and the emergence

---

[61] The other inscriptions referring to this philosophical club also seem to indicate that their meals were publicly financed. See Peter Marshall Fraser, *Ptolemaic Alexandria* (Oxford: Clarendon Press, 1972), 313–19.

[62] References to the philosophers from the Alexandrian Mouseion (or various other Mouseia) include: *IG* II² 3810 (Attica); *SEG* 21:703 (Athens, Attica; 100 CE); *TAM* V, 1 498 (Lydia, Asia Minor); *IGUR* I 241 (Rome; II CE). There is also reference to 'the Epicurean philosophers in Athens' (οἱ Ἀθήνησιν Ἐπικούρειοι φιλόσοφοι), who are one of the several social groups that honour Herakleitos son of Herakleitos oreios (*TAM* II 910.10–11; Lycia, Asia Minor; Imperial period); and other philosophical groups who banded together and performed activities characteristic of associations: *IPrusa* 17 (Bithynia, Asia Minor; II CE) and *IPrusa* 18 (Bithynia, Asia Minor; II CE); cf. Plutarch, *Adv. Col.* 117d–e; Matthias Klinghardt, *Gemeinschaftsmahl und Mahlgemeinschaft. Soziologie und Liturgie frühchristlicher Mahlfeiern*, TANZ 13 (Tübingen: Franke, 1996), 312; and Edwin A. Judge, 'What Makes a Philosophical School?' in *New Documents Illustrating Early Christianity, Volume 10 of New Documents Illustrating Early Christianity*; ed. S. R. Llewelyn and Jim R. Harrison (Grand Rapids, MI: Eerdmans, 2012), 1–5.

[63] Harland, *North Coast*, 377.

of the single classification, private associations: a category of highly diversified, often voluntary, groups that existed between civic and domestic spheres of life.

Differences would have existed between a group of Epicureans in imperial-period Athens, a συναγωγή of Judeans in Ephesos, and a σύνοδος of slaves in Ptolemaic Egypt. But for the purpose of this book, which is a study of money and leadership in the Corinthian *ekklēsia*, the value of grouping together associations into a single category is that most of the groups in this classification needed to find ways to buy food and wine for their meals corporately, and crowns and inscriptions for their service providers, and needed to secure recruits in order to generate income and fill couches on their *triclinia*. It is irrelevant that when they devised mechanisms to purchase food or select and honour leaders, they did it as representatives of different ethnicities or different cults or different intellectual persuasions. All associations are useful for controlling our speculation about how the Corinthian group – a private *ekklēsia*, not modelled exclusively on household organisation (see Chapter 2) – would have used money and selected leaders.

The flexibility of the category is one of its assets: we should prefer a heterogeneous analogy to Christ groups, one which can provide scholars of Pauline groups with data on a range of possibilities for how Paul's groups might have practised their activities. Some practices were rather generalised among the associations – such as collecting membership fees, selecting officers, and delivering formal commendation to service providers. However, there were multiple different ways to complete each of these common activities, and such diversity in association practices helps to control speculation about how Paul's groups might have addressed financial, leadership, disciplinary, and recruitment challenges.

2

HOUSE AND *EKKLĒSIA*

House and Association

Before situating the Corinthians' financial and leadership practices within the spectrum of activities practised by other private associations, the place of houses and families in shaping the identity and membership profile of the Corinthian group requires investigation – some researchers have argued that Christ groups were so modelled after ordinary domestic practices that Greco-Roman associations can offer little analogical value for social historians of Pauline groups. Peter Lampe, for instance, suggested that 'The community life of the Christians formed itself in many respects according to the *oikos* model . . . These assemblies are neither social gatherings of *collegiums* nor meetings of a philosophical *thiasos*, but simply the *private invitation of a host* to the fellow Christians in his district of the city.'[1] This claim necessitates a distinction between domestic cults and cultic associations that is highly problematic: it is well known that cult associations often assembled in domestic architecture,[2] that one variety of clubs (on Kloppenborg's and Harland's membership-based typologies) was the kind that recruited members primarily from kinship relations,[3] and that professional associations often consisted

---

[1] Peter Lampe, *From Paul to Valentinus. Christians at Rome in the First Two Centuries* (Minneapolis, MN: Fortress Press, 2003), 374 (original emphasis).

[2] See, e.g., *SIG*[3] 985 = *GRA* II 117 (Philadelphia, Lydia, Asia Minor; c.100 BCE); *LSAM* 72 (Thera, Aegean; III BCE); *IGUR* 160 (Rome; mid II CE); *IGBulg* 1864–1865 (Bizye, Thrace; III CE?); *TAM* V 71 (Lydia; 140 CE); *IG* X/2.1 255 = *GRA* I 77 (Thessalonica, Macedonia; I–II CE); *IG* XI/4 1299 (Delos, Asia Minor; c.200 BCE). See also the discussion of domestic associations in Philip A. Harland, *North Coast of the Black Sea, Asia Minor* (Volume 2 of *Greco-Roman Associations: Texts, Translations, and Commentary*; BZNT 204; Berlin: Walter de Gruyter, 2014), 178–93, esp. 187–8.

[3] John S. Kloppenborg, 'Collegia and *Thiasoi*: Issues in Function, Taxonomy and Membership', in *Voluntary Associations in the Graeco-Roman World*, ed. John S. Kloppenborg and Steven G. Wilson (London and New York: Routledge, 1996), 16–30 (23–26–7); Philip A. Harland, *Associations, Synagogues, and Congregations. Claiming a Place in Ancient Mediterranean Society* (Minneapolis, MN: Fortress, 2003), 30–3.

of more than one family member.[4] Therefore, rather than choosing either houses or associations as the model for understanding Corinthian behaviour, it is more responsible to employ the household as *one* model for interpreting some aspects of Corinthian behaviour,[5] such as the social usage of space on the theory that this group assembled in houses, and Paul's usages of household and family metaphors in his descriptions of social relationships in the Christ group, while using the association model to generate new questions about the Corinthians' finances and leadership practices when they assembled for meals as an *ekklēsia*.[6]

This chapter first highlights apologetic elements in the position that the Corinthian *ekklēsia* was a series of one-off private household dinners. Such a description is often accompanied by an ethical assumption, namely, that the Corinthians were a moral family-based group that was ethically superior to the kinds of people who joined associations. Second, I revisit the evidence behind the three convictions that generate the image of the Corinthians as a group of families who self-identified in household terms. These three convictions are: (1) the Christ group assembled for their meetings in members' houses rather than in rented space, temples, or clubhouses; (2) the local Corinthian *ekklēsia* comprised of several 'house churches'; and (3) Gaius was the host of the local *ekklēsia*. Portrayals of the Corinthian group as a moral, family, group depend on these three prior convictions; however, none of them finds adequate support from the Corinthian correspondence.

Third, membership numbers in the Corinthian group are recalculated. Presumptions about the group's membership size have typically spawned from usage of the household model. This results from the tendency in

[4] Philip F. Venticinque. 'Family Affairs: Guild Regulations and Family Relationships in Roman Egypt', *GRBS* 50 (2010), 273–94 (277–9). L. Michael White makes all three of these observations in his *Building God's House in the Roman World: Architectural Adaptation among Pagans, Jews, and Christians* (Volume 1 of *The Social Origins of Christian Architecture*; HTS 42; Valley Forge, PA: Trinity Press, 1996), 26–59.

[5] For this point, see John S. Kloppenborg, 'Greco-Roman *Thiasoi*, The *Ekklēsia* at Corinth, and Conflict Management', in *Redescribing Paul and the Corinthians*, ed. Ron Cameron and Merrill P. Miller (Early Christianity and Its Literature 5; Atlanta: Society of Biblical Literature, 2011), 187–218, 191–205. For discussion of models for understanding the practices of ancient Christ groups see also Wayne A. Meeks, *The First Urban Christians: The Social World of the Apostle Paul*, 2nd ed. (New Haven: Yale University Press, 2003 [1983]), 74–84; Richard S. Ascough, *What Are They Saying about the Formation of Pauline Churches?* (New York: Paulist Press, 1998); Ekkehard W. Stegemann and Wolfgang Stegemann, *The Jesus Movement: A Social History of Its First Century* (Minneapolis, MN: Fortress Press, 1999), 273–87; and Harland, *Associations*, 25–53.

[6] For the comparison of the Corinthian group with various models, see Kloppenborg, 'Greco-Roman *Thiasoi*', 191–205.

previous scholarship to calculate the size of the Corinthian *ekklēsia* after hypothesising that families joined the group in great numbers. This chapter finds that the Corinthian group was likely far smaller than what interpreters previously proposed. Indeed, a single *triclinium* would have been sufficient to accommodate the membership numbers evidenced by Paul.

The outcome of this chapter is not that the rich, recent work on domestic space by scholars of the Jesus movement fails to illuminate aspects of the social setting of the Corinthian group.[7] Rather, the chapter seeks to bring into focus some problematic assumptions intertwined in the theory of a wholly domestic setting for the early Jesus movement. Paul's letters to the Corinthians actually suggest a broader associative setting that includes but is not limited to families and houses.

The House: A Moral Meeting Location

Assertions that the Corinthian *ekklēsia* was a household group rather than an association, that it always assembled in domestic space, and that it comprised primarily of families who formed their own 'house churches', are not neutral. These claims have a specific apologetic role in distancing and exalting ancient Christ groups from non-house-based social formations. I begin in 1869, though the usage of houses for apologetic purposes might also be traced through earlier centuries[8] and, indeed, straight to Luke.[9] Arthur Cleveland Coxe, a nineteenth-century Episcopalian bishop, contended that 'Home is a Christian idea. Everything in a Christian's home should minister to thoughts of purity and truth.'[10] For

---

[7] Several excellent studies have been published recently that contribute significantly to our understanding of domestic aspects of Christ groups. For example, Markus Öhler, 'Das ganze Haus. Antike Alltagsreligiosität und die Apostelgeschichte', *ZNW* 102 (2011), 201–34; Peter Oakes, *Reading Romans in Pompeii: Paul's Letter at Ground Level* (Minneapolis, MN: Fortress and London: SPCK, 2009); David L. Balch, *Roman Domestic Art and Early House Churches* (WUNT I/228; Tübingen: Mohr Siebeck, 2008).

[8] John Bodel, speaking about the historiography of religion more generally, observes that 'A hundred years ago private religion was seen as a pristine, unfossilized form of popular religion, as yet untainted by institutionalization', in 'Cicero's Minerva, *Penates*, and the Mother of the *Lares*: An Outline of Roman Domestic Religion', in *Household and Family Religion in Antiquity*, ed. John Bodel and Saul M. Olyan (Malden, MA: Blackwell, 2008), 248–75 (249).

[9] Notice, e.g., the difference between Acts 17:17–34, 18:4–6, 17, 19:24–40 and Acts 16:12–15, 18:7–11.

[10] Arthur Cleveland Coxe, *Moral Reforms Suggested in a Pastoral Letter with Remarks on Practical Religion* (Philadelphia, PA: J.B. Lippincott and Co., 1869), 22. This

Coxe, the job of making the house a Christian home, and therefore a setting of moral purity, holds significance for the state, and falls upon women: women ought to 'make home happy; to fill it with pure delight . . . to teach children and husband to seek no external pleasure, and always to turn homeward for happiness; this is the work of woman; woman only can do this for the Church and for the Nation; and when this is done the Nation will also be a family'.[11] Citing evidence ranging from Jesus tradition to Tertullian and Clement of Alexandria, Coxe argued that family and domestic space were aspects of a distinctive early Christian morality – and he contrasted Christ believers' family values with the immorality of Greeks and Latins in antiquity.[12] For example, Coxes contended that the home originated out of pristine moral qualities of early 'Christian wives', and that it offered an alternative space in opposition to the settings of heathen immorality:

> [Jesus] taught the sanctity and blessedness of marriage and maternity, and the exceptional blessedness of the celibate when received as a gift of God, for a peculiar ministry. Thus heathen morals were rebuked and castigated, womanhood was lifted to a sphere of unwonted honour, and the home was created and sanctified in the purity and chastity of the Christian wife . . . The Lord prescribes to all, whether married or unmarried, a law of discipline and evangelical encraty. The Christian homes of England and America may be pointed out, thank God, as illustrating the divine wisdom; while the degraded monasteries of Italy and Spain and South America, with the horrible history of enforced celibacy in the Latin priesthood, are proofs of the unwisdom of those who imported into the Western churches the very heresies and abortive argumentations which Clement disdains, while he pulverizes them and blows them away, thoroughly purging his floor, and burning up this chaff.
>
> (*ANF* 2:405)

Coxe's argument was part of a broader attack on what he regarded as a later corruption of the earliest Jesus movement's emergence out of domestic settings and family morality. Specifically, the 'enormous

---

discussion of Coxe follows and builds upon Elizabeth A. Clarke, 'Early Christian Asceticism and Nineteenth-Century Polemics', *JECS* 17 (2009), 281–307.

[11] Coxe, *Moral Reforms*, 50.

[12] Arthur Cleveland Coxe, ed., *Ante-Nicene Fathers* (9 vols.; Buffalo, NY: Christian Literature Company, 1887–1896), 1:viii; 2:79, 405; 4:49, 73.

evils'[13] of modern Roman Catholic rules for enforced celibacy among clerics, and practices of asceticism, are traced by Coxe[14] to a minority of early Christ believers' extreme responses to supposed pagan sexual immorality and persecution during the initial centuries of the Jesus movement.[15] While this was a 'virtuous' response to pagan immorality, early Christ believers' ascetic practices were nonetheless 'morbid' in their rejection of the moral marriage, and therefore not part of a pristine original Jesus movement setting but rather part of a pagan milieu (even though they were reactions against it).[16] Coxe's practice of situating the earliest Jesus movement in family and house-based settings is a strategy for articulating the idea that the home is a particularly Christian and moral space that was, and still is, distinguishable from the settings of morally deprived heathenism. This apologetic can be located as well in mid-twentieth-century scholarship on ancient Christ groups.

For example, Gregory Dix, in his 1945 analysis of liturgy in the ancient Jesus movement, described the house as 'the ideal setting for the church's "domestic" worship at eucharist, in surroundings which spoke for themselves of the *noblest* traditions of family life'.[17] Dix does not explain why the house should be imagined as noble. But this rhetoric becomes especially hegemonic in later researchers' work where Christ groups are contrasted with associations, whose supposed moral depravity relates to their alternative meeting locations in non-domestic space (see pages 49–54 here).

It was Floyd Filson's short 1939 article published in the *Journal of Biblical Literature* that set in motion the contemporary social–historical study of 'house churches', including comparative enterprises.[18] In

---

[13] *ANF* 4:49.

[14] *ANF* 2:14, 35, 57–8; Arthur Cleveland Coxe, *The Criterion: A Means of Distinguishing Truth from Error, In Questions of the Times. With Four Letters on the Eirenicon of Dr. Pusey* (New York: H.B. Burand; Buffalo, NY: Martin Taylor, 1866), 49.

[15] *ANF* 2:57, 62, 4:38; 6:312 n.1.

[16] *ANF* 2:79. For Coxe, the modern implications of this reconstruction of Christian origins are clear: contemporary Protestant households are morally superior to Roman Catholic monasteries (*ANF* 2:405). Roman Catholicism, in fact, is consistently hostile towards the sacredness of the Christian family – even the institution of confession 'is unfavourable to the chastity of women and the peace of families'. See Arthur Cleveland Coxe, *The Vatican Council. A Letter to Pius the Ninth, Bishop of Rome* (London: James Parker and Co., 1870), 21, 37.

[17] Gregory Dix, *The Shape of the Liturgy*, 2nd ed. (London: Dacre Press, 1945), 23 (emphasis added).

[18] Floyd V. Filson, 'The Significance of the Early House Churches', *JBL* 58 (1939), 105–12.

Filson's article, the same presuppositions held by Coxe concerning Christ believers' distinctiveness and moral superiority over Greek, Latin, and Judean groups are expressed again by means of the house:

> The house church *enabled* the followers of Jesus to have a distinctively Christian worship and fellowship from the very first days of the apostolic age. Attention has often been called to the fact that the first believers continued to worship with their fellow-Jews in temple and synagogue . . . But the creative and controlling aspects of their faith and life were precisely those which other Jews did not share. These aspects found unhindered expression *not in temple or synagogue worship but in the house gatherings.*[19]

> It was the hospitality of these homes which *made possible* the Christian worship, common meals, and *courage-sustaining fellowship* of the group.[20]

> [M]any [house church] hosts in the earliest years of the Gentile church came from the 'God-fearers', who had shown *independence* enough to leave their ancestral or native faith and establish contact with the synagogues. They had thus shown themselves to be *men of initiative and decision.* In a mission movement which required *resourcefulness and courage*, they were likely candidates for leadership.[21]

> [The house] *provided the setting* in which the primitive Christians *achieved a mental separation from Judaism* . . . It gave added importance to the effort to *Christianize family relationships.*[22]

Although Filson's groundbreaking work contributed much to the modern study of house groups in the Jesus movement – including an explanation for why divisions might have happened in local Christ groups, and insights into the social status of Christ believers – his overall description of the domestic setting of the early Jesus movement is laced with moralistic assumptions that exalt Christ believers over their Judean, Greek, and Roman neighbours. First, Filson mobilises the house in order to separate Christ groups from other ethnicities and groups. He is uninterested in comparing usage of domestic space by ancient Christ

---

[19] Filson, 'Significance', 109 (emphasis added).
[20] Filson, 'Significance', 109 (emphasis added).
[21] Filson, 'Significance', 112 (emphasis added).
[22] Filson, 'Significance', 112 (emphasis added).

believers with employment of domestic space by Yahweh groups (and other associations, for that matter). Second, for Filson, the ancient house actually 'enabled' Christ believers to behave differently from their neighbours. Filson's description of Christ believers' behaviour is curiously idealistic: for Filson, individuals who provided cult to Jesus were 'courageous', 'men of initiative and decision', 'hospitable', and family people. Since Filson's work is the basis for more recent attention to the domestic setting of ancient Christ groups, it is apparent that the move to research the place of houses and families in the early Jesus movement cannot be documented as a netural or accidental scholarly development. Filson's research provided positive and lasting contributions to our understanding of the social setting of the earliest Christ groups, but it also set in motion hegemonic comparisons of Christ groups and Greco-Roman associations, and helped to ingrain in the household model an implicit assumption that Christ groups were superior morally to other ancient cult groups.

In Robert Banks's 1980 study, *Paul's Idea of Community*,[23] we locate the same apologetic moves observed in Coxe, Dix, and Filson. Banks, moreover, rejects the value of association data, a move which establishes the house as *the* morally acceptable setting for the ancient Jesus movement. For Banks, the Corinthians' meal (1 Cor 11:17–34) was a private household dinner party.[24] It was decisively not an association meal because Paul labelled it a δεῖπνον (11:20), a word that, according to Banks, designates private meals, not association meals.[25] Troublingly, Banks argues that the Corinthian group was religiously superior to other associations on the basis of the *ekklēsia*'s linkage to family identity:

[23] Robert Banks, *Paul's Idea of Community. The Early House Churches in Their Cultural Setting*, revised ed. (Peabody, MA: Hendrickson, 1994), 35; cf. 31–4.

[24] See also Lampe, *From Paul to Valentinus*, 192–3, 374; and Lampe, 'Das korinthinische Herrenmahl im Schnittpunkt hellenistisch-römischer Mahlpraxis und paulinischer Theologia Crucis (1 Kor 11, 17–34)', *ZNW* 82 (1991), 183–212 (191–4). In the later study, Lampe proposes that the Corinthian meal was organised as a potluck, a style of banqueting unattested in the association data (despite Lampe's claim that there is one example).

[25] For Banks, Paul's usage of this designator requires the meal to have been an ordinary meal where 'management was [not] in the hands of officials of any kind ... [but, rather] in the hands of the "host" in whose home the meal was held' (*Paul's Idea*, 82). The Corinthians' weekly banquet 'was in no respect different from the customary meal for guests in a Jewish home' (*Paul's Idea*, 81). Banks's identification of δεῖπνα as household meals is simply incorrect. *P.Tebt.* III/2 894, *Frag.4* recto, I.6 (Tebtynis, Egypt; 114 BCE); and *IG* XII, 3 330.129 = *AGRW* 243 (Thera, Asia Minor; 210–195 BCE) label association meals as δεῖπνα. Notably, the Tebtynis club's meal was organised around officials (e.g., ἄρχοντες, ἱεροποιοί).

[T]he meal that [the Corinthians] shared together reminded the members of their relationship with Christ and one another and deepened those relationships in the same way that participation in an ordinary meal cements and symbolizes the bond between a family or group.[26]

Since association meals were of a different typology of ancient banqueting practices, the 'deep' familial bonds established at the Corinthian meal, modelled on an ordinary household meal, were not possible in the context of associations that were less family oriented, less dependent on domestic architecture, and that met in rented spaces and clubhouses.[27] Indeed, the Corinthians' family bond was precisely what Paul sought to achieve when he founded the Corinthian group: 'So numerous are [household and family metaphors], and so frequently do they appear, that the comparison of the Christian community with a "family" must be regarded as the most significant metaphorical usage of all . . . More than any of the other images utilized by Paul, it reveals the essence of his thinking about community'.[28] Again, the special familial bond of the Corinthians made them unique from the associations: 'There are . . . occasional references in brotherly terms to members of the same religious society or guild. It can be concluded, however, that family terminology and the language of love nowhere occupy the central position or possess the intensive meaning that they do in Paul's writing'.[29]

Banks expresses some moral implications of his household model;[30] however, these were later articulated more explicitly by Peter Lampe. Lampe argued that one of the differences between Christ groups and associations was that 'pagan groupings did not develop ethics for everyday life to the extent that the Christians did.'[31] Lampe is speaking about the supposed practice in Christ groups of 'bringing the social strata . . .

---

[26] Banks, *Paul's Idea*, 83. With Banks's final phrase 'a family or group', the possibility is temporarily left open that an association, as a group, might have a similarly intensive religious experience at their meals. However, Bank later clarifies that the family-like bond among participants in the Corinthian dinner that 'reminded' them of their bond with their deity was unlike 'the common meals held under the aegis of a god by the members of a guild' (*Paul's Idea*, 84).

[27] Banks, *Paul's Idea*, 83. The Corinthian banquet was a meal 'to which guests were invited' by Gaius – in other words, it was a private meal in a house consisting of the host and his invited guests (*Paul's Idea*, 81).

[28] Banks, *Paul's Idea*, 49.

[29] Banks, *Paul's Idea*, 56.

[30] Banks, *Paul's Idea*, 112–14.

[31] Lampe, *From Paul*, 98.

nearer to each other' and the ideal that the 'wealthy should share from their possessions'.[32] Crucially, Lampe posits that in antiquity the physical setting where 'different social strata [came] close to each other, even to the extent that emotional bonds developed between masters and slaves ... was the *oikos*'.[33] In this way, the special linkage between the ancient Jesus movement and domestic space serves to exalt Christ believers morally and religiously from the pagan groups that were happy to meet outside of domestic space in temple dining rooms and clubhouses.

Hans-Josef Klauck's 1981 monograph was composed at the same time Banks was writing his monograph,[34] and he arrives at some similar conclusions. Klauck is interested in moving beyond the simple correlation of house church with family, a linkage that he documents in mid-twentieth-century Roman Catholic discourse from Heinz Schürmann to church documents such as the *Lumen Gentium* of the Second Vatican Council. He explores dynamics of the house church in light of broader usages of domestic space by associations and synagogues in order to nuance Catholic equations of family and house church. Oddly, Klauck carefully distances Christ groups from ancient analogies.[35] The 'Selbstverständnis' of Christ groups represents one important distinction, and this self-understanding is symbolised by their distinct domestic meeting location.[36] Members of Christ groups understood the house as a special location where Paul's idealistic propositions concerning social egalitarianism (e.g. Gal 3:28; 1 Cor 12:13) could be implemented. Since there was no opportunity for such egalitarian practices within the rigid hierarchy of other associations that met in houses,[37] Klauck insists that the ideal of 'Brüderlichkeit', and its social implications, differentiated the house churches from several analogies: 'missionierenden Bewegungen, Mysterienzirkeln, religiösen Konventikeln und philosophischen Schulen'.[38]

---

[32] Lampe, *From Paul*, 98

[33] Lampe, *From Paul*, 98.

[34] For Klauck's brief engagement with Banks, see *Hausgemeinde und Hauskirche im frühen Christentum* (Stuttgarter Bibelstudien 103; Stuttgart: Katholisches Bibelwerk, 1981), 12 n.4.

[35] Klauck's consideration of analogies can be found in *Hausgemeinde*, 83–97.

[36] Klauck, *Hausgemeinde*, 99.

[37] 'In Hausgemeinden wurde versucht, den kühnen Satz des Paulus, der selbst in Hausgemeinden lebte, zu verwirklichen' (Klauck, *Hausgemeinde*, 100). Klauck cites Gal 3:28, 1 Cor 12:13, and Col 3:11 as examples of the 'Satz des Paulus'.

[38] Klauck, *Hausgemeinde*, 99.

In Klauck's study, there is a special connection between 'churches' and family. He labels the house church as an 'Einzelfamilie',[39] but fails to justify why families of Christ believers deserve a special designator (i.e., 'house church/community') for their domestic cult practices, and, moreover, how Christ groups that meet in domestic space should be imagined as different from associations that assembled in houses. Noticeably, household associations come across not as nearly family-oriented as do Christ groups that assembled in domestic architecture.[40] Klauck mentions families only twice while discussing associations, and both references are made in passing. In the first instance, Klauck quotes Ernst Kornemann who calls the institution of the professional *collegium* figuratively 'eine Familie im grossen'.[41] In the second instance, he is discussing the well-known domestic association of Pompeia Agrippinilla, which includes the family's extended network, including clients.[42]

In their romantically minimal square footage, house churches began to create a new world of their own that was unlike anything else in outside society: 'Aber im eigenen Binnenraum, in ihren Häusern konnte sie damit beginnen, jene alles beherrschenden Schranken abzubauen und die antagonistischen Gruppen in eine christliche Bruderschaft zu integrieren.'[43] The crucial role of the household as a 'nichtkultischen Wohnraum' in the creation of this alternative society cannot be understated. It 'gewährleistet eine besondere Lebensnähe aller Glaubensäußerungen.'[44] Overall, this description requires the conviction that Pauline idealisations were 'nicht nur ein eschatologischer Wunschtraum' but an actual social program in these house churches.[45] On the whole, Klauck's framework for understanding Pauline groups privileges the household model but, confusingly, marginalises the value of analogous data that could potentially help to clarify routine behaviours practised by both *ekklēsiai* and associations, such as banqueting, securing

---

[39] Klauck, *Hausgemeinde*, 39.
[40] Klauck, *Hausgemeinde*, 86–7; cf. 87–91.
[41] Klauck, *Hausgemeinde*, 87.
[42] Klauck, *Hausgemeinde*, 91.
[43] Klauck, *Hausgemeinde*, 91.
[44] Klauck, *Hausgemeinde*, 101.
[45] Klauck, *Hausgemeinde*, 100. Schmeller (*Hierarchie*) would later show that associations embraced certain practices that might be termed (with heavy qualification) 'egalitarian', but Klauck merges Pauline idealisation with Christ group reality to an extent that the *ekklēsiai* appear socially unique with respect to the cultic analogies he explores earlier in the book.

funding, and establishing leaders. Indeed, for Klauck, Judean house–synagogues are the closest analogies among cult groups.[46]

Roger Gehring's 2004 monograph (originally published in 2000 under a German title), *House Church and Mission*, builds heavily on Klauck's work and uses the household model explicitly to distance Christ groups from associations.[47] Gehring believes that it is only *possible* that 'Hellenistic associations had an *indirect* influence on the early Christian house churches by way of the Jewish synagogue.'[48] Gehring briefly entertains the possibility that house churches might have been structured like *collegia*, but in the final analysis insists that early Christ groups 'understood themselves theologically not as an association but as an *ecclesia* or the family/house of God, which in turn would suggest a theological connection between the house church and the house synagogue'.[49] It is significant that Gehring uses 'family' and 'house' interchangeably. The implications of Gehring's model are that the Corinthian *ekklēsia* behaved like a household rather than an association in terms of its leadership organisation, the structure of its meals, and more.[50]

Disconcertingly, Gehring links his household model to the apologetic claim that Christ groups were especially loving in comparison to other associations In the following quote, 'family' is used descriptively of 'house churches' to emphasise the love that members had for one another:

> In the small, *family-like* setting of the house church, individuals from extremely different social backgrounds were united into one new community. Inwardly, early house churches provided Christians with a training ground for practicing *brotherly love* and had a powerful integrating effect.[51]

'House churches' are kind and compassionate – specifically, they are socially egalitarian – whereas associations, which were not 'family-like',

---

[46] Klauck, *Hausgemeinde*, 99.

[47] Roger W. Gehring, *House Church and Mission. The Importance of Household Structures in Early Christianity* (Peabody, MA: Hendrickson, 2004); Klauck, *Hausgemeinde und Mission: die bedeutung antiker Häuser und Hausgemeinschaften – von Jesus bis Paulus* (Giessen: Brunnen Verlag, 2000).

[48] Gehring, *House Church*, 21 (emphasis added).

[49] Gehring, *House Church*, 21.

[50] For instance, the perpetual leaders in the Corinthian *ekklēsia* were the οἴκων δεσπόται, not elected or appointed rotating offices. See Gehring, *House Church*, 190–4, 197–8, 202–5; cf. Klauck, *Hausgemeinde*, 101.

[51] Gehring, *House Church*, 294 (emphasis added).

seemingly lack the moral integrity naturally associated with domestic
life. How is Gehring able to make early Christ believers' households
more conducive to social egalitarianism than the houses in which some
clubs met? He follows Klauck in offering the following answer:

> Simply gathering in a house did not automatically lead to the
> reconciliation of individuals from diverse backgrounds in the
> church. Meetings in a house Mithraeum were exclusively for
> men; the members of *collegia* were most often from the same
> social level. The membership in house synagogues was a bit
> more socially diverse, but even here there was the tendency
> toward community formation according to profession and
> nationality, which also led to exclusiveness. As a result,
> Christian house churches integrated a large diversity of indivi-
> duals from a variety of backgrounds. This is primarily related
> to . . . the inner structure of this new faith (Gal 3:27–8).[52]

Although Gehring acknowledges that clubs sometimes assembled in
domestic architecture, he contends that the households of Christ groups
were especially family oriented, uniquely shaped by Pauline ideals (Gal
3:28; cf. 1 Cor 12:13), and, therefore, locations of superior morality. It
is worthwhile to provide one further quotation from Gehring that provides additional insights into the theological undertones of the trajectory
traced earlier:

> The integration into the family-like community of a house
> church can fulfill the universal need of all humankind to be at
> home, to belong, to be in a family with a sense of safety and
> security.[53]

With this sentiment, we return to Coxe's 1869 statement that the home
is a 'Christian concept'. For Gehring, the house church provides expression to a universal desire of humanity. The associations cannot offer the
same because they shared a different ethos, one which was not built on
family and house. This idea that the home is a 'Christian' innovation
naturalises the hegemonic perspective of Rudolf Sohm that ancient
Christ groups were destined to outlive pagan associations because of
their divine quality and utility for humanity.[54]

---

[52] Gehring, *House Church*, 295.
[53] Gehring, *House Church*, 304.
[54] Rudolf Sohm, *Outlines of Church History* (London and New York: MacMillan and
Co., 1895), 4–5.

The Theoretical Challenges of the Household Model

The function of domestic space in a particular trajectory of scholarship from Coxe to Gehring has been rather consistent: to distinguish Christ groups spatially and then moralistically from other ancient social formations. In short, houses have served to insulate the Corinthians from the practices and identities of other cult groups. In the 1990s, Jonathan Z. Smith and John Kloppenborg observed that some scholars utilised synagogues to this effect. After reviewing examples of this approach, Kloppenborg argued that 'The attempt to use either Qumran or the LXX to isolate primitive Christianity from the Graeco-Roman world should be recognized as apologetic.'[55] It is now apparent that houses have been employed in much the same way as Smith and Kloppenborg found the Yahweh groups to have been used in the past by some scholars, and this move needs to be recognised as apologetic, as well.

Edward Adams's recent monograph demonstrates that evidence for household gatherings in texts from the Jesus movement has been exaggerated by researchers.[56] Moreover, Adams shows that data suggestive of Christ believers assembling in alternative venues (e.g., rented dining rooms, inns, and bathhouses) are generally underrepresented by social historians. Adams's discovery complements the observations provided here. Both Adams and I have shown that there is reason to believe that ancient Christ groups were not as dependent on domestic space as previously imagined. I have shown apologetic reasons for imagining the house as the social setting of Christ groups; Adams has suggested that researchers have overlooked evidence indicating that Christ groups assembled in non-domestic buildings, a pattern that results at least in part from the apologetic interest of situating Christ groups in domestic architecture. Adams proposes that the phrase 'house church' be abandoned by researchers of the Jesus movement given the paucity of evidence for such a structure in the earliest centuries, and since the phrase is 'deeply associated with the modern house church movement'.[57] Scholarship on the Corinthian group certainly benefits little from the phrase.

---

[55] John S. Kloppenborg, 'Edwin Hatch, Churches and *Collegia*', in *Origins and Method: Towards a New Understanding of Judaism and Christianity. Essays in Honour of John C. Hurd*, ed. Bradley H. McLean (Journal for the Study of the New Testament: Supplement Series 86; Sheffield: JSOT Press, 1993), 212–38(226).

[56] Edward Adams, *The Earliest Christian Meeting Places. Almost Exclusively Houses?* (LNTS 450; London and New York: Bloomsbury T&T Clark, 2013).

[57] Adams, *Earliest Christian Meeting Places*, 202.

'House Churches' in the Corinthian Correspondence

Apart from the apologetic overtones of some descriptions of the domestic setting of the Corinthian *ekklēsia*, there is a second problem with the studies reviewed earlier. Namely, since Paul leaves us with little evidence for the presence of baptised families as members of the Corinthian *ekklēsia* and with no references to the Christ group actually assembling in domestic architecture, why do families and houses – particularly in the form of 'house churches' – factor so large in social descriptions of the Corinthians? In this section, I scrutinise the near consensus position that the 'whole' *ekklēsia* in Corinth was at its foundation a collection of smaller domestic cults, which researchers have called 'house churches'.

It is Paul's two references to the 'whole' (ὅλη) Corinthian Christ group (Rom 16:23; 1 Cor 14:23) that have lead Klauck and others to reconstruct the following two-tiered scenario of Corinthian *ekklēsia* organisation: individual domestic cults, also known as 'house churches' (i.e., Chloe's household [1 Cor 1:11]; Stephanas's household [16:15–18]), assembled several times each week to complete various activities including teaching, preaching, and baptisms.[58] These 'house churches' all came together once a week[59] to form the 'whole church' or the 'local church'. When this whole *ekklēsia* came together, it took part in the same activities practised in the domestic cults.[60]

Without analysing the data yet, there are already two serious problems with the two-tiered model. First, why did Chloe's people or Stephanas's household teach, preach, and baptise several days each week if these activities happened weekly in the ὅλη ἐκκλησία? The idea seems to be based on an assumption of a large presence of Christ believers in Corinth during the 50s CE. Second, why should the houses of Corinthian *ekkēsia* members be identified as 'churches', or as anything other than houses, for that matter? Klauck rightly observes a contrast in practices between the Corinthian ἐκκλησία and the households (οἰκίαι) of various members (e.g., 1 Cor 11:22); however, oddly, he also conflates the two, imagining each οἰκίαι as 'potentiellen Hausgemeinden'.[61] Domestic cultic practices obviously happened in the households of *ekklēsia*

---

[58] Klauck, *Hausgemeinde*, 38.
[59] Gehring, *House Church*, 142. Cf. Adolf Jülicher's commentary on Romans, posits that the 'whole church' met, at maximum, weekly. Adolf Jülicher, *Der Brief an die Römer*, in *Die Schriften des Neuen Testaments*, ed. Wilhelm Bousset and Wilhelm Heitmüller (Göttingen: Vandenhoeck und Ruprecht, 1917), 2:331.
[60] Klauck, *Hausgemeinde*, 39.
[61] Klauck, *Hausgemeinde*, 35. Indeed, Klauck's 'house churches' are not merely potential but definite realities in his reconstruction of the social situation in Corinth.

members,[62] but rather than describing the cultic identity of these house-holds anachronistically as 'churches', it is better to imagine households of Christ believers performing typical libations, prayers, sacrifices, and other domestic cultic activity in honour of Christ, and perhaps in devotion also of household and ancestral deities (1 Cor 10:14).

Apart from these difficulties, the evidence of smaller groups (i.e., 'house churches') in Corinth that assembled separately from the 'whole' local *ekklēsia* is minimal. It consists of Paul's use of ὅλη ('whole') to describe some meetings but not others.[63] Many researchers have taken this to mean that there was a 'whole' Christ group as well as smaller house groups. Smaller house 'churches' in Corinth are never mentioned by Paul, and so the idea that they existed stems only from the assumption that the opposite of an ὅλη *ekklēsia* is a smaller 'house church' consisting of a single family network. I have reproduced all of Paul's five references to the Corinthians' act of coming together below in order to clarify the discrepancy noticed by Klauck and others:

> 1 Cor 11:18: γὰρ συνερχομένων ὑμῶν ἐν ἐκκλησίᾳ
> 1 Cor 14:23: συνέλθῃ ἡ ἐκκλησία ὅλη ἐπὶ τὸ αὐτό
> 1 Cor 14: 26: ὅταν συνέρχησθε
> 1 Cor 16:19: ἀκύλας καὶ πρίσκα σὺν τῇ κατ᾽ οἶκον αὐτῶν ἐκκλησίᾳ [*not a Corinthian group*][64]
> Rom 16:23: Γάϊος ὁ ξένος μου καὶ ὅλης τῆς ἐκκλησίας

As previous scholarship has correctly observed, Paul only describes the Christ group as ὅλη in 1 Cor 14:23 and Rom 16:23. In the other instances, he speaks of local Christ believers coming together but does not explicitly state that these social formations comprised the grand total (ὅλη) of local Corinthians. Klauck's and others' assumption is that the semiotic opposition of ὅλη ἐκκλησία is a 'house church' such as Chloe's household and Stephanas's household.

A problem for that theory is 1 Cor 14:23–6. Here, it is clear that when Paul mentions a 'whole' *ekklēsia* meeting in 1 Cor 14:23, he is describing the same Christ group that he references three verses later without the

---

[62] For a fascinating study of the implications of this on so-called mixed-marriages in the early Jesus movement, see Caroline Johnson Hodge, 'Married to an Unbeliever: Households, Hierarchies, and Holiness in 1 Corinthians 7:12–16', *HTR* 103 (2010), 1–25.

[63] Klauck, *Hausgemeinde*, 34–5; Banks, *Paul's Idea*, 38.

[64] A similar formulation is found in a Latin inscription: *collegium quod est in domo Sergiae L.f. Paullinae* ('the collegium that is in the house of Sergia Paullina') (*CIL* VI 9148–9149.; IX 10260–4; Rome, II CE). Although this was a domestic *collegium*, there is nothing about its self-designation that would suggest that.

58   *House and Ekklēsia*

'whole' qualification.⁶⁵ Rather than taking 1 Cor 14:23–6 as indicating a
two-tiered organisation of Corinthian Christ believers, would it not be more
natural to posit that Paul's formulae for describing meetings of the local
Christ group varied? This alternative model finds analogical support from
association sources, which demonstrate that the language of the coming
together of an association could vary. A sample of associations' different ways to record their acts of coming together exemplifies this point:

> *BGU* IV 1137.2 (Alexandria, Egypt; 6 BCE): ἐπὶ τῆς γενηθείσης
> συναγωγῆς ('having come together in the assembly')⁶⁶
> *GRA* I 39 = *AM* 66:228 no. 4 (Athens, 138/7 BCE): ἐπὶ
> Τιμάρχου ἄρχοντος, Θαργηλιῶνος ἀγορᾶι κυρ[ίαι]. ('When
> Timarchos was archon, in the month of Thargelion at the
> regular assembly')
> *AGRW* 223 = *IDelos* 1519 (Delos, Asia Minor; 153/2 BCE): ἐπὶ
> Φαιδρίου ἄρχοντος, Ἐλαφηβολιῶνος ὀγδόει, ἐκκλησία ἐν
> τῶι ἱερῶι τοῦ Ἀπόλλωνος ('When Phaidrias was archon,
> during the 8th of Elphebolion, an assembly [was held] in the
> temple of Apollo')
> *SB* III 7182 *Frag.3*, l.43 (Philadelphia, Egypt; II BCE): ἐν] τῷ
> Ἰσιήῳ ('in the temple of Isis')
> *SB* III 7182, *Frag.4*. II.44–6: συνήχθησαν ἐν τῷ ἱπποκοιναρίῳ
> ἐν τῇ σχεοθήκῃ ('when they came together in the stable in the
> tool-chest')
> *SB* III 7182, *Frag.4*. III.62: ἐν τῷ θησαγρῷ ('in the store-house')
> *P.Tebt.* III/2 894 *Frag.1* recto, III.28 (Tebtynis, Egypt; 114
> BCE): ἐν Ἁρμύσι[...] ('in the house/shop of Harmiusis')
> *P.Tebt.* III/2 894 *Frag.2* recto, I.8: ἐν Μενοίτου ('in the house/
> shop of Menoitos')
> *P.Tebt.* III/2 894 *Frag.2* verso, II.45: ἐν τοῖς Ἅρπαλος ('in the ?
> of Harpolos')
> *P.Tebt.* III/2 894 *Frag.9* verso, II.15: ἐν Λυσανίου ('in the
> house/shop of Lysanios')
> *P.Tebt.* III/2 894 *Frag.10* recto, l.4: ἐν τῷ εργευτιγω
> ('in the ?')⁶⁷

⁶⁵ Marlis Gielen, 'Zur Interpretation der paulinischen Formel ἡ κατ' οἶκον ἐκκλησία',
ZNW 109–25 (113–14).
⁶⁶ See also *IAlexandriaK* 91.3 (Alexandria, Egypt; 3/4 CE).
⁶⁷ The fact that many of these texts employ ἐν rather than Paul's κατά is normal.
Hellenistic papyrological evidence indicates that these two prepositions were interchange-
able when designating a location. To demonstrate this point, Marlis Gielen cites two papyri

Paul's variances in describing the Corinthian group's act of coming together should not be taken as indicative of the presence in Corinth of 'house churches' assembling with one another apart from the 'whole' association.

There is also reason to believe that Paul's variations might have been deliberate. This argument has been made by Marlis Gielen, who proposes that Paul had 'Textpragmatik' reasons for using ὅλη in the two verses where this word shows up.[68] In Rom 16:23, Gielen proposes, Paul does not describe a 'whole' meeting in the sense of a collection of smaller individual household groups coming together but, rather, employs ὅλη to emphasise Gaius's generous act of hospitality. Gielen's interpretation of ὅλη works well in a verse wherein Paul extends Gaius's greetings to the Roman Christ believers and, in doing so, highlights Gaius's significance to the Corinthian group.[69]

In the only other instance of Paul describing a gathering as 'whole' (1 Cor 14:23), Gielen suggests that Paul's usage of ὅλη functions to supplement πάντες, which comes later ('the *whole* church ... *all* speak in tongues ... '). In 14:26, the whole *ekklēsia* is still signified but now *each* (ἕκαστος) individual is doing something different (e.g., a hymn, a teaching, a revelation), and so Paul drops the ὅλη. According to Gielen, the word, ὅλη is rhetorical and, at least in 14:23–6, functions to emphasise the opposition of a 'uniforme vs. pluriforme Gemeinde', not a local association vs. a domestic cult.[70]

---

where κατά indicates location. These texts show that κατ' οἶκον in Koine Greek occupied a 'feststehender, phraseologischer Ausdruck für ἐν οἴκῳ'. Gielen's examples are as follows: *P.Cair.Zen.* IV 59659.3–4 (Philadelphia, Egypt; after 241 BCE): ὄντων ἡμῶν κατὰ τὸ Νέστου ἐποίκιον ('when we sojourned in the country of Nestos'); *BGU* III 993. Col.3.10 (Hermonthis, Egypt; 127–126 BCE): τὰ κατ' οἰκίαν αὐτοῦ ἔπιπλα ('the household items in his house'). Gielen, 'Zur Interpretation', 112.

[68] Gielen, 'Zur Interpretation', 112–18.

[69] Gielen, 'Zur Interpretation', 112–13. Paul's description of Gaius as a ξένος ('guest') makes Gielen's exegesis slightly problematic. Later, I argue that Gaius was a guest (ξένος) rather than a host. Guests were very important participants at association meals. The papyri show that the difference between going into debt or collecting enough money to fund a dinner could be determined by an association's ability to secure enough guests. Moreover, guests sometimes became full members, and inviting guests therefore may have functioned as a recruitment technique. In other words, describing Gaius as Paul's guest at a meeting of *all* the Corinthians made Paul look good. It also clarified an important financial contribution made by Gaius to the *whole* Corinthian *ekklēsia*.

[70] Gielen, 'Zur Interpretation', 117.

Some larger associations may have held meetings at which only a selection of membership was required to be present,[71] but since Paul's occasional usage of ὅλη ἐκκλησία is the only evidence for the existence of smaller meetings of Christ cults (i.e., 'house churches') alongside a 'whole' local Christ group, the theory of a two-tiered structure of organising Christ believers in Corinth should probably be abandoned – especially in light of the reality that this group could very well have consisted of less than ten members in total (see section titled 'The Size of the Corinthian Group' in this chapter). In summary of the evidence from Paul concerning the make-up of the Corinthian *ekklēsia*, there is no reason to believe that the local Christ group comprised of separate 'house churches'. Some members may have had familial relations within the group's membership ranks (e.g., 1 Cor 1:11; 16:15–18); however, we should not assume that every member was able to afford membership for their entire households and establish 'house churches' (whatever that means). On the whole, the *ekklēsia* in Corinth is best understood as a single group, which Paul clarifies twice (1 Cor 1:2; 2 Cor 1:1).[72]

Did the 'Whole' Corinthian *Ekklēsia* Meet in Houses or Rented Space?

Edward Adams recently expressed doubt whether the Corinthians assembled exclusively in houses. Adams observes that since οἶκος and οἰκία 'can refer to a wide variety of dwellings, and not only "houses" strictly understood', Paul's phrase, ἡ κατ' οἶκον ἐκκλησία (which he never uses to describe a Corinthian meeting), could imply that an *ekklēsia* gathered in a workshop or other location.[73] In fact, as Adams shows, when Paul uses οἰκία to describe the domestic residents of Corinthian members in 1 Cor 11:22 ('Do you not have οἰκίαι to eat and drink in?

---

[71] There are hints of a two- or even three-level system of organising athletes, including a higher, σύνπαντος or σύμπας tier (e.g., *TAM* V.2 984.6–8 = *AGRW* 137; Lydia, Asia Minor; c.220 CE). This 'whole' tier might represent the coming together of athletes from around the world during festivals. There would seem to be little purpose for Paul's local Corinthian association, a group of nine or ten members, to organise itself on this model of the 'worldwide' organisation of athletes. See, Henry W. Pleket, 'Some Aspects of the History of the Athletic Guilds', *ZPE* 10 (1973), 197–227 (216 n.64).

[72] In contrast, see Rom 1:7 for Paul's address to a larger local network of Christ believers consisting of various smaller associations.

[73] Adams, *Earliest Christian Meeting Places*, 20.

Or do you show contempt for the *ekklēsia* of God?'), it actually seems as though Paul contrasts the *ekklēsia*'s space with that of οἰκία space.[74] To account for Paul's distinction between οἰκίαι and *ekklēsia*, Adams suggests that the Christ group may have rented rooms, such as in the Roman Cellar Building in the Roman forum, wherein they would hold their banquets. Paul does not tell us where the Corinthians met (see section 'Gaius: Host or Guest?' for a new reading of Rom 16:23), and so domestic space can at most be understood as only one option for the Corinthians' meeting location. Recent studies by Richard Ascough, Craig de Vos, and Lawrence L. Welborn also entertain the possibility that the Corinthian *ekklēsia* met in rented space.[75] It is unclear to me whether 1 Cor 11:22 really provides data of non-domestic meeting places for the Corinthians; however, there are two other pieces of evidence that point in that direction.

First, recent economic assessments of the Corinthians indicate that most of them lived below the middling strata of ancient society. Where did economically modest associations assemble in antiquity? Was it in the houses of members or in rental space or both? Fascinatingly, the usage of rental space is rather common for modest associations. I reserve presentation of these data until Chapter 3, but at this juncture I would suggest that analogies such as these, which clarify the types of space available to, and affordable for, economically modest clubs, help to control speculation about the locations of the Corinthians' meetings.[76] Second, Gaius, nearly unanimously known as the (only) host of the

[74] Adams, *Earliest Christian Meeting Places*, 29–30; cf. Edward Adams, 'Placing the Corinthian Common Meal', in *Text, Image, and Christians in the Graeco-Roman World. A Festschrift in Honor of David Lee Balch*, ed. Aliou Cissé and Carolyn Osiek (Princeton Theological Monograph Series; Eugene, OR: Pickwick, 2012), 22–35 (26–9); cf. Jorunn Økland, *Women in Their Place: Paul and the Corinthian Discourse of Gender and Sanctuary Space* (JSNTSup 269; London: T&T Clark, 2004), 141. Other texts are even more explicit about the difference between a regular house and an *ekklēsia* that meets within a house (e.g., 1 Tim 3:5).

[75] Richard Ascough, 'Sensing Space: Association Buildings and Socio-Rhetorical Interpretations of Christ-Group Texts' (paper presented at 2013 annual meeting of the Society of Biblical Literature; Baltimore, MD); Laurence L. Welborn, *An End to Enmity: Paul and the 'Wrongdoer' of Second Corinthians* (BZNW 185; Berlin: Walter de Gruyter, 2011), 247 – though he concludes that the group assembled in a *domus* (e.g., 377); Craig de Vos, *Church and Community Conflicts: The Relationships of the Thessalonian, Corinthian, and Philippian Churches with their Wider Civic Communities* (Atlanta, GA: Scholars Press, 1999), 203–4.

[76] See, for now, the association that meets in a 'Thoneion' for 10 drachmas (*P. Oslo* III 143.8; Oxyrhynchos, Egypt; I CE); and also the slave association that occasionally met in the 'Iseion' (*SB* III 7182, *Frag.3*, l.43; Philadelphia, Egypt; II BCE).

'entire' Corinthians (Rom 16:23), actually seems to have been a guest (ξένος) of the Christ group. In the absence of evidence for a householder who hosted the *ekklēsia* in domestic architecture, and in light of the apologetics in situating Christ groups exclusively within domestic settings, it is crucial not to jump to the conclusion that the Corinthians met in houses rather than used rental space, even if we cannot demonstrate where exactly they assembled.

Gaius: Host or Guest?

The notion that Gaius was a host represents one of the longest-standing consensus opinions in social descriptions of the Corinthians and has never really been scrutinised to my knowledge.[77] We can trace it back to Origen, who wrote the following:

> Gaius is understood to be the man concerning whom he relates when writing to the Corinthians saying, 'I thank God that I baptized none of you except Crispus and Gaius.' He seems therefore to be indicating about him that he was a hospitable man who had received in hospitality not only Paul and each of the individuals who had come to Corinth, but he also offered his own house as a meeting place for the entire church. It is of course related in the tradition of the elders that this Gaius was the first bishop of the church of Thessalonica (Romans 10.41).[78]

Origen identifies Gaius as a host not on the basis of Paul's description of him as a ξένος but, rather, from making a hypothetical connection

---

[77] Some recent studies have voiced the possibility that Gaius was the recipient of hospitality, but they ultimately conclude that Gaius himself was the host. See Welborn, *End to Enmity*, 242; and Julien M. Ogereau, *Paul's Koinonia with the Philippians* (WUNT II/377; Tübingen: Mohr Siebeck, 2014), 8 n.42. More regularly, interpreters debate the exact nature of Gaius's hosting role. Some posit that Gaius provided hospitality to Christian travellers rather than hosted local Christ group assemblies: Theodor Zahn, *Der Brief des Paulus an die Römer* (Kommentar zum Neuen Testament 6; Leipzig: Deichert, 1910), 614; Hans Lietzmann, *An die Römer* (HNT 8; Tübingen: Mohr Siebeck, 1928), 128; C. E. B. Cranfield, *A Critical and Exegetical Commentary on the Epistle to the Romans* (ICC; Edinburgh: T&T Clark, 1975–1979), 2.806–7 (Cranfield is undecided); Douglas J. Moo, *The Epistle to the Romans* (NICNT; Grand Rapids, MI: Eerdmans, 1996), 935; Robert Jewett, *Romans: A Commentary* (Hermeneia; Minneapolis, MN: Fortress Press, 2007), 980–1. Others argue that Gaius was host of the meetings of the 'whole Corinthian *ekklēsia*'. For support of this reading, see now, Welborn, *End to Enmity*, 243–4.

[78] Origen, *Commentary on the Epistle to the Romans* (2 vols.; The Fathers of the Church 104; Washington, DC: The Catholic University of America Press, 2002), 2:306.

between the Gaius in Rom 16:23 and the Gaius in 1 Cor 1:14. Modern scholarship has upheld Origen's conclusion regarding Gaius as an *ekklēsia* host but abandoned his rationale. Bruce Longenecker observes that 'The name "Gaius" appears in two of Paul's letters, and both occasions refer to someone based in Corinth. Although it is conceivable that both texts refer to the same person, this cannot be proved, since the name was exceedingly common in the ancient world.'[79] Steven Friesen provides reason to think that this is not the same Gaius as in 1 Cor 1:14: he observes that the supposed household of Gaius, the ξένος (Rom 16:23), is never mentioned in the Corinthian letter and that 'it is odd that Paul said he baptized Stephanas' whole house (1 Cor 1.16) but he did not say he baptized Gaius's whole house (1 Cor 1.14).'[80] Moreover, I would add, it is peculiar that Paul never commends Gaius's service as a host in the Corinthian correspondence, where he praises other service providers (1 Cor 3:1; 16:15–18). Most commentators will voice at least some measure of doubt regarding the link between Gaius the ξένος (Rom 16:23) and the baptised Gaius (1 Cor 1:14).[81]

The most significant challenge to identifying Gaius (Rom 16:23) as a host of the Christ group's gatherings is the language Paul employs to describe Gaius. It is as follows: ὁ ξένος[82] μου καὶ ὅλης τῆς ἐκκλησίας. The descriptor ξένος is a curious one to give to the host of a private cult group. Association hosts are referenced in a variety of ways but never as ξένοι.[83] Polycharmos, the host of the Macedonian Yahweh

[79] Bruce W. Longenecker, *Remember the Poor: Paul, Poverty, and the Greco-Roman World* (Grand Rapids, MI and Cambridge: Eerdmans, 2010), 239.

[80] Steven J. Friesen, 'Poverty in Pauline Studies: Beyond the So-called New Consensus', *JSNT* 26 (2004), 323–61 (356 n.108).

[81] Gordon D. Fee, *The First Epistle to the Corinthians* (New International Commentary on the New Testament; Grand Rapids, MI: Eerdmans, 1987), 62; Anthony Thiselton, *First Epistle, The First Epistle to the Corinthians* (NIGTC; Grand Rapids: Eerdmans, 2000), 140–1; Barrett, *First Epistle*; one exception is Wolfgang Schrage, *Der erste Brief an die Korinther* (4 vols.; EKKNT 7; Neukirchen-Vluyn: Neukirchener Verlag, 1991–2001), 1:155. Early Christian writings attest to several individuals named Gaius. For example, Paul's travel companion from Macedonia (Acts 19:29), a member of a church in Derbe (Acts 20:4), and a 'beloved Gaius' (3 John 1). Cranfield notes that Gaius is 'an extremely common Roman praenomen' (*Romans* 9–16, 807). Given this uncertainty, the most important information we have about the identity of Rom 16:23's Gaius is Rom 16:23 itself.

[82] The Vulgate is similarly ambiguous, referring to Gaius as a *hospes: Salutat vos Cajus hospes meus, et universa ecclesia.*

[83] Occasionally, interpreters suggest otherwise. This is done with reference to *IG* X/2 1 255.18 = *GRA* I 77 (Thessalonica, Macedonia; I–II CE), wherein a cognate (ξενισμός) is used to describe the hospitality a householder gave to a club. See Welborn, *End to Enmity*, 242 n.160; de Vos, *Church and Community Conflicts*, 204 n.100. This word is restored by

association is ὁ πατήρ, not ὁ ξένος.[84] Hosts could also be called
ἑστιάτωρ.[85] Other associations describe hosting duties variously but
avoid using ξένος to do so.[86] Some clubs entirely avoided designating
their hosts with titles. A certain Sosinike, who invited an association
into her house, was not called ὁ ξένος or by any other title.[87] A
Hellenistic Egyptian association from Tebtynis met in the houses of
various members, including Lysanios, Harmiusios, and Menoites, but
this club certainly did not call their hosts ξένοι.[88] That word was
reserved for a very different kind of participant at this club's dinners.

Since Origen's reason for identifying Gaius as a host has been rejected
by scholarship, and since hosts of associations were not called ξένοι as
far as our evidence permits, what reason is there to continue imagining
Gaius as an *ekklēsia* host? Generally, commentators take it for granted
that Gaius was a host without any argumentation.[89] In a recent commentary, Robert Jewett at least acknowledges that the word carried several
meanings in antiquity. Jewett contends that in Rom 16:23 'the Greek
term ξένος carries the connotation of the person granting hospitality
rather than of "stranger"'.[90] While not offering any original support for
this position, he cites Gustav Stählin's thirty-six-page *TDNT* entry on
ξένος and cognates.[91]

Sokolowski, so it is unclear what was actually in the inscription. In any case, it is a cognate
of ξένος and is not a title of a host.
    [84] *IJO* I Mac 1.4 = *GRA* I 73 (II–III CE).
    [85] This term tends to denote the office title of a rotating administrative position. For
example, in an early III BCE inscription from Athens, the duties of the host are outlined
(*Agora* 16:161.12–24 = *GRA* I 14; Athens, Attica) cf. Smith, *From Symposium*, 92;
Ferguson, 'The Attic Orgeones', 82–6; John S. Kloppenborg and Richard S. Ascough,
eds., *Attica, Central Greece, Macedonia, Thrace* (Volume 1 of *Greco-Roman Associations:
Texts, Translations, and Commentary*; Berlin and New York: W. de Gruyter, 2011), 82;
Geoffrey A. Woodhead, *Inscriptions: The Decrees* (Volume 16 of *The Athenian Agora*;
Athens: American School of Classical Studies at Athens, 1997), 231.
    [86] For example, see *IG* II² 1343.48 = *GRA* I 48 (Athens, Attica; 37–35 BCE): ἑστιάω;
IEph 3080 (Ionia, Asia Minor; 167 CE): ὑποδέχομαι; *IEph* 3080 (Ephoes, Ionia, Asia
Minor; 167 CE): ὑποδέχομαι; *IEph* 951 (Ephesos, Ionia, Asia Minor; unknown date).
    [87] *IG* X/2.1 255 = *AGRW* 77 (Thessalonica, Macedonia; I–II CE). Sosinike performs the
role of 'offering sacrifices' (ἔθυε Σωσινείκα τας θεσίας χρόον τινα; l.19) and perhaps held a
status-conferring title such as ἱέρεια (priestess) or ἑστιάτωρ (host).
    [88] *P.Tebt.* III/2 894 (Tebtynis, Egypt; 114 BCE). See Chapter 3.
    [89] For example, William Sanday asserts that Gaius 'is described as the host of St. Paul
and of the whole Church . . . In all probability the Christian assembly met in his house'
(*A Critical and Exegetical Commentary on the Epistle to the Romans* [New York:
C. Scribner's sons, 1923], 432); cf. Cranfield, *Romans*, 2:806–7.
    [90] Jewett, *Romans*, 980.
    [91] Gustav Stählin, 'ξένος κτλ.', *TDNT* 5 (1967): 1–36.

Stählin is unable to show that Paul uses ξένος to mean host. He takes it for granted presumably because Paul uses φιλοξενία earlier in the letter while urging the Romans to give 'hospitality towards strangers' (Rom 12:13). Though Stählin never explicates how Rom 12:14 should impact an interpretation of Rom 16:23, he perhaps assumed that Paul must have meant 'host' in Rom 16:23 since in the same letter he employed the cognate, φιλόξενος, to mean 'hospitality towards a stranger' rather than one of its five other meanings in Hellenistic Greek literature.[92] If this is the implied argument, it is untenable. We do not even need to leave the NT to find another author who uses φιλόξενος to mean 'hospitality towards strangers' and ξένος to mean 'stranger'. In Hebrews, the author makes an identical exhortation to the one found in Rom 12:13: 'Do not neglect to show hospitality to strangers (φιλοξενίας)' (Heb 13:2). Only seven verses later, the adjective ξένος modifies 'teachings' to mean 'strange': 'Do not be carried away by all kinds of strange (ξέναις) teachings' (Heb 13:7). Earlier in the same letter, the author used ξένος to mean 'strangers': 'They confessed that they were strangers (ξένοι) and foreigners on the earth' (Heb 11:13).

A New Reading of Rom 16:23

In addition to occasionally meaning 'host', ξένος more commonly denoted a group of related concepts that were similar in the sense that the denoted individuals were not at home: guest, foreigner, and stranger. Recently, Laurence Welborn acknowledged that the word 'mostly . . . applied to the "guest", less frequently to the "host"'.[93] Andrew Arterbury's study of ancient hospitality explains the Greeks' usage of the word as follows:

> the ancient Greeks seldom found it necessary to distinguish between the various roles in a hospitality interaction. This practice continued through the Roman period. Yet, by failing to demarcate the roles of the host and guest semantically, we can see the degree to which the Greeks (and Romans) considered this social convention to be based upon a fluid and reciprocal relationship. It should be noted, however, that when the Greeks were virtually forced to distinguish between the host and guest, 'they expressed the entertainer by the word ξενοδόκος,

---

[92] The five other meanings are: 'guest-chamber' (e.g., Phlm.22); lodging (e.g., Acts 28:23); soldier's quarters; inn, and monk's cell. See Stählin, 'ξένος κτλ.', 19.

[93] Welborn, *End to Enmity*, 242.

leaving ξένος for the person entertained' (e.g. Homer, *Od.* 8.542).[94]

Since ξένος never referred to a member of a cultic group who invited the association into his or her house for a banquet (see Table 2.1), Rom 16:23 would be one of those special instances where, if Paul wanted to call Gaius a 'host', he would need to use ξενοδόκος or a synonym to signify the host concept. In all circumstances, Arterbury concludes, ξένος was more often employed to denote 'guests' but 'occasionally used to refer to the host in a hospitality exchange'.[95] This concession makes it difficult to understand Arterbury's notion that Paul employed the word in its less-common sense in Rom 16:23: 'Paul refers to Gaius as his host, as well as the host of the whole church.'[96]

Given the range of meanings the word held, it is necessary to set some controls when looking for analogies that can illuminate the meaning of ξένος in Rom 16:23. Since Paul was a non-elite first-century writer, I will limit myself to evidence on the usage of ξένος in other first century sources written by non-elites. First, in the NT, we find fourteen occurrences of ξένος, including Rom 16:23. Ten instances mean 'strange, stranger'[97] and three mean 'foreign, foreigner'.[98] The fourteenth is Rom 16:23. Second, the noun and masculine adjective, ξένος, in all its declensions, appear in eleven first-century papyri from the Duke database of documentary papyri. Here, it never means 'host' but, rather, it denotes a foreign(er), strange(r), or guest.[99] In other words, the ξένοι of first-century papyri are people who are not at home.

Third, the instances from these papyri where the word means 'guest' (and guests) are from *SB* XXIV 16224, an association account. It is striking how consistently ξένος refers to guests in associations. Since

---

[94] Andrew Arterbury, *Entertaining Angels. Early Christian Hospitality in Its Mediterranean Setting* (New Testament Monographs 8; Sheffield: Sheffield Phoenix Press, 2005), 22; quote from St. George Stock, 'Hospitality (Greek and Roman)', in *Encyclopedia of Religion and Ethics* (12 vols.; New York: Charles Scribner's Sons, 1908–1922), 6: 808–12 (808).

[95] Arterbury, *Entertaining Angels*, 104. As examples, Arterbury provides Homer, *Od.* 1.214, *Il.* 15.532; Xenophon, *Anab.* 2,4,15; Dio Chrysostom, *Ven.* 68.

[96] Arterbury, *Entertaining Angels*, 104.

[97] Matt 25:35, 38, 43, 44; Eph 2:12, 19; Heb 11:13; 13:9; 1 Pet 4:12; 3 Jn 1:5.

[98] Matt 27:7; Acts 17:18, 21.

[99] *P.Oxy* VIII 1154.10 (Oxyrhynchos, Egypt; late I CE); *SB* XXIV 16224.60–1 (unknown provenance, Egypt; 76–125 CE); *O.Mich* II 712.1 (Karanis, Arsinoites, Egypt; 8–7 BCE or 36–37 CE); *P.Corn.* 22.1, 30, 128, 129 (Philadelphia, Egypt; 1–50 CE); *P.Oxy* XIV 1672.4 (Oxyrhynchos, Egypt; 37–40 CE); *P.Tebt.* II 401.22 (Tebtynis, Egypt; after 14 CE); *SB* XX 15130.3 (Tebtynis, Egypt; 1–25 CE) – this text is too fragmentary to translate.

Table 2.1 *The ξένοι of Associations*

Date	Type of Document	Type of Group	Source	Greek	Translation
269–246 BCE	Honorific Decree and Membership List	Association	*OGIS* 51.67–9 = *AGRW* 298 (269–246 BCE)	πρόξενος[100]	guest (perhaps honorary guest)
210–195 BCE	Regulation	Association	*IG* XII/3 330.140 = *AGRW* 243 (210–195 BCE)	οἶνος ξενικός	imported wine
180 BCE	Account	Association	*P.Ryl.* IV 589.63	ξένος	guest
170s BCE	Account	Association	*SB* III 7182.24	ξένος	guest
After 127 BCE	Honorific Decree	Association	*IDelos* 1528.11 = *AGRW* 230	ξένος	foreigner
114 BCE	Account	Association	*P.Tebt.* III/2 894 Frag.2 recto, I.5,12 (etc.)	ξένος	guest
112–111 BCE	Account	Association	*P.Tebt.* I 118.4, 12 = *Sel.Pap.* I 185 (112–111 BCE)	ξένος	guest
112–111 BCE or 76–75 BCE	Account	Association	*P.Tebt.* I 177 (112–111 BCE/76–75 BCE)	ξένος	guest
110–107 BCE	Account	Association	*P.Tebt.* I 224, r.3 (110–107 BCE)	ξένος	guest
II–I BCE	Honorific Inscription	Association	*IG* V.2 22.4	ξένος	foreigner
I BCE	Decree	Association	*IG* VII 190.18	ξένος	foreigner
37 BCE		Synagogue		ξένος	guest or foreigner

100 A πρόξενος was, in Athens, 'a person who for some time has assisted visitors from a *polis* [other than Athens] and has shown himself as a friend of that *polis* in general, [who] is now appointed *proxenos* by the *polis* in question'. Mogens Herman Hansen and Thomas Heine Nielsen, *An Inventory of Archaic and Classical Poleis* (Oxford and New York: Oxford University Press, 2004), 98; quoted from Kloppenborg and Ascough. *Attica*, 205.

Table 2.1 (cont.)

Date	Type of Document	Type of Group	Source	Greek	Translation
	Donations to a Synagogue		*IJO* II Aphrodisias 14 B.16		
41–54 CE	Honorific Decree	Association	*IMT* 1431.9 = *AGRW* 108	ξένος	foreigner
26 Aug 43 CE	Ordinance	Association	*P.Mich.* V 244. r. center column, l.7	ξένη	foreign meeting (i.e., not in the usual village or city locations in the Arsinoite nome)
18 Aug 47 CE	Ordinance	Association	*P.Mich.* V 245.31, 34, 36	ξένη	outside the village (i.e., in a foreign area)
25–26 CE	Honorific Decree	Association	*IDidyma* 272	πρόξενος	guest or honorary guest
c.55 CE	Epistle	Christ-group in Corinth	Rom 16:23	ξένος	
c.60 CE	Epistle	Christ-group in Philemon's house	Philemon 22	ξενία	guest room
Before 70 CE	Honorific Decree	Synagogue	*CIJ* 1404.5 = *AGRW* 270 (before 70 CE)	ξενών	guest room
76–125 CE	Account	Association	*SB* XXIV 16224.60–61	ξένος	guest
I–II CE	Foundation Narrative	association	*IG* X/2 1 255.18 = *GRA* I 77	[ξενισμός – restored]	[entertainment of a guest or stranger – restored]
II–III CE	Legal document	Association	*P.Giss.* I 99.25	ξένος	guest
II–III CE			II–III CE		
II–III CE	Account	Association	*O.Narm.* I 49.10 = *SB* XXVI 16373	θεῶν ξένοι	guests of the gods

Paul refers to Gaius as the ξένος of an *ekklēsia*, the following chart is instructive. It lists instances where the word ξένος or πρόξενος, and some other words with a ξεν-root, appear in sources from 250 BCE to 250 CE that also contain an association designator (e.g., σύνοδος, συναγωγή, κοινόν). This chart is not comprehensive of the association data; however, it is representative of the ways associations used these words, and it demonstrates the overall absence of the 'host' meaning in this context.

The data from the NT, from first-century documentary papyri, and from association sources remain consistent with Arterbury's conclusion that the word ξένος most often denoted someone who was not at home (i.e., guest, foreigner, stranger), and it always carried this connotation in situations that called for specificity such as in the writings of associations.[101] I suggest that Rom 16:23 was one of those instances where, to use Arterbury's words, Paul was 'virtually forced' to call Gaius a ξενοδόκος if Gaius really was a host. But Paul chose the word ξένος. This usage of the word in Rom 16:23 should be understood with the data from Table 2.1 in mind.

If Paul referred to Gaius as the guest of both Paul and the entire Christ group, this two-level function of a guest requires further investigation. It is understandable how a person could provide hospitality to Paul as well as to the Corinthian group, but how could a person be a guest in this double sense? Guests were commonly invited to club banquets by *collegiati*, and it is likely, I would suggest, that Gaius was invited to an *ekklēsia* meeting by Paul. This makes him both Paul's and the Christ group's guest: Paul's guest because Paul invited him, and the *ekklēsia*'s guest because he paid to attend one of their banquets. We do not need to imagine two separate occasions where Gaius was a ξένος – a personal ξένος to Paul, and later, a communal ξένος to the Christ group. In fact, associations could record attendance of ξένοι both in a general manner and by the name of the invitee. In a slave association, we have two references to ξένοι. One attestation shows how an individual could be perceived as ξένος of the entire association:

---

[101] When we turn to non-'Christian', Judean literature from the first century, the results are similar to what we have already discovered. For example, Josephus and Philo use the noun and masculine adjective, ξένος, eighty-two times. The word holds a range of meanings including guest (e.g., Philo, *Moses* 1.275; Josephus, *Ant.* 5.145 [twice]), stranger (e.g., Philo, *Moses* 1.58; Josephus, *Ant.* 1.246), and foreigner (e.g., Philo, *Virtues* 1.173; Josephus, *Ant.* 3.214). Only once out of eighty-two usages does the term signify a host (Josephus, *Ant.* 5.243), but this is not in reference to the host of a private cultic group, where the word most often means guest and never host.

in the treasury of a temple when Hermias was the epimeletes,
[the following were present]: Hermias, Bacchos, Demas,
Karpos, Kamax, Psammetichos, Dikaios. [They came to] 7.
[Their] ξένοι [were] Thibron, and ... son of Horion (*SB* III
7182, *Frag.1.* II.12–26).

Here, Thribon was invited by someone but identified as the entire
association's guest. Later in the papyrus we discover Thibron was promoted to a full member, as is indicated by his presence at subsequent
meetings without ξένος status (ll. 65, 83).
In another association (*P.Tebt.* III/2 894; Tebtynis, Egypt; 114 BCE),
we have evidence of guests being identified both in conjunction with
their invitee and also without mention of the invitee. The following entry
in this club's account identifies a guest of the entire club:

ξένος α σ (*Frag.2* recto, I.12; *Frag.2* recto, II.37).
One guest, 200 (drachmas)

This is an attestation to a guest who contributed 200 drachmas at the
banquet he or she attended. In other locations of this same club's account,
ξένοι were recorded according to the member who invited them. At a
meeting on Mecheir 1, the Tebtynis club records a certain Herakleides
to have brought nine guests (ξένοι Ἡρακλείδ[ου]; *Frag.4* recto, l.8).
Although Herakleides was the invitee, another club member, a certain
Patynis, paid for parts of the admission for three ξένοι (*Frag.4* recto, l.3).
In a second instance, four different members each invited one ξένος on
Mecheir 14. The names of these four guests are lost but we know that the
member, Kagos, invited one of them. It would appear that a fellow
member, a certain Pomous, put 60 drachmas towards each of their
admissions (*Frag.5* verso, II.11–20). These individuals were ξένοι
of the member whom invited them as well as ξένοι of the entire
congregation.

Gaius the Guest of Paul and the Entire Christ Group

When Gaius's role in the Corinthian group is understood in light of
evidence of ξένοι in the first-century papyri, in light of ancient associations' signifiers for hosts and guests from III BCE to III CE, and in light
of NT literature, it is difficult to maintain the assumption that he had
any hosting role at all for the Corinthian *ekklēsia*. The reasons for
mentioning Gaius's guest role in the Corinthian group (Rom 16:23)
would have been manifold for Paul. First, guests were essential

participants at association meals: the papyri show that the difference between going into debt or collecting enough money to fund a dinner could be determined by an association's ability to secure enough guests (*P.Tebt.* I 118.15–18; Tebtynis, Egypt; 112–111 BCE). Gaius, therefore, would have been an important participant in the small Corinthian group even if he were only as a guest. Second, it was prestigious for an association to be able to recruit guests to sit in on their meal. These participants often paid their own way and sometimes became full members (see *SB* III 7182, *Frag. 1*, ll.12–26, 65, 83; Philadelphia, Egypt; II BCE). Invitation of guests, therefore, was a recruitment technique: it provided Gaius an opportunity to try out membership in the Christ group without actually committing for any longer than one evening. Identifying Gaius as a guest of the Corinthian *ekklēsia* signified that he was a potential recruit, and also that the Corinthian group was successful in expanding. Finally, describing Gaius as Paul's guest made Paul look valuable to the Roman hearers of his letter. It highlighted Paul's ability as a recruiter and demonstrated that he held financial value to Roman Christ groups with whom he planned to meet soon.

The Size of the Corinthian Group

The notion that several houses of families comprised the ὅλη ἐκκλησία results in inflated estimates of the group's membership size. Even Jerome Murphy-O'Connor's comparatively modest estimation of the Corinthian group's size is still too large. He based his number on his assumption that families dominated the make-up of the Christ group: after finding fourteen male members in the *ekklēsia* from Pauline and Lukan evidence, he reasons that 'We must suppose that, like Aquila, all were married. This brings us to twenty-eight persons, which is obviously the minimum figure.'[102] Others have made similar arguments and have arrived at a membership size of 40–100 members.[103] What is lost in this methodology is the difference between marriage and association membership. The

---

[102] Jerome Murphy-O'Connor, *St. Paul's Corinth: Texts and Archaeology* (Good News Studies 6; Wilmington, DE: Glazier, 1983), 156.

[103] Branick suggests a total of about thirty (*The House Church in the Writings of Paul* [Wilmington, DE: Glazier, 1989], 64); Banks proposes 40–45 (*Paul's Idea of Community*, 35); and several suggest up to 90–100 members: see Bradley B. Blue, 'Acts and the House Church', in *The Book of Acts in Its Graeco-Roman Setting*, ed. D. W. J. Gill and C. Gempf (Volume 2 of *The Book of Acts in Its First Century Setting*; Grand Rapids, MI: Eerdmans, 1994), 119–222 (175 n.219); Gehring, *House Church*, 139; and Welborn, *End to Enmity*, 377.

former usually does not result in the latter. When it does, the association tends to be rather wealthy.[104] In modest clubs, if the spouses and other family members of recruits wanted to join the association, their households may not have had enough surplus economic resources to cover two to four rounds of subscription dues each week and, in such situations, they would have been prevented from joining.

A second problem with the idea that the Corinthian group was between 30 and 100 members is the assumption that there were many members whom Paul did not name in First and Second Corinthians. This is possible, but it should not be assumed that a new cult group devoted to a Galilean hero, that is otherwise unknown in Roman Corinth, would be on the larger side of association membership size ranges.[105] Add to this the unlikely idea that the Corinthian *ekklēsia* failed to provide members with attractive, normative, forms of symbolic capital, such as offices, crowns, and proclamations, and it becomes questionable whether such a group could even survive in a city where other associations offered these attractors to potential recruits (e.g., *ICorinth* III 308 = *AGRW* 26; Corinth, Greece; 44 BCE–267 CE).

A third problem relates to the second one. Membership size varied dramatically in Greco-Roman associations, and the idea that the Corinthians consisted of 30–100 members tends to be made without consideration of the association data. Philip Venticinque suggests that in Roman Egypt, associations 'tended to be small – roughly 10–25 individuals'.[106] John Kloppenborg has collected fifty-five association inscriptions and papyri that provide indications of membership size in associations from throughout the Mediterranean in Hellenistic and Roman periods. Membership numbers in these groups varied from single to triple digits.[107] Kloppenborg argues that certain factors would limit the maximum number of members an association could accept. These included the space the group used for assemblies and banquets and also the group's ability to recruit – especially for occupational guilds whose maximum potential number was the total number of local workers affiliated with the guild's common trade.[108] Kloppenborg argues that

[104] See *Agora* 16:161.17–23 = *GRA* I 14 (Athens, Attica; early III BCE); and *IG* XII, 3 330.94–108 = *AGRW* 243 (Thera, Asia Minor; 210–195 BCE).
[105] See next paragraph for average association sizes.
[106] Venticinque, 'Family Affairs', 278.
[107] John S. Kloppenborg, 'Membership Practices in Pauline Christ Groups', *Early Christianity* 4 (2013), 183–215 (211–15).
[108] Kloppenborg, 'Membership Practices', 190–5.

these data 'can serve to discipline our imaginations when we think about the membership size of Christ groups'.[109]

One significant way in which Kloppenborg's data controls speculations about the size of the Corinthian group concerns the minimum number of Corinthian *ekklēsia* members. The traditional notion that the minimum number of Corinthian members was around thirty is now demonstrably arbitrary: the minimum number of members in an association is approximately four (*IG* VII 33; Megara, Attica; late I BCE) or six (*SB* III 7182; Philadelphia, Egypt; II 174 BCE),[110] not thirty.

The Minimum Number of Corinthians

Were there only four or six Corinthians? The association data are helpful as a first step in analysis for showing that very small associations did exist, and for clarifying the range of possibilities for imagining the size of the Corinthian group. The *ekklēsia* surely fit somewhere within – not outside of – the spectrum of membership sizes presented in the appendix of Kloppenborg's study (i.e., 4–402).[111]

In order to clarify the size range of the Corinthian group, we first explore data from the Corinthian correspondence in order to estimate the minimum number of *ekklēsia* members. Below, it is suggested that Paul's descriptions of Corinthian membership can be fully accounted for by ten individuals and, therefore, that the minimum membership size is ten, not thirty. The ten members of the Christ group in Corinth would need to have identity markers similar to the following individuals: Stephanas, Fortunatus, Achaiacus, Crispus, Chloe, Gaius (1 Cor 1:14),[112] Phoebe, two unnamed women, and Erastus. Our knowledge about these individuals is not ideal, and some of them were not even members, but for the purpose of establishing a minimum size of the Corinthian group, these names can function heuristically as placeholders.

Paul's descriptions of Corinthian members include the following details. In 1 Cor 1:26 and in various other places, Paul assumes some level of status heterogeneity in terms of σοφία, δυνάτης, and εὐγένεια.

---

[109] Kloppenborg, 'Membership Practices', 195.

[110] *SB* III 7182: 6 members; *P.Mich.* V 248 (Tebtynis, Attica; I CE): 9 members; *IG* VII 33 (Megara, Attica; I BCE): 4 members; *TAM* Suppl III 201 (Direvli Kalesi; Western Rough Cilicia; I CE): 10 members. Cf. Kloppenborg, 'Membership Practices', 211–15.

[111] Kloppenborg, 'Membership Practices', 211–15.

[112] There is reason to believe that Gaius in Rom 16:23 is not the same person as this Gaius. See section 'Gaius: Host or Guest?'

Erastus, a civic οἰκονόμος, need not have been an *aedile* to have been regarded as elevated socially from Fortunatus (for example) with respect to the first two categories. It would be enough for him to be a public slave holding a civic role such as *arcarius*.[113] With regard to the third category, putting names to the 'well-borns' is guess work – though names such as Achaiacus and Fortunatus, deriving from geography and personality attributes, certainly fall within the range of typical slave naming practices and therefore might be excluded.[114] Since Paul states that 'not many' (οὐ πολλοί) were well born (1:26), he surely means less than half – perhaps 25 per cent of the membership. We only need a total of eight members if we imagine the 'well-borns' (plural) to represent 25 per cent of total group membership. We could speculate about which of the ten above-mentioned named members were born slaves (1 Cor 7:21), and which were εὐγένειαι, and still have no evidence for the group's membership size other than that it was at least eight (on the 25 per cent εὐγένειαι assumption).

It is commonplace to depict fractionation in the Corinthian *ekklēsia* along social lines (i.e., the socially strong division and socially weak division). We could speculate that these divisions were large, but any size attributed to the divisions is arbitrary. Discussions of Corinthian divisions tend to include consideration of 1 Cor 1:12, where the divisions seem to be fourfold. Here, Paul states that each (ἕκαστος) member of the Corinthian group held allegiance towards Paul, Apollos, Cephas, or

---

[113] Friesen has revived the proposal that Erastus, the οἰκονόμος of Corinth, was more likely a Corinthian *arcarius* than an *aedile*. Since there is no evidence equating the οἰκονόμος office with the *aedile* position, that needs to be ruled out (see Steven J. Friesen, 'The Wrong Erastus: Ideology, Archaeology, and Exegesis', in *Corinth in Context: Comparative Studies on Religion and Society*, ed. Steven J. Friesen, Daniel N. Schowalter, and James C. Walters (Leiden and Boston: Brill, 2010), 231–56 (245 n.42). The other possibility, that Erastus was a *quaestor*, is unlikely since the Urso charter does not mention the *quaestores* in Julian colonial administrations. John Goodrich's discussion of Neikostratos (*SEG* 45 418) of Patras (a first-century οἰκονόμος of Patras (a Greek city under Roman rule) who was a *quaestor* and was very wealthy, may be relevant but it is difficult to make a case for attributing more weight to this evidence from Patras than to data suggesting that Erastus was a lower-level civic administrator. For recent developments in identifying Erastus, see Friesen, 'Wrong Erastus', 231–56; John Goodrich, 'Erastus, Quaestor of Corinth: The Administrative Rank of ὁ οἰκονόμος τῆς πόλεως (Rom 16.23) in an Achaean Colony', *NTS* 56 (2010), 90–115; Alexander Weiss, 'Keine Quästoren in Korinth: Zu Goodrichs (und Theißens) These über das Amt des Erastos (Röm 16.23)', *NTS* 56 (2010), 576–81.

[114] See Bradley Hudson McLean, *An Introduction to Greek Epigraphy of the Hellenistic and Roman Periods from Alexander the Great down ot the reign of Constantine (323 B.C.–A.D. 337)* (Ann Arbor: University of Michigan, 2002), 102–3.

Christ (1 Cor 1:12). Paul makes no mention of 'parties', as in a Paul-party and Apollos-party; rather, Paul states that 'each' of the group's (ten? one hundred?) members was affiliated to one of the four teachers. This requires a minimum of four members, who overlapped certainly with the so-called strong and weak divisions (e.g., 1 Cor 8:1–13).[115] When imagining the size of the divisions, a smaller estimate holds value since it can pull exclusively from named individuals, and therefore depends less on arguments from silence than do larger estimates.

In 1 Cor 7, Paul describes various marital statuses among members. First, in 7:8, Paul assumes the presence of unmarried individuals (ἄγαμοι) in the Christ group. The plural suggests more than one and, of the ten individuals listed earlier, we only need two – perhaps Fortunatus and Achaiacus. In 7:8, Paul also mentions widows (χῆραι). The minimum number of widows is also two. Since Paul does not mention the spouses of Chloe or Phoebe, we could use their names heuristically to signify the Corinthian widows.

In 7:10–11, Paul mentions the presence of Christ believers who were married to other Christ believers. These individuals cannot be the four names already used for widows (Phoebe, Chloe) and for the unmarried (Fortunatus and Achaiacus). The minimum number of members needed to account for the presence of married affiliates is two (one partner in at least two married couples). We know that Stephanas's entire household was baptised (1 Cor 1:14), and the same might have been true for the household of Crispus (Acts 18:8), so these individuals can be imagined as the married members addressed in 7:10–11.[116] In case it seems likely that more than 25 per cent of Christ group members were 'well-born' (see above), Gaius (1:14) can be counted here for good measure as a place-holder for a (well-born) member married to another Christ believer, even though we do not need him. The spouses of these three affiliates need not have been – and probably were not – members in the Christ group.

In 7:12–13, Paul assumes that some Christ believers were married to non-Christ believers. Again, the minimum number here is two. Since

---

[115] Some commentators doubt the existence of Christ allegiance as a separate option because in 1 Cor 3:4–5 Paul mentions allegiance only to himself and Apollos; and in 3:22 mentions only Paul, Apollos, and Cephas as heads of subgroups.

[116] I hesitate to imagine baptism as the only requirement for admittance into a Christ group. Kloppenborg recently demonstrated that a Corinthian would likely know she or he were a member of the local *ekklēsia* not by being baptised but by having their name written on a membership list, which, I argue in the next chapter, would have come at a financial cost. See, Kloppenborg, 'Membership Practices', 206–10.

Chloe and Phoebe have already been accounted for as widows, we need two additional individuals, probably women,[117] to account for this information. Paul does not mention any individuals fitting this description, so they will be left unnamed. Of course, the presence of Chloe, Phoebe, and two unnamed women can account for Paul's assumption elsewhere that women were represented in the Corinthian group's membership list (e.g., 1 Cor 14:34).

In 1 Cor 7:18, Paul mentions a 'rule in all the churches' pertaining to members who were circumcised prior. The presence in the Christ group of Luke's ἀρχισυνάγογος, Crispus (Acts 18:7–8; cf. 1 Cor 1:1), might merit Paul's mention of this rule to the Corinthians – but we need not add arbitrarily other Judeans to the membership list. So far, we have needed nine or ten names to account for Paul's assumptions concerning the Corinthian group's membership profile. One could easily imagine additional members, such as Stephanus's unnamed spouse, if he were married (16:15–18), but no direct evidence exists for more than ten members.

What about the other names that Paul mentions in First and Second Corinthians and Romans 16? When Jerome Murphy-O'Connor's argued that the Christ group consisted at minimum of fourteen male members' names, he followed Gerd Theissen's earlier list, which included the following male individuals whom Paul does not describe as members of the Corinthian Christ group and whom I have left off my heuristic membership list: Jason (Rom 16:21), Lucius (Rom 16:21), Sosthenes (1 Cor 1:1), Titius Justus (Acts 18:7), and Tertius (Rom 16:22).[118]

We should imagine the Corinthian *ekklēsia* to have had a fluctuating number of members. In addition to a minimum of nine or ten core members, the Corinthian *ekklēsia* was rounded off by participants who came and, for various reasons, left. Aquila and Prisca moved to West Asia (1 Cor 16:19; Rom 16:3–5), Chloe (whose name was used only heuristically earlier) and her people somehow affiliated themselves to the Christ group but Paul never mentioned them as members (1:11); Phoebe (whose name was employed heuristically earlier) lived about a two-hour walk Southeast and perhaps made occasional appearances but we cannot be sure (Rom 16:1–2); guests periodically dined with the group: Gaius (Rom 16:23), various itinerants (2 Cor 11:4–5), and

---

[117] See Johnson Hodge, 'Married', 9–10.

[118] Gerd Theissen, *The Social Setting of Pauline Christianity* (Philadelphia: Fortress, 1982), 94–5.

unnamed individuals (1 Cor 14:16–24) joined in occasionally. The Corinthians' guests may have been invited to replace the absence of regular members (1 Cor 14:16) or to fill in for those who were expelled after failing to change their misbehaviour (1 Cor 5:1–13; 2 Cor 7:9–16).

The Maximum Number of Corinthians

The question of maximum size should be recognised as impossible as well as prone to apologetic estimates deriving from the notions that the Jesus movement was destined to succeed, and that the attractiveness of the Corinthian group is self-evident. I do not believe that it is proper to provide a specific number for the maximum membership size since, as has been pointed out already, the group's size fluctuated based on the presence of guests and the migration as well as expulsion of former members. Nonetheless, we can consider some limiting factors and, in this way, indirectly imagine the maximum size of the group.

Several factors suggest that we should imagine the maximum size of the Corinthian group close to the minimum size (i.e., ten). First, let us look at the statistics. An association consisting of ten names fits within the typical range Philip Venticinque finds in Roman Egypt (ten to twenty-five).[119] Some of the associations in Venticinque's database existed far longer than did the Corinthian group at the time Paul wrote his letters and also had the benefit of taking on patron deities/heroes far more recognisable than Christ. Neither of these factors should be dismissed when imagining limitations to the size of the Corinthian group. Unfortunately, we do not know the typical size of associations in Roman Corinth; our extant Hellenistic and Roman association inscriptions from Corinth amount to eighteen; however, they do not inform us of average membership size.[120] It would be special pleading to suggest that Corinthian associations were larger on average than Hellenistic and Roman era Egyptian ones.

Second, Kloppenborg has argued that a limiting factor would be the space available to an association.[121] As well, Dennis Smith recently proposed a small membership size for the Corinthians on the basis of available dining space. He observes the following:

---

[119] Venticinque, 'Family Affairs', 278.

[120] *ICorinth* I 1,2,3,4,5,6,7,8,9,10; *ICorinth* III 46, 62, 306, 307, 308, 309, 310; *GCRE* 47. For Yahweh associations, see Acts 18:4–8 (a συναγωγή of Greeks and Judeans); and, possibly, *NewDocs* IV 113; *CIJ* I 718; *SEG* 981.

[121] Kloppenborg, 'Membership Practices', 190–2.

Our starting point should be the potential capacity of the dining space. The standard *triclinium* was designed for nine diners, three couches with three spaces for diners per couch. However, as indicated in vase paintings and in literary references, it was not unusual for diners to share couches and crowd in closely.[122]

Our information from the Corinthian letters independently suggests a minimum size that corresponds almost perfectly to the number of diners that would fit at a *triclinium*. Before arbitrarily suggesting that the minimum size of ten is far lower than the actual size, Smith's insights would need to be addressed. Ten members is nearly ideal for the space at an average-sized *triclinium* but also on the verge of overcrowding the group's dining space. If the Christ group only consisted of ten full members, already there would have been weeks when its members would have required to share couches and crowd together when its participant numbers fluctuated upwards from ten because of invitations of guests and other factors. But if the group assembled at a *triclinium* – for example, in one of the dining room at the Asklepeion, in a rented private dining room, or otherwise – a total of ten participants would have been close to ideal.

In the event that the Christ group had access to more space than it needed for the names Paul mentions as members, such as House I. 10.7 in Pompeii,[123] or a location such as the Anaploga villa in Corinth,[124] the evidence shows that they still might not have accepted 40–100 members.[125] These data have been compiled and presented recently by

---

[122] Dennis E. Smith, 'The House Church as Social Environment', in *Text, Image, and Christians in the Graeco-Roman World. A Festschrift in Honor of David Lee Balch*, ed. Aliou Cissé and Carolyn Osiek (Princeton Theological Monograph Series; Eugene, OR: Pickwick, 2012), 3–21 (13).

[123] Peter Oakes does not suggest that the Corinthians had access to such a space, but does identify the owner of this house as living in a rather elevated stratum of non-elite society (where Corinth's Gaius is often situated), and uses this house heuristically for imagining a 'house church' See Oakes, *Reading Romans*, 32–3.

[124] Murphy-O'Connor, *St. Paul's Corinth*, 153–61.

[125] Scholars, who have followed Murphy-O'Connor's usage of the Anaploga villa as 'typical', tend to assume that large spaces need to be filled to their architectural capacity, and argue that the Corinthian *ekklēsia* had the space for, and therefore recruited, forty to more than a hundred members. More recently, David Horrell imagined a 10 × 5m room 'equipped perhaps with some tables and benches' wherein 'it would by no means be impossible to cram in 50 or so people, though this would probably be pretty crowded' (David G. Horrell, 'Domestic Space and Christian Meetings at Corinth: Imagining New Contexts and the Buildings East of the Theatre', *NTS* 50 [2004], 349–69 [367–8]). Dennis Smith is rightly critical of these assumptions, as well as unpersuaded by the argument that a

Richard Ascough. He observes that even associations that were wealthy enough to acquire large amounts of space preferred not to cram their dining rooms to capacity, favouring intimate nine to twelve-person banquets. For example, the clubhouse of the Dionysiac 'cowherds' in Pergamon measured 24m × 10m, and consisted of two *triclinia* rooms, with two meters between them (*AGRW* B6; II–IV CE). Wolfgang Radt estimated that these rooms had a combined capacity of seventy members.[126] Ascough shows, however, that in the first century (*IPergamon* 485 = *AGRW* 115) this association consisted of twenty-four members, despite having the space to fit many more members uncomfortably. In the second century, by which time the second dining room had presumably already been added,[127] a fragmentary inscription lists only seventeen members but probably included up to twenty before it broke (*IPergamonSupp AM* 24, no. 31 = *AGRW* 116).[128] This means that although the rooms could be filled with seventy diners in theory, the group's actual preference and practice seems to be to maintain the intimacy of smaller banquets.[129] Ascough's analysis of associations' dining space, along with inscriptional evidence attesting to associations' membership size, leads him to conclude that groups whose membership was higher than twenty preferred to hold their banquets in multiple dining rooms so that the intimacy of a small banquet might be preserved.[130]

The Corinthians may have lived below the socio-economic levels of association who possessed the banquet halls and spaces explored by Ascough. Nonetheless, economically modest associations also find themselves dining in *single* rooms: rented temple banquet rooms,[131] rental dining rooms attached to domestic buildings,[132] storerooms, tool

---

Corinthian banquet would use space in an atrium as in Murphy-O'Connor's Anaploga model. See Smith, 'The House Church', 11–12.

[126] Richard S. Ascough, 'Implications of Association Meeting Places for Imagining the Size of Pauline Christ Groups' (paper presented at the annual meeting of the SNTS, Szeged, Hungary, 2014), 1–35(12). Ascough cites Wolfgang Radt, *Pergamon: Geschichte und Bauten einer antiken Metropole* (Darmstadt: Primus, 1999), 197.

[127] Ascough, 'Implications', 12; cf. Radt, *Pergamon*, 196.

[128] Ascough notes that the missing text amounts to just one line. The total membership was therefore no more than twenty. See Ascough, 'Implications', 14.

[129] Ascough, 'Implications', 14.

[130] Ascough, 'Implications', 26.

[131] *P.Oslo* III 143.8 (Oxyrhynchos, Egypt; I CE); *SB* III 7182, *Frag. 3* (Philadelphia, Egypt; II BCE).

[132] This is most likely in mind in *SB* X 10278.12–14 (Heptacomia, Egypt; c.114–119 CE).

chests, and other locations.[133] Some of economically modest associations, such as a slave club, consisted of less than ten members.[134] Others were larger than this but still smaller than typical estimates of the Corinthians' size. If modest associations' dining practices resembled middling associations' banquets, then we can imagine a *triclinium* arrangement in their single-room meetings, which would have limited their membership size accordingly. Dennis Smith has recently rejected the notion that an association would use spaces for meals other than *triclinia*, such as *atria*, because of lack of evidence of dining in atria from antiquity – and, of course, lack of evidence from Paul.[135]

Returning to the impossible question of the Corinthian group's maximum size, we could go as high as twenty-four if we imagine the group to have been wealthy enough to secure two of the dining rooms at the Asklepeion for its members, or even thirty-six members if we imagine the *ekklēsia* to have secured even more dining space. There are some problems with these estimates, however, since they would put the group's size on par with some of the wealthier associations on record who could afford substantial clubhouses. Our association data also include modest clubs that attracted twenty or thirty members.[136] But these groups probably offered cult towards recognised deities/heroes, unlike the Corinthians.

Considering the fact that a forty-member association was higher than average, we need to ask whether forty Roman Corinthians would have been interested in yet another new cult group in their city, this one devoted to an unknown Galilean hero, and with a founder whose behavioural ideals in 1 Cor 12 would have appeared unattractive to most Corinthians seeking normative forms of status affirmation.[137] The evidence points towards 'no'; however, the pervasive assumption that Corinth's Christ group was destined to succeed and enjoy great recruitment success masks this observation.

Conclusions

Investigations of ancient household practices can help to clarify issues surrounding the social usage of space at Corinthian meetings that might

---

[133] *SB* III 7182, *Frag. 4*.II.44–6; *Frag. 5*, recto, l.79 (Philadelphia, Egypt; II BCE).
[134] *SB* III 7182 (Philadelphia, Egypt; after 174 BCE).
[135] Smith, 'The House Church', 11–14.
[136] For example, eighteen members in *P.Tebt.* I 118 (Tebtynis, Egypt; 112–11 BCE); and twenty to thirty members in *P.Tebt.* III/2 894 (Tebtynis, Egypt; 114 BCE).
[137] Especially if they provided no symbolic capital to its members, as researchers often assume.

have happened in domestic architecture,[138] reactions to Paul's instruction that believers who live with their non-believing spouses should remain together,[139] the daily lives of Christ believers,[140] the architectural evolution of the Jesus movement,[141] and more. However, some scholarship has confined the Corinthian group to a domestic setting, perhaps, in some instances, for the apologetic purpose of portraying the Corinthian Christ group as a moral and noble family-based group. During its very early history, in 49–51 CE,[142] the group may have assembled occasionally in the household of Prisca and Aquila (Acts 18:2–3) but neither Paul nor Luke provides this information. The notion that the group later met in Gaius's alleged house rests on the inaccurate identification of Gaius as a host.

In this chapter, evidence from the Corinthian correspondence has been shown to counter two assumptions about the domestic setting of the Corinthian group: (1) the notion that the local Corinthian *ekklēsia* comprised of several 'house churches', and (2) the idea that Gaius was the host of the larger local *ekklēsia* in the city. Finally, this chapter proposed that the Corinthian group, a new association, comprised of nine or ten members approximately, rather than scores of families amounting from 40 to 100 individuals. Since nine was the ideal size for participants at a *triclinium*, which is where association meals often happened in antiquity, we should not imagine the maximum number to be much higher than ten without considering the issue of dining space, and without addressing head on why we should assume that the Corinthian *ekklēsia* of all associations should have attracted several more recruits than those whom Paul names. One wonders if assumptions concerning triple-digit scores of Corinthian Christ believers' meeting in Gaius's house have in mind Luke's report of 120 adherents meeting in a room of a Jerusalem house with Peter, James, and John (Acts 1:12–15).[143] The actual size of a

---

[138] Key recent contributions include Murphy-O'Connor, *St. Paul's Corinth*, 153–72; Horrell, 'Domestic Space', 349–69; Daniel N. Schowalter, 'Seeking Shelter in Roman Corinth: Archaeology and the Placement of Paul's Communities', in *Corinth in Context: Comparative Studies on Religion and Society*, ed. Steven J. Friesen et al. (NovTSup 134; Leiden: Brill, 2010), 327–41; and Smith, 'The House Church', 3–21.

[139] Johnson Hodge, 'Married to an Unbeliever', 1–25.

[140] Oakes, *Reading Romans*.

[141] White, *Social Origins*.

[142] See Joseph A. Fitzmyer (*First Corinthians* [Anchor Bible Commentary 32; New Haven and London: Yale University, 2008], 38–44) for a review of the literature on Paul's arrival in Corinth, as well as an analysis of the literary and epigraphic evidence.

[143] For discussion of the impact of Luke's myth of the evolution of the Jesus movement on scholarship, see Ascough, 'Implications', 3–4.

Christ group, by contrast, would not have been a static round number – it would have fluctuated due to absenteeism, invitations of guests, expulsions of members, and migration of former members. A core group of ten is most likely since it accounts for Paul's data about the membership size, it is close to the ideal number of participants around a *triclinium*, and it falls within the typical range of association membership size.

3

TWO ECONOMICALLY MODEST ASSOCIATIONS

What Could the Christ Group Afford?

If the Corinthian group elected officers, purchased wreaths, and collected subscription dues from its members, as Chapters 4–7 argue, then *ekklēsia* members must have possessed surplus economic resources. Do Steven Friesen's, Bruce Longenecker's, and others' low assessment of Corinthian socio-economic status allow for such a proposal? For Longenecker, who recently suggested that *ekklēsia* members, on average, came from lower social registers than did association members,[1] the answer is 'no'. Longenecker contends that the Pauline groups' low economic standing would have put honorific rewards such as crowns and inscriptions out of reach,[2] that membership fees were not collected in Christ groups,[3] and that benefactors were less inclined to provide services to the Pauline groups than they were to associations.[4]

A problem with Longenecker's analysis is its general lack of engagement with evidence of non-elites spending, saving, and possessing money in antiquity. Friesen's model suffers from the same omission. Without examining cases of financial behaviour among non-elites from

[1] Bruce W. Longenecker, *Remember the Poor: Paul, Poverty, and the Greco-Roman World* (Grand Rapids, MI and Cambridge: Eerdmans, 2010), 259–68.

[2] Longenecker, *Remember*, 266–8. This argument is made by several other scholars. See, e.g., William L. Countryman, 'Patrons and Officers in Club and Church', in *Society of Biblical Literature 1977 Seminar Papers*, ed. Paul J. Achtemeier (SBLSP 11; Missoula, MT: Scholars Press, 1977), 135–43; Thomas Schmeller, *Hierarchie und Egalität: eine sozialgeschichtliche Untersuchung paulinischer Gemeinden und griechisch-römischer Vereine* (Stuttgart: Verlag Katholisches Bibelwerk, 1995), 73–4; and Thiselton (*First Epistle*, 1342), who notes that in the Corinthian group 'often loyal hard work is simply taken for granted rather than publicly and consciously recognized'.

[3] Longenecker, *Remember*, 271. See also Peter Pilhofer, *Die frühen Christen und ihre Welt: Greifswalder Aufsätze 1996–2001* (Tübingen: Mohr Siebeck, 2002), 207–8; Charles Kingsley Barrett, *The First Epistle to the Corinthians* (Black's; London: Hendrickson, 1968), 24–6; and Chapter 4.

[4] Longenecker, *Remember*, 266.

papyri and epigraphy,[5] Friesen proposed a 'nearly complete absence of wealth'[6] in Pauline groups. Assuming that the Corinthians actually did live where Friesen places them – that is, between middling and destitute categories on Friesen's poverty scale (i.e., categories 5–7; explained later in the chapter) – how can we imagine what a 'nearly complete absence of wealth' looked like unless we explore the financial records of non-elites living in the economic strata in which Friesen places the Pauline groups? Peter Oakes addressed this lacuna partially by offering an excellent descriptive assessment of the various sizes of non-elite houses in Pompeii, and, as a result of this engagement with the data, he constructed a nuanced and highly stratified economic scale.[7]

Unfortunately, the poverty scales of Friesen, Longenecker, and Oakes neglect association data. This omission is surprising since association inscriptions and papyri provide key sources of information on the financial behaviours of non-elites. Poverty scales that rank individuals (Friesen, Longenecker) or houses (Oakes) are useful, but since the Corinthian *ekklēsia* was a private cult group whose income came from the *surplus resources of individuals*, the lowest strata of individuals in current economic scales are irrelevant for modelling the economic stability of Pauline Christ believers because paid membership in a Christ group would seem out of the question for most of them.[8] Koenraad Verboven articulates the centrality of collecting membership dues in all associations: 'Even the most humble associations demanded relatively substantial financial contributions from their members and favoured the "better" to do. The more important a *collegium* was, the more exclusive and expensive membership became.'[9] Upon realisation that Christ group membership was not free (see Chapter 4), we must narrow our focus to the economic strata wherein club membership was

---

[5] Friesen acknowledges the importance of these data in 'Poverty in Pauline Studies: Beyond the So-called New Consensus', *JSNT* 26 (2004): 323–61 (346 n.77).

[6] Steven J. Friesen, 'The Wrong Erastus: Ideology, Archeology, and Exegesis', in *Corinth in Context: Comparative Studies on Religion and Society,* ed. Steven J. Friesen, Daniel L. Scholwalter, and James C. Walters (Leiden and Boston: Brill, 2010), 256.

[7] For Oakes's economic scale, see *Reading Romans* in *Pompeii: Paul's Letter at Ground Level* (Minneapolis, MN: Fortress and London: SPCK, 2009), 61.

[8] See Koenraad Verboven, 'The Associative Order, Status and Ethos of Roman Businessmen in Late Republic and Early Empire', *Athenaeum* 95 (2007): 861–93 (882); and C. C. Edgar, 'Records of a Village Club', *Raccolta di scritti in onore di Giacomo Lumbroso (1844–1925)* (Pubblicazioni di 'Aegyptus'. Serie scientifica 3; Milano: Aegyptus, 1925), 369–76 (371).

[9] Verboven, 'Associative Order', 882.

affordable. Wayne Meeks provides an additional basis for this re-description of economics in Pauline groups: 'there is ... no specific evidence of people who are destitute – such as the hired menials and dependent handworkers' in Pauline groups.[10] Meeks based his assessment on the Pauline evidence, whereas my assessment in Chapter 4 comes from an independent dataset – namely, that of the financial requirements of association membership (since the Corinthians fall within the association *genus*) and from evidence for the presence of a common fund kept by the Corinthians, which would have required members to have possessed surplus economic resources.

In this chapter, I explore two financial records of economically modest Egyptian associations living below the middling stratum and above the level of subsistence. These documents provide significant data on the financial behaviour of individuals whose economic standing reflected Pauline Christ believers. To be sure, Friesen proposed that 'the vast majority of the people in [Paul's] assemblies lived just above or just below the level of subsistence',[11] and Longenecker suggested that 65 per cent of people in the average Pauline group lived at or below the level of subsistence,[12] so these scholars might argue that even the associations explored in this chapter lived above the economic strata of most Pauline groups. The amount of freeloading required on their proposals makes their models untenable, but Friesen's and Longenecker's observations that members of Pauline groups lived between middling and subsistence economic ranks remains viable. This chapter helps illuminate how people in these economic strata used their surplus money. An investigation of their financial behaviour allows us to imagine economic activity among Pauline groups whose members were mostly not middling but cannot have lived directly at or below the level of subsistence.

The overall outcome of these two case studies is the insight that clubs living between middling and subsistence categories found cheap ways to do similar things that middling clubs did. For economically modest associations (like the Corinthians), this meant purchasing crowns instead of marble tablets for inscriptions, providing opportunities to hold cheap offices instead of expensive ones, and collecting modest subscription dues rather than hefty ones. Exploring the income and expenditures of

---

[10] Wayne A. Meeks, *The First Urban Christians: The Social World of the Apostle Paul*, 2nd ed. (New Haven: Yale University Press, 2003 [1983]), 73.

[11] Friesen, 'Poverty', 357.

[12] Longenecker, *Remember*, 295.

economically modest clubs demonstrates that, contrary to Longenecker's assumption, economic modesty would not have prevented Pauline groups from delivering honorifics and collecting subscription dues.

Middling Associations and Poor Christ Groups

In the following pages, I introduce two modest clubs: an association of slaves from Philadelphia (*SB* III 7182, II BCE), and a cult club from Tebtynis that met in houses, workshops, and temple dining rooms (*P.Tebt.* III/2 894, 114 BCE). Since these papyri offer more information about economic life below the middling strata than does Paul, they can serve heuristic ends to control speculations about the economic activities of *ekklēsia* members living in the same economic categories.[13] However, first, we need to explore further why the suspicion persists that associations could afford to do things the Corinthians could not.

In the following sections, I argue that this assumption results from the type of associations with which scholars prefer to compare the Corinthians: we typically find our wealthiest associations in epigraphy, and the four of the associations most commonly compared with the *ekklēsia* are known from inscriptions.[14] These four middling associations enjoyed a kind of economic prosperity that Pauline groups did not experience, and their famous inscriptions tend to shape generalisations about associations' universal economic superiority to Christ groups. This, in turn, generates the idea that Christ groups lacked offices, crowns, and fees due to their perceived economic inferiority to associations.

Comparisons between the *Ekklēsia* and Middling Associations

One example of an association commonly compared with the Corinthian Christ group is the Lanuvium *collegium* of Diana and Antinoüs (*CIL* XIV 2112 = *AGRW* 310; Lanuvium, Italy; June 9, 136 CE). Thomas Schmeller and Eva Ebel view the Lanuvium group as one with relatively low

---

[13] The wealth of information on non-elite financial practices in associations runs counter to Georg Schöllgen's claim that too little is known about ancient urban economics to speak confidently about social status among Pauline Christ believers, though, admittedly, we still know far less than we would like. See Georg Schöllgen, 'Was wissen wir über die Sozialstruktur der paulinischen Gemeinden?' *NTS* 34 (1988), 71–82 (72–3).

[14] *CIL* XIV 2112 = *AGRW* 310 (Lanuvium, Italy; 136 CE); *IG* II² 1368 = *GRA* I 51 (Athens; 164/5 CE); *SIG*³ 985 = *AGRW* 121 (Philadelphia, Lydia, Asia Minor; late II–early I BCE); *IGUR* 160 = *AGRW* 330 (Torre Nova, Sicily, Italy; 160–170 CE).

status,[15] however they both acknowledge that all members of the *collegium*, even the slaves, were resourceful enough to provide benefactions on rotation: four members provided an amphora of good wine, two loaves of bread, and four sardines for each member six times a year when it was their turn to take up the rotating offices of *magistri cenarum* (I.3, II.2, 8–23). These expenses were in addition to hefty entrance fees (100 sesterces) and modest monthly subscription dues of 1.5 sesterces (I.20–1). Social–historical descriptions of the Corinthians rarely claim *all members* could afford all three sets of expenses. In fact, Bruce Longenecker assumed that members in early Christ groups could not even spare from their household incomes modest subscription fees.[16] Thus, even though the Lanuvium *collegium* comprised of somewhat a cross section of ancient society (at least in terms of legal status), the members behaved approximately like Friesen's Gaius, who was exceptionally wealthy compared to other Corinthians,[17] in the sense that he provided banquets for the Corinthians and enjoyed a fair amount of surplus economic resources. We do not know if everyone in the Lanuvium group possessed a house like the one Friesen assumes Gaius inhabited, but they certainly demonstrated their economic prowess by paying high entrance fees upon admittance, and by consistently contributing various dues to their group.

When we explore other associations selected for comparisons with the Corinthians, we find Thomas Schmeller's choice of a Roman club devoted to Asklepios and Hygiae (*CIL* VI 10234 = *AGRW* 322; Rome, Italy; 153 CE). Schmeller identifies this group as a 'sozial höhergestellter Verein',[18] enjoying the support of two rich donors, Salvia Marcellina and Publius Aelius Zenon, who gave benefactions of 50,000 and 10,000 sesterces, respectively. Marcellina also donated a clubhouse to the association. There is little evidence of this type of benefaction or infrastructure in the Corinthian group.[19]

---

[15] Schmeller, *Hierarchie*, 26; Eva Ebel, *Die Attraktivität früher christlicher Gemeinden: Die Gemeinde von Korinth im Spiegel grichisch-römischer Vereine* (Wissenschaftliche Untersuchungen zum Neuen Testament II/178; Tübingen: J. C. B. Mohr Siebeck, 2004), 55.

[16] This is such a consensus that Eva Ebel calls it 'unübersehbar' (*Attraktivität*, 217). See also Schmeller, *Hierarchie*, 72–8; Pilhofer, *Die frühen Christen*, 207; and Chapter 4.

[17] Friesen ('Poverty', 356–8) places Gaius in the highest middling category (PS4).

[18] Schmeller, *Hierarchie*, 26; cf. 37–8.

[19] See David Horrell, 'Domestic Space and Christian Meetings at Corinth: Imagining New Contexts and the Buildings East of the Theatre', *NTS* 50 (2004), 349–69; Edward Adams, 'Placing the Corinthian Common Meal', in *Text, Image, and Christians in the Graeco-Roman World. A Festschrift in Honor of David Lee Balch*, ed. Aliou Cissé and Carolyn Osiek (Princeton Theological Monograph Series; Eugene, OR:

Schmeller and Eva Ebel also compare the Corinthians to the Athenian Iobacchoi (*IG* II² 1368 = *GRA* I 51; Athens, Attica; 164/5 CE), whose status in mid-second-century Athens attracted the 'berühmten Herodes Atticus' as their patron.[20] Schmeller portrays the Iobacchoi's social standing as 'nicht schlecht gestellten', presumably in contrast to the Lanuvium *collegium*.[21] For Schmeller, a distinguishing feature of wealthier associations was the presence of a president who was wealthy enough to hold an office for life, or at least a long time.[22] The Iobacchoi meet this criterion – they selected priests who held offices between seventeen and twenty-three years, which is far longer than the Lanuvium group's *quinquennalis* (three years) and *magistri cenarum* (one year).[23] The Iobacchoi, moreover, have certain features that for socio-economic reasons were long regarded as absent in the Christ group: every member was required to pay entrance and monthly fees (ll.37–41, 46–7); the group was structurally organised with rotating magistrates who owed services to the group; and they honoured their officers with gifts,[24] possessed a clubhouse (*Baccheion*, l.56), and enjoyed meat at certain of their banquets (ll.117–27).[25]

In summary, Schmeller and Ebel compare the Corinthians primarily with middling associations living above the socio-economic position of typical *ekklēsia* members. The same trend appears in other comparisons between the Corinthians and associations.[26] This comparative work lends the impression that all association members were more

Pickwick, 2012), 22–37; and John M. G. Barclay, 'Money and Meetings: Group Formation among Diaspora Jews and Early Christians', in *Vereine, Synagogen und Gemeinden in kaiserzeitlichen Kleinasien*, ed. Andreas Gutsfeld and Dietrich-Alex Koch (Studien und Texte zu Antike und Christentum 25; Tübingen: Mohr Siebeck, 2006), 113–27 (120).

[20]   Schmeller, *Hierarchie*, 26.

[21]   Schmeller, *Hierarchie*, 38.

[22]   This office was usually a priest in cultic associations, according to Schmeller.

[23]   Schmeller, *Hierarchie*, 36–8.

[24]   Unlike the Corinthians, see Schmeller, *Hierarchie*, 74.

[25]   Kloppenborg and Harland recently suggested the following concerning the Athenian Iobacchoi's social status: 'The honors for which a member was required to provide wine are all offices open only to citizens (ll. 127–36): the ephebate; (a grant of) citizenship; rod-bearer, Council member, president of the games, member of the elders' council (*gerousia*), *thesmothesia*, peace officer, and other magistracies. This perhaps means that membership in the group was limited to (male) citizens.' John S. Kloppenborg and Richard S. Ascough, eds., *Attica, Central Greece, Macedonia, Thrace* (Volume 1 of *Greco-Roman Associations: Texts, Translations, and Commentary*; Berlin and New York: W. de Gruyter, 2011), 254.

[26]   See, e.g., Stephen J. Chester, *Conversion at Corinth: Perspectives on Conversion in Paul's Theology and the Corinthian Church* (London and New York: T&T Clark, 2003), 227–66; David J. Downs, *The Offering of the Gentiles: Paul's Collection for Jerusalem in*

financially stable than most Pauline Christ believers, which, in turn, allows Longenecker's statements concerning differences between associations and Christ groups in terms of structural organisation to go unchallenged.[27] The four (or so) best-known associations were middling. The act of characterising all associations according to this very small sampling of our association data leaves us in the dark when imagining the financial situation of the Corinthians. Uncontrolled assumptions then proliferate, particularly, the notion that supposedly poorer Pauline groups simply went without key features characteristic of the associations' structural organisation.

The Rising Social Status of Association Members in Scholarship

It is not only comparative work that gives the impression that associations recruited members from higher economic registers than did Pauline groups. Scholars of *collegia* are beginning to recognise the economic prowess of typical association members who are attested in epigraphic sources.[28] Onno Van Nijf depicts association affiliates as moderately wealthy and 'mainly from among the upper levels of the urban plebs'.[29] John Patterson and others note that the financial cost of joining an association made membership tenable mostly to those with moderate wealth.[30] Andreas Bendlin has shown that even the Lanuvium group, long

Its Chronological, Cultural, and Cultic Contexts (Tübingen: Mohr Siebeck, 2008), 79–119; and Longenecker, *Remember*, 259–78.

[27] See section 'What Could the Christ Group Afford?' of this chapter.

[28] For the older view on the economic status of *collegiati*, see, e.g., Paul Foucart, *Des associations religeuses chez les Grecs: thiases, éranes, orgéons, avec le texte des inscriptions rélative à ces associations* (Paris: Klingksieck, 1873), 5–7; Jean-Pierre Waltzing, *Étude historique sur les corporations professionelles chez les Romains depuis les origines jusqu'à la chute de l'empire d'Occident* (4 vols.; Mémoires Couronnés et Autres Mémoires Publié par l'Académie Royale des Sciences, des Lettres et des Beaux-Arts de Belgique 50; Bruxelles: F. Hayez, 1895–1900), I:32–56; Ernst Kornemann, 'Collegium', *Paulys Realencyclopädie der classischen Altertumswissenschaft* 4 (1901), 380–479 (386–403); George La Piana, 'Foreign Groups in Rome during the First Centuries of the Empire', *HTR* 20 (1927), 183–403 (239–44); Schmeller, *Hierarchie*, 26; and Ebel, *Attraktivität*, 55.

[29] Onno M. Van Nijf, '*Collegia* and Civic Guards. Two Chapters in the History of Sociability', in *After the Past: Essays in Ancient History in Honour of H.W. Pleket*, ed. Willem Jongman and Marc Kleijwegt (Mnemosyne Supplement 233; Leiden: Brill, 2002), 305–40 (307); cf. Onno M. Van Nijf, *The Civic World of Professional Associations in the Roman East* (Amsterdam: J.C. Gieben, 1997), 18–22.

[30] John R. Patterson, *Landscapes and Cities: Rural Settlement and Civic Transformation in Early Imperial Italy* (Oxford: Oxford University Press, 2006), 255; cf. van Nijf, '*Collegia* and Civic Guards', 308.

held to be an association of poorer individuals, was actually a *collegium* of rather well-off affiliates.[31] Jinyu Liu's 'main body of information concerning *collegia* [*centonariorum*] comes from inscriptions',[32] and her careful analysis of social status in these groups reveals many instances of high social standing: members from equestrian ranks,[33] epigraphic dedications with 'high-quality carvings',[34] and large sums of money transferred from members to their associations.[35] These studies generate the impression that even in those associations that comprised members living in a relative cross section of ancient society, the bottom-end was still higher than the Corinthians 'who have nothing' (οἱ μὴ ἔχοντες, 1 Cor 11:22).

With regard to minimum requirements for association membership, Koenraad Verboven recently characterised the bottom-end comprising of people who were far from 'having nothing'. Rather, they were distinguished from their fellow *humiliores* who could not afford the time and money required for membership.[36] For Verboven, 'the rank and file of the *collegia* was composed of ... "working-class" people, making enough money to cover living expenses and in addition to engage in social activities such as college membership, but hardly enough to live in luxury'.[37] Philip Venticinque observes from the Egyptian data that 'members in Egypt or elsewhere needed a baseline of wealth in order to sustain even the most basic membership in such groups.'[38]

Typical association members in these studies, it would seem, were of a 'middling' variety. The top-end of association membership consisted

[31] Andreas Bendlin, 'Associations, Funerals, Sociality, and Roman Law: The *collegium* of Diana and Antinous in Lanuvium (CIL 14.2112) Reconsidered', in *Das Aposteldekret und das antike Vereinswesen*, ed. Markus Öhler and Hermut Löhr (WUNT I/280; Tübingen: Mohr Siebeck, 2011), 207–96 (265–8, 283).

[32] Jinyu Liu, *Occupation, Social Organization, and Public Service in the Collegia Centonariorum in the Roman Empire (First Century BC–Fourth Century AD)* (PhD Diss.; Columbia University, 2004), 13.

[33] Liu, *Occupation*, 239.

[34] Liu, *Occupation*, 242.

[35] Liu, *Occupation*, 243–4.

[36] Koenraad Verboven, 'Magistrates, Patrons and Benefactors of Collegia: Status Building and Romanisation in the Spanish, Gallic and German Provinces', in *Transforming Historical Landscapes in the Ancient Empires. Proceedings of the First Workshop Area of Research in Studies from Antiquity, Barcelona 2007*, ed. I. B. AntelaBernárdez and T. Ñaco del Hoyo (British Archaeological Reports; International Series 1986; Oxford: John and Erica Hedge, 2009), 159–67, 161; cf. Robert Parker, *Athenian religion. A History* (Oxford: Clarendon, 1996), 340.

[37] Verboven, 'Associative Order', 882.

[38] Philip Venticinque, 'Family Affairs: Guild Regulations and Family Relationships in Roman Egypt', *GRBS* 50 (2010), 273–94 (293).

of individuals who 'possessed fortunes surpassing those of many *decuriones*', some of whom entered the *ordo decurionum* or established a precedent that would allow future generations of their families to do so.[39]

The Falling Social Status of *Ekklēsiai* Members

Alongside this recent recognition of economic stability within associations comes a shift in Pauline scholarship away from the 'new consensus'. As is now well documented, many Pauline interpreters currently emphasise poverty among early Christ believers.[40] Justin Meggitt's 1998 contribution was a nuancing and rejuvenation of the so-called old consensus, forwarding the notion that all members of Pauline groups struggled with meeting requirements for subsistence on a daily basis. Meggitt supposed a '*harsh existence*' for members of Pauline groups, as was typical for everybody outside of the elite strata of society.[41] Meggitt's well-known and clear thesis requires no further description for present purposes, other

[39] Verboven, 'Magistrates', 160; cf. 'Associative order', 885–7.

[40] Meggitt describes material poverty in the ancient world as ' an absolute rather than relative phenomenon. It is present where the basic essentials necessary for supporting human life are not taken for granted but are a continuous source of anxiety' (Meggitt, *Paul*, 5). See also Peter Garnsey and Greg Woolf's definition: 'The poor are those living at or near subsistence level, whose prime concern it is to obtain the minimum food, shelter, and clothing necessary to sustain life, whose lives are dominated by the struggle for physical survival' ('Patronage of the Rural Poor in the Roman World', in *Patronage in Ancient Society*, ed. Andrew Wallace-Hadrill [London: Routledge, 1989], 153–70 at 153). Scholars who regard the Corinthians as 'poor' tend to make their case on the basis of a few ambiguous texts. The main verse is 1 Cor 1:26: 'not many were well-born (εὐγενής).' Karl Kautsky uses this verse to support his contention that 'die christliche Gemeinde ursprünglich fast ausschließlich proletarische Elemente umfaßte und eine proletarische Organisation war' (*Der Ursprung des Christentus* [Hannover: J. H. W. Dietz, 1910], 338). Scholars now recognise that εὐγενεῖς were 'die aus angesehenen Familien Stammenden, die aristokratische Bourgeoisie' (Schrage, *Der erste Brief*, I:209), and therefore the fact that not many were εὐγενεῖς tells us little about where they fit in the highly differentiated lower strata of society. This is the conclusion drawn by several scholars of Pauline groups. See, e.g., Andrew D. Clarke, *Secular and Christian Leadership in Corinth. A Socio-Historical and Exegetical Study of 1 Corinthians 1–6* (Arbeiten zur Geschichte des antiken Judentums und des Urchristentums 18; Leiden, New York, and Köln: Brill, 1993), 41–5; Gerd Theissen, *The Social Setting of Pauline Christianity* (Philadelphia: Fortress, 1982), 71–3; Abraham J. Malherbe, *Social Aspects of Early Christianity*, 2nd ed. (Philadelphia: Fortress Press, 1983), 30; John K. Chow, *Patronage and Power: A Study of Social Networks in Corinth* (Sheffield: JSOT Press, 1992), 145; Edwin A. Judge, *The Social Pattern of the Christian Groups in the First Century: Some Prolegomena to the Study of New Testament Ideas of Social Obligation* (London: Tyndale Press, 1960), 59; Dale B. Martin, The *Corinthian Body* (New Haven: Yale University Press, 1995), 61.

[41] Meggitt, *Paul*, 75 (original emphasis).

than to point out that it shared more commonalities with Steven Friesen's later stratification model of ancient poverty than overviews of it (including mine here) tend to imply.[42]

Steven Friesen nuanced and relativised the term 'poverty', but agreed in substance with Meggitt's conclusions concerning Pauline groups.[43] Friesen describes economic status in relation to subsistence. It is 'defined as the resources needed to procure enough calories in food to maintain the human body'.[44] People need between 1,500 and 3,000 calories per day, but can survive below the subsistence level for some time.[45] The outcome of Friesen's (and others') studies is the realisation that we need more than a single category ('the poor') to describe 97–99 per cent of the urban population that fell below the ruling elite. Friesen's 'poverty scale' stratifies the people whom historians of Pauline groups formerly called 'the poor' into four groupings:

> PS4 denotes those with 'Modern surplus resources'
> PS5 denotes individuals who were 'Stable near subsistence level'
> PS6 denotes people 'at subsistence level'
> PS7 denotes those 'Below subsistence level'[46]

He proceeds to suggest, 'the vast majority of the people in [Paul's] assemblies lived just above or just below the level of subsistence.'[47] Bruce Longenecker, while allowing for a larger middling demographic in the ancient world than does Friesen,[48] surmises that 'It is unlikely . . . that, among urban Jesus-followers, the percentage for ES4 [=middling

---

[42]   See Justin M. Meggitt, 'Response to Martin and Theissen', *JSNT* 84 (2001), 85–94.

[43]   See Friesen, 'The Wrong Erastus', 256.

[44]   Friesen, 'Poverty', 343.

[45]   Friesen, 'Poverty', 343; cf. Peter Garnsey, *Food and Society in Classical Antiquity* (Cambridge: Cambridge University Press, 1999). A person requires economic resources for other necessities, as well, and so Allan Chester Johnson has analysed wage scales in Roman Egypt in relation to food as well as other requirements, such as clothing, and the ability to pay taxes (i.e., living costs) in *Roman Egypt to the Reign of Diocletian*. Volume 2 of *An Economic Survey of Ancient Rome* (Baltimore: The Johns Hopkins Press, 1936), 301–22.

[46]   Friesen, 'Poverty', 341.

[47]   Friesen, 'Poverty', 357.

[48]   Friesen supposes 7 per cent in 'Poverty', 347. In a more recent article co-authored by Walter Scheidel, Friesen and Scheidel estimate the middling category at 6–12 per cent. See Walter Scheidel and Steven J. Friesen, 'The Size of the Economy and the Distribution of Income in the Roman Empire', *JRS* 99 (2009), 61–91. Longenecker proposes 17 per cent (*Remember*, 46). Even more recently, Guy R. D. Sanders has suggested that Roman Corinth's middling strata represented 20 per cent of the population, in 'Landlords and Tenants: Sharecroppers and Subsistence Farming in Corinthian Historical Context', *Corinth in Contrast: Studies in Inequality,* ed. Steven J. Friesen, Sarah A. James, and Daniel N. Schowalter (NovTSup 155; Leiden: Brill, 2014), 103–26.

people] would have risen much above 10%'.[49] This means 1 or 2 Corinthian members lived at an ES4 level if we imagine the *ekklēsia* as a ten- to twenty-member Christ group.

Textual Basis for Poverty in the Corinthian Ekklēsia

In Friesen's and Longenecker's prosopographic surveys, most named individuals affiliated with the Corinthian *ekklēsia* lived around middling

Table 3.1 *Corinthians in Economic Scales*

Name	Source	Economic Status according to Friesen[50]	Economic Status according to Longenecker[51]
Chloe	1 Cor 1:11	4	4–5[52]
Gaius	Rom 16:23	4	4
Erastus	Rom 16:23	4–5	4
Prisca and Aquila	Rom 16:3–5	4–5	5–6[53]
Phoebe	Rom 16:1–2	4–5	4
Chloe's people	1 Cor 1:11	5	4–5
Stephanas	1 Cor 16:17–18	5–6[54]	4–5
Household of Stephanas	1 Cor 16:17–18	5–6	4–5[55]
Crispus	1 Cor 1:14; Acts 18:8	N/A	4–5

[49] Longenecker, *Remember*, 57.

[50] Friesen, 'Poverty', 357.

[51] Longenecker, *Remember*, 235–49.

[52] Longenecker, *Remember*, 249, n.93.

[53] Longenecker, *Remember*, 235–49. His placement of Prisca and Aquila in ES5/ES6 is curious. Others have found the data to indicate they enjoyed economic stability on par with other householders such as Gaius and Stephanas. See Carolyn Osiek and Margaret Y. MacDonald, with Janet H. Tulloch, *A Woman's Place: House Churches in Earliest Christianity* (Minneapolis, MN: Augsburg Fortress, 2006), 32; and Peter Oakes, 'Methodological Issues in Using Economic Evidence in Interpretation of Early Christian Texts', in *Engaging Economics: New Testament Scenarios and Early Christian Reception*, ed. Bruce W. Longenecker and Kelly D. Liebengood (Grand Rapids, MI: Eerdmans, 2009), 9–34 (33). Longenecker's assessment is based on his synthesis of data from Acts 18:3 and 2 Cor 11:9, which produces a scenario where Paul was in need even while staying at Aquila and Priscilla's house in Corinth. In this scenario, one must conclude that the householders made too little profit at their workshop to sustain their guest, Paul. Cf. Peter Lampe, *From Paul to Valentinus: Christians at Rome in the First Two Centuries* (Minneapolis, MN: Fortress, 2003), 191.

[54] Friesen concedes, 'The most appropriate category for Stephanas is PS5, and PS6 is not to be excluded as a possibility' ('Poverty', 352).

[55] Longenecker does not explicitly discuss Fortunatus and Achaicus apart from Stephanas. See *Remember*, 243–4.

levels. Indeed, we should expect as much since possession of surplus economic resources was a requisite for joining an association.

According to Friesen's and Longenecker's surveys, every Corinthian member named by Paul lived around ES4 ('surplus economic resources'), a phenomenon recognised as problematic by Longencker for himself and others who propose that most Christ believers lived in economic categories lower than this.[56] Both researchers suggest that percentages of *ekklēsia* members from the various non-elite economic classifications would resemble percentages of overall urban populations in these strata. However, since many people in ancient cities could not afford club membership, this equation fails to persuade.

In a speculative move, Longenecker claims that named individuals were exceptionally well-off relative to unnamed members and attempts to show that when Paul imagines the 'general economic profile' of specific Christ groups, he presupposes a lower average economic status.[57] He argues that Paul's description of entire Christ groups 'seem[s] to drop a level, gravitating towards the ES5 level primarily, with some resonance with ES6'.[58] Very little evidence is provided for this. One piece of support is apparently Paul's instruction in 1 Cor 16:1–2 that the Corinthians should save money for the Jerusalem collection on a weekly basis. For an unstated reason, Longenecker believes that this sort of measure would be taken by members in very low economic categories.[59] Friesen does the same: 'The instructions to the Corinthian saints about how to save up money for the poor among the Jerusalem saints presuppose people in categories 5 or 6 of the poverty scale.'[60] Both fail to take seriously the economic dynamics behind contributing to the Jerusalem collection. To be a donor to the Jerusalem λογεία, an individual needed to meet subsistence requirements and possess still more money each week for the collection. Such people did not live at or below the level of subsistence. This is especially clear if the argument

---

[56] 'Most of the individuals whom Paul mentions by name, and whose economic profile can be tentatively reconstructed, seem to fall within ES4 or ES5.' (Longenecker, *Paul*, 253). Meeks contends only that 'there is ... no specific evidence of people who are destitute – such as the hired menials and dependent handworkers ... There may well have been members of the Pauline communities who lived at the subsistence level, but we hear nothing of them' (*First Urban*, 73).

[57] Longenecker, like others, imagines scores of Corinthian members whom Paul failed to name.

[58] Longenecker, *Remember*, 253.

[59] Longenecker, *Remember*, 253–4.

[60] Friesen, 'Poverty', 350–1.

in Chapter 4 is correct – namely, that membership fees were required from all Corinthians at every banquet.

The other evidence put forward by Longenecker and Friesen is equally uncertain: Paul's reference to οἱ μὴ ἔχοντες (1 Cor 11:22) among the Christ group's members. Friesen takes this phrase 'in an absolute sense as "those who have nothing" '[61] and Longenecker renders it 'in absolute terms as "those who have nothing" '.[62] The problem with identifying these individuals as literally having nothing in an absolute sense is that it does not match up well with Paul's 'mental averaging'[63] in 2 Cor 8:14–15, where he speaks of the Corinthians in their entirety as individuals with an abundance, nor with 1 Cor 16:1–2 where Paul expects all Corinthians to contribute money they have been able to save for the Jerusalem collection. Longenecker notes that Paul's comment about Corinthian abundance in 2 Cor 8:14 is made in relation to the inferior economic standing of the Macedonian groups. But how poor were the Macedonians? In Phil 4:15–17 Paul references a voluntary λόγος ('account')[64] to which the Philippians alone contributed. This account was debited when the Philippians supported Paul's early travels 'more than once' (4:15–16), when they 'paid' Paul 'in full' (4:17), and when they sent Paul gifts through Epaphroditos (4:18).[65] It is fascinating that the Philippians' ability to establish two voluntary λόγοι (the Paul collection and the Jerusalem collection) has not factored more prominently in socio-economic analyses of Pauline Christ believers, and that 'poverty', or 'subsistence-living', still seem fitting descriptors of the Philippians. Since the Macedonian groups were able to contribute quite generously to voluntary financial accounts, these individuals were not as destitute as Paul and Longenecker characterise them. So Second

---

[61] Friesen, 'Poverty', 349.

[62] Longenecker, *Remember*, 232 n.41.

[63] This is Longenecker's phrase (*Remember*, 258).

[64] Paul uses the standard term for a financial account. For other examples, see *P.Oslo* III 143.1 (Oxyrhynchos, Egypt; I CE); *P.Oslo* III 144.2 (Oxyrhynchos, Egypt; 272–5 CE); *P. Mil. Vogl.* III 188.2 (Tebtynis, Egypt; 125 CE); and *O.Theb.* 142.1 (Thebes, Egypt; II CE). Non-association papyri: *P.Hibeh* I 51.2 (Oxyrhynchos, Egypt; 245 BCE); *P.Oxy.* II 239.8 (Oxyrhynchos, Egypt; 66 CE); and *SB* XVI 12675.1 (Tebtynis, Egypt; 100 BCE).

[65] For analogies to λόγος δόσεως καὶ λήμψεως (Phil 4:15) in civic and association inscriptions, see Peter Pilhofer, *Philippi. Der erste christliche Gemeinde Europas* (WUNT I/87; Tübingen: Mohr Siebeck, 1995), 148–51. See also Richard Ascough's analysis of what this language reveals about the social position of the Philippians in *Paul's Macedonian Associations. The Social Context of Philippians and 1 Thessalonians* (WUNT II/161; Tübingen: Mohr Siebeck, 2003), 118–22.

Corinthians 8:14 actually pushes the Corinthians higher than a Philippian group with noteworthy amounts of surplus economic resources. Paul's mention of Corinthians possessing 'nothing' cannot be taken in 'absolute terms'. It needs to be interpreted in the context in which Paul places it: the Corinthian banquet. The Corinthians with nothing were the ones left without food portions (i.e., with nothing) at the Christ group's meals. Poverty did not cause their lack, but, rather, the Christ group's food distribution policies did, which will be discussed later in the chapter in comparison with a range of food distribution practices in associations (see Chapter 7).

The current shift towards upgrading the social status of association members while downgrading the social status of Pauline Christ believers has culminated in Longenecker's recent argument that association members, on average, came from higher social registers than Pauline Christ believers,[66] a conclusion that also could be drawn from Schmeller's and Ebel's comparisons. Does this mean that association members could afford to structure their groups in ways unaffordable for Pauline Christ believers? According to Longenecker, the answer is 'yes', as we have observed.

Two Modest Clubs

Comparative scholarship almost entirely ignores the existence and practices of economically modest associations. These clubs lived below the economic level of the middling Iobacchoi association, the Lanuvium *collegium*, and the other middling cults most often compared with Corinth's Christ group. Modest clubs were not rare – papyrological evidence attests to a variety of associations consisting of individuals living below middling strata. Consideration of the finances of these associations can provide some controls for speculating what the Corinthians could not afford, since these associations fit the socio-economic context into which many Pauline scholars place the Corinthians.

My focus in this chapter centres on two detailed financial accounts written by modest associations: the account of an association of slaves (*SB* III 7182; Philadelphia, Egypt; II BCE); and the account of a modest cultic and dining club from Tebtynis (*P.Tebt* III/2 894; c.114 BCE). I first provide a brief introduction to some of their status indicators and economic activities.

---

[66] Longenecker, *Remember*, 259–68.

My primary question is this: Did the low economic profile of the modest Egyptian associations prevent them from building organisational apparatuses such as offices, formal presentations of honorific rewards, and collections of subscription dues? The clubs introduced below clarify that the economics of life below the middling strata did not hinder these associative practices.

SB III 7182

SB III 7182 was found in the Fayum town of Philadelphia in middle Egypt along with the Zenon papyri. The Zenon papyri contain documents dating from 261 BCE to 229 BCE, including letter correspondences involving Zenon, an assistant to a Ptolemaic official; accounts connected to Apollonios, Zenon's employer; and other documents related to government operations in the early Ptolemaic period. This archive, along with other texts from Philadelphia, such as *SB* III 7182, was discovered by villagers in 1914–1915. *SB* III 7182 was shortly thereafter sent to C. C. Edgar by Italian papyrologist G. Vitelli, who hoped it was part of, or could illuminate, other Zenon texts that were (and still are) housed in the Cairo Museum. Edgar found that since the papyrus uses the copper standard (which was introduced in 210 BCE), it cannot have been a Zenon text. Zenon texts, which date to the mid-third century, record wages and prices in silver drachmas as was common during this century regardless of whether payment was in gold, silver, or copper coins. Near the end of the second century BCE, a silver shortage that had been developing for some time led to an abandonment of efforts to convert copper prices and wages into their silver equivalents. As a result, accounting became completed in less valuable copper drachmas. Tony Reekmans has calculated the approximate conversion of silver to copper drachma according to time period:

> 210 BCE–183 BCE – 1 silver drachma: 60 copper drachmas
> 183/2 BCE–174 BCE – 1 silver drachma: 120 copper drachmas
> 173 BCE–c. late I BCE – 1 silver drachma: 480 copper drachmas[67]

The high subscription and commodity fees in *SB* III 7182 reflect copper's inflation in this later period.[68] This means that when Kamax, one of the

---

[67] Tony Reekmans, 'Monetary History and the Dating of Ptolemaic Papyri', *Studia Hellenistica* 5 (1948), 15–43 (17, 33–43).

[68] Reekmans, 'Monetary History', 26–7. Reekmans ('Monetary History', 17) proposes, 'If we can discover and date stages in the development of the currency from the level of prices and wages recorded in dated texts, we find definite criteria by which undated texts

club members, pays 270 drachmas in subscription fees at one meeting, it was worth just a little more than half a silver drachma (*Frag.1.*I.2). This papyrus dates to 173 BCE or later, and Edgar can 'safely assume that it comes from Philadelphia ... like the Zenon papyri among which it was purchased'.[69] Edgar published the papyrus in 1925 along with a short commentary. His publication consists of five fragments from the text arranged in arbitrary order. Unfortunately, no full record of a single club meeting survives, however much information about this association's typical proceedings at banquets is provided in these fragments, including meeting locations, names of members, and items of expenses. The club consisted of seven or eight affiliates. All recorded members have the type of 'fanciful names' characteristic of slaves.[70] Edgar argues, 'when we find a whole group of men with such names, the chances are that they belonged to the menial class.'[71]

P.Tebt. III/2 894

P.Tebt. III/2 894 is the most extensive of the published Greek club accounts. After initial usage by the association around the first-century BCE, the papyrus was thrown away, later to be found in the late Ptolemaic period and reused with many other texts as 'papyrus mâché' to form part of a shell that made a mummy case or mask. It was in this form when Bernard P. Grenfall and Arthur S. Hunt discovered it in 1900 along with many others in fifty mummies. Only twelve fragments of the account have been published so far from what was a narrow roll. The editors deemed the remaining pieces 'too monotonous' for inclusion

can be approximately dated, according to the information which they give about prices and wages.' See Reekmans, 'Monetary History', 34–43 for a chart outlining these currency stages.

[69] C. C. Edgar, 'Records of a Village Club', *Raccolta di scritti in onore di Giacomo Lumbroso (1844–1925)* (Pubblicazioni di 'Aegyptus'. Serie scientifica 3. Milano: Aegyptus, 1925), 369–76 (369).

[70] For servile names, see Heikki Solin, *Die stadtrömischen Sklavennamen: Ein Namenbuch* (3 vols.; Forschungen zur antiken Sklaverei 2; Stuttgart: Franz Steiner, 1996); Heikki Solin, *Die griechischen Personennamen in Rom: Ein Namenbuch* (3 vols.; Berlin: W. de Gruyter, 1982); and Bradley H. McLean, *An Introduction to Greek Epigraphy of the Hellenistic and Roman Periods from Alexander the Great down to the Reign of Constantine (323 B.C.–A.D. 337)* (Ann Arbor, MI: University of Michigan Press, 2002), 102–3.

[71] Edgar, 'Records', 369.

in the original publication.[72] Grenfall and Hunt's publication appeared in 1938 as part of the third volume of Tebtynis papyri. *P.Tebt.* III/2 894 is dated to approximately 114 BCE. The published fragments mention forty-nine dates, many of which appear to denote the days of club meetings. Some entries include wide-ranging information about the association's assemblies, such as the meeting location, total number of attendees, and items purchased for banquets (*Frag.2* recto, I.1–22); others just consist of amounts of unidentified beverages bought by the group (*Frag.6* verso, I.21–35). All figures are recorded in copper drachmas and reflect the inflationary levels found in *SB* III 7182. The club could expect between twenty and twenty-five attendees when it assembled: in the first fragment, twenty-three members are listed before the papyrus breaks off (*Frag.1* recto, II.1–22); elsewhere, the group records total attendance numbers of twenty-two (*Frag.2* recto, I.3–5),[73] and still elsewhere twenty (*Frag.2* verso, II.43). The contents of the papyrus reveal this was a cultic group that met to dine as a group in the houses or shops of its members, and made small sacrifices at nearby altars.[74]

Socio-economic Indicators in the Egyptian Associations

There are at least four reasons to categorise both groups below the economically middling associations commonly compared with Pauline Christ groups. I briefly review the evidence that these clubs consisted of people below middling strata – as represented by the Lanuvium, Iobacchoi, and other clubs reviewed above – and then I show that their modest economic status neither prevented them from collecting subscription dues and selecting officers who had financial responsibilities, nor from taking part in activities such as vying for honour, and presenting commendatory rewards to peer benefactors.

Expenses, Membership Fees, and Treasuries

One indication of these clubs' economic modesty comes from the low amount of money they spent on banquets and collected from subscription

---

[72] Bernard P. Grenfall, Arthur S. Hunt, and J. Gilbart Smyly, eds., *Tebtynis Papyri* (Cambridge: Cambridge University Press, 1902–1938), 3.2:170.

[73] This includes one guest (*Frag.2* recto, l.5).

[74] The cultic aspect of this group is highlighted by the fact that they chose 'sacrifice-makers' for meetings and used altars. The dining component is revealed most clearly by their references to two types of meals: the midday meal (ἄριστον; *Frag.4* recto, l.4); and supper (δεῖπνον; *Frag.4* recto, l.6; *Frag.6* recto II.8).

dues. C. C. Edgar identifies one fragment from the Philadelphia slave club's financial account (*SB* III 7182) as an expense report outlining the finances for one of their meetings,[75] though its function as an expense report does not explain why it includes mention of income generated from the meeting, too. In any case, the final line in the entry seemingly indicates that the group's expenditures came to 1,590 copper drachmas at this meeting (*Frag.2*, l.41). The relevant lines appear as follows:

[-ca.?-] ǫ   35
[-ca.?-] υν
[-ca.?-]ῳ η αὐλη(τῇ) Ψα-
[μ]μητίχου συμβο(λὴ) σο,
[ἄ]λλου ξένου σο,
[-ca.?-] μα . . καὶ τρυ(γὸς) ρ,   40
(γίνονται) Αφϱ

[An account of what the club has spent at this banquet]
. . . . 90 drachmas
. . . 450 drachmas
. . . contribution of Psammetichos to the flute-player
, 270 drachmas
of another guest, 270 drachmas
. . . and of new wine, 100 drachmas
Total: 1,590 drachmas

Unfortunately, we are missing the first items of the group's expenses for this meeting. The surviving lines only add to 1,180 drachmas, leaving 410 drachmas uncharted. We can imagine what this full entry looked like because the group seemingly recorded information about each meeting according to the same order.[76] Their procedure was to begin with meeting details (date and location), and an attendance list (officers, members, and guests). This component is missing from the quoted fragment. The club followed their attendance list with the phrase εἰς οὕς ἀνήλωται, meaning something like '[an account] of what the club has spent [at this meeting]' (see *Frag.4* recto, IV.67; *Frag.5* recto, l.92). This is also missing in the quoted fragment. The last component included financial records from the meeting, including expenditures often in the dative case, which survives and has been quoted above.

Using the conversion ratio of 1 silver drachma: 480 copper drachmas, which was likely in effect at the time, the above meeting's expenditures

75 Edgar, 'Records', 371.
76 Edgar, 'Records', 370.

of 1,590 copper drachmas were equivalent to 'rather more than three drachmae in silver' in total.[77] With seven contributors in the club, such an amount equals an approximate financial commitment of 0.43 silver drachma per person (198 copper drachmas per person).[78] Edgar surmises that the slave club's members earned the equivalent of 5 silver drachmas a month, making club membership 'quite a serious ontlay'[79] for them despite how cheap it would seem to members of the clubs more commonly compared with the Corinthians. If Edgar's supposition is accurate, membership fees represented 10 per cent of their modest income, assuming that they gathered once a month, and 20 per cent if they assembled biweekly (which they sometimes did).

Outside of partially obscure entries such as this, *SB* III 7182, unfortunately does not provide much insight concerning the cost of subscription; rather it is taken for granted that members knew the rates.[80] To be sure, we know that participation in each of the club's feasts required payments from most members and, as demonstrated above, the club kept the total cost of assembling low. The recto of fragment 5 clarifies that the club did indeed require subscription dues from members. It reads as follows:

Χοία[-ca.?-]κ[-ca.?-]	
ἐν τῇ σ[κευοθήκῃ] —	
ἱερο͙π[ο]ι̣[ο]ῦ [Δ]ι̣[καίου]	80
Ἑρμίας,	
Βάχ[χος],	
Θίβρων,	
Δημᾶς,	
Κάρπος,	85
Κάμαξ,	

---

[77] Edgar, 'Records', 371. Edgar values 1 silver drachma at 530 copper drachmas, which is close to the 1:480 general ratio proposed by Reekmans.

[78] This is almost exactly what members in *P.Tebt.* III/2 894 seem to have contributed in *Frag.1* recto, II.22–38.

[79] Edgar, 'Records', 371. This is an educated guess on Edgar's part (amounting to around 1 obol per day) that warranted no explanation in his article. My review of slave wages confirms Edgar's supposition, though there was great variety in the jobs and wages of slaves. On the lower end, see *P.Hamb.* I 114 (Philadelphia, Egypt; 256–248 BCE), where *paidaria* (young slaves) earn 0.5 obols a day for their labour. See also *P.Cair.Zen* III 59398 (Philadelphia, Egypt; 260–258 BCE) and *P.Cair.Zen* I 59059 (Philadelphia, Egypt; 257 BCE).

[80] Unless *Frag.1*, I.1–9 represent subscription payments. This seems unlikely since these payments amount to much more than the club's typical banquet expenditures (see section 'Membership Dues' and Chapter 4).

Ψαμμήτιχος,
Δίκαιος,
(γίνονται) η, (τούτων)
ἀσύμβολος Ἑρμίας,   90
λ(οιποὶ) ζ,

[On the? day of] Choiak [they were brought together]
at the stables when Dikaios was sacrifice-maker
Hermias
Bacchos
Thibron
Demas
Karpos
Kamax
Psammetichos
Dikaios

They came to eight, of these Hermias was exempt from contribution,[81] the rest (came to) seven.

Hermias's exemption from dues represents an exception to the regular practice of contributing fees at the feast. Eight members came to this dinner, Hermias did not pay but 'the rest came to seven', meaning these seven contributed fees. The club placed its subscription dues ἐν κοινῷ ('into the treasury', *Frag.4* recto, III.59) when the income generated by fees exceeded expenses from holding a meeting.

When we turn to the Tebtynis group, we find that members made payments correlating to their place in the association's current hierarchical order. The following columns from fragment 1 (verso) of *P.Tebt.* III/2 894 demonstrates their subscription structure. The first column records an attendance list, and the following column outlines who paid what amount of subscription:

(Col. II)
Φαρμοῦθι κη   35
Ἁρμιῦσις
Πανεῦις
Ψεναμοῦνις

Πετεσοῦ(χος) Κα(γῶτος)
Τιτάκ 40
Ὀνῶφρις Γλυ()
Θέων
Σιλοῦς
Ἀμενεύς
Πατῦνις Χο() 45
Ἀπῦγχις Τε(ῶτος)
Θορτᾶις νέο(ς)
⟦Εὔδημος⟧
Ὧρος Πακύ(σιος)
Ψενεθώτ(ης) 50
Τράλλις
Φατρῆς
(Col. III)
(ὧν(?)) ἔχομεν
ἀρχῶν \τοῦ/ Παχών·
Σοκμῆνις ρ 55
Ἀπῦγχις Τε(ῶτος) φ
Πανεῦις ξ
Φατ[ρῆς] ν
Τρά[λλις] μ
Ὧρος Πακύ(σιος) ξε, 60
(γίνονται) ωιε ἀπὸ Βσ,
λο(ιπαὶ) Ατπ[ε],
ἀνδρῶν ιᾳ ἀνὰ (δραχμὰς) ρ, (γίνονται) Α[ρ].

(Col. II)
28th of the month of Pharmouth:
Harmiysis, Paneuis, Psenamounis, Petesouchos son of Kagos,
    Titak, Onophris Glu(), Theon, Silous, Ameneus, Patynis Cho(),
    Apygchis son of Teos, Thortais the younger (?), Eudemos,
    Horos son of Paky(sis), Psenethotes, Trallis, Phatres
(Col. III)
we have [the following] from the archons of the month of
    Pachon:
Sokmenis, 100 drachmas[82]
Apygchis son of Teos 500 drachmas
Paneuis 60 drachmas

[82] Sokmenis does not appear in col. II, indicating that he was absent but still paid 100
drachmas.

Phatres 50 drachmas
Trallis 40 drachmas
Horos son of Pakysis 65 drachmas
Their contributions came to 815 drachmas out of a total of 2,200 drachmas in total contributions. The rest of the drachmas: 1,385. Of the men there were 11 at 100 drachmas each, the total came to 1,100 drachmas.

The 100 drachmas collected from regular members is lower than the financial contributions made by the slave club; however, at other meetings of the Tebtynis association, the fees elevated to 200 drachmas (see following paragraphs). Four of the six officers (ἄρχοντες) contributed less-than-ordinary members because, I suggest, their office required them to carry out other financial activities. In comparison with the associations behind *SB* III 7182 and *P.Tebt.* III/2 894, middling *collegiati* paid lofty fees. Membership in the Lanuvium association demanded three sets of fees: entrance dues, monthly subscriptions of 1.5 sestertii (= c.237.6 copper drachmas),[83] and requirements to fund six dinners with four colleagues over the course of a year when it was one's turn in the rotation to do so (*CIL* XIV 2112 = *AGRW* 310, I.3, 20–1, II.2, 8–23). It is most unlikely that any individual member of the slave and Tebtynis groups, or even four acting together, would have been in a position to underwrite one of their monthly meals.

The contrast between modest and middle clubs' subscription rates is illustrated, as well, by the high fee rates collected by the middling group behind *P.Mich.* V 243 (Tebtynis, Egypt; 14–37 CE). This group required its members to contribute 12 silver drachmas per month (1.2). Some other clubs known from the papyri also collected more income at their meetings than did our economically modest groups. An account of expenses from a club of priests reveals a purchase of 50 keramia of wine for 200 silver drachmas, far beyond the cost of any single expenditure in the slave and Tebtynis associations (*P.Mil. Vogl.* III 188.4; Tebtynis, Egypt; 125 CE). The members of another association contributed between 10 and 22 silver drachmas at one of their banquets, which greatly exceeds any single payment provided by any member in our modest clubs (*P.Mich.* V 246; Arsinoites, Egypt; 26–75 CE).

---

[83] For conversion mechanisms, see McLean, *Introduction to Greek* Epigraphy, 373; and Roger S. Bagnall, ed., *The Oxford Handbook of Papyrology* (New York: Oxford University Press, 2011) 189–91.

If we can characterise the Lanuvium *collegium*, and the Egyptian associations mentioned in the previous paragraph as middling, then the slave association and Tebtynis club need to be positioned lower down one's economic scale of choice. The substantially lower financial obligations of the slave and Tebtynis associations suggest their members possessed less surplus economic resources than did middling association members. Yet their possession of modest surplus drachmas indicates that they belong above the level of subsistence, on the whole.

Richard Duncan-Jones calculates the subsistence level in Roman Egypt at 2.98–6.66 silver drachmas per month per person.[84] If C. C. Edgar is correct about the monthly income of the slaves in *SB* III 7182 (5 drachmas), then they (as well as the Tebtynis association members) may have lived just marginally above the level of subsistence.[85] Although they only earned 5 drachmas (or so) a month, they could satisfy subsistence requirements and still afford an extra 0.42 silver drachmas per month for membership in a modest club.

Researchers who propose that the Corinthians did not pay subscription fees due to poverty will need to adjust their economic profiling of the *ekklēsia* in light of the wide range of fee rates collected by associations of different economic strata. In Chapter 4, I provide evidence from the Corinthian correspondence that the *ekklēsia* did, indeed, collect subscription dues.

Food

A second indicator of modest socio-economic standing among these *collegiati* is their food and drink. Their banquets contained less impressive menu items than those consumed by associations typically compared with the Corinthians. For example, the Lanuvium and Iobacchoi associations regularly drank wine. In contrast, the slave club makes five references to wine, but two of which are to τρύξ ('unfermented wine'; *Frag.2*, l.40; *Frag.4* verso, l.77) – a cheap but

---

[84] This is based on the finding that the typical person (not accounting for gender, age, or any other variable) needs ten artabas of wheat in a year. One artaba costs between 3.5 to 8 drachmas in Roman Egypt. See Richard P. Duncan-Jones, *Structure and Scale in the Roman Economy* (Cambridge: Cambridge University Press, 1990), 144. In the earlier Ptolemaic period, one artaba of wheat sold at an *official* rate of 2 drachmas. See Sitta von Reden, *Money in Ptolemaic Egypt. From the Macedonian Conquest to the End of the Third Century BC* (Cambridge and New York: Cambridge University Press, 2007), 123 n.27.

[85] Edgar's supposition is based on the club's expenses and income, as well as other economic indicators that are discussed later, such as meeting locations.

high-quality grape drink.[86] Unfermented wine cost the group 50 (*Frag.4* verso, l.77) and 100 drachmas (*Frag.2*, l.40),[87] which is significantly less than the price of wine in the same region (Philadelphia) and time (early II BCE).[88]

The Corinthians supposedly bought wine for their banquets, some members even became 'drunk on wine' (μεθύειν; 1 Cor 11:21). However, if 1 Cor 16:2 indicates weekly meetings, it remains possible that they found the cost of wine burdensome and opted for less-expensive alternatives occasionally.

The Tebtynis club consumed foods regularly associated with members of low non-elite strata. For example, at one meeting the group ate cabbage (*Frag.2* recto, I.8). Several ancient authors associate cabbage and other inexpensive vegetables with low status.[89] At another meeting, the Tebtynis association members ate beans and celebrated with beer (*Frag.5* verso, II.11–20). Beans, Peter Garnsey notes, were 'the poor man's meat'.[90] Higher up the economic scale, the Lanuvium *collegium* purchased seafood over beans;[91] and the Iobacchoi association occasionally consumed meat (*IG* II² 1368.117–27 = *GRA* I 51; Athens, Attica; 164/5 CE).

So we can again distinguish economically modest associations from the middling associations this time on the basis of the menu.[92] The Christ group's common meal presumably lacked meat since group members with dietary restrictions (1 Cor 8:13) brought no concerns to Paul about meat consumption at *ekklēsia* meals.

---

[86] The other three references are to οἶνος twice (*Frag.4* recto, IV.70; *Frag.5* verso, II.112) and Memphite wine (*Frag.5* recto, I.94). Unfortunately the price paid by this club for wine does not survive but the papyrus from the Tebtynis group, from sixty years later, records the price of οἶνος at 3,000–4,000 per keramion.

[87] We do not know the unit of measure, but a keramion would be standard.

[88] Although these copper figures come from a period of lesser copper inflation (see p.23 in this chapter), they nonetheless provide some insight into the slave association's savings when they bought unfermented wine: 1 keramion: 400 drachmas (*BGU* VII 1501; Philadelphia, Egypt; 189/8 BCE); 2 keramia: 1,000 drachmas (*BGU* VII 1506; Philadelphia, Egypt; 206–189 BCE); 1 keramion: 600 drachmas (*BGU* VII 1545; Philadelphia, Egypt; 210–187 BCE). Wine cost the Tebtynis club between 6 and 8 silver drachmas (*Frag.2* recto, I.6; *Frag.2* verso, II.44; *Frag.3* verso, I.4–19; *Frag.6* recto, II.1; *Frag.7* verso, II.2; and *Frag.10* recto, l.3–5).

[89] Juv. 1.134; 3.283; 5.87; Pers. 3.114; Mart. 13.13.1; Plaut. *Poen.* 1314; cf. Peter Garnsey, *Cities, Peasants, and Food in Classical Antiquity: Essays in Social and Economic History* (Cambridge and New York: Cambridge University Press, 1998), 242.

[90] Garnsey, *Cities*, 225.

[91] The Lanuvium association ate sardines, which, to be fair, were 'a fish conspicuously lacking in prestige' (Bendlin, 'Associations', 269).

[92] There is no indication what the slave club ate, though references to sacrifice makers (ἱεροποιοί; *Frag.4* recto, II.46; *Frag.5* recto, l.80) suggest that food was present.

Meeting Locations

A third way to differentiate economic status among associations is to compare their meeting locations. The slave association from Philadelphia did not possess a clubhouse. They settled for what was available when they met. This meant assembling in a storehouse (θησαυρός, *Frag.1*.II.12, *Frag.4* recto, III.62), in the harness-room in a stable (ἱπποκοινάριον ... σχεοθήκη[93], *Frag.4* recto, II.45–6, *Frag.5* recto, l.79), and in a room in an Isis temple ("Ισιῆον[94], *Frag.3* l.43). C. C. Edgar concludes, 'I think we may fairly infer that a society which held its meetings in the stables and the barn was mainly recruited from the servants' quarters.'[95] The physical locations in which the Tebtynis group dined suggests the modest economic positions of its members, as well. The club's papyrus records meetings at the house or shop of members, such as a certain Menoites (*Frag.2* recto, l.7) and a certain Harpalos (*Frag.2* verso, II.45); at the ἐργευτίγῳ[96] (*Frag.3* verso, I.3; *Frag.10* recto, l.4), and at a storehouse (θηγαρόν[97]; *Frag.6* recto, II.10). The group also references many visits to altars, sometimes singular (βομός;[98] e.g., *Frag.10* recto, l.2) sometimes plural (e.g., *Frag.11* verso, II.6).

The rotating physical space of modest clubs results from their lack of funds to secure a consistent meeting location. In contrast, the Lanuvium *collegium* enjoyed the stability of a set location: the temple of Antinoüs.[99] The Iobacchoi association secured their own hall.[100] The household Zeus association in Philadelphia (Lydia, Asia Minor) assembled in its founder's house (*SIG*[3] 985 = *AGRW* 121); and the association of Asklepios and Hygiae (*CIL* VI 10234 = *AGRW* 322; Rome; 153 CE) benefited from a patron who gave them land, a chapel, and solarium for banqueting.

---

[93] This is a misspelling of σκευοθήκη.

[94] This appears to be a misspelling of "Ισειον.

[95] Edgar, 'Records', 370.

[96] The meaning of this word is unknown. It is possibly a misspelling of ἐργαστηρίῳ ('in the workshop').

[97] This is a misspelling of θησαυρός.

[98] This is a misspelling of βωμός.

[99] It is possible but unlikely that the *collegium* owned the temple. See Bendlin, 'Associations', 273–8.

[100] For the Iobacchoi's meeting place, see Richard S. Ascough, Philip A. Harland, and John S. Kloppenborg, *Associations in the Greco-Roman World. A Sourcebook* (Waco, TX: Baylor University Press, 2012), 221–2.

If the Corinthians assembled perpetually in a house such as the Pompeiian cabinet-maker's home, which Peter Oakes described so eloquently (House I.10.7),[101] or in the Anaploga Villa outlined by Jerome Murphy-O'Connor,[102] their meeting space would fit within the range of physical locations used by middling associations. However, the Corinthian correspondence provides no information concerning the *ekklēsia*'s meeting location, and so it is best to imagine the location of their dinners in the context of other associations at the economic strata the Corinthian *ekklēsia* is imagined to have lived in. Current reconstructions of economic status in Pauline groups by Justin Meggitt, Steven Friesen, and Bruce Longenecker necessitate the possibility that the Corinthians rotated the locations of their meeting as did the slave association and the Tebtynis club.

Activities of Modest Associations

Since *SB* III 7182 and *P.Tebt.* III/2 984 attest to modest associations that occupied the economic categories into which the Corinthians belong, it will be instructive to analyse what these clubs could afford to do. Specifically, could they manage fees, officers, and honorifics?

Membership Dues

Koenraad Verboven observes that both middling and economically modest associations needed to collect subscription dues from all members.[103] This rather generalised associative practice should not be contrasted with Corinthian financial activities. But this is exactly what happens when associations are assumed to be homogeneous and taxonomically separate from individual Christ groups. For example, Eva Ebel has argued that the Corinthian *ekklēsia* was different from associations with respect to its 'openness'. Anyone could join the Corinthian group, regardless of social status, since membership was free.[104] For Ebel, free membership represented an attraction for individuals living near the level of subsistence and, as a result, the Corinthian group comprised of many individuals who were poorer than the lowest strata of association members.

---

[101] Oakes, *Reading*, 15–33.
[102] Murphy-O'Connor, *St. Paul's Corinth*, 153–61.
[103] Verboven, 'Associative Order', 882.
[104] Ebel, *Attraktivität*, 216–17.

It is highly unlikely that the Corinthian group found a way to offer free membership and, therefore, to recruit members from the lowest economic strata. Exemption from dues tended to be offered to generous members as an honorific reward for their service.[105] For example, in the slave association, a certain Hermias is exempt from dues; he is ἀσύμβολος three times (*Frag.5* recto, l.90; cf. *Frag.4* recto, II.58; *Frag.5* verso, II.114). Hermias's exemption from dues was likely a reward for his financial service as ἐπιμελητής (*Frag.1*.II.15).[106] He ate for free not because membership was free to the poor, but because his previous generosity earned him exemption from the dues everyone else was paying. Paul alludes to a similar pattern of exemptions in Christ groups.[107]

The slave group records the collection of membership dues at its meetings (*Frag.1*. I.1–9; *Frag.1*.III.33–*Frag.2*, l.9), and also references its usage of a common fund (*Frag.1*. III.30–2). While the Tebtynis club does not mention a common fund, it does record the subscription fees paid by its members at various places (e.g., *Frag.1* recto, II.1–24; *Frag.3* verso, I.5–19). In Chapter 4, I discuss in greater detail fee structures in these papyri as well as in other accounts produced by modest clubs.

Officers

Economically modest associations also selected temporary magistrates. The slave association appointed or elected ἱεροποιοί (sacrifice makers). In the existing fragments, this position was held by a certain Dikaios (*Frag.4* recto, II.47; *Frag.5* recto, l.80). The fragments of their financial accounts also attest to an ἐπιμελητής (supervisor) post, which was held by Hermias for a time (*Frag.1*, II.15).

At several places, the Tebtynis account records ἄρχοντες.[108] The association had either five (*Frag.6* recto, II.15–20) or six ἄρχοντες at a time (*Frag.1* verso, III.54–60; *Frag.2* recto, I.14–21; *Frag.2* recto, II.29–35). These magistrates were appointed to one-year terms.[109] The group also appointed or elected sacrifice makers (ἱεροποιοί). On one

---

[106] Sometimes members accepted administrative positions precisely to be exempted from paying more expensive membership fees that they could not afford (*P.Mich.* VIII 511; Karanis, Egypt; first half of III CE).
[107] 1 Cor 9:2–4; cf. 2 Thess 3:9.
[108] They often use the genitive plural of ἀρχός (ἀρχῶν). See, e.g., *Frag.1* verso, III.54; and *Frag.6* recto, II.15.
[109] For the length of this office, see, e.g., *Frag.6* recto, II.15–20.

occasion they had five of them (*Frag.2* recto, II.22), and on another occasion they had two (*Frag.7* verso, II.7). We do not know what responsibilities the sacrifice makers accepted, however, their incumbency came at a financial price. Perhaps by coincidence, the sacrifice makers were responsible for 1,000 drachmas (2.08 silver drachmas) at each of two meetings where their contributions are recorded, regardless of how many people held these offices at a time: when there were five of them, each paid 200 drachmas (*Frag.2* recto, II.22–3); when there were two, each paid 500 drachmas at a meeting held on Ephiphi 27 (*Frag.7* verso, II.7–11).

Although officers in the Tebtynis and slave clubs may have carried financial responsibilities beyond what was expected of regular members, these associations seem to have devised strategies to make office-holding affordable for their economically modest members. First, it would appear that the rate of subscription dues for members serving as an ἄρχων in the Tebtynis group,[110] and as an ἐπιμελητής in the slave association, were left to the discretion of the officers themselves or were waived. As a result, if the standard subscription fees were 200 drachmas at each meeting, these officers were given the freedom to pay a little less or nothing, perhaps on the understanding that they would properly fulfil their additional financial responsibilities, which were built into their roles as officers. For example, the supervisor Hermias (*SB* III 7182, *Frag.1*, II.12–16) enjoyed ἀσύμβολος status[111] (*Frag.5*, recto 90), which provided him exemption from subscription dues.

The difference between modest and middling associations is not that modest groups lacked officers while middling clubs appointed magistrates. Rather, the difference is in fee rates and policies. In the middling Lanuvium association, the *magistri cenarum* were responsible for entrance fees, regular dues, *and* the additional expenses that came with their offices. In the modest slave and Tebtynis clubs, financially burdensome offices could come with exemptions from regular dues. The data concerning the ἱεροποιοί office in the Tebtynis group are suggestive of another strategy for keeping the cost of office-holding low.[112] There seems to have been no set financial contribution from each incumbent of this office. Rather, the group expected 1,000 drachmas from the magistrates on both recorded occasions. When poorer members were

---

[110] We see a range of subscription payments from these officers, spanning 40–500 drachmas. See, e.g., *Frag.1*, III.53–60.

[111] For ἀσύμβολος in associations, see n.81 from this chapter.

[112] For references to these officers in the papyrus, see *Frag.4*.II.46; *Frag.5* recto, I.80.

selected to hold the position, perhaps the club allowed for a greater number of incumbents in order to make the extra fees more manageable.

Material Rewards for Service Providers

In the Tebtynis association, we find three attestations to crowns. In one fragment, the club records the cost 'of crowns for the 19th (of Payni)' (*Frag.1* recto, III.31). Elsewhere, crowns (plural) are listed as an expense costing 125 drachmas on the 27th of Epiphi (*Frag.7* verso, II.3). On this date, the association perhaps presented the honorific rewards to the two sacrifice makers who were present at this meeting (*Frag.7* verso, II.7–11). Finally, on the 2nd of Hathyr, reference is made to crowns worth 130 drachmas (*Frag.10* recto, l.7). The Tebtynis club seemingly rewarded officers and other service providers with cheap crowns when required.

Unfortunately, in the five surviving fragments from the slave association we do not find the complete records for any single meeting, and this might explain why we do not hear of rewards in their lists of expenses.[113] The group was not opposed to the honorific practices so common to ancient associations. They elected members to prestigious roles in the club, and they made a practice of naming their ἐπιμελητής, Hermias, first in their meeting minutes.[114] These acts demonstrate a concern for hierarchy, honour, and status.

A distinction should not be made between middling associations that offer rewards, and modest Christ groups that do not. Rather, associations from all strata rewarded service with formal commendation. The real distinction is in the value and type of honorific prizes. Middling associations could occasionally afford gold crowns,[115] though olive wreaths were much more common, as well as honorific inscriptions. The cost of honorific inscriptions varied according to quality and size. A simple monumental inscription, that is, a marble slab in rectangular shape and lacking decoration, might not have incurred high cost for the actual inscribing of text on the stone. However, a club would need to pay for the stone itself, and the cost of transporting the stone, which seems to have amounted to approximately 10–20 silver drachmas in the early

---

[113] For the purchase of crowns by another economically modest club, see *P.Tebt.* I 118.9, 16 (Tebtynis, Egypt; 112–111 BCE).

[114] *Frag.1*.I.1; *Frag.1*.II.16; *Frag.4* recto, II.48; *Frag.4* recto, III.63; *Frag.5* recto, l.82; and *Frag.5* verso, II.103.

[115] See, e.g., *IG* II² 1255 = *GRA* I 2 (Piraeus, Attica; 337/6 BCE); *IG* II² 1256.9 = *GRA* I 5 (Piraeus, Attica; 329/8 BCE); *IRhamnous* II 59.8, 23 = *GRA* I 27 (Rhamnous, Attica; after 216/15 BCE).

Hellenistic period.[116] The more modest associations used wreaths of a cheaper brand that cost less than 1 drachma. They perhaps also performed proclamations of honours during their meetings, which were free of charge.

Conclusions

Steven Friesen's recent insistence on the 'nearly complete absence of wealth'[117] in Pauline groups seriously underestimates the financial capital of people who could afford the luxury of membership in a Christ group. Many associations existed below the middling strata of society.[118] The two associations outlined in this chapter show that economically modest associations were able to elect officers, reward magistrates with honorifics, and attract members willing to show financial zeal.

Further analyses of economically modest associations may prove illuminating to understand social relationships in the Corinthian group as they relate to finances. For example, the modest clubs explored in this chapter illustrate how social heterogeneity *below* the middling strata might have led to different roles, based on personal wealth, within these associations. At the 'socially strong' end of the spectrum, we find members who were able to pay subscription dues and, in addition, provide contributions to various voluntary collections (e.g., *P.Tebt.* III/2 894, *Frag.3* verso, I.4–19; *Frag.4* verso, II.11–27; *Frag.8* recto I.1). A certain Sokmenis represents an affiliate from a socially strong stratum of the modest Tebtynis association. He kept up to date with his subscription fees (*Frag.1*, recto, II.2) and contributed to two of the club's voluntary λόγοι: one for wine (*Frag.5*, I.6) and one for an unidentifiable item (*Frag.4*, II.22). Other members fell somewhere in the middle: they paid what was expected of them and little or nothing more. Perhaps Harmiusis should be fitted here. He paid his fees and also helped pay off a fellow member's debt (*Frag.12* recto, II.13). He also allowed the club to use his house or shop as a meeting venue (*Frag.1* recto,

---

[116] See Thomas Heine Nielsen et al., 'Athenian Grave Monuments and Social Class', *GRBS* 30 (1989), 411–20; Brian T. Nolan, 'Inscribing Costs at Athens in the Fourth Century B.C.', (PhD. Diss.; Ohio State University, 1981), 57–9; Kloppenborg and Ascough, *Attica*, 98–100.

[117] Friesen, 'The Wrong Erastus', 256.

[118] Additional papyri attesting to the expenditures of modest associations exist but are far shorter and less detailed than the ones overviewed in this chapter. See *P.Tebt.* I 224 (Arsinoites, Egypt; 109–108 BCE); *CPJ* I 139 (Apollinopolis Magna, Egypt; I BCE); *P.Tebt.* I 118 (Tebtynis, Egypt; 112–111 BCE).

III.28). Hareos may be categorised here, too: he paid his fees and helped Theon pay a fine (*Frag.5* recto, II.10). Neither Harmiusis nor Hareos contributed to the group's voluntary collections.

Still other affiliates seemingly inhabited lower social registers and might be counted among the 'socially weak'. In an account of debts owed to the club, several members are named (*Frag.12* recto, II; *Frag.12* verso, I). The name of a certain Mares appears on this list, and he is recorded to have been 2,000 drachmas in debt. Mares paid off about 300 drachmas each meeting after his debt was recorded (*Frag.12* recto, II.5). It is no surprise that Mares does not show up as a contributor to any of the club's voluntary collections. To be sure, we cannot safely place Mares among the socially weak because we do not know why he was in debt. Did he fail to pay membership fees about ten times? If so, he was likely among the socially weak at least temporarily. Did he take out a loan? If so, this would complicate matters. Nonetheless, his financial contributions to the club ranked lower than the others' since his debt drained any assets he might otherwise provide. Imagining the socially weak Corinthians as poorer than Mares, who possessed enough surplus resources to pay off a debt rather consistently, can only be done arbitrarily, and with the anachronistic assumption that membership in a Christ group was as free as membership in a church.

4

THE COSTS OF *EKKLĒSIA* SURVIVAL

Introduction

If Justin Meggitt's, Steven Friesen's, and Bruce Longenecker's place-ment of most Corinthians below the middling strata of ancient society is accurate, then the associations that represent the closest analogies to the *ekklēsia* with respect to socio-economic status are the economically modest ones. There were some variances between associations of differ-ent socio-economic strata (e.g., types of meeting places, cost of member-ship dues, and banquet menus); however, clubs at all strata established an organisational apparatus that could handle collections for income. Associations managed their expenditures and income in a variety of ways, but these differences generally existed on top of the basic organi-sational requirement that all members pay subscription fees. Koenraad Verboven's insight on the minimum economic requirement of club membership merits repetition: 'Even the most humble associations demanded relatively substantial financial contributions from their mem-bers and favoured the "better" to do. The more important a *collegium* was, the more exclusive and expensive membership became.'[1] Having established in Chapter 3 the presence of financial structures and various strategies for generating income in modest associations, this chapter focuses on one specific inquiry: Did the *ekklēsia*'s survival depend on its ability to secure subscription fees from its members? Data from economically modest Egyptian associations help to clarify what is at stake in the question.

A Not-So-Obvious Difference

There presently stands a peculiar discrepancy between association and *ekklēsia* scholarship on the necessity of subscription dues in ancient

[1] Koenraad Verboven, 'The Associative Order, Status and Ethos of Roman Businessmen in Late Republic and Early Empire', *Athenaeum* 95 (2007), 861–93 (882).

clubs. On the one hand, scholars of associations recognise the centrality of membership fees to the life of associations. In his commentary on the slave association from Philadelphia (*SB* III 7182), C. C. Edgar states, 'The club was *of course* kept up by subscription.'[2] We observed in Chapter 3 (and will see more examples in this chapter) that membership in modest clubs could require as little as 10 per cent of their members' rather low monthly wages as subscription fees. Although we are dealing with modest figures, the survival of low-strata associations nonetheless depended on them.

Curiously, several scholars of Pauline groups have reached an opposite consensus regarding the place of subscription dues in *ekklēsiai*. Hans Conzelmann states, without providing support, that the Corinthian *ekklēsia* 'obviously as yet [had] no organized system of finance.'[3] Eva Ebel surmises it is 'unübersehbar' that the Corinthian *ekklēsia* did not charge fees.[4] Conzelmann's and Ebel's conclusions reflect an accepted consensus that the Corinthians did not pay membership dues.[5] Rarely do scholars betray their reasons for drawing this conclusion.[6]

In a study on financial practices within Yahweh groups, other associations, and Christ groups, John Barclay takes steps forward. He acknowledges that the Corinthian *ekklēsia*'s survival depended on the income it could generate – not only for banquets but for other expenses, as well.

---

[2] C. C. Edgar, 'Records of a Village Club', in *Raccolta di scritti in onore di Giacomo Lumbroso (1844–1925)* (Pubblicazioni di 'Aegyptus.' Serie scientifica 3; Milan: Aegyptus, 1925), 369–76 (371) (emphasis added).

[3] Hans Conzelmann, *1 Corinthians. A Commentary on the First Epistle to the Corinthians* (Hermeneia; Philadelphia: Fortress Press, 1975), 296.

[4] Eva Ebel, *Die Attraktivität früher christlicher Gemeinden: Die Gemeinde von Korinth im Spiegel grichisch-römischer Vereine* (Wissenschaftliche Untersuchungen zum Neuen Testament II/178; Tübingen: J. C. B. Mohr Siebeck, 2004), 217.

[5] See also, e.g., Bruce W. Longenecker, *Remember the Poor: Paul, Poverty, and the Greco-Roman World* (Grand Rapids, MI and Cambridge: Eerdmans, 2010), 271; and David J. Downs, *The Offering of the Gentiles. Paul's Collection for Jerusalem in Its Chronological, Cultural, and Cultic Contexts* (Wissenschaftliche Untersuchungen zum Neuen Testament II/248; Tübingen: Mohr Siebeck, 2008), 101. C. K. Barrett cites 1 Cor 16:2 as evidence that 'There was no treasurer to whom subscriptions could be paid' (*First Epistle*, 24), though, he proposes that fees were contributed in an unstructured format. The meal was procured by 'a pooling of resources by rich and poor members' (*First Epistle*, 26).

[6] Gordon Fee is one exception. For him, subscription dues would necessitate *ekklēsia* officials in charge of the collections. This, for him, is 'a contemporary picture of the church' (*First Epistle*, 813, n.22). One result of recent research on associations is knowledge of ancient financial practices, which commonly involved treasurers, common funds, and subscription fees.

He also explains some of the convictions that may be behind the position taken by Conzelmann, Ebel, and others:

> Not surprisingly, there are no institutional structures concerning money apparent in the first generation of the Christian movement: without buildings to construct or maintain, and without a membership fee or annual dues to collect, there was no reason for the earliest Christians to handle money on other than an *ad hoc* basis. But that is not to say that money was irrelevant to the social formation of the Christian movement . . . Paul's church in Corinth seems to have relied on members bringing their own food, or on the wealthier supplying food for others . . . But as well as the regular expense of meals (Christian cultic activity, fortunately, cost next to nothing!), there were the occasional, but significant costs of travelling 'prophets' and 'apostles'.[7]

Barclay seems right that the *ekklēsia* did not build or lease a clubhouse – this was a feature characteristic of middling, not modest associations. He also correctly remarks that the banquet would have been just one of several expenses the Christ group would need to somehow cover. But the supposition that the Corinthian meal was styled as a potluck or was procured by a minority of wealthy members cannot be maintained. These theories, especially the former, rest on Paul's reference to each banquet participant's act of προλαμβάνειν ('taking') his or her ἴδιον δεῖπνον (1 Cor 11:21). Paul says nothing about how the food was financed in this verse or anywhere else in 1 Cor 11:17–34, but two related theories have emerged from Paul's description of Corinthian 'taking' in 11:21. The first is Peter Lampe's reconstruction and the second is Gerd Theissen's:

(1)   All Corinthians were supposed to bring their own meal for the first part of the banquet (*prima mensa*) and those 'who have nothing' ate what was left for them when they arrived later.[8]

[7] John M. G. Barclay, 'Money and Meetings: Group Formation among Diaspora Jews and Early Christians', in *Vereine, Synagogen und Gemeinden in kaiserzeitlichen Kleinasien*, ed. Andreas Gutsfeld and Dietrich-Alex Koch (Studien und Texte zu Antike und Christentum 25; Tübingen: Mohr Siebeck, 2006), 113–27 (120).

[8] Peter Lampe, 'Das korinthinische Herrenmahl im Schnittpunkt hellenistisch-römischer Mahlpraxis und paulinischer Theologie Crucis (1 Kor 11, 17–34)', *ZNW* 82 (1991), 183–212 (191–3).

(2)   The wealthy members 'whose contribution made the meal
        possible in the first place'[9] acted as hosts of the banquet
        and decided among themselves that it was only
        appropriate that they should enjoy larger portions, higher
        quality food, and that they should start before poorer,
        non-contributors arrived.[10]

These conclusions are similar since Lampe's freeloaders (the latecomers)
are, like Theissen's freeloaders, generally regarded as having no food to
bring to the Christ group banquet due to poverty and work schedules.[11]
One difference, though, is Lampe's understanding that the Lord's Supper
was *supposed to be* a potluck (even though some members brought
nothing).[12] Theissen distinctively emphasises that the wealthier
Corinthians agreed in advance to fund the whole meal from their own
resources. Longenecker, who supports Theissen's reconstruction, nicely
emphasises the direction to which that model leads us: 'those in ES5
could enjoy the benefits of a benefactor's generosity [at common meals]
without being expected either to make membership payments or to be
involved in public acclaim of the benefactor.'[13] The oddities of this
description will become clearer as this book progresses.

   This chapter reviews ways in which associations financed their
banquets. As John Kloppenborg observes, Christ groups were not the
first 'to confront problems of how to organize communal eating, [and]
how to fund it'.[14] Consideration of funding mechanisms in other

---

[9] Gerd Theissen, *The Social Setting of Pauline Christianity* (Philadelphia: Fortress, 1982), 154.

[10] Theissen argues, 'the ἴδιον δεῖπνον is most likely the meal which individual Christians bring with them. If some Christians have no ἴδιον δεῖπνον, that suggests that not all contributed to the Lord's Supper but that the wealthier Christians provided for all ἐκ τῶν ἰδίων' ('from their own resources'; see *Social Setting*, 148). Theissen further argues, 'The wealthy Christians not only ate separately that food which they themselves had provided, but it appears that they began doing so before the commencement of the congregational meal' (*Social Setting*, 153); cf. Suzanne Watts Henderson, '"If Anyone Hungers ... "': An Integrated Reading of 1 Cor 11.17–34', *NTS* 48 (2002), 195–208; Thomas Schmeller, *Hierarchie und Egalität: eine sozialgeschichtliche Untersuchung paulinischer Gemeinden und griechisch-römischer Vereine* (Stuttgart: Verlag Katholisches Bibelwerk, 1995), 66–73; and Downs, *Offering*, 101.

[11] See Lampe, 'Korinthische', 194 n.34.

[12] Lampe, 'Korinthische', 192–3; followed by David Horrell, The *Social Ethos of the Corinthian Correspondence: Interests and Ideology from 1 Corinthians to 1 Clement* (Edinburgh: T&T Clark, 1996), 103–4, and others.

[13] Longenecker, *Remember*, 271.

[14] John S. Kloppenborg, 'Associations and their Meals' (paper presented at the annual meeting of the SBL, Chicago, IL, 2012), 1–54 (48).

associations will allow for fresh perspectives on Lampe's and Theissen's models of free Corinthian banquets and free Corinthian membership.[15] After reviewing the range of ways in which associations funded their banquets, it becomes clear that both Theissen's and Lampe's explanations of the Corinthians' funding strategy falls outside of known associative funding mechanisms. The chapter then explores finances in associations beyond meal expenses to help generate questions about other non-food items the Christ group may have needed to procure in order to function. The Christ group would have required income from members for these additional expenses, too, and we cannot expect a handful of Corinthian benefactors to have paid for everything perpetually, thus allowing free membership for the majority. In other words, even if Theissen's or Lampe's explanation for the Corinthians' procurement of food were reliable, we would still need to account for the Corinthians' possession of other necessary purchases. Given the Corinthians' array of expenses, it is unlikely that the group would have found a way to offer free membership to the majority.

Finally, the chapter provides a new analysis of 1 Cor 16:2 in light of association financial practices. My interest with this verse is in understanding why Paul would instruct Christ group members to collect funds on a specific day of the week rather than at any time during each week. Moreover, how might have Paul's instruction to keep the Jerusalem λογεία apart (παρ' ἑαυτῷ) been heard by members of an association? Commentators struggle with these questions. Approaching Paul's directives in 1 Cor 16:2 in light of collections in associations helps to provide some helpful insights. Specifically, I suggest that these formerly awkward instructions become comprehensible in the theory that the Corinthians were in the habit of making regular payments of subscription fees from which the money for the Jerusalem collection was to be kept separate.

Financing Dinners in Associations

This section draws extensively from a recent study of association meals by John Kloppenborg.[16] In one section of this article, Kloppenborg searches for attestation in association sources to the food procurement

---

[15] Both Lampe's and Theissen's models have been submitted to little scrutiny. Even for Lampe, 'Etliche Elemente der Theißenschen Rekonstrucktion der korinthischen Situation warden wiederkehren' ('Korinthische', 194).

[16] Kloppenborg, 'Associations and their Meals', 1–54.

mechanisms suggested by Lampe and Theissen.[17] I shall begin with
Kloppenborg's findings concerning Lampe's *eranos* meal.

Lampe contested that a potluck version of the *eranos* meal explains
Paul's detail in 1 Cor 11:21 that each Corinthian banquet participant
took an ἴδιον δεῖπνον. The ἔρανος meal, first attested by Homer
(*Od.* 1.227, 11.415), could be formatted in one of two ways: 'Die
Gäste bringen ihren Beitrag entweder in Geld mit ... oder als Speisen
in Körben.'[18] Dennis Smith's description of the ἔρανος meal favours its
more common variant: 'The term *eranos* is used in Homer to refer to a
meal paid for by the common contributions of the participants.'[19] In a
series of articles, Lampe suggests that the other, less common, practice
of guests bringing their own meals – the potluck dinner – was practised
by the Corinthians; hence each member ate their own meal (τὸ ἴδιον
δεῖπνον, 1 Cor 11:21) because they brought their own meal.[20] While
ἔρανος meals, where participants make monetary contributions,
were common among the associations (see p. 124 in this section),
Kloppenborg found 'no clear parallels' to potluck dinners in
associations.[21]

Lampe's sources on potluck banquets almost all concern private meals
such as the one Paul references in 1 Cor 10:27–33,[22] not the Christ group
meal in 11:17–34. A possible exception is Aelius Aristides's description
of a sacrificial Sarapis cultic meal (*Orations* 45.27–8 = *AGRW* L.13).
Aristides describes the banquet as an ἔρανος meal where participants
bring food donations and Sarapis distributes 'was diese als Spenden
mitgebracht haben'.[23] As Kloppenborg observes, though, Aristides actually says nothing indicative of a potluck meal.[24]

[17] Kloppenborg, 'Associations and their Meals', 35–42.

[18] Lampe, 'Korinthische', 195.

[19] Dennis E. Smith, *From Symposium to Eucharist: The Banquet in the Early Christian
World* (Minneapolis, MN: Fortress Press, 2003), 89.

[20] Lampe, 'Korinthische', 183–213; and Peter Lampe, 'The Corinthian Eucharistic
Dinner Party: Exegesis of a Cultural Context (1 Cor 11:17–34)', *Affirmation* 4 (1991),
1–15.

[21] Kloppenborg, 'Associations and their Meals', 36.

[22] Aristophanes, *Wasps* 1085–1149; Lucian, *Lexiphanes* 13; Xenophon, *Memorabilia*
3.14.1. The potluck dinners were only one funding option even in private dinners. Paul
assumes that the Christ believer at a private dinner will be served by the host. For the
structure of typical private banquets, see Smith, *From Symposium*, 13–46.

[23] Lampe, 'Korinthische', 196.

[24] This point is made in a forthcoming version of the paper, John S. Kloppenborg,
'Precedence at the Communal Meal in Corinth' (paper presented at the Annual Meeting of
the SNTS, Seged, Hungary, 2014), 1–35 (19–20).

The most significant problem with Lampe's reconstruction is not necessarily the fact that this was a rare – or even unattested – practice for private associations. Most problematic is the fact that Lampe's reconstruction only works if it is imposed onto Paul's description of the *ekklēsia*'s banquet: Paul only mentions that members 'took' (προλαμβάνειν) food, he says nothing about who paid for the food or where it came from. Indeed, the detail that each member 'took' ἴδιον δεῖπνον ('an individual meal') has been interpreted by Dennis Smith and others to suggest food procurement procedures other than the potluck. As Smith persuasively argued, Paul's point when describing 'private meals' was that each member had their own *portion* as determined by their place in the Christ group's present hierarchy.[25] This was a very common practice in associations, with officers and other leaders receiving double or, sometimes, unlimited portions (see Chapter 7).[26] An 'individual meal' (τὸ ἴδιον δεῖπνον) was one 'in which portions are not equal and activities are not shared by all . . . the inequality signified by the situation at Corinth where "some are hungry and others are drunk" qualifies this meal as an "individual" one'.[27] Theissen observed that was the way Plutarch used the adjective, ἴδιον, when he described dinner portions at private banquets:

> When I was holding the eponymous archonship at home, most of the dinners (τῶν δείπνων) were portion-banquets, and each man at the sacrifices was allotted his share of the meal. This was wonderfully pleasing to some, but others blamed the practice as unsociable and vulgar . . . [For Hagias said] 'where each guest has his own private portion (ἴδιον), companionship fails' (*Quaest. conv.* II.10.1, 2).[28]

The scholarship of Theissen, Smith, and Kloppenborg create significant challenges for the viability of the *current version* of Lampe's reconstruction. A better way to reconstruct Lampe's scenario is to maintain the idea of a meal where each member makes an individual contribution but to presume in place the mechanism that almost all other associations used – namely, bringing payments, not food, to banquets.

It is also difficult to support aspects of Theissen's reconstruction. Theissen suggested that a small, though unspecified, number of

[25] Smith, *From Symposium*, 191–3.
[26] See also Theissen, *Social Setting*, 154.
[27] Smith, *From Symposium*, 193.
[28] Quoted from Theissen, *Social Setting*, 149.

Corinthians bought all the food for all participants at *ekklēsia* banquets.[29]
If we are to imagine middling Corinthians as the benefactors, as
Bruce Longenecker has done, then only 7–10 per cent of Corinthian
members would have funded the weekly meals (if we agree with
Friesen's and Longenecker's percentages).[30] For a Christ group with
ten members, this would mean that one member paid for everything.
Kloppenborg locates a few analogies to Theissen's payment method, but
they, in fact, reveal significant problems with Theissen's theory rather
than prop it up with support – even if scholarship is to maintain the idea
that the Corinthian group consisted of 40–100 members and therefore
enjoyed the support of more than one middling member.

Perhaps the closest analogy that Kloppenborg finds to Theissen's
model is a fragmentary inscription from Ionia produced by a Dionysiac
club (*SEG* 31:983 = Kloppenborg 2012, p. 31; Söke, Ionia, Asia Minor;
II–I BCE).[31] This inscription attests to three people who had promised
(προεπηγγείλεσθαι) wine to the association, and who made good on their
commitments. The third donor, a certain Dionysios, also provided bread
(ἄριστον, l.11), cooks (ἐργάτης, l.10), and musicians (μουσικός, l.10).
Like Theissen's notion of a handful of Corinthian benefactors providing
all of the food and drink, this Dionysiac club, at first glance, seems to
have relied on a few of its wealthy affiliates for its banquet expenses.

The quantities of the benefactions to the Dionysiac club are lost except
for one donation of 100 *metretai* (3,900 litres) of wine by a certain son
of Protamachos whose name is missing (ll.5–7). Since 3,900 litres of
wine would be an exorbitant amount for just one banquet, Kloppenborg
suggests that it was meant to be consumed at several dinners.[32]

This wine donation is worth exploring further since it represents the
kind of benefaction Theissen imagines the middling *ekklēsia*'s members
to have made *every year* – crucially, the Dionysiac club secured food

---

[29] Theissen, *Social Setting*, 147–51.

[30] Friesen posits approximately 7 per cent, Longenecker suggests 10 per cent. See
Chapter 3.

[31] Other notable analogies are middling associations who were wealthy enough to rotate
the duty of funding club banquets among leaders. For example, members in the Lanuvium
group needed to pay 1.5 sesterces per month (in addition to entrance fees) even though
rotating *magistri cenarum* funded some of their meals (*CIL* XIV 2112.I.20). Another type
of analogy is the association whose leaders (e.g., officers, peer benefactors) paid for entire
banquets, though these were not perpetual benefaction that saved members from having to
make contribution fees. See *SEG* 31:983 (Ionia, Asia Minor; II–I BCE); *IG* II² 1343.24–7 =
GRA I 48 (Athens, Attica; 37/6 or 36/5 BCE); *IPergamon* II 274 = *AGRW* 117 (Pergamon,
Asia Minor; 129–138 CE).

[32] Kloppenborg, 'Associations and their Meals', 31.

benefactions from these patrons for only a single year. How much money did the Dionysiac wine donor spend on his promised wine? The economically modest Tebtynis club (*P.Tebt.* III/2 894) purchased one keramion of wine for its banquets of twenty-five to thirty participants.[33] Protomachos's son's 3,900 litres of wine is equivalent to 534.25 monochoron keramia.[34] Keramia of wine could be purchased by the monochoron (7.3 litres) or dichoron (14.6 litres), however, it was usually the monochoron in clubs. In Philadelphia (Egypt), one keramion of wine sold for 400–600 copper drachmas (6.66–10 silver drachmas) between 210 BCE and 187 BCE.[35] This is the same price range the Tebtynis club recorded for their wine purchases – they bought one keramion of wine in 114 BCE for 3,000–4,000 copper drachmas or 6.25–8.33 silver drachmas. Since we know, approximately, the size and price of the Tebtynis club's wine purchases, we can convert the Dionysiac benefactor's gift into 114 BCE prices and compare it with the contributions made by the Tebtynis club. Given the cost of wine in 114 BCE, Protomachos's son's donation of 3,900 litres would be valued at approximately 3,896 silver drachmas. This is equivalent to the income of twenty *P.Tebt.* III/2 894 members over the course of thirty-nine years.[36] The Tebtynis club, it will be remembered, consisted of members from strata below the middling economic category, just like the Pauline Christ believers on Meggitt's, Friesen's, and Longenecker's models. The fact that Theissen's method of paying for banquet menu-items was so rare in associations results from the enormity of the donation.

The procedure proposed by Theissen, in fact, necessitates greater generosity than what is attested in the Dionysiac inscription. The benefactors in this inscription are not said to have made these donations perpetually, and there is certainly no evidence that they did. More

---

[33] *P.Tebt.* III/2 894, *Frag.2* recto, I.6; *Frag.2* verso, II.44; *Frag.6* recto, II.1.

[34] Dominic Rathbone suggests that this size of jar held 7.3 litres. See *Economic Rationalism and Rural Society in Third-Century AD Egypt: The Heroninos Archive and the Appianus Estate* (Cambridge and New York: Cambridge University Press, 1991), 469; see also Kenneth W. Harl, *Coinage in the Roman Economy, 300 B.C. to A.D. 700* (Baltimore: Johns Hopkins University Press, 1996), 316; and Philip Mayerson, 'The Monochoron and Dichoron: Standard Measures of Wine Based on the Oxyrhynchition', *ZPE* 131 (2000), 169–72.

[35] See *BGU* VII 1501 (Philadelphia, Egypt; 206–188 BCE), *BGU* VII 1506 (Philadelphia, Egypt; 205–188 BCE), and *BGU* VII 1545 (Philadelphia, Egypt; 210–187 BCE).

[36] This is if the Tebtynis club members' income resembled what C. C. Edgar supposes of the members in the slave association (5 drachmas per month). See Chapter 3 for socio-economic similarities between these two clubs.

probably, given the value of their donations, they accepted the temporary kind of responsibilities held by the middling Lanuvium association's four annual, rotating, *magistri cenarum.*

What happens when we apply Protomachos's son's donation to Christ group practices? First, the Christ group did not require 3,900 litres of wine per annum, unless the majority of scholars are correct in arbitrarily assuming that the Christ group consisted of between 40 and 100 members. If they consisted of twenty members, which is still probably too large, then perhaps they ordered a keramion for each meeting, which was enough for twenty-five to thirty participants at the Tebtynis club's banquets. Let us assume with many scholars that *ekklēsia* assemblies were held at weekly intervals (see section 'Temporal Aspects of Paul's Instructions in 1 Cor 16:2'). Since one keramion was approximately 7.3 silver drachmas for the Tebtynis group, fifty orders at this quantity in 114 BCE would cost 365 silver drachmas. If two Corinthians shared the expense, it would be the equivalent of 181.25 drachmas for the Tebtynis group. This is almost equal to the annual income of all the Tebtynis recruits over the course of two years. Even if the Christ group was a socially heterogeneous group, this type of perpetual, year-after-year, benefaction was seemingly beyond the level of available resources held by typical middling (let alone modest) individuals, which is why it is so rarely found as a food procurement method even in middling associations.

Of course, scholars could tweak their numbers to make the idea of Corinthian freeloading financially feasible for the middling Corinthian benefactors – for example, one could arbitrarily posit four Corinthian benefactors and only twelve Christ group meetings throughout the year. This would amount to meal donations costing 22 drachmas per year per benefactor. At that annual rate, the benefactors' financial commitments would actually resemble spendings of subscription dues within the range of modest associations. The problem with tweaking the numbers in this way is that it still produces an oddity. The crucial datum is that no association financed meals year after year the way that Theissen proposed.[37] Even a rare bylaw from a late antique Christian association

---

[37] Apologetic literature provides no data to contradict this finding. For example, in Justin's description of Christ group banquets (*Apol.* 67), he mentions payments of contributions (τὰ συλλεγόμενα), but these are voluntary payments for mutual aid activities, and they are paid after the meal itself – Justin is silent on how the groups funded their meals. Tertullian (*Apol.* 39) speaks about contributions (*stipes*), but these are the same voluntary payments for mutual aid that Justin described.

of craft workers explicitly attests to an equal distribution of the burden of financing club meals:

> When it is our desire to drink wine together and enjoy each other's company, then each man in turn, for a day at a time, entertains us in his house. He provides for us out of his own pocket, in accordance with the custom and usage we have. But any of us who does not entertain his companions in his house gladly shall pay a monetary fine of 10 staters. If there is anyone among us who complains about the equal helping which has been set before him and in his greed it seems to small, then let that helping be taken from him; let him stand up and give his companions three draughts to drink, and then sit down again.[38]

Longenecker's notion that the Corinthians found two or four individuals who agreed to perpetually fund all *ekklēsia* banquets, and who also approved of the Christ group's failure to provide them with honorific rewards, tests the limits of credulity.

Kloppenborg shows that collection of subscription fees from all members was the preferred way to fund club expenses,[39] an argument that is consistent with Koenraad Verboven's analysis of financial behaviour in associations.[40] Not even the presence of some 'socially weak' members in the Corinthian group would have meant financial exemptions. In the Tebtynis group, as noted, some members paid regular fees and contributed to additional collections; some members paid only modest fees, and others found themselves in debt – though they attempted to pay it back. Despite their socially heterogeneous membership profile, all members paid a base level of dues. The theory that a few wealthy Corinthians purchased all the banquet items from their own resources, allowing '50 free meals'[41] for all other members, is not a plausible scenario in light of these analogous data.

An alternative way to understand Theissen's theory may be to imagine the *ekklēsia*'s one or two meal providers as donors of *sportulae*

---

[38] Sebastian Brock, 'Regulations for an Association of Artisans from the Late Sasanian or Early Arab Period', in *Transformations of Late Antiquity: Essays for Peter Brown*, ed. Philip Rousseau and Manolis Papoutsakis (Surrey, England and Burlington, Vermont: Ashgate, 2009), 51–62 (59). I thank Richard Ascough for pointing out this article to me.

[39] Kloppenborg, 'Associations and their Meals', 36.

[40] Verboven, 'Associative Order', 882.

[41] Peter Pilhofer, *Die frühen Christen und ihre Welt: Greifswalder Aufsätze 1996–2001* (Wissenschaftliche Untersuchungen zum Neuen Testament II/145; Tübingen: Mohr Siebeck, 2002), 207.

(gifts)[42] or endowments. But endowments given to associations were generally modest and did not relieve recipients from the necessity of collecting entrance and monthly fees from their members in order to fund their activities.[43] Moreover, it is doubtful that the Christ group would have come into possession of endowments; Jinyu Liu observes that endowments

> were not made out of charity or in response to particular finan-
> cial difficulties, but . . . donors tended to favor the wealthier and
> more prominent associations and often obliged the recipients
> to perform certain services in return. The more prominent and
> well off the association, the larger and more frequent the dona-
> tions it tended to receive.[44]

Sportulae and endowments were more than a modest *ekklēsia* could expect and, in any case, did not eliminate banquet expenses. On this last point, it is fascinating that the Tebtynis club seems to have come into the possession of a vast amount of money at some point in their history: in one very obscure fragment, the club seems to record the possession of eighteen talents (*Frag.8* recto, II.34). The papyrus provides no hints concerning the source of this money or where it was used. Indeed, it is so much higher than the club's other recorded funds that it may be erroneous to read the 'eighteen' as a number of talents rather than the date of the month. On the theory that it was a sum of money, perhaps an endowment and other gifts, it is nonetheless clear that the club still depended on subscription fees to fund their dinners, and that this association consistently behaved as an economically modest group (e.g., meeting in a storehouse and a workshop;[45] and collecting very low amounts of

---

[42] These could be in the form of money (more common) or food (less common). See Kloppenborg, 'Associations and their Meals', 33–4; cf. John Donahue, *The Roman Community at Table during the Principate* (Ann Arbor: University of Michigan Press, 2004), 133.

[43] Jinyu Liu, 'The Economy of Endowments: The Case of Roman Associations', in *'Pistoi dia tèn technèn'. Bankers, Loans and Archives in the Ancient World. Studies in Honour of Raymond Bogaert*, ed. Koenraad Verboven, Katelijn Vandorpe, and Véronique Chankowski-Sable (Studia Hellenistica 44; Leuven: Peeters, 2008), 231–56 (238); cf. Kloppenborg, 'Associations and their Meals', 41.

[44] Liu, 'Economy of Endowments', 239.

[45] For the storehouse (θησαυρός) meeting, see *P.Tebt.* III/2 894. *Frag.6* recto 2, l.10. The slave association also uses this term for their meeting in a storehouse (*SB* III 7182 *Frag.1*.II.12; *Frag.4* recto, III.62). For a possible workshop (ἐργαστήριον) meeting, see *P.Tebt.* III/2 894, *Frag.3* verso, 1; *Frag.10* recto, l.4. The Tebtynis club misspells both words (especially undecipherable is the misspelling of the latter term) so it is possible that

subscription dues). In summary, club members paid for their dinners. This was partially a financial necessity, and partially a distinctive aspect of association meals that differed from private household dinner parties.

Expenditures and Funding Strategies in Modest Associations

It is far from 'obvious' that the *ekklēsia* managed to avoid 'the most commonly attested practice for funding banquets', namely, collections of membership dues.[46] C. C. Edgar, Jinyu Liu, Koenraad Verboven, and John Kloppenborg have all found collection of subscription payments to be typically prerequisite for holding association meals. In the documentary papyri and epigraphic evidence, associations never or only rarely record the potluck dinners that Lampe described of the Corinthians, and in this database we never locate associations who secured perpetual meal funding through benefaction akin to Theissen's portrayal of the Corinthian meals.

The association data require us to re-examine how the *ekklēsia* paid for their weekly meals. But more to the point, even if Theissen's or Lampe's implausible scenario concerning funding for the Corinthian *meals* should be maintained, neither could be cited any longer as an explanation for why the Christ group supposedly offered free membership. Associations were responsible for financing several non-banquet expenses that were also necessary for survival, and subscription dues most likely covered these expenses, too. The data outlined in the following pages help to broaden contemporary understandings of financial pressures that were felt by ancient cult groups including the Corinthians. I also propose some new ideas about how the Corinthians strategised to meet these challenges.

Non-Menu Expenses

Economic descriptions of Pauline groups rarely take into account the kinds of things these groups needed to purchase (other than food) in order to survive. The following papyrus generates ideas concerning various

---

they did not intend to signify meetings in a storehouse and workshop. Nonetheless, we know that they met in the shops or houses of various members at other times. See, e.g., *Frag.2*.II.45; *Frag.2* recto, I.7.

[46] Kloppenborg, 'Associations and their Meals', 36.

expenditures that the Corinthians may have needed to make on a regular basis. This document was written by an association of priests from first-century Oxyrhynchos (*P.Oslo* III 143; Oxyrhynchos, Egypt; I CE):

λόγο[ς π]αστοφό(ρων) συγόδο(υ)
Θῶνις Τεῶτος (δραχμαὶ) πδ
Θομπαχράτῃ (δραχμαὶ) ξς
γραμματεῖ (δραχμαὶ) ε
ἱστιατορίας κοινω() (δραχμαὶ) ιβ   5
χειρογραφίας (δραχμαὶ) δ
λεπτῆς δαπάνη(ς) ὀβο(λοὶ) κδ∠
συνόδωι ἐντῷ Θωγιείου (δραχμαὶ) ι
Σενθεῖ Θοω() συνόδ(ου) Δαμαρίω(νος) (δραχμαὶ) η
Οὐερεθώνει (δραχμαὶ) μ   10
γ(ίνονται) (δραχμαὶ)σλβ(ὀβολοὶ) γ∠

Account of a *pastophoroi* σύνοδος. Thonis son of Teos 84 drachmas; to Thompakhrates 66 drachmas; to the secretary 5 drachmas; for the common feast 12 drachmas; for writing expenses 4 drachmas; for small expenses 24.5 obols; to the σύνοδος in the temple of Thonis 10 drachmas; to Sentheus son of ? of the Damarion σύνοδος 8 drachmas; to Ouerethonis 40 drachmas. The total comes to 232 drachmas and 3.5 obols.[47]

The price figures in this papyrus could be recorded in copper drachmas,[48] but do not represent the inflationary copper levels during II–I BCE. The value of copper apparently stabilised itself by this date. At least, this is the impression one gets from a farm account from 78 to 79 CE – approximately the time of *P.Oslo* III 143 – where copper expenditures were converted to silver drachmas at the approximate rate of 1.13 copper drachmas to 1 silver drachma (*P.Lond.* I 131; Hermopolis, Egypt). In this

[47] The author of the account places a ∠ at the end of lines 7 and 11. This symbol is sometimes taken to mean 'one-half', and other times it serves to remind the author that he or she made an abbreviation in the line (see *P.Tebt.* II 401 and the editors' comments on l.18 in *Tebtunis Papyri* II, 272). In *P.Oslo* III 143, it means 'one-half' – the total sum calculated at the end adds up if the group reckoned a 7-obol drachma. See Verne B. Schuman, 'The Seven-Obol Drachma of Roman Egypt', *CP* 47 (1952), 214–18 (214).

[48] 'Payments in copper were frequently recorded in Roman times, although it is probable that such entries were the survivals of Ptolemaic practice, and copper was no longer actually current. Usually these sums were converted to their equivalent in silver or bullion' (Allan Chester Johnson, *Roman Egypt to the Reign of Diocletian* [Volume 2 of *An Economic Survey of Ancient Rome*; Baltimore: The Johns Hopkins Press, 1936], 431).

farm account, 68 copper drachmas and 4.5 obols is converted to 59 silver drachmas.[49] The expenditures in *P.Oslo* III 143 begin with payments to three club members (Thonis, Thompakhrates, and the secretary).[50] Club officers regularly paid up front for various items needed by their associations[51] and were later reimbursed. In the event that one or two elected officers or regular members brought the food for the Corinthian meals, this would not necessarily indicate that they were acting as benefactors. Rather, it could mean that these members purchased food using funds from the group's treasury, or that they used their personal funds and later would receive compensation.

The second expense on the list is a banqueting fee. Here, the *pastophoroi*[52] record one of their feasts to have cost 12 drachmas, which may mean their 20 (?) members' subscription fees were about 0.5 silver drachmas, but not anywhere near the fees that could be charged by middling associations (e.g., 12 drachmas each in a first-century Egyptian guild[53]), and in a different world from the Dionysiac donor of 3,896 silver drachmas worth of wine.

Third, the club records writing expenses, presumably for the material to compose financial accounts, bylaws, and other documents. These amounted to one-third the cost of a banquet. Fourth, in an obscure entry, the Oxyrhynchos club pays money 'for the/to the σύνοδος in the Thoneion'. The editors of the text take σύνοδος here to denote another association and suggest, 'the *pastophori* had borrowed some implements necessary for their feast for which the other club received dr. 10 as remuneration.'[54] A

---

[49] It is not always possible to know the copper to silver ratio. The conversion rate in *P.Lond.* I 131 is at odds with other near-contemporary texts. For example, in *P.Fay.* 101 (Euhemeria, Egypt; 18 BCE), the ratio is 1850:1; *P.Fay.* 44 (Theadelphia, Egypt; 6 BCE) uses a ratio of 400:1, and *SB* III 6951 (Theadelphia, Egypt; II CE) employs a ratio of 300:1.

[50] It is curious that Thonis is not in the dative. The spelling of a member's name in the nominative followed by a sum makes it difficult to know if the individual owes the sum or is being paid back money.

[51] E.g., *P.Tebt.* II 401.23 (Tebtynis, Egypt; early I CE).

[52] The *pastophoroi* were priests responsible for carrying shrines in processions. The editors understand these to be 'subordinate priests'. This papyrus is our earliest attestation to Greek associations of priests in Egypt. See Franz Poland, *Geschichte des griechischen Vereinswesens* (Leipzig: Teubner, 1909), 40–4; Mariano San Nicolò, *Ägyptisches Vereinswesen zur Zeit der Ptolemäer und Römer* (2 vols.; Münchener Beiträge zur Papyrusforschung und antiken Rechtsgeschichte 2; Munich: Berk, 1972), 1, 11–12; Walter von Otto, *Priester und Tempel im hellenistischen Ägypten: Ein Beitrag zur Kulturgeschichte des Hellenismus* (2 vols.; Leipzig and Berlin: Teubner, 1905), 1, 94–5.

[53] *P. Mich.* V 243.2 = *AGRW* 300 (Tebtynis, Egypt; 14–37 CE).

[54] S. Eitrem and Leiv Amundsen, eds., *Papyri osloenses* (Oslo: J. Dybwad, 1925–), 3:222.

second possibility is that the 4 drachmas were paid to the temple as a rental fee for a date when they held their σύνοδος ('meeting') in a dining room in the Thoneion. Fifth, the association later records remuneration for two named individuals, Sentheus and Ouerthonis, for an unknown reason. Finally, 'small expenses' are listed in obols and did not warrant specificity. In all, these fees signify some of the costs in keeping up an association. The two modest associations explored in Chapter 3 provide additional examples of non-food expenditures. The slave club (*SB* III 7182) records the prices for flute players and public dancers,[55] and the Tebtynis group (*P.Tebt*. III/2 894) lists costs of crowns,[56] a lamp,[57] perfume,[58] and a flute player.[59] Other club accounts mention crowns (*P.Tebt*. I 118; Tebtynis, Egypt; late II BCE) and clothing items for cultic rituals (*P.Lund*. IV 11; possibly Bakchias, Arsinoites, Egypt; 169/170 CE).

The financial accounts produced by associations show that food and wine were only two of the many expenditures for which associations needed income. Evidence of the Corinthians' non-banquet expenses are explored later but, first, an investigation into strategies that associations developed in order to fund all of their expenses are outlined.

Strategies for Generating Income

The financial records of associations show that clubs often required more money than they took in from subscription dues. Their strategies for collecting extra revenue are outlined in the following sections.

Voluntary Contributions and Collections

An informative papyrus carries the title ἔκθεσις οἰνικῶν συνόδου ὀνηλατῶν (*P.Athen*. 41; unknown provenance; I CE).[60] This text records the names and contributions by nineteen association members for wine that was consumed at their club meetings. As far as we can tell, members contributed what they could spare to this wine collection, and these monetary donations would have been over and above the regular fees each of them paid. Areios son of Ptolemaios is listed first. He contributed 4 drachmas and 11 obols (l.3). Several lines down, we find a certain

---

[55] *Frag.5* recto, ll.95–6.
[56] *Frag.1* recto, III.30.
[57] *Frag.2* recto, I.9.
[58] *Frag.2* verso, II.45.
[59] *Frag.2* verso, II.47.
[60] 'List of Wine-Payments of a σύνοδος of Donkey-Drivers'.

Dionysios son of Apollos, who contributed 20 drachmas (1.16). Some members contributed as little as 1 drachma and 1 obol (1.6).

Certainly, this association needed more than wine: funeral costs, lamps, entertainment, bread, writing materials, dining space, and more. Presumably, those necessities were funded some other way. We do not know if this association of donkey drivers included more than nineteen members. If it did, then the non-contributors may have lived too close to the level of subsistence to provide fees for wine on top of subscription dues – though they would have been still above the level of subsistence since they could afford the luxury of joining a club.

Another example of a wine collection is found in *P.Tebt.* III/2 894. Fourteen of the club's twenty-five (or so) members contributed to a monetary collection for wine as this passage indicates (*P.Tebt.* III/2 894; *Frag.3* verso, I.1–19):

> (ἔτους) δ̅ Μεχ[εὶρ ,]
> ἐν τῷ βομῷ
> καὶ ἐν τῷ ε[. . . . .]γῳ.
> συ(μβολαὶ) τῶν οἰν[-ca.?-]
> (γίνονται) . . .αγελις συ(μβολαὶ) τμε   5
> Σοκμῆνις συ(μβολαὶ) σμε εις
> Πανεῦις συ(μβολαὶ) σμε
> Φατρῆς συ(μβολαὶ) σμε
> Τράλλις συ(μβολαὶ) σμε
> Σιλοῦς συ(μβολαὶ) σμε   10
> Φῖβις συ(μβολαὶ) ρμε
> Νααρῶς συ(μβολαὶ) σμε
> ζημία υ (γίνονται) χμε
> Πομβᾶς συ(μβολαὶ) σμε
> Θορτᾶις νεὸ(ς) συ(μβολαὶ) ρμε   15
> Εὔδημος συ(μβολαὶ) σμε
> Σαρᾶς συ(μβολαὶ) σμε
> Πτόλλις ἀδελ(φὸς) συ(μβολαὶ) σμε
> Πετεσοῦ(χος) Καγῶ(τος) σμε

Membership dues in this club were approximately 100 drachmas for regular members. Those fees would have been used for other expenses and would have been mandatory for everyone (*Frag.1* verso, III.63). The practice of making additional monetary collections indicates that income from subscription dues was a bare minimum for some groups' survival, and that subscription dues sometimes did not even cover the cost of essential items needed for banqueting. Special collections represented a strategy for closing the gap between income from subscription dues and overall expenses.

Guests at Association Banquets

A fascinating mechanism for generating income outside of membership fees, and outside of voluntary collections, was to invite guests to club dinners. The short club account, *P.Tebt.* I 118 (Tebtynis, Egypt; late II BCE), lists expenses for three meetings at which guests were present. Subscription rates sat at 100 copper drachmas per participant per meeting, which is comparable to the modest dues expected from Chapter 3's slave association and Tebtynis club. Given copper's value at the time (late II BCE), this amounts to 0.20–0.25 silver drachmas. The income and expenses of this modest club over the course of three meetings are placed in Table 4.1. At each meeting, guests proved decisive for keeping the books balanced.

Table 4.1 *The Finances of a Modest Association (P.Tebt. I 118; Tebtynis, Egypt; late II BCE)*

Meeting Date	Occasion	Expenses	Attendance and Income (100 dr. per participant)	Balance
Hathyr 17	Funeral feast	– 6 chöes of wine (2000 dr.) – 6 dinner loaves (190 dr.) Total: 2190 dr.	– 18 members – 4 guests Total: 2200 dr.	10 dr. surplus
20th day of unknown month	Regular banquet	– 6 chöes of wine (2000 dr.) – Crown (120 dr.) Total: 2120 dr.	– 18 members – 3 guests – Nephoreges – Sen(yris?)[61] Total: 2300 dr.	180 dr. surplus that 'remain with the treasurer' [ἐν οἴκο(νόμῳ), l.15]
Tybi 25	Regular banquet	– 6 chöes of wine (2,000 dr.)[62] – crown (120 dr.) Total: 2,120 dr.	– 21 attendees Total: 2,100 dr.	20 dr. deficit [ὑπὲρ ἀνη-(λώματος) κ]

[61] Nephoreges and Senyris are neither listed as ξένοι nor grouped in with the members. They paid 100 drachmas – the same fee as all other participants.

[62] The quantity of wine at the third meeting is not stated in the papyrus, but its price indicates the same six chöes as was procured at the previous two dinners.

Instructively, fees from all eighteen members were never enough to cover the expense of holding these three meetings. Instead of increasing subscription fees, which were low but presumably burdensome enough already, the club encouraged its members to invite guests. Guests would not sign up initially for full membership but would nonetheless pay fees to participate in the meal. Participation in this association's feasts at the rank of a guest cost 100 drachmas, which could have been paid by the guest or by the regular member who invited the guest – it did not matter as long as the fee was paid.

Crucially, the club ordered no additional food or drink when guests came – six chöes of wine were purchased for all three meetings even though the attendance numbers fluctuated from twenty-one to twenty-three. In this papyrus, guests are always listed as sources of income rather than as added expenses,[63] which signifies how their participation in feasts allowed the association to purchase the resources they already needed for their own members without going into debt. Interestingly, at the association's third meeting, they were only able to secure the participation of three guests – a lower number than at previous meetings. The result is a deficit that needed to be paid from the common fund.

P.Tebt. III/2 894 further demonstrates the significance of guests as sources of additional income. The Tebtynis club shared with the association behind *P.Tebt.* I 118 the practice of spending more money than its core membership could afford. Guests' fees helped the group to underwrite their expenses. Here is a tally of a meeting's *income* from a banquet that cost 4,140 drachmas (*Frag.2* recto, II.36–8):

(γίνονται) Αωιε,
ξένου α σ, (γίνονται) Βιε,
λο(ιπαὶ) Βρμ.

Total money (i.e., from the officers)[64]: 1,815 drachmas.
one guest whose participation brought us 200 drachmas. Total (from officers and a guest): 2,015 drachmas.

---

[63] For example, line 8 reads: (γίνονται) κβ ἀνὰ ρ Βσ ('The total number of members were 22 at the rate of 100, for a total of 220 drachmas'). Each of the 22 participants, including four guests, paid 100 drachmas. Another example of guests reckoned as income is from *P.Tebt.* I 224 (Tebtynis, Egypt; late II BCE). This is a very fragmentary account of the expenses of a banquet. It comes from a modest association that charges members and guests 105 drachmas (0.20–0.25 silver drachmas) for attending.

[64] The five ἄρχοντες contributed 815 drachmas in total (*Frag.2* recto, I.14–21), the five ἱεροποιοί paid 200 each for a total of 1,000 (*Frag.2* recto, I.22).

The remaining (income from regular members): 2,140 drachmas. If we add up the club's total income from this meeting, we arrive at 4,155 drachmas. Their expenditures (4,140 drachmas) were on wine, cabbage, and a lamp (see *Frag.2* recto, I.6–10). If they did not secure 200 drachmas from their guest, they would have been in debt by almost 200 drachmas. Moreover, we know that they did not order extra wine for their guests. Here, they totalled twenty-two and ordered their standard 7 litre (one keramion) jar of wine, which cost 4,000 drachmas (I.6), while at another banquet, they totalled twenty and ordered the same quantity of wine (*Frag.2* verso, II.44).

Varying Subscription Dues

While some modest clubs charged a uniform rate from every member (e.g., *P.Tebt.* I 118, 224), others collected different amounts of fees based on members' position in the association's hierarchy. Perhaps these clubs depended less than other associations on special collections and on the presence of guests. One example of hierarchy-based fee rates comes from the financial records of an association of *Dioskouroi*. This club purchased several items for one of its banquets, held on the first day of Mesore (*P.Lund.* IV 11; possibly Bakchias, Arsinoites, Egypt; 169/170 CE): oil (ll.7, 16), condiments or seasoning (l.17), a vessel for some type of liquid (l.21), dried fruits (l.24), grain (ll.25–6), and two dichora of wine (l.4). In the second column, the association lists twenty members who contribute either 100, 80, 60, or 20 silver drachmas (*P.Lund.* IV 11. II.1–23):

οἱ δὲ συ[ντε]λο[ῦντες]		
εἰς τὸν ἐγ[γεγραμ-]		
μένον στολισμ[όν ·]		
Διόσκ[ο]ρος οὐετ(ρανὸς)	(δραχμαὶ) ρ	
Διόσκορος Ἰσί[ω]νος	(δραχμαὶ) ρ	5
Φιλ[ό]ξενος	(δραχμαὶ) ρ	
Ν]εφωτιαν[ὸ]ς	(δραχμαὶ) ρ	
Δῖος ...	(δραχμαὶ) ρ	
Σερῆνο[ς ο]ὐετ(ρανὸς)	(δραχμαὶ) ρ	
Ἀπολινάριος οὐετ(ρανὸς)	(δραχμαὶ) π	10
Πτολεμαῖος [οὐ]ετ(ρανὸς)	(δραχμαὶ) ξ	
Ἀπολινάριος οὐ[ε]τ(ρανὸς)	(δραχμαὶ) ξ	
Ὠρίων οὐετ(ρανὸς)	(δραχμαὶ) ξ	
Διόσκορος Ἡφαιστ[()]	(δραχμαὶ) ξ	

Διογένης	[(δραχμαὶ) ξ	15
Ζωίλος Ἡφαιστ[()]	(δραχμαὶ) ξ	
Δεῖος Μάρων(ος).	(δραχμαὶ) [ξ	
Ὠ]ρίων ἐλαιου[ργὸς	(δραχμαὶ) ξ	
Διονύσιος	(δραχμαὶ) [ξ	
Π]τολεμαῖος οὐετ(ρανὸς)	(δραχμαὶ) ξ	20
.ονας	(δραχμαὶ) κ	
Ἀκῆς	(δραχμαὶ) κ	
Ἑρμείας	(δραχμαὶ) κ	

The ones who have paid for the equipping (of the gods in new clothing and the sacrificial feast) have been written below . . .[65]

Erik Knudtzon believes that the different contribution rates reflect the group's current hierarchical structure ('Klasseneinteilung') rather than members' position in society outside of the community.[66] If some Corinthians contributed slightly more to the Lord's Supper than others, might that be because they occupied a higher place in the Christ group's current hierarchical arrangement rather than an elevated social standing outside of the *ekklēsia*?

Menu Alterations

When an association needed more income than what was generated through subscription fees, guest participants, and voluntary collections, it could downgrade its menu in order to avoid over-expenditure. In Chapter 3, it was observed that the slave association occasionally ordered cheap wine (e.g., *Frag.2*, l.40) possibly for this very reason. More strikingly, the club behind *P.Tebt.* I 118 (see Table 4.1) met without

---

[65] The numerals indicate the following payments: ρ = 100 drachmas; π = 80 drachmas; ξ = 60 drachmas; κ = 20 drachmas. Some idea of these members' social status can be gained from wage information from 170 CE. Two examples are as follows: a bricklayer earned 40 drachmas per day (*P.Tebt.* I 42; Tebtynis, Egypt; 172 CE); and a laborer hired for mowing work earned 10–14 obols (about 1.5–2 drachmas) per day (*P. Mil. Vogl.* III 153 col. 2+3; Tebtynis, Egypt; 169/170 CE). For attestation to wages before and after 170 CE, see Hans-Joachim, Drexhage, *Preise, Mieten/Pachten, Kosten und Löhne im römischen Ägypten* (St. Katharinen: Scripta Mercaturae, 1991), 402–39; and Johnson, *Roman Egypt*, 306–10.

[66] 'Obwohl natürlich auch bei einmaligen Festen eine solche Gliederung der Zahler in verschiedene Gruppen nach Vermögensverhältnissen denkbar ist, scheint sie mir doch am besten als Klasseneinteilung eines Kultvereins erklärt warden zu können' (Erik Johan Knudtzon, *Bakchiastexte und andere Papyri der Lunder Papyrussammlung* [Volume 44 of *Aus der Papyrussammlung der Universitätsbibliothek in Lund*; Lund: Hakan Ohlssons Boktryckeri, 1946], 58).

bread on occasion in order to stay out of debt. During this association's second and third meetings, crowns were required for officers or service providers, which pushed bread outside of their budget for the banquets on those evenings. When the club needed to choose between rewarding service providers with formal honours and providing bread to participants, it chose crowns.

Summary of Associations' Financial Practices

One reality beginning to emerge from associations' financial records is the foundational importance of collecting subscription dues from all members as a bare minimum requirement for existence as a club. It is not surprising that in club bylaws one of the most consistently prohibited activities was showing up at banquets without fees.[67] Even with income from membership dues, some economically modest clubs needed to assemble without bread or without the quality of wine that they were accustomed to drink. Even when middling associations received exceptionally large donations, such as Dionysios's 3,896 drachmas worth of wine (*SEG* 31:983; Söke, Ionia, Asia Minor; II–I BCE), they still needed subscription fees in order to cover other expenses. The same would be true in the unlikely scenario that the economically modest Christ group managed to attract the patronage of two or four members who covered wine and bread expenses for a temporary period of time.

The Corinthian Christ Group's Expenses

The association data raise new questions about the economic structure of the Corinthian *ekklēsia*. When the Christ group wrote a letter to Paul (1 Cor 7:1), or composed their own meeting minutes,[68] were these regarded as 'writing expenses' as in *P.Oslo* III 143.7? When Stephanas and others travelled to Paul on behalf of the *ekklēsia* (16:17–18), or when

---

[67] For bylaws prohibiting participation in an association without paying fees, see *IG* II²
1339.5–15 = *GRA* I 46 (Athens, Attica; 57/56 BCE); *P.Mich.* V 243.2–3 = *AGRW* 300
(Tebtynis, Egypt; 14–37 CE); *P.Mich.* V 244.18–20 = *AGRW* 301 (Tebtynis, Egypt; 43
CE); *P.Mich.* V 245.37–42 = *AGRW* 302 (Tebtynis, Egypt; 47 CE); *CIL* XIV 2112, col.
2.20–3 = *AGRW* 310 (Lanuvium, Italy; 136 CE); *SEG* 31 [1981], no. 122.42–5 = *GRA* I 50
(Liopesi, Attica; early II CE); *IG* II² 1368.45–9 = *GRA* I 51 (Athens, Attica; 164/165 CE);
and *P.Tebt.* III/2 894, *Frag.4* verso, II.19, 24 (Tebtynis, Egypt; 114 BCE).

[68] For an investigation of record-keeping in Pauline groups, see Richard Last and Sarah
Rollens, 'Accounting Practices in *P.Tebt.* III/2 894 and Pauline Groups', *Early Christianity*
5 (2014), 441–74.

members gave provisions to visiting teachers (e.g., 16:10–11; 2 Cor 11:20), were their expenses reimbursed by the *ekklēsia* as was done by the Egyptian σύνοδος for their secretary who paid 5 drachmas of club expenses out of his pocket (*P.Oslo* III 143.4)? When Paul told the Christ group to recognise Stephanas, Fortunatus, and Achaicus (16:18), would this have implied purchasing cheap crowns? If so, how would the Christ group afford that extra expense? Would they order less food than usual, as was done by the modest club behind *P.Tebt.* I 118 when that club needed crowns? Or was there pressure to invite an extra ξένος ('guest') so that the Christ group could order crowns for Stephanas, Fortunatus, and Achaiacus as well as provide the typical amount of food?[69]

Turning to the Christ group's banquet expenses, the papyri discussed earlier raise the possibility that the Corinthians hired musicians. Dennis Smith observes that ancient banquets 'presupposed entertainment as part of the event'.[70] C. C. Edgar, commenting on the meals of the slave association, suggests that in 'little provincial towns no social gathering was complete without the flute-player and the effeminate dancer'.[71] Paul does not (need to) tell the Corinthians that they hired flute players at their gatherings. And it may just be an arbitrary coincidence that Paul compares Corinthian tongue-speaking with poor musical performances (1 Cor 14:7–12). On the other hand, since tongue-speaking likely happened during the symposium section of Corinthian meetings, when musicians would have been performing, further warrant is provided for reimagining how the Corinthians might have heard 14:7–12 in light of the typical presence of musicians at ancient banquets, including, possibly, their own common meals.[72] A second non-menu expense from holding a banquet is rental fees. Paul never mentions where the Corinthians assembled, which leaves open the possibility that they sometimes needed to negotiate the price of rental dining space in local houses or temples.[73]

---

[69] *P.Tebt.* I 118 shows that any Christ group with enough financial resources for wine and bread were well endowed to provide crowns. Crowns took precedence over bread in this Egyptian club when the choice needed to be made between the two.

[70] Smith, *From Symposium*, 12.

[71] Edgar, 'Records', 370.

[72] Smith observes, '[a] full, formal banquet that included both a *deipnon* and a symposium, as the Corinth banquet surely did, would have to include some form of banquet entertainment during the symposium' (*From Symposium*, 179).

[73] For the rental of private dining rooms see, e.g., *P.Oxy.* VIII 1128 (Oxyrhynchos, Egypt; 173 CE). These rooms could be subleased on nightly bases. For an opportunity to rent a private dining room as a dinner party or association, see *SB* X 10278.8–17 (Heptakomia, Egypt; c.114–119 CE).

Table 4.2 *Expenditures of the Corinthian* Ekklēsia

Expense	Source
Cheap wine	1 Cor 11:20–2
Bread	1 Cor 11:20–2
Reimbursement for members' out-of-pocket expenses on behalf of *ekklēsia*	1 Cor 16:3, 10–11, 15–18; 2 Cor 11:7–9
Cheap crowns and/or inscriptions for officers/ service-providers	1 Cor 16:17–18 (cf. 11:19 and Chapter 6)
Entertainment	1 Cor 14:7–12?
Funerary meals and related expenses	1 Cor 15:17–18
Writing expenses (letter, accounts, bylaws)	1 Cor 4:6[74]; 7:1

I tentative suggest the expenses in Table 4.2 as the primary ones for which the Christ group would likely need to find income.

I have intentionally omitted other typical association expenditures that may have been too burdensome for the *ekklēsia*, though we cannot be sure. These include *ekklēsia* contributions to civic honours for public officials such as Erastus and participation in civic events such as the Isthmian games. This small chart is not meant as a full reconstruction of the *ekklēsia*'s expenses, rather, it hopefully substantiates the earlier suggestion that neither Lampe's nor Theissen's interpretation of the Corinthian banquet would free the Christ group from having to collect subscription dues unless it is assumed that the Corinthian group secured uniquely generous patrons who paid for everything the *ekklēsia* required.

Evidence of *Ekklēsia* Fees

An investigation into associations' financial lives – their monetary pressures and funding strategies – makes it difficult to imagine how a Christ group would survive for long if it offered free meals and open membership. But it is not only the broader economic setting of associative life that calls into question the dominant portrayal of a Corinthian group that upheld a lax attitude towards membership fees. There is also evidence directly from Paul that the *ekklēsia* kept a common fund. When giving

---

[74] James C. Hanges, '1 Corinthians 4:6 and the Possibility of Written Bylaws in the Corinthian Church', *JBL* (1998), 275–98.

instructions about contributing to the out-of-the-ordinary Jerusalem collection, Paul presupposes that the Corinthians would be simultaneously making ordinary collections of subscription dues. His formerly obscure instructions to the Corinthians concerning the Jerusalem λογεία become comprehensible when considered in light of the organisational difficulties that would be faced by a club attempting to make two different monetary collections at the same time. Paul's directives read as follows (1 Cor 16:2):

κατὰ μίαν σαββάτου ἕκαστος ὑμῶν παρ' ἑαυτῷ τιθέτω θησαυρίζων ὅ τι ἐὰν εὐοδῶται, ἵνα μὴ ὅταν ἔλθω τότε λογεῖαι γίνωνται.

Every first day of the week, let each of you put[75] aside[76] money, storing up whatever profit each makes, in order that when I come collections do not take place.

These instructions include spatial as well as temporal aspects, which need to be considered in turn.

Temporal Aspects of Paul's Instructions in 1 Cor 16:2

Paul's mention of weekly payments on Sundays seemingly attests to the *ekklēsia*'s practice of holding meetings on this day each week.[77] For many interpreters, this verse marks the earliest evidence of weekly Christ

---

[75] I understand τιθέναι to mean 'pay' or 'deposit' rather than just 'put'. Therefore, in the full sentence, the idea of 'putting away' for Jerusalem means more specifically to 'put aside money' or to 'deposit' money in a specific location away from some other location. The verb means 'pay' or 'deposit' in several texts, including *P. Enteux* 32.7 (Pharbaithos, Arsinoites, Egypt; III BCE); *PCair.Zen* II 59218.33 (Crocodilopolis, Arsinoites, Egypt; 254 BCE); *PCair.Zen* IV 59753.64 (unknown provenance, Egypt; mid III BCE).

[76] See Stephen R. Llewelyn, 'The Use of Sunday for Meetings of Believers in the New Testament', *NovT* 43 (2001), 205–23 (209). For other usages of παρ' ἑαυτῷ carrying this meaning, see Xenophon, *Mem.* 3.13.2; Philo, *Cherubim.* 48; *Embassy.* 271; cf. Gordon D. Fee, *The First Epistle to the Corinthians* (New International Commentary on the New Testament; Grand Rapids, MI: Eerdmans, 1987), 813 n.24.

[77] Willy Rordorf, *Sunday, The History of the Day of Rest and Worship in the Earliest Centuries of the Christian Church* (London: SCM Press, 1968), 193–6; Conzelmann, *1 Corinthians*, 296; Fee, *First Epistle*, 813–4; Anthony Thiselton, *The First Epistle to the Corinthians* (New International Greek Testament Commentary; Grand Rapids: Eerdmans, 2000), 1321; Wolfgang Schrage, *Der erste Brief an die Korinther* (4 vols.; Evangelisch-katholischer Kommentar zum Neuen Testament 7; Neukirchen-Vluyn: Neukirchener Verlag, 1991–2001), 4:428; Pilhofer, *Die frühen Christen*, 207.

group meetings.[78] But why did Paul care what day the Corinthians made their weekly contributions? Adolf Deismann suggested that this was their pay day, but provided no data in support of weekly wages distributed on Sundays.[79] Charles Hodge argued that each member was supposed to bring their private donation to the *ekklēsia*, which happened to be the first day of the week[80] We return in the following paragraphs to the attractive thesis that members brought their pay for the Jerusalem fund to the Christ group's meeting location.

Gordon Fee's answer also seems on the right track: 'this day marked for them the specifically Christian day in their week that probably made it convenient for Paul to note it as the time for them to remember the poor among the brothers and sisters in Jerusalem.'[81] It was typical for associations to collect dues on the days they gathered, which means the Corinthians likely would not have found anything odd in Paul's instruction to make collections for Jerusalem on Sundays (the days they apparently assembled). To use Fee's word, they might have heard Paul's directive as 'convenient'. The following documents provide some examples of associations collecting money on the dates they assembled:

(*P.Tebt.* I 118, ll.16, 17; Tebtynis, Egypt; 112–111 BCE)

Τῦβι κε ... εἰσὶν ἄνδρες κα ἀνὰ ρ ['Βρ,

25th day of Tybi ... there are 21 men at 100 drachmas each. Total: 2,100 drachmas.

(*P.Tebt.* I 224 recto II; Kerkeosiris? Egypt; 109–108 BCE)

Τῦβι ιγ ... εἰσ<ὶν> ἄνδρες ιθ ἀν(ὰ) ρε Βμε

13th day of Tybi ... There are 19 men at 105 drachmas each. Total: 2,045 drachmas.

(*P.Lund.* IV 11, I.1–2, II.1–3; Bakchias, Egypt; 169–170 CE)

λόγος δ[απάν]ης στολισμ[οῦ] θεῶν Διο[σ]κ[ο]ύρων (ἔτους) ι
Με[σο(ρὰ)] α ... οἱ δὲ συ[ντε]λο[ῦντες] εἰς τὸν ἐγ[γεγραμ]
μένον στολισμ[όν] ·

---

[78] See also Acts 20:7 and Rev 1:10. In the second century, attestations to weekly church gatherings accumulate: *Didache* 14:1; Ignatius, *Magnesians* 9:1; Irenaeus, *Fragments* 7; Pliny, *Epistles* 10.97; Justin, *Apology* 1:65–7.

[79] Adolf Deissmann, *Light from the Ancient East: The New Testament illustrated by Recently Discovered Texts of the Greco-Roman World*, revised ed. (London: Hodder and Stoughton, 1927), 361.

[80] Charles Hodges, *1 Corinthians* (Wheaton: Crossway Books, 1995), 364.

[81] Fee, *First Epistle*, 813–14.

An account of expenditure of the equipping of the Dioskouroi gods (in new clothing and the sacrificial feast) during the 10th year, 1 Mesore ... The ones who have paid for the equipping (of the gods in new clothing and the sacrificial feast) have been written below ...
(*SB III 7182, Frag.5* recto, ll.78, 89–91; Philadelphia, Egypt; II BCE)

Χοία[-ca.?-]κ[-ca.?-] ... (γίνονται) η, (τούτων) ἀσύμβολος Ἑρμίας, λ(οιποὶ) ζ,
On the 7th day of Choiak ... they came to 8, of whom Hermias was without contribution. The rest came to 7.
(*P.Tebt.* III/2 894, *Frag.1* recto, II.1–24; Tebtynis, Egypt; 114 BCE)

Παῦνι ιη ... [-ca.?-]
[Σοκ]μῆνις τ̄
Θέων τ
Μαρῆς ρξ
Ὧρος Πακύ(σιος) σ   5
ọ λạτạς ρ κ Ἀρτέμω(ν) σ
Πεκῦσις σ Εὔδημος σ
Πομοῦς τ
Νααρῶς τ
Φατρῆς σ   10
Τράλλις σ
Πατῦνις Χο() τ
Πανεῦις τ
Πομβᾶς τ
Ἀμενεὺς τ   15
Ἀπῦγχις τ
Πετεσοῦ(χος) Κα(γῶτος) τ
Πατῦνις μέ(γας) τ
Πατμοῦις τ
Τεραῦς ρ   20
Ψενεθώτ(ης) τ
Σιλοῦς σιε
Ψεναμοῦνις ρϙ
Τιτὰκ ρϙ

18th day of the month of Payni: Sokmenis 300 drachmas, Theon 300 drachmas, Mares 160 drachmas, Horos son of Pakysis 200 drachmas, ... o.latas 120 drachmas, Artemon

200 drachmas, Pekusis 200 drachmas, Eudemos 200 drachmas, Pomous 300 drachmas, Naaros 300 drachmas, Phatres
200 drachmas, Trallis 200 drachmas, Patynis Cho() 300
drachmas, Paneuis 300 drachmas, Pombas 300 drachmas,
Ameneus 300 drachmas, Apynchis 300 drachmas, Petesou
(chos) son of Ka(gos) 300 drachmas, Patynis the elder 300
drachmas, Patmouis 300 drachmas, Teraus 100 drachmas,
Psenethotes 300 drachmas, Silous 215 drachmas,
Psenamounis 190 drachmas, Titak 190 drachmas

Paul's temporal instruction seems standard in light of typical collection
practices in other associations. To be sure, if the Corinthians were not in
the habit of already making subscription payments on the day they met,
Paul's temporal instruction might have appeared odd to them. As outlined in the Chapter 3 and here, though, the financial difficulties of an
association unable to collect subscription dues when they assembled
would have been enormous. It seems most likely that the 'convenience'
of collecting money for Jerusalem on the day that the *ekklēsia* assembled
comes from the reality that collections of subscription dues were already
being made that day. Now, Paul instructs the Corinthians, members
should bring payments both for the ordinary (i.e., subscription) and
voluntary (i.e., Jerusalem donations) accounts on the days they assemble.
Certainly, it was convenient for the Tebtynis association to pay both
mandatory and, when necessary, voluntary fees – such as wine contributions (*P.Tebt.* III/2 984, *Frag.3* verso, I.1–19) – on meeting dates.[82]
Further details in Paul's instructions about the Jerusalem collection
strengthen the theory that the *ekklēsia* collected membership fees.

Spatial Aspects of Paul's Instructions in 1 Cor 16:2

Paul suggests that on the first day of each week contributions should be
paid παρ' ἑαυτῷ. When παρά modifies a dative such as ἑαυτῷ, the
construction designates the location at which something happens.[83] In
1 Cor 16:2, therefore, Paul insists that each person's weekly contribution
towards the Jerusalem λογεία (16:1) should be placed 'aside', 'by itself',
or 'at one's own home'.[84] But why did Paul care *where* collections were
made? The detail has baffled exegetes who prefer to discuss the temporal

---

[82] For this group's payment of subscription dues on meeting dates, see, e.g., *Frag.1*,
III.53–63.

[83] Though see Llewelyn, 'Use of Sunday for Meetings', 205–23.

[84] See n.76 in this chapter.

aspects of Paul's instruction in 16:2 rather than spatial aspects.[85] Anthony Thiselton observes, 'It is not entirely clear why this collection should take place at home.'[86] He concludes that it must be to ensure that there 'is to be no last-minute, superficial scraping around for funds as an unplanned off-the-cuff gesture ... Each is to play his or her part *in a planned strategy of regular giving*'.[87] John Chow reaches a similar determination about the timing of donations:

> Paul suggests that the money should be saved up bit by bit in keeping with one's gains until he comes ... in asking members of the church to save up in order to give to the collection, Paul gives the impression that his audience is not very well off, and may include poorer people and slaves who may not have stated income.[88]

Thiselton's and Chow's explanation perhaps account, for why Paul wanted *ekklēsia* members to collect money each week as opposed to making donations at the eleventh hour, but it clarifies little about why he asked them to keep each donation to the Jerusalem λογεία 'by itself'.[89] Special collections for wine, beer, or other items happened at the general assembly of other private cultic groups, not apart from it.

C. K. Barrett attempts to answer the question more directly. He suggests that the donations were made away from the *ekklēsia* in order to 'avoid the possibility of accusations with regard to misappropriation, and perhaps to avoid misappropriation itself'.[90] While this response to potential corruption seems reasonable in modern contexts, and while associations shared the concern, they did not address it by avoiding communal collections and asking their members to make collections at home. Rather, they elected treasurers, stored excess income safely in the common fund, and required any officers who had access to the common fund to keep transaction records and to submit them to the association for scrutiny at the expiry of their terms. The association would then honour

---

[85] For a review, see Schrage, *Der erste Brief*, 4:428–30.

[86] Thiselton, *First Epistle*, 1324.

[87] Thiselton, *First Epistle*, 1324 (original emphasis).

[88] John K. Chow, *Patronage and Power: A Study of Social Networks in Corinth* (Sheffield: JSOT Press, 1992), 187–8.

[89] Thiselton entertains another possibility but is correctly dismissive of it: 'Perhaps sensitivities about patrons, the wealthy, and relations with other churches suggested a quiet, noncompetitive strategy on pastoral grounds' (*First Epistle*, 1324).

[90] Charles Kingsley Barrett, *The First Epistle to the Corinthians* (Black's; London: Hendrickson, 1968), 387.

financial officers if the records proved that they held their office with honesty. Frequently, treasurers were honoured specifically for their honesty since this was such an important attribute for them to possess.[91] The difficulty Barrett finds in communal collections was shared by association members, but their solution was to select honest treasurers and keep tabs on them rather than to instruct members to make collections at their homes.

The direction forward in interpreting 1 Cor 16:1–2 is to place Paul's instruction within the spectrum of collection activities practised by associations. Associations collected two types of fees: mandatory συμβολαί and voluntary contributions. Sometimes voluntary collections (e.g., for wine) were inconveniently merged with mandatory fees and placed into a club's common treasury along with subscription dues. This seems to have been the practice of the Tebtynis club when they made a voluntary wine collection, which is quoted earlier. Two lines taken from the club's records of the wine collection are particularly relevant here (*P.Tebt.* III/2 894; *Frag.3* verso, I.12–13):

Νααρῶς συ(μβολαὶ) σμε
ζημία υ (γίνονται) χμε

Naaros' contribution (to the wine collection), 245 drachmas
Fine: 400 drachmas; total: 645 drachmas

Although this is specifically a wine collection (*Frag.3* verso, I.4),[92] the group collected (or at least recorded) Naaros's fine alongside the wine collection, rather than *apart* from it. This raises questions about where Naaros's fees went: did the fine go to the common fund while the wine contribution went to a separate location or fund? It also raises new questions about Paul's spatial directive, παρ' ἑαυτῷ, which could have been understood by the Corinthians as advice to keep contributions for Jerusalem away from the common fund.

But, again, why did it matter where the Jerusalem contributions were stored as long as they were made? There are several reasons for Paul and the Corinthians to prefer a separate location for the Jerusalem contributions. One reason is that associations sometimes spent more money on

[91] For example, see *SEG* 2:9.5–6 = *GRA* I 21 (Salamis, Attica; 243/242 BCE); *SEG* 2:10.6–7 (Salamis, Attica; 248/247 BCE); *SEG* 31:122 = *GRA* I 50 (Liopesi, Attica; early II CE).
[92] The fact that only fourteen of the group's more than twenty members contributed to the collection further suggests that contributions to this fund were not mandatory for all members.

banquets than they collected in weekly subscriptions. In these situations, they paid the difference from funds sitting in their treasury. For example, in *P.Tebt.* I 118 one banquet cost 20 drachmas more than the group collected that evening (see Table 4.1). They paid the balance by using fees stored in their treasury. In *P.Tebt.* I 224 (recto II, ll.1–4), a banquet of bread and wine cost 2,400 drachmas on a day the club in question only collected 2,045 drachmas. This club also would have paid its debts from money in their treasury. C. C. Edgar identifies the practice of digging into the common fund as typical when associations incurred debt: 'if a surplus was left over, [the club] went into the treasury; if there was a deficit, it was made good out of the common funds.'[93]

Associations made payments from their treasuries for more than just deficits caused by bread and wine expenses. In *P.Oslo* III 143, we observed that three group leaders were reimbursed from the common fund: a certain Thonis, Thompakhrates, and a treasurer were owed a total of 155 drachmas that came from the treasury. If this group made a wine collection and stored it in their common fund along with excess income from subscription dues, it would not take much for an official to accidentally reimburse these members with money specially collected for a different purpose.

A solution to the problem of misdirected money would be to keep the common fund separate from voluntary or unordinary funds. In the slave association, it seems as though the common fund was, at one point, kept in the house of a certain Thorax (*SB* II 7182, *Frag.1*.III.31–2). Any voluntary collections made by the slave association could easily be stored elsewhere. The θησαυρός referenced in the Tebtynis club's financial account (*P.Tebt.* III/2 894, *Frag.6* recto II, l.10) could designate a storehouse where the group assembled. Alternatively, the word also denoted treasury boxes for the storage of valuables.[94] Perhaps the group stored income from subscription dues in a movable treasury box. Since this group did not possess a clubhouse or temple, it is conceivable that one of the club's functionaries took the treasury box home with them. Again, it would not take much for this club to find an alternative place to store members' donations to extraordinary collections.

In light of the associative financial behaviours reviewed, it is possible that Paul was worried about the location where Jerusalem contributions were stored because if these funds were placed within the Christ group's common fund, they might have been used for routine financial

---

[93] Edgar, 'Records', 371.
[94] For this usage of the word, see Matt 2:11 and Herodotus 7.190.

transactions. That would mean that Jerusalem contributions might be used to cover various operating expenditures – for example, reimbursing Stephanas for his travelling expenses, paying for any letters the *ekklēsia* wrote to Paul, or covering deficits or rent payments from banquets. Paul's advice is that the Jerusalem collection be kept by itself (παρ' ἑαυτῷ), apart from the Christ group's other financial activity.

Paul's directive to keep the voluntary Jerusalem contributions separate from other sources of income stored in the group's treasury may not have appeared especially nitpicky to the Christ group. Such a measure was taken by an association of donkey drivers contemporary to the Corinthians, whose wine collection reads as follows (*P.Athen.* 41; unknown provenance, Egypt; I CE):

ἔκθεσις οἰνικῶν συνόδου ὀνηλατῶν
τῶν ἕως Φαρμοῦθ(ι) ιγ
Ἄρειος Πτολεμαίο(υ) (δραχμαὶ) δ κ̣αὶ ὀβ(ολοὶ) ια
Σαρᾶς ἀδελφὸς (δραχμαὶ) ϛ (τριώβολον)
Δίδυμο(ς) Διδύμο(υ) (δραχμαὶ) ιε ὀβ(ολὸς) 1   5
Ἀραβᾶς Τιμ̣ο̣κ(ράτους) (δραχμαὶ) ι̣ ὀβ(ολὸς) 1
Διόσκορο(ς) Πάπου (δραχμαὶ) ζ (τριώβολον)
Ἀπολλώ(νιος) Φρόντ(ωνος) (δραχμαὶ) δ ὀβ(ολὸς) 1
Λεονίδ(ης) Φίλω(νος) (δραχμαὶ) β (τριώβολον)
Σωκράτ(ης) Τιμοκ(ράτους) (δραχμαὶ) ζ ὀβ(ολὸς) 1   10
Ἀπολλω( ) Ἥρω(νος) (δραχμαὶ) ιη ὀβ(ολὸς) 1
. . . . . Σμαρ . (δραχμαὶ) ζ (τετρώβολον)
Δίδυμο(ς) Τιμοκ(ράτους) (δραχμαὶ) δ (ὀβολοὶ) ιε
Πτολεμ(αῖος) Δωρίω(νος) (δραχμαὶ) ιδ
Χ̣ᾶρις Ἰσχυρίω(νος) (δραχμαὶ) ε [ὁ]β(ολὸς) 1   15
Διονύσιο(ς) Ἀπόλλω(νος) (δραχμαὶ) κ (τριώβολον)
Ἀκουσίλ(αος) Διδύμο(υ) (δραχμαὶ) ζ .
Πάπος ἀδελφὸς (δραχμαὶ) ζ ὀβ(ολὸς) 1
Διονύσιο(ς) Ἥρωνο(ς) (δραχμαὶ) . . .
Σκαπλ() Πεκ(ύσιος) (δραχμαὶ) [-ca.?-] ὀβ(ολὸς) 1   20
Μυσθ(ᾶς) Σωκ(ράτους) (δραχμαὶ) [-ca.?-] ὀβ(ολὸς) 1

Wine list of the σύνοδος of donkey-drivers until the 13th day of Pharmouthi . . .

Unlike collections of subscription fees, which, as we have seen, were due on specific meeting dates, the donkey drivers' wine collection was an ongoing collection *until* a certain date. Noticeably absent from the papyrus is a date at which the collections took place – the secretary recorded voluntary contributions as they came in, presumably on dates when the club gathered.[95] The Jerusalem collection shares several similarities. Not only was the wine collection of the donkey drivers recorded (and possibly stored) separately from the association's other sources of income (παρ' ἑαυτῷ), it was also ongoing (16:2; 2 Cor 8–9) and had a deadline (1 Cor 16:3; 2 Cor 9:3, 5).

Paul's Assumed Role during Collections

An additional, small, detail in Paul's instruction concerning the Jerusalem collection merits brief reflection. When Paul imagines what will take place if the Corinthians do not listen to his instructions, he envisions a passive role for himself. He does not say 'start early otherwise I will need to take collections when I get there.' Rather, he assumes that, in the imagined worst-case scenario, the Corinthians would do their own last-minute collecting. Paul asks them to begin early:

ἵνα μὴ ὅταν ἔλθω τότε λογεῖαι γίνωνται

so that collections do not happen when I arrive (1 Cor 16:2).

The unstated presupposition is that the Corinthians will know how to collect contributions as an association, and that Paul could assume a sideline role in such a situation – he simply arrives and thereby triggers the Jerusalem collection, the structure for completing it being already in place.

If we imagine how 1 Cor 16:2 would sound to an association, several insights can be gained. First, the pervasive notion that the Corinthians' practice of gradually collecting money for Jerusalem says something about the Corinthians' supposedly low economic status plainly cannot be maintained. Putting money into a fund over time was neither unusual nor very indicative of association members' economic standing.[96] Second, Paul's selection of Sunday as the day when the *ekklēsia* should collect money for Jerusalem would have been interpreted as inconvenient by an association unless the association met on that day each week. It was typical practice for an association to collect money on

[95] This is why, unlike the mandatory collections in *P.Lund.* IV 11, there was no ranking of wine contributors by the amount they paid. The secretary marked them down in the order they arrived. The largest contribution is by Dionysios son of Apollos in line 16. The smallest contribution was 1 drachma and 1 obol, which is listed in line 5.

[96] For associations and gradual collections, see, e.g., *P.Athen.* 41 (unknown location; I CE); *P.Oslo* III 144 (Oxyrhynchos, Egypt; 272–275 CE).

the days they met – whether subscription dues or otherwise. Finally, Paul's instruction to keep money for Jerusalem 'by itself' or 'apart' does not mean that individual piles of money were being stashed away for Jerusalem at each member's house. Interpreters often assume that but fail to consider mechanisms for completing extraordinary collections in other ancient cult groups. The Corinthians probably understood Paul to mean that they should keep the money for Jerusalem away from the Christ group's other income, which seems to have been typical practice in associations. The fact that Paul tells the Corinthians to keep the Jerusalem collection 'separate', moreover, raises the strong possibility that other collections were happening at the *ekklēsia* from which the Jerusalem collection should be kept apart. The most natural supposition is that these other collections were membership fees, which the group would have needed in order to stay alive.

Conclusions

It is not 'unübersehbar' that the *ekklēsia* offered free membership. In fact, without collecting subscription dues from each member, it is difficult to explain how the Christ group would have funded the Lord's Supper or any other activities it performed. Given the particular economic challenge of assembling so often (weekly), the Corinthian group required income at minimum from subscription fees, and even membership fees may have been insufficient for covering all of the group's expenses.

The implications of this reassessment of Corinthian finances are manifold and cannot be explored here. Broadly, the study of finances in Pauline groups needs to shift away from emphases on charitable initiatives (e.g., offering free meals, providing free membership, love patriarchalism and economic mutualism). Charity was largely out of the question for an economically modest cult group whose primary financial concerns were self-preservation and temporary assistance to fee-paying members.[97] The Christ group could not have afforded to enrol as members any freeloaders who were interested in devotion to Christ; recruits to Christ groups and other associations came exclusively from economic strata wherein club membership was affordable.

Chapter 5 marks a transition from the Corinthians' financial organisation, which has proven to be more pronounced than previous scholarship

---

[97] For mutual aid among associations members who were wealthy enough to join clubs, see Andrew Monson, 'The Ethics and Economics of Ptolemaic Religious Associations', *Ancient Society* 36 (2006), 221–36.

imagined, to the group's leadership organisation and social hierarchy. Social descriptions of the Corinthian group often explicitly deny the presence of officers, opportunities for the so-called weak to become strong, and delivery of formal commendation. What tends to be overlooked, again, are the practical challenges for an association that behaved the way that the Corinthians tend to be described. Recruitment pressures, in particular, would have made it difficult for the Corinthians to survive without offering to its members the kinds of social benefits provided by contemporary associations in Roman Corinth.

5

KEEPING UP WITH THE θιασῶται

Another Lack

Wayne Meeks suggested that an association would 'reward its patron with encomiastic inscriptions, honorary titles, [and] wreaths' but that a 'Christian congregation was quite different, and the patrons [of Christ groups] may have had reason to feel somewhat slighted'.[1] More recently, Eva Ebel supposed the same distinction between associations and Pauline groups: 'die Ehrerbietung, die ihnen [i.e., patrons] im Rahmen der christlichen Gemeinde entgegengebracht wird, nicht so ausgeprägt wie in den Vereinen: Ehreninschriften oder Festmähler am Geburtstag sind nicht zu erwarten.'[2] Anthony Thiselton puts it best: in the Corinthian church 'often loyal hard work is simply taken for granted rather than publicly and consciously recognized'.[3]

These quotations represent the majority opinion on the matter. Scholars agree, though, that the Corinthians at least gave service providers something in return for their favours. Namely, the *ekklēsia* recognised them with abstract attitude changes: 'special esteem' was won by

---

[1] Wayne A. Meeks, *The First Urban Christians: The Social World of the Apostle Paul*, 2nd ed. (New Haven: Yale University Press, 2003 [1983]), 78.

[2] Eva Ebel, *Die Attraktivität früher christlicher Gemeinden: Die Gemeinde von Korinth im Spiegel grichisch-römischer Vereine* (Wissenschaftliche Untersuchungen zum Neuen Testament II/178; Tübingen: J. C. B. Mohr Siebeck, 2004), 220.

[3] Anthony Thiselton, *The First Epistle to the Corinthians* (New International Greek Testament Commentary; Grand Rapids: Eerdmans, 2000), 1342. See also William L. Countryman, 'Patrons and Officers in Club and Church', in *Society of Biblical Literature 1977 Seminar Papers*, ed. Paul J. Achtemeier (Society of Biblical Literature Seminar Ppapers 11; Missoula, MT: Scholars Press, 1977), 135–43; Thomas Schmeller, *Hierarchie und Egalität: eine sozialgeschichtliche Untersuchung paulinischer Gemeinden und griechisch-römischer Vereine* (Stuttgart: Verlag Katholisches Bibelwerk, 1995), 73–4; Elizabeth Schüssler Fiorenza, *In Memory of Her: A Feminist Theological Reconstruction of Christian Origins* (New York: Crossroad, 1983), 181; and Bruce W. Longenecker, *Remember the Poor: Paul, Poverty, and the Greco-Roman World* (Grand Rapids, MI and Cambridge: Eerdmans, 2010), 271.

the first Corinthians to be baptised;[4] 'voluntary subordination' was given to leaders;[5] 'Achtung und Ansehen' was given to hosts of banquets and providers of food;[6] and 'warrants of authority' were the prizes for πνευματικοί.[7] Would this have been enough, though, to keep up with the θιασῶται, so to speak?

In this chapter, I analyse honorific epigraphy to dectect hints about what would have been at stake if the Corinthians decided to avoid the delivery of formal honours to their leaders. Contrary to previous estimations, a refusal on the part of the *ekklēsia* to provide crowns to service providers seems to have been scarcely an option. Delivery of honorific rewards functioned to create generosity among members, to establish a positive relationship between an association and outsiders, and to manufacture an 'associative order' for non-elites disqualified from entry into the civic order.

A Strategy to Create Peer Benefactors

Members expected their associations to prioritise the purchase of honorific rewards when necessary (i.e., when a member's generosity deserved recognition) – even if this meant forgoing food at banquets during times of financial distress.[8] In response to recruits' expectations, formal recognition tended to become a matter of policy for successful associations.[9] The following inscription from a group of θιασίται in Scythia Minor demonstrates the level of specifity with which some associations would promise symbolic capital to their generous members – and it illustrates well how any Christ believers with previous knowledge of associative practices might bring to their new Christ group expectations of the same formalities:

> [T]he society members resolved that a temple should be constructed for the god. Let those of the society members who want to contribute toward the construction promise whatever amount each chooses. Those who have promised a gold coin (stater) are

[4] Hans Conzelmann, *1 Corinthians. A Commentary on the First Epistle to the Corinthians* (Hermeneia; Philadelphia: Fortress Press, 1975), 298.

[5] Conzelmann, *1 Corinthians*, 298.

[6] Ebel, *Attraktivität*, 219–20.

[7] Meeks, *First Urban*, 138.

[8] For example, *P.Tebt.* I 118.8–18 (Tebtynis, Egypt; 112–111 BCE).

[9] Honorific decrees constitute somewhere between one-third to one-half of extant ancient association epigraphy. Franz Poland estimates one-half in *Geschichte*, 423; Onno Van Nijf supposes one-third in *Civic World*, 74.

granted a crown of honor for life and their name inscribed on the monument. Those promising less than a gold coin up to thirty silver pieces (drachmas) are granted their name inscribed and a crown of glory during the triennial festival for life. The rest who have promised less are granted their name inscribed on the monument (*IGLSkythia* III 35.3–13 = *AGRW* 73; Kallatis, Scythia Minor, Danube and Black Sea regions; late III BCE [Ascough, Harland, and Kloppenborg]).

This announcement is followed by thirty names of honourees who answered the call by contributing gold coins, silver drachmas, and other benefactions. Their names were inscribed on the monument, just as advertised (ll.20–41). The association of θιασῖται, therefore, generated the donations it needed for the construction of a temple by promising to its donors the delivery of the recognition they desired.

We can call the thirty donors to the Scythian club, 'peer benefactors'. This term was employed in a recent article by John Kloppenborg to describe benefaction from individuals who were not elite patrons. Whereas the elite patron provided large gifts such as clubhouses or *sportulae*, the peer benefactor agreed to hold administrative functions, and offer small amounts of their own resources to help fund club activities or to finance purchases beyond materials brought in from membership fees.[10] Signfiicantly for present purposes, peer benefactors could be anyone in an association: officers, ordinary members, socially strong, or socially weak.

One function of the delivery of honorific rewards, then, was to encourage members to become peer benefactors. That is, to encourage members to make the financial contributions that their club needed in order for its survival or reputational enhancement. In return, having one's name inscribed on an honorific stone represented one way for a club member to improve (or, at least, maintain) their social ranking in their club. Numerous associations guaranteed commendation to their members for the same explicitly referenced purpose of motivating them to step up to become peer benefactors in the present or future.[11] If the Corinthian

---

[10] John S. Kloppenborg, 'Greco-Roman *Thiasoi*, The *Ekklēsia* at Corinth, and Conflict Management', in *Redescribing Paul and the Corinthians*, ed. Ron Cameron and Merrill P. Miller (Early Christianity and Its Literature 5; Atlanta: Society of Biblical Literature, 2011), 187–218 (212–13).

[11] See, *IDelos* 1519.27–34 = *AGRW* 223 (Delos, Asia Minor; 153/2 BCE); *IDelta* I 446 (Psenamosis, Egypt; 67 and 64 CE); *IG* II² 1273A B.9–21= *GRA* I 18 (Piraeus, Attica; 265/4 BCE); *IG* II² 1277.27–33 = *GRA* I 15 (Athens, Attica; 278/7 BCE); *IG* II² 1327.20–3 = *GRA* I 35 (Piraeus, Attica; 178/7 BCE); *IG* II² 1263.27–31 = *GRA* I 11 (Piraeus, Attica; 300 BCE);

ekklēsia failed to offer this type of recognition to members willing to enhance the Christ group's reputation, it would scarcely have been able to motivate members to contribute to the Jerusalem collection or any other project that required financial committments over and above subscription dues.

A Strategy to Enhance the Association's Reputation

A second function of honorifics, in addition to motivating current members to be generous, relates to controlling outsiders' impression of the association's attractiveness. Specifically, delivering honorific rewards to members publicly – either at a festival or in a temple or in a clubhouse – generated among passersby assumptions about the group's commitment to the social enhancement of its members. Monika Trümper's description of the Delian Poseidoniasts' clubhouse as its 'business card' articulates this function well. The courtyard of the association's building housed

> many statue bases, and honorary exedra, steles with honorary decrees, and three altars ... it figured as a kind of grand vestibule and 'business card' of the association: every visitor had to pass through it when he came from the narrow entrance corridor ... and wanted to proceed to the sanctuary or to the peristyle courtyard complex.[12]

It was likely partially for reputational reasons, and the need to generate recruits, that Paul was concerned about how the Corinthian group looked to non-members (1 Cor 14:23), including, perhaps, anxiety about the visibility of their honorific practices (16:18).

Since local associations competed with one another for the resources of (peer) benefactors such as Stephanas (16:15–18), whose financial

---

IG II² 1271.18–21 = *GRA* I 13 (Piraeus? 299/8 BCE); *IG* II² 1292.18–23 = *GRA* I 26 (Athens or Piraeus, Attica; 215/4 BCE); *IG* II² 1315 = *GRA* I 29 (Piraeus, Attica; 211/0 BCE). In light of data such as these, Ilias Arnaoutoglou, '*Between* Koinon *and* Idion: Legal and Social Dimensions of Religious Associations in Ancient Athens', in *Kosmos. Essays in Order, Conflict and Community in Classical Athens,* ed. Paul Cartledge, Paul Millett, and Sitta von Reden (Cambridge: Cambridge University Press, 1998), 63–83 (81), correctly observes that 'Associations were a venue in which accumulation of ... symbolic capital was highly desirable and was therefore promoted.'

[12] Monika Trümper, 'Negotiating Religious and Ethnic Identity: The Case of Clubhouses in Late Hellenistic Delos', *Hephaistos* 24 (2006), 113–40 (119).

capital was not limitless,[13] clubs tended to advertise to prospective (peer) benefactors that they had reputations for reliably converting financial capital into symbolic capital. We find this strategy employed by an association of ὀργεῶνες from Piraeus (Attica) that wanted 'to be seen' by potential recruits honouring a peer benefactor:

> in order, then, that the *orgeōnes* might be seen (φαίνεσθαι) to have rendered thanks appropriate to those who, at any time, have been ambitious (towards the association); for good fortune, be it resolved by the *orgeōnes* of Bendis and Deloptes and the other gods to commend Stephanos for the zeal that he has shown towards the *orgeōnes* (and) to crown him with an olive wreath (*IG* II² 1324.11–20 = *GRA* I 32; Piraeus, Attica; c.190 BCE [Kloppenborg and Ascough]).

The ὀργεῶνες' desire for outsiders to see them honouring their members was shared by many other clubs who explicitly mention the same motivation for making their honours visible to outsiders.[14] By participating responsibly in exchange relationships, clubs generated reputations as institutions that potential peer benefactors could depend upon for reciprocity.[15] One can imagine the poor reputation of the Corinthian

---

[13] Philip A. Harland, *Dynamics of Identity in the World of the Early Christians. Associations, Judeans, and Cultural Minorities* (New York and London: T&T Clark, 2009), 149.

[14] For example, *IRhamnous* II 59.19–26 = *GRA* I 27 (Rhamnous, Attica; after 216/15 BCE); *IG* XII/1 155.dface I.1.8–13 = *AGRW* 255 (Rhodos on Rhodes, Aegean; II BCE); *IG* II² 1314.9–12 = *GRA* I 28 (Piraeus, Attica; 213/2 BCE); *IG* II² 1315.16–18 = *GRA* I 29 (Piraeus, Attica; 211/0 BCE); *AM* 66: 228.12–18 = *GRA* I 39 (Athens, Attica; 138/7 BCE); *IG* II² 1337.9–12 = *GRA* I 44 (Piraeus, Attica; 97/6 BCE); *IG* II² 1334. 11–19 = *GRA* I 45 (Piraeus, Attica; after 71/70 BCE); and Franz Poland, *Geschichte des griechischen Vereinswesens* (Leipzig: Teubner, 1909), 423–505 (440).

[15] The following inscription was designed to convince prospective recruits not only that the association had the resources and willingness to reward service providers, but also that it would protect a member's receipt of honour even in the event of factions: 'the sacrifice makers are to announce publicly their names [i.e., the names of the treasurer, secretary, and supervisor who were voted honours] at each sacrifice after the ceremony; and ... if they should not announce them or if they should not crown them, each [sacrifice maker] shall pay fifty (?) drachmae sacred to the *Sarapiastai*, so that there might be rivalry among those who are ambitious in respect to them [the members], knowing that they will be honored in a way that is appropriate' (*IG* II² 1292 = *GRA* I 26; Athens or Piraeus, Attica; 215/4 BCE). This *Sarapiastai* group was one of many associations that levied fines for failure to announce voted honours. See: *IG* XII/1 155.dface III 90–104 (Rhodes, Aegean; II BCE); *IG* II² 1273.21–2 = *GRA* I 18 (Piraeus, Attica; 265/4 BCE); *IG* II² 1292.16–18 = *GRA* I 26 (Athens or the Piraeus, Attica; 215/4 BCE); *IG* II² 1297.17–18 = *GRA* I 24 (Athens, Attica; 236/5 BCE). For broader dynamics of competition among associations, see Harland,

group in its city if Bruce Longenecker's claim, cited earlier, that 'those [Corinthians] in ES5 could enjoy the benefits of a benefactor's generosity [at common meals] without being expected either to make membership payments or to be involved in public acclaim of the benefactor'[16] were an accurate description of the group's honorific practices.

A Strategy for Manufacturing Status Differentiation among Non-elites

Third, the receipt of honorific rewards from an association actually helped to shape the honouree's position in society. Koenraad Verboven identifies three levels of status generation fostered through affiliation to a local association.[17] First, individuals who joined associations were differentiated and elevated socially above those in their city or village who could not afford to join a club;[18] second, holding a fixed-term association office was an honourable, financial commitment, and it temporarily elevated magistrates above regular members; and, third, contributing a service to a club differentiated oneself above peers who

Dynamics, 145–60; and Jinyu Liu, *Collegia Centonariorum. The Guilds of Textile Dealers in the Roman West*, (Columbia Studies in the Classical Tradition 34; Leiden and Boston: Brill, 2009), 229–42.

[16] Longenecker, *Remember*, 271.

[17] The process of status generation extends from the concept of social status as a multidimensional social construction comprising of 'power (defined as "the capacity for achieving goals in social systems"), occupational prestige, income or wealth, education and knowledge, religious and ritual purity, family and ethnic-group position, and local community status' (*First Urban* 54). Thomas Schmeller highlights dimensions of legal status (freeborn, freed, enslaved) and gender identity (*Hierarchie*, 44). A person can rank high or low in any status category and the overall status of an individual 'is a composite of his or her ranks in all the relevant dimensions' (Meeks, *First Urban*, 54). Koenraad Verboven's argument concerning status generation takes as its starting point the observation that 'Generosity in general and evergetism in particular was indissolubly linked to the Roman status system' ('Associative Order', 866), and his description of honorific practices in associations highlights ways in which clubs allowed members to use their economic assets to appropriately display their wealth and generosity so as to generate symbolic capital.

[18] 'At the bottom end, membership of a *collegium* . . . served to distinguish members . . . socially from those who were unable to participate in the activities of *collegia*.' See Koenraad Verboven, 'Magistrates, Patrons and Benefactors of Collegia: Status Building and Romanisation in the Spanish, Gallic and German Provinces', in *Transforming Historical Landscapes in the Ancient Empires. Proceedings of the First Workshop Area of Research in Studies from Antiquity, Barcelona 2007*, ed. I. B. AntelaBernárdez and T. Ñaco del Hoyo (British Archaeological Reports; International Series 1986; Oxford: John and Erica Hedge, 2009), 159–67 (160).

had not shown generosity to their club.[19] Verboven does not explicitly identify the receipt of honorifics as generative of status differentiation, but this much is implied since officers and peer benefactors stereotypically received formal commendation to mark their status achievements. On this point, Ilias Arnaoutoglou explains that 'the process of honouring resulted in an adjustment of the attitudes of the honoured, as well as in the attitudes of the other members towards him in conformity with his new status.'[20] In these three ways, then, associations 'institutionalised' status differentiation in the lower strata of a city or village's society.[21] The presence of associations in a location created an 'associative order' below the civic order, Verboven argues. This associative order clarified a person's position in the social order of resident non-elites and, thereby, provided a field on which non-elites competed with one another for honour.

Honorific Behaviour and Recruitment

For the three reasons overviewed above, it was not a viable option for an association to be structured the way that most scholars describe Paul's Corinthian group. The Corinthians' supposed policy of denying crowns, proclamations, honorific inscriptions, and other normative forms of commendation, would have decreased *ekklēsia* members' willingness to show zeal towards their Christ group, tarnished the reputation of the Christ group to prospective recruits, and would have prohibited the very social benefits that made membership in an association attractive. An association that failed to offer commendation to service providers, such as the Corinthian *ekklēsia* on previous readings, put itself at a serious disadvantage when competing with local associations for recruits. This competitive reality helps to explain why the Egyptian club reviewed in Chapter 4 held a banquet without food on an occasion when it was short on money and needed to choose between purchasing food and buying a crown for a service provider.[22] Failure to reward a crown to its deserving peer benefactor would have posed a reputational problem for this Egyptian club that was already so short on members

---

[19] Koenraad Verboven, 'The Associative Order, Status and Ethos of Roman Businessmen in Late Republic and Early Empire', *Athenaeum* 95 (2007), 861–93 (871–2); cf. Sandra R. Joshel, *Work, Identity, and Legal Status at Rome: A Study of the Occupational Inscriptions* (Norman, OK: University of Oklahoma Press, 1992), 114–15.

[20] Ilias Arnaoutoglou, 'Koinon *and* Idion', 80–1.

[21] Verboven, 'Associative Order', 870.

[22] *P.Tebt.* I 118.1–8 (Tebtynis, Egypt; 112–111 BCE).

that it required four fee-paying guests at their banquets just so that it could afford wine.

There were, no doubt, multiple factors affecting recruitment to Christ groups and other associations, including fictive-family connections,[23] social compensation,[24] and patronage,[25] but opportunities for status achievements represented an important factor driving recruits to associations. For this reason, Franz Poland, in his classic work on Greek associations, spoke 'des Eifers der Vereine für die Ehre der Genossen'.[26] Recent scholarship elaborates on the centrality of honorific behaviour in associations, and I would suggest that the following statements concerning associations apply directly to the Corinthian group:

> The bestowal of honours was not only a formal and standardized custom; its purpose was twofold, in the first place to honour the official and in this way to increase his or her social esteem among the members of the association or in an even larger community, and secondly to encourage others to act as officials in the association.[27]

---

[23] For slightly different articulations of this attractor, see Meeks, *First Urban*, 191; and Karl Olav Sandnes, 'The Role of the Congregation as a Family within the Context of Recruitment and Conflict in the Early Church', in *Recruitment, Conquest, and Conflict: Strategies in Judaism, Early Christianity, and the Greco-Roman World*, ed. Peder Borgen, Vernon K. Robbins, and David B. Gowler (Atlanta, GA: Scholars Press, 1998), 333–45.

[24] For a recent assessment of social compensation as an attractor to associations, see Philip Venticinque, 'Family Affairs: Guild Regulations and Family Relationships in Roman Egypt', *GRBS* 50 (2010), 273–94 (275); Onno M. Van Nijf, *The Civic World of Professional Associations in the Roman East* (Amsterdam: J.C. Gieben, 1997), 3–28; Verboven, 'Associative Order', 861–93; John S. Kloppenborg and Richard S. Ascough, ed., *Attica, Central Greece, Macedonia, Thrace.* Volume 1 of *Greco-Roman Associations: Texts, Translations, and Commentary* (Berlin and New York: W. de Gruyter, 2011), 8; Andreas Bendlin, 'Gemeinschaft, Öffentlichkeit und Identität: Forschungsgeschichtliche Anmerkungen zu den Mustern sozialer Ordnung in Rom', *in Religiöse Vereine in der römischen Antike: Unversuchungen zu Organisation, Ritual und Raumordnung*, ed. Ulrike Egelhaaf-Gaiser and Alfred Schäfer (STAC 13; Tübingen: Mohr Siebeck, 2002), 9–40 (32–3); Markus Öhler, 'Antikes Vereinswesen', in *Neues Testament und antike Kultur II: Familie, Gesellschaft, Wirtschaft*, ed. Kurt Scherberich (Neukirchen-Vluyn: Neukirchener, 2005), 79–86.

[25] Zeba A. Crook, *Reconceptualising Conversion: Patronage, Loyalty, and Conversion in the Religions of he Ancient Mediterranean* (Berlin and New York: De Gruyter, 2004), 186–90.

[26] Poland, *Geschichte*, 445.

[27] Ilias N. Arnaoutoglou, *Thusias Heneka Kai Sunousias: Private Religious Associations in Hellenistic Athens* (Yearbook of the Research Centre for the History of Greek Law 37/4; Athens: Academy of Athens, 2003), 117.

associations likely served as vehicles by which various populations in the polis replicated and internalized the hierarchical structures of the ancient city and mimicked its honorific practices. This is a strategy for 'claiming a place in ancient Mediterranean society' (Harland 2003) rather than one of compensation or resistance.[28]

By joining these organizations, members most likely augmented an already strong position in their communities.[29]

Der Beitritt zu einem Verein war für die meisten Mitglieder mit einem sozialen Aufstieg verbunden.[30]

Most scholars would probably agree that commensality was one of the major attractions of Roman *collegia* ... commensality helped to establish group identity, but it also served to create social distance.[31]

The associations created a social environment with constraints and possibilities that for the vast majority of the population constituted the social order par excellence ... The hierarchies of [associations] were publicly expressed and displayed. Patrons, magistrates and former magistrates were rewarded by visible tokens of honour; seats of honour were reserved for them at banquets, larger portions were given them, honorific decrees were voted, busts and statues of them were erected in club houses.[32]

It is striking that Paul's silence on the routine practice of reciprocating service providers with honorifics has been interpreted by scholars to mean that the Christ group avoided normative forms of honorific behaviour, rather than the more natural conclusion that the Corinthians'

[28] Kloppenborg, and Ascough, *Attica*, 8. The quotation is a reference to the subtitle of Philip A. Harland's book: *Associations, Synagogues, and Congregations. Claiming a Place in Ancient Mediterranean Society* (Minneapolis, MN: Fortress, 2003).

[29] Venticinque, 'Family Affairs', 275.

[30] Schmeller, *Hierarchie*, 40.

[31] Onno M. Van Nijf, '*Collegia* and Civic Guards. Two Chapters in the History of Sociability', in *After the Past: Essays in Ancient History in Honour of H.W. Pleket*, ed. Willem Jongman and Marc Kleijwegt (Mnemosyne Supplement 233; Leiden: Brill, 2002), 305–40 (324, 330). Some other recent studies that arrive at similar conclusions include Martti Leiwo, 'Religion, or Other Reasons? Private Associations in Athens', in *Early Hellenistic Athens: Symptoms of a Change,* ed. Jaakko Frösén (Papers and Monographs of the Finnish Institute at Athens; Helsinki: Finnish Institute at Athens, 1997), 103–17; and Nicholas Tran, *Les membres des associations romaines. Le rang social des collegiate en Italie et en Gaules, sous le Haut-Empire* (Rome: École française de Rome, 2006), 49–210.

[32] Verboven, 'Associative Order', 872, 887.

honorific behaviour, which Paul rarely had opportunities to discuss, fell somewhere within the spectrum of typical activities practised by ancient associations.

Competing for Recruits in Roman Corinth

Anthony Thiselton's distinction between positive attitudinal changes towards service providers in Christ groups versus the practice of presenting actual material rewards to officers and benefactors in associations is a false dichotomy.[33] Ilias Arnaoutoglou points out that attitude changes more likely occurred *as a result of* honorific ceremonies in associations, not independent of them.[34] Given the nearly ubiquitous practice of honouring benefactors, the oddly prevalent suspicion that the Corinthian group indeed failed to participate in the practice of honour exchange must be documented, not assumed a priori.

One reason to believe that Stephanas and other Corinthian service providers were crowned or honoured with inscriptions or proclamations is the level of competition for recruits among associations in Roman Corinth in the 50s CE. The *ekklēsia* grew up in a city whose inhabitants regarded competition for honour as a 'most important' cultural value,[35] and the nine or ten people who joined the Christ group behaved the way socially ambitious people did: they vied for status at public courts (1 Cor 6:1–8), argued about distinctions of place and food portion at club banquets (11:17–34), put themselves in positions to be invited to private dinners (10:27–30), tried to impress their peers by speaking in tongues (14:2–33), as well as strove for honour in ways explored in Chapters 6 and 7.[36] Eva Ebel has observed that 'die Christinnen und Christen sind somit keineswegs konkurrenzlos, sondern müssen sich einem Wettbewerb um potentielle Mitglieder stellen. Beliebt, weit verbreitet und damit ein ernstzunehmender Konkurrent der christlichen Gemeinden sind Vereine.'[37] Wolfgang Schrage identifies Corinth as

---

[33] Thiselton, *First Epistle*, 1341–2.

[34] Arnaoutoglou, '*Between* Koinon *and* Idion', 80–1.

[35] Donald Engels, *Roman Corinth: An Alternative Model for the Classical City* (Chicago: University of Chicago, 1990), 86. For a similar conclusion concerning Corinthian cultural values, see Andrew D. Clarke, *Secular and Christian Leadership in Corinth. A Socio-Historical and Exegetical Study of 1 Corinthians 1–6* (Arbeiten zur Geschichte des antiken Judentums und des Urchristentums 18; Leiden, NY, and Köln: Brill, 1993), 23–39.

[36] Edwin A. Judge's famous description of the Corinthians (and other Pauline groups) as 'socially pretentious', in *Social Pattern*, 60, seems to be an accurate assessment.

[37] Ebel, *Attraktivität*, 1.

'ein Ort zahlreicher Kulte und Tempel',³⁸ which no doubt made the city a challenging location for the establishment of a new cult group looking for recruits. One of the 'Konkurrenen' vying specifically with the Corinthian *ekklēsia* for recruits was a local θίασος. This club is known to us exclusively from a fragmentary inscription, possibly dating to the first-century CE:

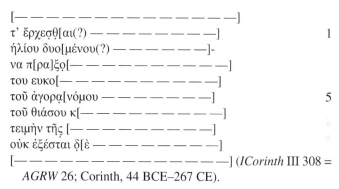

```
[— — — — — — — — — — — — — — —]
τ' ἔρχεσθ[αι(?) — — — — — — — —]            1
ἡλίου δυο[μένου(?) — — — — — —]-
να π[ρα]ξο[— — — — — — — — — —]
του ευκο[— — — — — — — — — —]
τοῦ ἀγορα[νόμου — — — — — — —]             5
τοῦ θιάσου κ[— — — — — — — — —]
τειμὴν τῆς [— — — — — — — — —]
οὐκ ἐξέσται δ[ἐ — — — — — — —]
[— — — — — — — — — — — — — —] (ICorinth III 308 =
AGRW 26; Corinth, 44 BCE–267 CE).
```

The inscription contains only eight legible words, however, it reveals that the θίασος' members were appointed or elected to communal offices that mimicked titles from the civic order (ἀγορανόμος, 1.5)³⁹ and that the club honoured (τειμή, 1.7) patrons and peer benefactors with status-generating prizes. In a Corinthian culture characterised by an 'obsessive concern to win reputation and status in the eyes of others'⁴⁰ this θίασος would have been tough competition for a Christ group that supposedly offered its members few opportunities to win formal honours and, in any case, was unable to fund the purchase of crowns and honorific inscriptions given its apparent policy on free membership. The θίασος is just one of several known associations from Roman Corinth who were competing for recruits with Paul's group.⁴¹

---

³⁸ Schrage specifies, 'Gottheiten und Kulte des alten Griechenlands waren ebenso vertreten wie die ägyptischen Mysterien-religionen und die Institutionen des Kaiser-Kults', in *Der erste Brief*, 1:27.

³⁹ The inscription is so fragmentary that we do not know for certain if the ἀγορανόμος is a club official or a civic magistrate.

⁴⁰ Thiselton, *First Epistle*, 21.

⁴¹ For other Greek and Latin associations from Hellenistic and Roman Corinth, see Chapter 2, n.120.

Assumptions in Previous Scholarship

Why is there such a consensus among scholars concerning the *ekklēsia*'s peculiar act of denying formal honours to its service providers? Apart from Paul's supposed silence on the group's selection of officers (see Chapter 7), and his supposed silence on their practice of reciprocating benefactors (see Chapter 6), the consensus seemingly results from a combination of two long-held and misguided opinions. The first is the conviction that other associations reserved formal recognition exclusively for officers and so-called distant patrons (i.e., patrons who did not show up at all meetings).[42] Two inscriptions cited already in this chapter (*IGLSythia* III 35 = *AGRW* 73 and *IG* II² 1324 = *GRA* I 32) expose this perception as false since they highlight how regular members (not just officers) were recipients of formal commendation in return for the generosity they showed to their clubs. The principal requirement in associations for receiving formal commendation is showing zeal for the group, not holding a title within it. If officers failed to show zeal for their association, they would be denied honour.[43] Plenty of evidence shows that regular members without any titles earned symbolic capital comparable to that which magistrates earned.[44] For present purposes, the implication of these data is that even if there were no officers in an association, presumably there still would be honorific ceremonies when individual affiliates distinguished themselves by showing generosity to their club.

The second, widely held, view that generates the idea that the Corinthian Christ group did not provide formal honours to their most generous members is that the Christ group did not have officers[45] – and since there were no officers, there must have been no one to crown or otherwise reward formally. As the theory goes, the Corinthians did enjoy

---

[42] The contemporary focus on title-holders as recipients of honours from associations seems to be shaped by nineteenth-century scholarship. See, e.g., Foucart, *Des associations religieuses*, 20–40; and Erich Ziebarth, *Das griechische Vereinswesen* (Stuttgart: S. Hirzel, 1896 [1969]), 143.

[43] *IG* II² 1277.27–33 = *GRA* I 15 (Athens, Attica; 278/7 BCE). Fines for members who neglect their duty of honouring officers also suggest that sometimes magistrates were denied honour. See *IG* II² 1292 = *GRA* I 26 (Athens or Piraeus, Attica; 215/4 BCE) and *IDelos* 1520.66–8, 88–9 = *AGRW* 22 (Delos, Asia Minor; after 153/2 CE). Some officers were praised in inscriptions that did not even mention their titles, which confirms that their reward was for service rather than for holding a title. See *ICorinth* III 62 (Corinth, Peloponese, Greece; c.120 CE); *IG* II² 1273AB = *GRA* I 18 (Piraeus, Attica; 266 BCE).

[44] For other examples, see *CIL* III 633 I = *GRA* I 68 (Philippi, Macedonia; II CE); *SEG* 17:823 = *AGRW* 307 (Berenice, Cyrenaica, Egypt; 3 December 55 CE).

[45] See Chapter 6 for my discussion of officers in the *ekklēsia*.

the support of patrons,[46] however, the group probably failed to recognise them with material rewards. This is supposedly a result of the fact that *ekklēsia* patrons did not 'auf Distanz bleibt' but rather served leadership functions in the community.[47] It is not clear to me why it would be acceptable to treat engaged patrons – or, as John Kloppenborg describes them, peer benefactors – differently from patrons who were mostly absent. Officers and regular members were constant presences at club meetings, and their services merited symbolic capital. In any case, Stephen Chester and Andrew Clarke explicitly combine both theories in recent works. Chester, for example, asks, 'Does the absence of offices within the church indicate that those who provided services to it, and to Paul, were expected to do so without receiving any recognition or honour?'[48] The assumption here is that only title-holders could win honorific rewards. Chester answers his question as follows: 'there appears to have been no identifiable mechanism within the church by which such benefactions could be honoured.'[49]

Conclusions

Acts of reciprocity were not luxuries with which the Corinthians could dispense. Patterns of reciprocity in modest and middling associations show how Longenecker's claim about the lack of reciprocity received by the Corinthians' peer benefactors[50] would be dangerous to the reputation of the Christ group in the unlikely event that it was a reality. Indeed, such a practice would be detrimental to the *ekklēsia*'s ability to recruit the very

---

[46] John K. Chow, *Patronage and Power: A Study of Social Networks in Corinth* (Sheffield: JSOT Press, 1992); and Clarke, *Secular and Christian*.

[47] Schmeller (*Hierarchie*, 73) is followed by Ebel in *Attraktivität*, 220.

[48] Stephen J. Chester, *Conversion at Corinth. Perspectives on Conversion in Paul's Theology and the Corinthian Church* (London and New York: T&T Clark, 2003), 240. See also Andrew D. Clarke's monograph (*Serve the Community of the Church. Christians as Leaders and Ministers* [Grand Rapids, MI: Eerdmans, 2000]) where he notes a lack of references to offices in the Christ group (176, n.11) and proceeds to argue that informal praise was given to Corinthian patrons in the form of boasting, with the implication that formal honorific rewards were not available (178).

[49] Chester, *Conversion*, 240. Elsewhere Chester argues that the Corinthians' desire for status and honour was satisfied by 'a competition for honour which was no less intense, but which was a great deal less clearly channelled and regulated' (245). Chester's examples of unstructured competition for honours include the rivalries for honour at the banquet and status competitions settled in public courts (245–56).

[50] Longenecker, *Remember*, 271.

people whom Longenecker supposes to have funded all of the group's activities.

In Chapters 6 and 7, I explore *ekklēsia* members' opportunities to generate status by means of providing services with or without holding offices. The provision of these opportunities, and the ceremonial honours to follow, would have appeared attractive to passers-by (1 Cor 14:24) and guests (Rom 16:23). Moreover, the maintenance of an ethos where generosity was valued and rewarded would have kept current members from discontinuing their membership. For a new group with a relatively small membership size, an unknown patron hero, and a divisive founder (1 Cor 1:12; 2 Cor 10:10–12; 11:4–5), the Corinthian group was especially pressured to establish a reputation for providing its members with opportunities to win status achievements comparable to what was being offered by contemporary associations. The following chapters document some of the ways in which the Corinthian group built up such a reputation.

6

STRENGTHENING THE WEAK

Fixed and Fluid Social Hierarchies

In this chapter and the next, I re-describe mechanisms of social differentiation in the Corinthian group. As the traditional theory goes, the *ekklēsia* comprised of socially heterogeneous members whose various individual positions in the group's social hierarchy were fixed according to their positions in relation to one another in society outside of the Christ group: the weak (ἀσθενεῖς, 1 Cor 8:7–12) were outranked by the (unattested) strong in outside society, and, as a result, they were perpetually socially inferior to them in the *ekklēsia*, as well.[1] Previous interpreters suppose that the so-called socially strong always controlled the food at the banquet[2] and that it was they who monopolised hosting responsibilities in the *ekklēsia*[3] and that it was they whose demonstrations of philosophical wisdom were perceived as status achievements in the minds of their social inferiors.[4] Generally, little to no consideration is given to ways in which the so-called socially weak could win status achievements in the Christ group.

---

[1] For a recent articulation and variation of the theory, see Volker Gäckle, *Die Starken und die Schwachen in Korinth und in Rom: Zu Herkunft und Funktion der Antithese in 1Kor 8,1–11,1 und in Röm 14,1–15,13* (WUNT II/200; Tübingen: Mohr Siebeck, 2004), 39–109, who suggests that the strong minority identified the others as weak due to their lack of education, especially in philosophy. Overall, Gäckle is less certain than other interpreters on the point that the weak were economically inferior to the strong (*Die Starken*, 183–218).

[2] The classic formulation of this theory is Gerd Theissen, *The Social Setting of Pauline Christianity* (Philadelphia: Fortress, 1982), 145–74.

[3] Theissen (*Social Setting*, 76, 89,158) identifies the supposed banquet host, Gaius, as one of the socially strong members of the congregation. See also Jerome Murphy-O'Connor, *St. Paul's Corinth. Texts and Archaeology* (Good News Studies 6; Wilmington, DE: Michael Glazier, 1983), 153–61; Wayne A. Meeks, *The First Urban Christians: The Social World of the Apostle Paul*, 2nd ed. (New Haven: Yale University Press, 2003 [1983]), 57–8; Roger W. Gehring, *House Church and Mission. The Importance of Household Structures in Early Christianity* (Peabody, MA: Hendrickson, 2004), 194.

[4] Gäckle, *Die Starken*, 216.

If the traditional description of the Corinthian group's social hierarchy is correct, then a problem arises, which interpreters have yet to confront: *ekklēsia* membership offered few, if any, opportunities to the majority of affiliates to earn the types of honorific rewards that we saw to be so central to recruitment in associations. Since clubs throughout the ancient Mediterranean went so far as to advertise their practice of offering commendation to all generous members, the Corinthians' supposed reputation for avoiding this practice might have deterred potential recruits. In contemporary societies, a church might prevail without offering proclamations, crowns, and/or honorific inscriptions to generous members. But in Corinth's honour–shame society, the survival of a Christ group structured as a modern church with respect to honorific behaviour would be rather remarkable.

My concern in this chapter is to show that social hierarchy in the Christ group was fluid, not finalised in the fixed modern categories of 'strong' and 'weak'. Opportunities for status generation and honorific rewards were regularly available to all members: including the ones in modest economic categories,[5] the ones in slightly elevated economic strata, the group's current officers, and the group's current regular members. As a result of dynamic and constantly developing competitions for honour in the Christ group, social–hierarchical relationships would have been determined by recent service to the *ekklēsia*, and there never would have been a stable status quo. Both officers and regular members possessed opportunities to impress and win formal recognition, however, for officers and non-officers alike, occasions to contribute to the next big financial endeavour needed to be exploited, and there was only a limited amount of honour and recognition to go around.

Bruce Malina's concept of acquired honour frames the association evidence rather well.[6] Malina characterises competitions for superior status in ancient Mediterranean societies as 'ongoing'[7] and as component to 'every social interaction that takes place outside one's family or

---

[5] These individuals would still be above the level of subsistence since the Christ group depended on income from all members in order to procure necessities.

[6] 'Acquired honor . . . is the socially recognized claim to worth that a person acquires by excelling over others in the social interaction that we shall call challenge and response. Challenge and response is a sort of social pattern, a social game, if you will, in which persons hassle each other according to socially defined rules in order to gain the honor of another.' See Bruce J. Malina, *The New Testament World: Insights from Cultural Anthropology* (Atlanta, GA: John Knox Press, 1981) 37.

[7] Malina, *New Testament World*, 37.

outside one's circle of friends'.[8] In light of agonistic tendencies in ancient Mediterranean society more broadly, the routine activities practiced in associations, such as elections, banquets, opportunities for peer benefaction, and honorific ceremonies, would have kept social relations among members in an association in a constant state of instability and fluidity. Whichever members were weak and strong in the *ekklēsia* when Paul wrote 1 Corinthians might not have been so for long. In the following pages, my labelling of some Corinthians as weak and others as strong is to designate their supposed positions outside the Christ group, as traditionally understood. The point of this chapter is to demonstrate that even if the Christ group brought together a socially heterogeneous group of individuals, social–hierarchical relations in the *ekklēsia* would not have been fixed according to members' positions outside of the group.

Honorific Behaviour in the Jesus Movement and Early Christianity

Christ believers produced multitudes of inscriptions that attest to the currency of honour in the Jesus movement and early Christianity.[9] In later centuries, Christians adopted imagery of crowns (στέφανοι) as part of their honorific customs (*SB* IV 7315; St. Persburg, Egypt; end III CE), though we do not know as much as we would like about their actual crowing practices.[10] They also heroised (ἀφηρωΐζειν) fellow believers (*IG* XIII, 3 942; Thera, unknown date), though the meaning of heroisation in late antiquity is debated.[11] Even into the sixth century when we might expect Pauline idealisations, such as 1 Cor 12–14, to have gained some traction, Christian groups still commended service providers with honorific inscriptions such as the following one:

---

[8] Malina, *New Testament World*, 36.

[9] John S. Creaghan and A. E. Raubitschek, 'Early Christian Epitaphs from Athens', *Hesperia* 16 (1947): 1–51; Anastasius C. Bandy, 'Early Christian Inscriptions of Crete', *Hesperia* 32 (1963): 227–47; Giovanni Battista de Rossi, *Inscriptiones Christianae urbis Romae septimo saeculo antiquiores* (Rome: Libaria Pontificia, 1822–1894).

[10] See Denis Feissel, 'Notes d'e épigraphie chétienne (II)', *BCH* 101 (1977) 209–28 (209–14).

[11] For an argument of continuity with earlier practices, see Dennis D. Hughes, 'Hero Cult, Heroic Honors, Heroic Dead: Some Developments in the Hellenistic and Roman Periods', in *Ancient Greek Hero Cult: Proceedings of the Fifth International Seminar on Ancient Greek Cult, Organized by the Department of Classical Archaeology and Ancient History, Göteborg University, 21–23 April 1995*, ed. Robin Hägg (Stockholm: Svenska Institutet i Athen, 1999), 167–75.

ἐπὶ [τοῦ ——— ἐτελει]ώθη τὸ ἄγ(ιον) θυσιαστ(ήριον) σπουδῇ
Ἰωάννου διακ(όνου) ὑπὲρ σωτη(ρίας) τῶ[ν κα]ρποφορ
(οὗντων) (*SEG* 29: 1610; Palestine, mid VI CE).

The holy altar was completed with zeal by John, deacon, for the
sake of the salvation of the ones who bear fruit.

Formulaic honorific language even appears in Christian funeral inscriptions from late antiquity.[12]
Any honorific inscription produced by the first-century Corinthian
group remains lost to us. While this epigraphic silence helps drive
the perception that the *ekklēsia* failed to recognise peer benefactors, it
cannot go unnoticed that if the Christ group inscribed honours on stone,
archaeologists will probably never locate them in useable condition.
During the combined reigns of Claudius and Nero (41–68 CE), only
thirty-eight inscriptions were located in Corinth by the time of John
Harvey Kent's publication of the material[13] – this amounts to an average
of just over one extant inscription per year. Of the surviving Corinthian
epigraphy, Kent bemoans its particularly poor condition. He finds it
'difficult to think of any other ancient site where the inscriptions are so
cruelly mutilated or broken'.[14]

Re-description of Service and Recognition
in the Christ Group

The unfortunate archaeological record is not a blockade to exploring
the *ekklēsia*'s honorific customs. Instructively, Paul reveals that the
Corinthians performed services we frequently find praised in civic and
association honorific inscriptions. His usage of formulaic honorific language while praising instances of Corinthian peer benefaction shows that
even Paul accepted the practice of commending service providers.

This chapter focuses on two occasions where all Corinthians were
given the opportunity to earn commendation and symbolic capital,
regardless of the social category (i.e., strong and weak) in which we
place them. First, the Jerusalem collection will be explored in comparative context. This collection is placed within the framework of voluntary
collections made by various other ancient associations for different

---

[12] See, e.g., Bandy, 'Early Christian Inscriptions', 242.

[13] John Harvey Kent, *Corinth: Results of Excavations. The Inscriptions 1926–1950*.
Volume 8/3 of *American School of Classical Studies at Athens* (Cambridge, MA: Harvard
University Press, 1966), 18–19.

[14] Of 1,500 Roman period inscriptions, only 14 remain intact. See Kent, *Corinth*, 17.

construction and financial projects, especially the λογεία attested by *P.Oslo* III 144 (Oxyrhynchos, Egypt; 275 CE). Researchers often depict the Jerusalem λογεία as an act performed out of concern for the poor.[15] An outcome of this mislabelling is that the so-called weak members of the Christ group who contributed funds to the Jerusalem collection are imagined to have earned minimal symbolic capital for their generosity, and to have experienced no upward social mobility. Yet, one can imagine how a financial contribution by an economically modest member in the Corinthian group, coupled with negligence by a slightly wealthier Corinthian, would temporarily impact the social positions of these two members in the context of the Christ group. In this way, the *ekklēsia*'s social–hierarchical structure was being generated from the very practices of the Christ group, and social rankings in the group changed as fast and often as opportunities for honour arrived. The Corinthians were associates in an organised network of fluid social relations.

A second opportunity for the Corinthian members to generate status was when the group decided to send emissaries to visit Paul in Ephesos (1 Cor 16:17–18). While commentators believe that the travelling of Stephanas, Fortunatus, and Achaiacus was met with 'respect' rather than material rewards by the *ekklēsia*,[16] this seems to be an understatement. Greeks and Romans rewarded emissaries with a range of normative forms of symbolic capital, and the practice of delivering commendation (ἔπαινός; cf. 1 Cor 11:22) to emissaries involved more than attitudinal changes. Moreover, the possible presence of slaves in this committee (Fortunatus and Achaiacus) ought not to be overlooked

---

[15] For example, see Bruce W. Longenecker, *Remember the Poor: Paul, Poverty, and the Greco-Roman World* (Grand Rapids, MI and Cambridge: Eerdmans, 2010), 60–107; and James R. Harrison, *Paul's Language of Grace in its Graeco-Roman Context* (WUNT II/172; Tübingen: Mohr Siebeck, 2003), 323.

[16] Attitudinal changes are all that scholars typically posit when discussing forms of reciprocity for service in the Christ group. See Anthony Thiselton, *The First Epistle to the Corinthians* (New International Greek Testament Commentary; Grand Rapids: Eerdmans, 2000), 1341–2; Ben Witherington III, *Conflict and Community in Corinth: A Socio-Rhetorical Commentary on 1 and 2 Corinthians* (Grand Rapids, MI: Eerdmans, 1995), 320; Eckhard J. Schnabel, *Der erste Brief des Paulus an die Korinther* (Wuppertal: R. Brockhaus, 2006), 1024; Wolfgang Schrage, *Der erste Brief an die Korinther* (4 vols.; Evangelisch-katholischer Kommentar zum Neuen Testament 7; Neukirchen-Vluyn: Neukirchener Verlag, 1991–2001), 4, 458–9; Johannes Weiss, *Der Erste Korintherbrief* (Göttingen: Vandenhoeck & Ruprecht, 1910), 386; Gordon D. Fee, *The First Epistle to the Corinthians* (New International Commentary on the New Testament; Grand Rapids, MI: Eerdmans, 1987), 832–3.

as an instance of so-called weak members of the group finding an opportunity to behave honourably and, thereby, enhance their status.

The Jerusalem Collection

Interpreters tend to gravitate towards Paul's understanding of the collection rather than the dynamics surrounding the Corinthians' decision to participate in it.[17] However, some researchers have attempted to analyse the Jerusalem collection from the perspective of its contributors. Curiously, they propose that the Corinthians engaged in charity rather than benefaction. Bruce Longenecker understands charity and benefaction as mutually exclusive in the ancient world: the Corinthians' donations were 'charity'[18] whereas benefaction and patronage 'do not qualify as charitable'.[19] Longenecker defines charity as care for the poor that aims 'to offset the needs of those who had for long been enmeshed within economic levels ES6 and ES7 specifically', which marks it off from the exchange relationships forged by acts of benefaction.[20] A similar distinction is made by James Harrison. In Harrison's work, a line is drawn between the ethos of civic benefaction and Paul's description of the collection, even though Paul employed the discourse of the former. Paul 'feared' that the Corinthians would contribute to the λογεία 'due to the silent demands of Graeco-Roman reciprocity system' as opposed to doing it for Paul's idealised reason, namely, out of a 'sense of gratitude for the divine grace revealed in the impoverished Christ'.[21] To be sure, the contributing Corinthians did behave as benefactors but, on Harrison's theory, Jerusalem was not obligated to 'return favour for the

[17] For example, Karl Holl, *Gesammelte Aufsätze zur Kirchengeschichte*, 2 vols. (Tübingen: J. C. B. Mohr, 1928–1932), 2:44–67; Oscar Cullmann, 'The Early Church and the Ecumenical Problem', *AThR* 40 (1958): 181–9, 294–301; Johannes Munck, *Paul and the Salvation of Mankind* (Atlanta: John Knox, 1959), 301–3; Witherington, *Conflict and Community*, 423; Victor Furnish, *II Corinthians: Translated with Introduction, Notes, and Commentary* (AB 32A; Garden City: Doubleday, 1984), 412; David Horrell, 'Paul's Collection: Resources for a Materialist Theology', *Epworth Review* 22 (1995), 74–83; Stephen Joubert, *Paul as Benefactor: Reciprocity, Strategy, and Theological Reflection in Paul's Collection* (WUNT II/124; Tübingen: Mohr Siebeck, 2000), 6–7; Longenecker, *Remember*, 135–53; David J. Downs, *The Offering of the Gentiles. Paul's Collection for Jerusalem in Its Chronological, Cultural, and Cultic Contexts* (Wissenschaftliche Untersuchungen zum Neuen Testament II/248; Tübingen: Mohr Siebeck, 2008), 158.

[18] Longenecker, *Remember*, 60–107.

[19] Longenecker, *Remember*, 67–74. For an explanation of ways in which benefaction differed from patronage, see Joubert, *Paul as Benefactor*, 68–9.

[20] Longenecker, *Remember*, 73.

[21] Harrison, *Paul's Language*, 313.

collection'.[22] The reciprocity earned by the Corinthians would come from God, who 'in the disposal of His blessings upon the Corinthians (2 Cor 9:7–11), undergirds their beneficence by His grace ... and as a result will reward both the Corinthians (9:10, 11a, 13a) and their beneficiaries (9:12, 14a)'.[23] It is unclear why Harrison deems that it needs to be one or the other, from God or Jerusalem. Indeed, Richard Ascough provides evidence of benefactors who expected/earned reciprocity from both the deity and the cult group to whom the donor showed generosity.[24]

For Harrison, the Corinthians' own motivations were mirror-reflections of Paul's idealisation. He concludes that 'the beneficence of believers is not motivated by the obligation to return favour or, conversely, the expectation of the return of favour.'[25] To be sure, this was a bit of a one-off in Harrison's estimation: he agrees that the Corinthians usually acted out of self-interest.[26]

If Longenecker and Harrison are correct, then Corinthian contributors from the *ekklēsia* showed an interest in charity that ancient historians rarely find among Greeks and Romans.[27] Gillian Clark observes, 'No Roman cult groups, not even those that were primarily mutual groups, are known to have looked after strangers and people in need.'[28] A re-description is needed especially since a recent re-examination of the ancient data finds little evidence to overturn Clark's statement about the relative lack of charitable initiatives by private citizens in antiquity.[29]

The following sections show that the classification of the Corinthians' contributions to the Jerusalem collection as charity is misleading and incomplete. Even if the Corinthians somehow knew that the Jerusalem

[22] Harrison, *Paul's Language*, 324.

[23] Harrison, *Paul's Language*, 321.

[24] For present purposes, Ascough's data show that an association member could 'complete' (ἐπιτελεῖν; cf. 2 Cor 8:6, 11) a benefaction that was found to be 'worthy of a god', such as when a treasurer from a Piraean club made repairs to a Zeus temple, and still earn reciprocity from their cult group (*IG* II² 1271.6–7 = *GRA* I 13; 298/97 BCE). See Richard S. Ascough, 'The Completion of a Religious Duty: The Background of 2 Cor 8.1–15', *NTS* 42 (1996), 584–99.

[25] Harrison, *Paul's Language*, 324.

[26] James R. Harrison, 'The Brothers as the "Glory of Christ" (2 Cor 8:23) Paul's *Doxa* Terminology in Its Ancient Benefaction Context', *NovT* 52 (2010), 156–88 (163).

[27] William Woodthorpe Tarn, *Hellenistic Civilization* (New York: Plume, 1974), 110; Paul Veyne, *Bread and Circuses: Historical Sociology and Political Pluralism* (London: Penguin, 1990), 31; Gillian Clark, *Christianity and Roman Society* (Cambridge: Cambridge University Press, 2004), 23–4; cf. Longenecker, *Remember*, 60–7.

[28] Clark, *Christianity*, 23. To be sure, the Corinthians were notionally connected to the Jerusalem group, if only through both groups' ties to Paul, Peter, and Barnabas.

[29] See Longenecker, *Remember*, 74–86.

Christ group would not reciprocate their generosity with material honours, the contribution signalled the Corinthians' achievement of superior
status and honour over the Jerusalem *ekklēsia*.[30] Formal commendation
could have been expected by the donors *from their own group*, delivered
to them in return for exalting the Corinthian group's reputation and status
in relation to another cult group.

A New Analogy to the Jerusalem Collection

P.Oslo III 144 (Oxyrhynchos, Egypt; 272–75 CE) generates several new
questions about the Jerusalem collection. It is a fragmentary papyrus that
is missing the whole right side. The surviving portion reads as follows:

> A list of those who have made gifts [to the association] of sacred
> victors[31] during the . . . year of Aurelianos Augustus. The con-
> tributors are as follows: Aurelioi:
>
> Neilos, a carpet weaver (gave) . . .
> Pammenes, a perfume dealer (gave) . . .
> Ammonios, a dyer (gave) . . .
> Ammonios, son of Sarapa the dyer (gave) . . .
> Philosarapis, a goldsmith (gave) . . .
> Sarapammon, a copper worker (gave) . . .
> Heras, an oil merchant (gave) . . .
> the sons of Syros, a baker (gave) . . .
> Theodoros son of Sakaon, a manufacturer of oil (gave) . . .
> Eros from Seryphis[32] [who is currently residing in] Hypsele (in
>   the Thebaid gave) . . .
> Papontos, a craftsman (gave) . . .
> the son of Demes from the Arsinoite nome (gave) . . .
> a wine merchant . . .
> Ploteinos residing in the house of Hippeus (gave) . . .
> Souchammon, a forwarding-agent (gave) . . .
> Laskarios son of Souchammon, a baker (gave) . . .

[30] For discussion of a similar dynamic between two associations, see *OGIS* 595 = *AGRW*
317 (Campania, Italy; 174 CE) and commentary in Richard S. Ascough, *Paul's
Macedonian Associations: The Social Context of Philippians and 1 Thessalonians*
(Wissenschaftliche Untersuchungen zum Neuen Testament II/161; Tübingen: Mohr
Siebeck, 2003), 95, 141; and George La Piana, 'Foreign Groups in Rome during the First
Centuries of the Empire', *HTR* 20 (1927), 183–403 (257–8).
[31] Λόγος τῶν δεδωκότω[ν . . .] ἱερονικῶν
[32] Of the Oxyrhynchite nome.

a broiderer (gave) . . .
. . . son of Phainole the daughter of Harendotes (gave) . . .
Hierax son of Epimachos, ex-exegetes, (gave) . . .
Papontos in Kerk . . . (gave) . . .
. . . son of Diogenes, a huckster (gave) . . .
the son of Kephalon, a collector (gave) . . .
the son of Achilleus (gave) . . .
. . . an ex-exegetes (gave) . . .
. . . a purple-dyer (gave) . . .
. . . son of Mono . . ., a forwarding agent (gave) . . .
. . . son of Pausanias from Pa . . . (gave) . . .
. . . son of Sarapion . . . (gave) . . .
The son of Nemesion . . . (gave)
[--]
. . . seller . . .
[--]
[--]

The association of sacred victors (ἱερονεῖκαι), named in the first line of
the papyrus, presumably wrote and kept the document. The list records
names of donors, many of whom held jobs similar to those presumably
held by members of Pauline groups. The donors gave gifts to the sacred
victors' association for some unattested reason. Significantly for us, the
donors were not affiliated with the guild to which they made contributions. Owing to the lacunae, we do not know as much as we would like
about the beneficiary association, such as whether these victors were
athletes or artistic performers.[33] There is merit to both options, but the
issue is ultimately irrelevant for present purposes.[34]

[33] As Clarence Forbes observed, 'The term *hieronikai* was equally applicable to athletic
victors and to winners in the musical and dramatic festivals where the contestants were
members of the centuries-old guild of the Artists of Dionysus.' Clarence A. Forbes,
'Ancient Athletic Guilds', *CP* 50 (1955), 238–52 (240).

[34] In support of these being artistic victors, at least one member of the worldwide artists
and sacred victors lived in Oxyrhynchos around the time of this text – a certain Aurelius
Hatres (*P.Oxy* XXVII 2476, ll.12–17; 289 CE). Slightly earlier, a papyrus attests to
'Tiberius Claudius Didymus . . . from the Dionyseum and the sacred association of victors
(τῆς ἱερᾶς συνόδου ἱερονεικῶν)' (*P.Oxy* VI 908, ll.4–10; 199 CE). Given its connection to
the Dionyseum it is perhaps appropriate to imagine this association as having consisted
exclusively of artistic victors. On the other hand, in *BGU* IV 1074.19 (Oxyrhynchos, 273/4
CE), there is attestation to an Oxyrhynchite guild of athletes (ξυστόν) who are urged to
attract as many victors as possible to compete in the games. If the beneficiaries were
athletes, perhaps we should understand that these donations were directed towards assisting

How do we know that the donors were unaffiliated with the victors' association to which they provided contributions? If they were honorary affiliates, such as the φιλοτεχνῖται or πρόξενοι mentioned in other guilds of Dionysiac artists (e.g., *OGIS* 51, ll.67, 75 = *AGRW* 298; Ptolemais Hermou, Egypt; 269–246 BCE), it would be odd for the scribe of the papyrus to identify them by their professions, and never by honorary designations as is usually done with honorific affiliates. The occupational identifications further confirm that none of the contributors were professional artists or athletes – it goes against our knowledge about membership in occupational guilds to assume that hucksters and perfume dealers would be full-time members of an artists' or athletes' guild.[35] *P.Oslo* III 144 seems to be our only list of benefactions to an association from non-members.[36] For this reason, the editors, Samson Eitrem and Leiv Amundsen, describe the association of ἱερονεῖκαι as recipients of 'an extraordinary collection of contributions ... [from] non-members'.[37]

A further striking similarity to the Jerusalem collection is that some donors did not live in the same town inhabited by the beneficiary association: Eros was originally from the Oxyrhynchite nome but was living in the Thebaid when he made his contribution (ll.16–17); another contributor was from the Arsinoite nome (l.19); Ploteinos was living παρεπίδημος in Hippeos's house (l.22); and Papontos seems to have been residing in Kerkeosiris (l.32).

How does this list illuminate the Jerusalem collection, which was also an act of benefaction by donors to a cult group with which they were unaffiliated? I suggest three insights from this papyrus for an understanding of the Corinthian groups' mechanics of putting together donations for the Jerusalem *ekklēsia*.

Making a List

When we come across lists of subscription payments in association papyri, we often find that the contributions were dated because they

members from a guild of athletic victors to compete in the games. The editors of this papyrus, S. Eitrem and Leiv Amundsen, understand the association of *hieronikai* to have been involved somehow with the Capitoline games, which came to Oxyrhynchos in 274 or 275 CE for the first time. Both artists and athletes competed in these games.

[35] Philip A. Harland, *Associations, Synagogues, and Congregations. Claiming a Place in Ancient Mediterranean Society* (Minneapolis, MN: Fortress, 2003), 38–44.

[36] Erich Ziebarth, *Das griechische Vereinswesen* (Stuttgart: S. Hirzel, 1969), 160–2; S. Eitrem and Leiv Amundsen, ed., *Papyri osloenses* (Oslo: J. Dybwad, 1925–), 3:224.

[37] Eitrem and Amundsen, ed. *Papyri osloenses*, 3:224.

were all due the same day. In contrast, *P.Oslo* III 144 does not list a specific date on which all collections arrived. This may indicate that the ἱερονεῖκαι guild received contributions gradually over time, which is similar to the payment mechanism in other non-subscription collections (see *P.Athen.* 41; 2 Cor 8:10–11, and Chapter 4). As donations came in, the victors made note of them. What was the point in recording donors' names and the amount they donated over a period of time?

Eitrem and Amundsen suggest that the function of this list was for the ἱερονεῖκαι guild to keep track of the donors so that they could remunerate them somehow,[38] as a way to affirm the honour and status achieved by contributors. Their suggestion seems plausible since voluntary donations and benefactions such as this typically merited reciprocity.[39] Their suggestion about the function of the sacred victors' list also raises a new question for researchers of Pauline groups. Would the Jerusalem *ekklēsia* have liked to know the individual names of donors to their group? Moreover, would an economically modest, small shop owner in the Corinthian group not insist that the Jerusalem group be given a list of donors with his or her name on it? How many other opportunities would there be for such a person to behave as a generous benefactor outside of the opportunities organised by their association?

Steven Friesen argued that the Jerusalem collection represented an alternative to patronage because of the supposedly low economic status of the donors: 'Paul envisioned a system of average saints helping the desperately poor-saints ... The practice here is not that of benefaction, where families with huge amounts of capital or resources distribute a fraction of their surplus.'[40] This understanding of benefaction seems too restrictive. In light of our evidence from modest associations, it would seem that the status of donors is irrelevant in determining whether a gift was benefaction or representative of an alternative economic relationship.[41] *P.Oslo* III 144 lists several non-elites – a baker, an oil manufacturer, and a carpet weaver – who were likely honoured as

[38] Eitrem and Amundsen, *Papyri osloenses*, 3:224.
[39] To name a couple: *IGLSkythia* III 35 = *AGRW* 73 (Kallatis, Scythia Minor, Danube, and Black Sea regions; late III BCE); *CIL* III 633 I = *GRA* I 68 (Philippi, Macedonia; II CE).
[40] Steven J. Friesen, 'Paul and Economics: The Jerusalem Collection as an Alternative to Patronage', in *Paul Unbound: Other Perspectives on the Apostle*, ed. Mark D. Given (Peabody, MA: Hendrickson, 2010), 27–54 (50).
[41] See the reciprocity won by peer benefactors (i.e., non-elites) over and over again in associations, found in scores of honorific inscriptions and also in the papyri attesting to delivery of cheap crowns as symbolic capital in return for the expenditure of economic resources by economically modest club members functioning as peer benefactors (cf. Chapter 4).

benefactors in some way that fit within the range of honours won by hundreds if not thousands of other non-elite benefactors from associations throughout the ancient Mediterranean.[42] The Corinthians' financial donations may have been placed in the same treasury box as the contributions from Macedonia (Rom 16:31; 2 Cor 9:4), or they may have arrived at Jerusalem in a separate box with Paul's letter (1 Cor 16:3). Either way, both the Corinthian donors and the Jerusalem recipients might have reasons for wanting a list to accompany the delivery of the money. This brings us to the related point of the necessity of two lists. Perhaps we should imagine the co-workers whom Paul sent to 'prepare' (προκαταρτίζειν) the collections as helpers who would copy the names of Corinthian donors onto a second list that would be presented to the Jerusalem community along with the gift (2 Cor 9:5). Since generosity towards the Jerusalem group would merit reciprocity from both the Corinthian *ekklēsia* (to which the donors brought honour) and the Jerusalem Christ believers (to whom the donations were given), both groups needed their own list of donors. The Corinthians required the names of contributors, and the specific amount that each donated, in order to script proclamations, and/or draft commendations to be inscribed on stone.

John Kloppenborg suggested that the Corinthians drafted their own list of contributors to the Jerusalem collection for an additional practical reason. He observes that Paul requested that the Corinthians complete their donation to Jerusalem (ἐπιτελεῖν, 2 Cor 8:11). But how would a Christ group know when the collection for Jerusalem was complete? Kloppenborg suggests, 'The simplest way to signal that the collection was completed is to produce a contributor list with or without the contributions of each member.'[43] He shows that clubs often recorded the names of all members who contributed their subscription payments at banquets, as well as those who failed to pay and owed their fee at the next meeting.[44] *P.Oslo* III 144 illustrates that associations could make

[42] For a large digital collection of these, see http://philipharland.com/greco-roman-associations/category/type-of-document/honorary/

[43] John S. Kloppenborg, 'Membership Practices in Pauline Christ Groups', *Early Christianity* 4 (2013), 183–215 (210).

[44] For example, *P.Cairo dem.* 30606 = *AGRW* 299 (Tebtynis, Egypt; 158/57 BCE); *P.Mich.* V 246 (Arsinoites, Egypt; 43–49 CE); *IEph* 20 = *AGRW* 162 (Ephesos, Asia Minor; 54–59 CE); *SB* III 7182 (Philadelphia, Egypt; early II BCE); *P.Tebt.* III/2 894 (Tebtynis, Egypt; 114 BCE); *P.Athen.* 41 (unknown provenance, Egypt; I CE); *P.Lund.* IV 11 (Bakchias?, Egypt; 169/70 CE); cf. Kloppenborg, 'Membership Practices', 210.

contributor lists even when the payments were for an external group, as was the Jerusalem collection.

Recognition for Strong and Weak Corinthians

A second, new question raised by the papyrus concerns the content of the list that was delivered to Jerusalem. Would each *ekklēsiai* get a single row on the left column, and a corresponding tally of contributions on the right? Or would each donor receive individual recognition? Friesen would assume the former: 'the contributor was communal: the money came from several groups of people rather than from an individual or family ... So the Jerusalem collection did not incorporate the patronage system's focus on the named contributor.'[45] Our papyrus helps us to control speculation on this point because some of the donors to the ἱερονεῖκαι were members of their own associations. By the early fourth century just about every profession in Oxyrhynchos was organised into a guild – from tavern keepers to potters.[46] Some of the donors to the sacred victors are mentioned as artisans and merchants whose professions had guilds in Oxyrhynchos at the time. For example, the donor Pammenes, the perfume dealer (μυροπώλης, 1.7), was in a profession organised around an Oxyrhynchite guild (*P.Oxy.* LIV 3744, 318 CE); while Souchammon and a contributor whose name is lost were both forwarding agents (ἐκδοχεύς, ll.23, 38), another profession organised around a guild (*P.Oxy.* LIV 3772, 338 CE).

The pair of donors from the same association (the forwarding agents) is most interesting for the present purposes. How odd would it be if our papyrus listed the combined donation from the forwarding agents and attributed it to the forwarding agent guild? Rather than doing this, the writer of the list recorded the forwarding agent (ἐκδοχεὺς) Souchammon (1.23) and the forwarding agent in l.38 (whose name is lost) separately, and listed their specific, individual contributions.

It seems likely that some Corinthians donated money to the Jerusalem fund while others did not (2 Cor 8:10–11). Of the group's ten members, the weakest ones very well might have volunteered more money than the strongest owing to any one of a variety of scenarios. Whatever happened, the Christ group's social hierarchy fluctuated as a result of the different levels of zeal that donors committed to the Christ group. The delivery of

---

[45] Friesen, 'Paul and Economics', 49–50.
[46] See *P.Oxy.* LIV 3731–40, 3742–5, 3747–53, 3755, 3760–3, 3765–6, 3768, 3772, 3776.

honours to some and not to others would have altered attitudes towards
donors and non-donors accordingly – and as a result, it would have
impacted social and hierarchical rankings in the *ekklēsia* – at least until
the next competition for honour altered it once more, and so on.
Collections such as this highlight the fluidity of social rankings in
associations.

A Long List

Previously, interpreters attributed to Paul a greater concern for the total
amount of monetary donations from the Corinthians than for a high
percentage of the group's members to participate in the benefaction.
Gordon Fee, for example, argues, 'Although [Paul] does not say as
much', his objective is that 'by their weekly setting aside from their
"success" of that week, there will be a sum worth the effort of sending
people all the way to Jerusalem'.[47] Contrary to this assumption, Paul
repeatedly insisted that it did not matter how much each individual
contributed as long as they participated in the gift (1 Cor 16:2; 2 Cor
8:3, 8:11–12). The impact that would be created by the delivery of a long
list of contributors to the Jerusalem collection, presented alongside the
box of money, should not be overlooked when analysing Jerusalem's
overall impression of the effort. The more donors, the longer the list, even
if the overall sum of the benefaction is modest.

We have located a fairly illuminating analogy to the Corinthian
group's Jerusalem collection. This papyrus shifts the focus from a debate
over whether the contributions were benefaction or an alternative economic activity, towards questions concerning how the so-called strong
and weak might have viewed the Jerusalem project as one of many
opportunities to enhance individual status within the *ekklēsia* at the
expense of those who failed to show zeal and generosity for the Christ
group.

Travelling on Behalf of the *Ekklēsia* (1 Cor 16:17–18)

In support of his claim that the Corinthians did not furnish officers and
peer benefactors with material forms of honour, Wayne Meeks
observed that 'Paul even admonishes the Corinthians to show a little
more respect for such people such as Stephanas.'[48] Meeks's reading of

---

[47] Fee, *First Epistle*, 814.
[48] Meeks, *First Urban*, 78.

1 Cor 16:17–18 takes some liberties: Paul simply encouraged the group to commend the emissaries; he said nothing about the Corinthians' supposed usual avoidance of delivering reciprocity to peer benefactors. As the beneficiary of the travellers' service, Paul expressed to the *ekklēsia* his evaluation of the emissary's service. The Christ group required this from Paul since he was the only one who could scrutinise whether the emissaries enhanced or diminished the reputation of the *ekklēsia*. Honorific rewards were not given to service providers before their association performed a formal scrutiny of the quality of their service.[49] So before deciding how to reciprocate the emissaries, the Christ group (if it followed typical procedure) would have considered carefully what Paul said of their service. Paul hammers his point home by not only praising the quality of their service (see the following paragraph) but also stating rather bluntly that the emissaries deserve recognition from the Christ group.

Interpreters generally agree that Stephanas, Fortuantus, and Achaicus would have received a type of commendation from the *ekklēsia* – Meeks's interpretation of 1 Cor 16:17–18 leaves open this possibility, as well. But they tend to stop short of the rather natural conclusion that the Christ group's commendation for the travellers would look like the range of prizes described over and over again in associations' honorific inscriptions. Anthony Thiselton blatantly described the reward in light of modern church practices rather than in a proper comparative context:

> The Corinthian church should show due recognition [to the travelers], then (ἐπιγινώσκετε οὖν), in the sense of *appreciation* (NJB), of people such as these … it is a live issue in the church today to what extent, if at all, Christian congregations wish to 'honor' leaders in the Christian sphere. Such *respect* or recognition has more to do with *attitude* than financial provision … However it is shown, Paul urges its propriety; indeed, he directs that it be shown. This may apply at any level of service to the church, where often loyal hard work is simply taken for granted rather than publicly and consciously recognized.[50]

[49] The evidence for associations' procedure of first scrutinising and then honouring is massive. See, though, e.g., the following inscriptions that clearly imply a consideration of the quality of the honouree's service before the decision to honour them: *SEG* 2.9.4–6 = *GRA* I 21 (Salamis, Attica; 243/2 BCE); *IG* II² 1284.21–8 = *GRA* I 22 (Piraeus, Attica; 241/0 BCE); *IG* II² 1329.3–19 = *GRA* I 37 (Piraeus, Attica; 175/4 BCE); *IByzantion* 31.1–9 = *GRA* I 90 (Rhegion, Thrace; 85–96 CE).

[50] Thiselton, *First Epistle*, 1341–2 (emphasis in original).

Thiselton's preference to call the *ekklēsia*'s reciprocity for Stephanas, Achaicus, and Fortunatus 'appreciation' and 'respect' rather than formal recognition, and to imagine it as an 'attitude' adjustment rather than a material reward can be located in several other pieces of scholarship, as well.[51] Ben Witherington remarks, 'The Corinthians are urged to "recognize" these men, which likely means to obey them and accept their leadership and work.'[52] Eckhard Schnabel insists that 'Die "Anerkennung" in v.18 should be equated with v.16's "Unterordnung."'[53] Wolfgang Schrage draws a parallel between Paul's general usage of ἐπιγινώσκειν ('to recognise') in 1 Cor 14:37 and here in 16:18, despite the different context: in 14:37, it is said that anyone who is a prophet (προφήτης) or 'of the spirit' (πνευματικός) should 'recognise' that Paul's commendation is from a divine source, whereas in 16:18 the group is asked to recognise the three people who performed commendable behaviour that was commonly reciprocated with honorific inscriptions and other material rewards.[54] What is missed in all of this is attention to the actual mechanics of recognition in ancient cult groups contemporary with the Corinthians. As Ilias Arnaoutoglou observes, attitudinal changes (i.e., respect) happened as a positive response to watching fellow association members receive customary honorific rewards – respect, in the abstract, did not replace formal delivery of crowns, proclamations, honorific inscriptions, honourable seats at banquets, and exemptions.[55]

The Service of the Emissaries

Paul frames Stephanas, Fortunatus, and Achaicus's trip to Ephesos as a service on behalf of their Christ group, not a visit for the household's personal reasons. In Paul's perspective, their presence functioned to ἀναπληροῦν ('fill in for') the absence (ὑστέρημα) of the other members (16:17). He attributes to the Corinthians the responsibility to recognise

---

[51] For example, Johannes Weiss concedes that the travellers 'received prestige' (*Der Erste Korintherbrief*, 386). See also Fee, *First Epistle*, 832–3.

[52] Witherington, *Conflict and Community*, 320.

[53] Schnabel, *Der erste Brief*, 1024.

[54] Schrage, *Der erste Brief*, 4:458–9. Schrage stops short of saying that Paul's meaning is the same in both verses but provides no elaboration on the word's function in 16:18.

[55] Ilias Arnaoutoglou, '*Between* Koinon *and* Idion: Legal and Social Dimensions of Religious Associations in Ancient Athens', in *Kosmos. Essays in Order, Conflict and Community in Classical Athens*, ed. Paul Cartledge, Paul Millett, and Sitta von Reden (Cambridge: Cambridge University Press, 1998), 63–83 (80–1).

the emissaries (ἐπιγινώσκειν οὖν τούς τοιούτους, 16:18), and he provides them with the information they would require in order to do so: he speaks not about their status within or outside of the group (i.e., office titles, surplus economic resources)[56] – which was not worthy of recognition in itself – but about the quality of the travellers' service. Specifically, he relates that their presence at Ephesos refreshed (ἀνεπαύειν) his spirit and did the same for the entire congregation (16:18).

Paul's silence on how the Corinthians should commend the emissaries is striking. He is explicitly concerned with proper delivery of honours to the emissaries, and so the silence cannot be explained on the theory that he had knowledge of the Christ group's supposed custom of avoiding honorifics. If this were the case, then Paul would need to teach the Corinthians how to provide Stephanas and his household fitting honours as opposed to being silent about the matter. We can turn to comparative material in order to gain a sense of the range of ways in which emissaries were 'recognised' by civic and private organisations in antiquity.

Honorific Rewards for Emissaries

We begin in Corinth with an honorific decree from the Hellenistic period that commends a team of Corinthian ambassadors. These travellers were deployed to a foreign polis in order to solve by arbitration a dispute involving Corinth somehow (*ICorinth* I 65; mid II BCE).[57] Although the inscription is fragmentary, the spelling of δῆμος gives away its foreign provenance – δᾶμος was typical in Corinth until the Roman period, which means that the foreign polis made the inscription and sent it to Corinth where it would have been publicly displayed.[58] Kendall Smith summarises the function of the epigraph as follows:

> The preservation of such records on stone is commonly due, as I assume was the case in the present instance, to the publication in this manner of honors conferred on the visiting commission by the state whose citizens have thus been laid under obligation. The place of discovery is not necessarily the city which

---

[56] Although Paul mentions Stephanas's household's status as the 'first in Achaia' (16:15), this is not the reason he believes that they deserve recognition.

[57] Kendall K. Smith, 'Greek Inscriptions from Corinth II', *American Journal of Archaeology* 23 (1919), 331–94 (344).

[58] See Smith, 'Greek Inscriptions', 345.

promulgates the decree. It is as likely to be the home of the arbitrators.[59]

In this case, the Corinthian travellers received recognition for their service from the location to which they travelled.

We find another civic example from Athens. Here, the shipper and benefactor, Heracleides of Salamis, is honoured by Athens for many things, including speedy travel to the port during a grain shortage, where he honourably sold items at less than market value (SIG³ 304; 325 BCE). Heracleides is praised for being πρῶτος τῶν καταπλευσάντων ἐνπόρων ('the first [i.e., most distinguished and, probably, fastest] of the maritime merchants'). Several other examples of civic honours for travelling and travellers are known.[60]

Associations also provided material rewards to their travellers. In Dibio (Gaul), two altar inscriptions were established by the *ferrarii Dibione consistentes* and the *lapidarii pago Andomo consistentes* for the travelling exploits of the patron, Ti. Flavius Vetus (*CIL* XIII 5474; *CIL* XIII 4375). These associations gave thanks to Jupiter and Fortuna Redux for the emissary's successful return. Since Flavius's travel was likely partially on behalf of the *collegium*,[61] we might expect that the associations rewarded him somehow, perhaps with a crown or proclamation.

In another instance, an association of Tyrian ship owners and traders in Delos honoured a certain Patron, son of Dorotheos, for several services, among which was the completion of a travel assignment as part of the association's embassy to Athens to ensure a grant of land for the guild (*IDelos* 1519.10–16 = *AGRW* 223; 153/2 BCE). A description of Patron's travelling was placed into an honorific decree that his association awarded him:

> Being elected (αἱρεθεὶς) ambassador to the Council and the People of Athens, he sailed, readily taking upon himself the

[59] Smith, 'Greek Inscriptions', 344.

[60] See, e.g., *SIG* 762 = Frederick W. Danker, *Benefactor: Epigraphic Study of a Graeco-Roman and New Testament Semantic Field* (St. Louis, MO: Clayton: 1982), 77–9 (no. 12); *SIG* XVII, 315 = Danker, *Benefactor*, 75 (no. 11).

[61] See Koenraad Verboven, 'Magistrates, Patrons and Benefactors of Collegia: Status Building and Romanisation in the Spanish, Gallic and German Provinces', in *Transforming Historical Landscapes in the Ancient Empires. Proceedings of the First Workshop Area of Research in Studies from Antiquity, Barcelona 2007*, ed. I. B. AntelaBernárdez and T. Ñaco del Hoyo (British Archaeological Reports; International Series 1986; Oxford: John and Erica Hedge, 2009), 159–67 (166).

expenses from his own resources and demonstrating the good-will of the synod toward the People. In this way he accomplished the will of the association members and increased honor for the gods, just as it suited him (ll.16–21 [Kloppenborg and Ascough with slight adaptions]).[62]

These are only some examples of travellers rewarded by associations and ancient cities.[63]

Service in the form of travel was likely not a regular occurrence in the Christ group. Rather, it represented a single instance of a more systematic occurrence: the announcement of a new opportunity to provide service to the group. Such opportunities could arise on the spot and would quickly set in motion an alteration of social rankings in the *ekklēsia*. Proclamations or crowns for the weak members, such as the (possible) slaves who travelled to Ephesos and the weak contributors to the Jerusalem collection, would have enhanced their standing relative to others who failed to respond to the Christ group's call for generosity.

Conclusions

The presence of social heterogeneity within the Corinthian group may be true – it was certainly true of most associations. It tells us very little about social–hierarchical relationships within the *ekklēsia*, though. The Jerusalem collection and the excursion by Stephanas, Achaiacus, and Fortunatus represent two occasions where any member in the Christ group could have provided a service that typically generated status in other associations. Responding with generosity in opportunities such as these could enhance a member's social ranking and honour in the *ekklēsia*, depending, of course, on the manner in which other members responded (i.e., did they contribute as much or anything at all?). In other words, there were ongoing opportunities for the so-called weak to strengthen themselves.

An additional attestation to honorific zeal among the Corinthians – as well as a further indication of the group's social–hierarchical fluidity – comes in 1 Cor 11:18–19, the focus of the Chapter 7. These verses probably indicate that the *ekklēsia* elected officers whose duties partially

---

[62] I altered the *AGRW* translation slightly by rendering αἱρεθείς as 'being elected' rather than 'being chosen'. See Chapter 7 for election terminology in associations.

[63] Others include *IG* XI/4 1299 = *AGRW* 221 (Delos, Asia Minor; c.200 BCE) where a certain Apollonius's travel from Egypt to Delos is commemorated as the central event in the community's origin; and *IG* X/2 255 = *GRA* I 77 (Thessalonica, Macedonia; I–II CE).

consisted of administrative services in preparation for and during the Lord's Supper (11:17–22). The presence of temporary officers in the group's hierarchical structure again illustrates that all members would have had regular opportunities to be strong for a temporary period of time. If they performed their offices' duties well – some did not (11:17–22) – then they could expect a form of reciprocity falling within the range of rewards provided to officials of other associations.

7

THE ELECTION AND CROWNING
OF OFFICERS[1]

Yet Another Lack

Were there officers in the Corinthian *ekklēsia*? On the whole, past scholarship has found no evidence for such,[2] and some pivotal works over the last century argue that the Corinthians did not elect temporary, rotating, officers as the associations did.[3] In the 1970s, Gerd Theissen showed that portrayals of an egalitarian *ekklēsia* by Rudolf Sohm and others[4] did not adequately account for the dominance of leadership roles enjoyed by a minority of socially powerful Corinthians. Although Theissen finds hierarchy among the Corinthians, he distinguishes its form from what he observes in associations. He describes the Christ group's order in the following way: 'When, by contrast [to the associations], everything is left to the free sway of the "Spirit" [as it is in the Corinthian group], those who are of privileged status are much more

---

[1] The first part of this chapter is based on an article previously published. The version here is revised and supplemented with additional sources in support of the original thesis.

[2] Some interpreters have briefly considered the possibility of officers in 1 Cor 12:27–8. See Bradley H. McLean, 'The Agrippinilla Inscription: Religious Associations and Early Church Formation', in *Origins and Method: Towards a New Understanding of Judaism and Christianity. Essays in Honour of John C. Hurd*, ed. Bradley H. McLean (Journal for the Study of the New Testament: Supplement Series 86; Sheffield: JSOT Press, 1993), 239–70 (259); and Rachel M. McRae, 'Eating with Honor: The Corinthian Lord's Supper in Light of Voluntary Association Meal Practices', *JBL* 130 (2011), 165–81 (172–3, 181).

[3] Edwin Hatch, *The Organization of the Early Christian Churches: Eight Lectures Delivered before the University of Oxford in the Year 1880 on the Foundation of the Late John Bampton* (London: Rivingtons, 1881), 119–20; Johannes Weiss, *Der Erste Korintherbrief* (Göttingen: Vandenhoeck & Ruprecht, 1910), xxiv–xxvi, 386; Eduard Schweizer, *Church Order in the New Testament* (London: SCM, 1961), 99.

[4] For this early literature, see the present book's Introduction. It continues to hold sway. For example, recently, Jan Bremmer argued, 'everything we know about early Christianity indicates that the early congregations were relatively egalitarian and supplied important bridging and bonding opportunities', in Jan N. Bremmer, 'The Social and Religious Capital of Early Christians', *Hephaistos* 24 (2006), 269–78 (276).

likely to have things their way.'[5] More recently, Bengt Holmberg, Wayne Meeks, Thomas Schmeller, Eva Ebel, and many others have followed Theissen in acknowledging social hierarchy while simultaneously insisting that the Corinthians' organisational structure was less defined than what is found in ancient associations.[6]

Whether interpreters prefer Corinthian egalitarianism by means of diverse permanent gifts or hierarchical order on the basis of social status, they agree that leadership roles in the Christ group did not have annual expiry dates. On this point, Theissen draws the following conclusion: 'Fortunately it is obvious that the officials in early Christianity were permanent officials.'[7] In other words, once a leader (i.e., a teacher, a prophet, one of the socially strong), always a leader.

One might expect that clear evidence exists confirming the absence of rotating, elected officers in the group, but no such data has been offered. The most commonly cited validation of the *communis opinio* is Paul's silence on the issue:[8] he fails to mention titles

---

[5] Gerd Theissen, *The Social Setting of Pauline Christianity* (Philadelphia: Fortress, 1982), 155.

[6] Wayne A. Meeks (*The First Urban Christians: The Social World of the Apostle Paul*, 2nd ed. (New Haven: Yale University Press, 2003 [1983], 134) observes, 'Acts and the Pauline letters make no mention of formal offices in the early Pauline congregations. This fact is striking when we compare these groups with the typical Greek or Roman private association.' Holmberg is open to the existence of offices in Pauline groups. Like others, though, he downplays their significance: 'The general impression we get when reading Paul's letters is that the local offices were rather unimportant.' For Holmberg, this was apparently especially true in Corinth (*Paul and Power*, 113–17, cf. 205). See also, Stanley K. Stowers, 'Kinds of Myth, Meals, and Power: Paul and the Corinthians', in *Redescribing Paul and the Corinthians* (Early Christianity and Its Literature 5; Atlanta: Society of Biblical Literature, 2011), 105–49 (109); Thomas Schmeller, *Hierarchie und Egalität: eine sozialgeschichtliche Untersuchung paulinischer Gemeinden und griechisch-römischer Vereine* (Stuttgart: Verlag Katholisches Bibelwerk, 1995), 77–8; Ben Witherington III, *Conflict and Community in Corinth: A Socio-Rhetorical Commentary on 1 and 2 Corinthians* (Grand Rapids, MI: Eerdmans, 1995), 243–7; 453–8; Stephen J. Chester, *Conversion at Corinth. Perspectives on Conversion in Paul's Theology and the Corinthian Church* (London and New York: T&T Clark, 2003) 227–66 (240); and Eva Ebel, *Die Attraktivität früher christlicher Gemeinden: Die Gemeinde von Korinth im Spiegel grichisch-römischer Vereine* (Wissenschaftliche Untersuchungen zum Neuen Testament II/178; Tübingen: J. C. B. Mohr Siebeck, 2004), 220.

[7] Theissen, 'Social Structure', 78. Theissen is informed by Thomas Schmeller's theory (*Hierarchie*, 36–8) that permanent offices were characteristic of the wealthiest associations while rotation was used in associations of lower social registers as a way to share the financial cost of magistracy responsibilities.

[8] For example, Ekkehard W. Stegemann and Wolfgang Stegemann, *The Jesus Movement: A Social History of Its First Century* (Minneapolis, MN: Fortress Press, 1999), 281; Hans Conzelmann, *An Outline of the Theology of the New Testament*, 2nd

held by Stephanas, Fortunatus, and Achaicus when he recognises them (1 Cor 16:17–18); and he remains silent on titles held by members in charge of the food at the Lord's Supper (1 Cor 11:17–34). This chapter contends that, despite occasional silences, Paul does provide evidence of the group's practice of electing officers. It is demonstrated that Paul's language in 1 Cor 11:19 makes better sense as election discourse than as apocalyptic discourse. Indeed, the existence of a flat hierarchy of temporary and rotating magistrates in the Corinthian group helps to clarify an otherwise awkward sentence in 1 Cor 11:19.

The Problem of 'Factions' (αἱρέσεις) in 1 Cor 11:19

First Corinthians 11:19 is traditionally rendered in a way that defies logic and obscures Paul's technical terminology. The full verse reads as follows: δεῖ γὰρ καὶ αἱρέσεις ἐν ὑμῖν εἶναι, ἵνα [καὶ] οἱ δόκιμοι φανεροὶ γένωνται ἐν ὑμῖν. A common translation is, approximately, 'It is necessary for there to be factions (αἱρέσεις) among you, for only so will it become (γίνεσθαι) manifest (φανεροί) who among you are genuine (οἱ δόκιμοι).' Denoting αἱρέσεις as 'factions' or 'Parteien' is nearly unanimous in standard Bible translations,[9] commentaries,[10] and

---

ed. (New York: Harper & Row, 1969), 267–8; Bengt Holmberg, *Paul and Power: The Structure of Authority in the Primitive Church as Reflected in the Pauline Epistles* (Philadelphia: Fortress, 1980), 113–17; Meeks, *First Urban*, 134; Schmeller, *Hierarchie*, 77; Bremmer, 'Social and Religious', 276; and James R. Harrison, *Paul's Language of Grace in its Graeco-Roman Context* (Wissenschaftliche Untersuchungen zum Neuen Testament II/172; Tübingen: Mohr Siebeck, 2003), 323.

[9] For example, 'heresies' in KJV; 'factions' in NRSV, RSV, ESV, and NASB95; and 'differences' in NIV.

[10] See Weiss, *Der Erste Korintherbrief*, 279–80; Charles Kingsley Barrett, *The First Epistle to the Corinthians* (Black's; London: Hendrickson, 1968), 261; Hans Conzelmann, *1 Corinthians. A Commentary on the First Epistle to the Corinthians* (Hermeneia; Philadelphia: Fortress Press, 1975), 194; Gordon D. Fee, *The First Epistle to the Corinthians* (New International Commentary on the New Testament; Grand Rapids, MI: Eerdmans, 1987), 538; Anthony Thiselton, *The First Epistle to the Corinthians* (New International Greek Testament Commentary; Grand Rapids: Eerdmans, 2000), 859; Wolfgang Schrage, *Der erste Brief an die Korinther*, 4 vols. (Evangelisch-katholischer Kommentar zum Neuen Testament 7; Neukirchen-Vluyn: Neukirchener Verlag, 1991–2001), 3.21–2; Jean Héring, *The First Epistle of St. Paul to the Corinthians* (London: Epworth, 1962), 113; Richard Horsley, *1 Corinthians* (Nashville: Abingdon, 1998), 158–9; Joseph A. Fitzmyer, *First Corinthians* (Anchor Bible Commentary 32; New Haven and London: Yale University, 2008), 433.

social–historical studies.[11] While 'factions' is a possible interpretation for αἱρέσεις, it requires interpreters to confront a difficult question about how the Corinthians would have heard the verse: how can factions reveal who is genuine among the Corinthians? R. Alastair Campbell has spoken of the 'enormous psychological difficulty' of the standard interpretation.[12] Strategies for salvaging the αἱρέσεις-as-factions translation have been nearly identical for more than a century: the verse apparently makes sense once it is assumed that Paul was alluding to a well-known Jesus saying about αἱρέσεις at the end of the age.[13] While Judean apocalyptic literature widely attests to the idea that hardships accompanied the coming of the ἔσχατον,[14] the key terminology in 1 Cor 11:19 is not found in those texts. For this reason, scholars have searched for closer analogies from Jesus tradition that might be able to clarify the meaning of the verse.

The search for a parallel in the Jesus tradition has been unsuccessful. To be sure, scholars do observe that Q records a possibly authentic saying where Jesus claims that he will be responsible for intergenerational familial disruption (Matt 10:34–9 = Luke 12:51–3, 14:25–7 cf. Mic 7:6). But the problem is that none of the key terminology from 1 Cor 11:18–19 shows up (e.g., σχίσματα, αἱρέσεις, οἱ δόκιμοι, φανεροὶ) in the Q saying. The words used by the gospel writers for 'divisions' are

---

[11] Meeks, *First Urban*, 67; Theissen, *Social Setting*, 168; Peter Lampe, 'Das korinthinische Herrenmahl im Schnittpunkt hellenistisch-römischer Mahlpraxis und paulinischer Theologia Crucis (1 Kor 11, 17–34)' *ZNW* 82 (1991), 183–212, (211 n.78); Dennis E. Smith, *From Symposium to Eucharist: The Banquet in the Early Christian World* (Minneapolis, MN: Fortress Press, 2003), 197; Chester, *Conversion*, 218; Kenneth E. Bailey, *Paul through Mediterranean Eyes. Cultural Studies in 1 Corinthians* (Madison: InterVarsity, 2011), 318; David Horrell, *The Social Ethos of the Corinthian Correspondence: Interests and Ideology from 1 Corinthains to 1 Clement* (Edinburgh: T&T Clark, 1996), 150–1; Margaret M. Mitchell, *Paul and the Rhetoric of Reconciliation. An Exegetical Investigation of the Language and Composition of 1 Corinthians* (Louisville: Westminster/John Knox, 1992), 80. The only exception of which I am aware is R. Alastair Campbell, 'Does Paul Acquiesce in Divisions at the Lord's Supper', *NovT* 33 (1991), 61–70. Campbell's translation is 'choices'. It is peculiar that he does not consider 'elections' since he admits that his 'choices' rendering makes for an 'unusual use of αἱρέσεις'. See 'Acquiesce', 66.

[12] Campbell, 'Acquiesce', 70.

[13] See Joachim Jeremias, *Unknown Sayings of Jesus*, 2nd ed. (London: SCM, 1964), 76–7; Weiss, *Der Erste Korintherbrief*, 279–80; Henning Paulsen, 'Schisma und Häresie. Untersuchungen zu 1 Kor 11:18, 19', *ZTK* 79 (1982), 180–211; Witherington, *Conflict and Community*, 248; Thiselton, *First Epistle*, 858–9; Fee, *First Epistle*, 537–9; Barrett, *First Epistle*, 261–2.

[14] See W. D. Davies and D. C. Allison, *Matthew 8–18* (ICC; Volume 2 of *The Gospel According to Matthew*; London and New York: T&T Clark, 1991), 217–24.

διχάζειν (Matt 10:35) and διαμερισμός (Luke 12:51–3). There are also no ideas in common between the two texts unless the prior decision is made to translate Paul's αἱρέσεις as 'factions'. Even with this allowance, there stands only one common element between Q and Paul: strife between people who already know each other. Q neither describes factions as necessary nor as phenomena that will generate knowledge of genuineness.

Matthew 24:9–13 (cf. Mark 13:13; Luke 21:17–18) is also sometimes cited as a parallel. Here, there is mention of betrayal (παραδιδόναι), false prophets (ψευδοπροφῆται), lawlessness (ἀνομία), and salvation for the ones who endure this hardship. Relating this text to 1 Cor 11:18–19 raises all the problems of Q's supposed parallel and, in addition, brings the added issue of the text's redactional history that postdates 1 Corinthians.[15]

Approximately a hundred years after Paul wrote 1 Corinthians, Justin records Jesus to have predicted σχίσματα and αἱρέσεις (*Dial.* 35.3): Ἔσονται σχίσματα καὶ αἱρέσεις.[16] Here, Justin uses αἱρέσεις to mean heresies – a later development of the word's usage – and, more to the point, he does not connect any dots left unconnected by Paul on the dominant reading of 11:19: why are heresies (or, factions, in Paul's time) necessary? And how do they make known the genuine Christ believers in a divided Christ group? In his text, Justin's point in 35.3 was that the very presence of heresies actually strengthens the faith of authentic Christ believers because Jesus is said to have predicted heresies. Crucially, the presence of heresies does not show Justin's heretics anything about who in the second century were *genuine* Christ believers – the logion simply strengthens the *prior convictions* of the Christ believers with whom Justin identifies.

Recently, Timothy Brookins proposed that Justin's logion represents an authentic Jesus saying to which Paul later alluded in 11:19.[17] This is a singly attested and very late logion. Moreover, Paul does not claim to be quoting Jesus in 11:19, which sets this verse apart from passages in the letter where Paul tells the Corinthians that he is pulling from Jesus tradition (i.e., 1 Cor 7:10, 9:14, 11:23–5, 14:37). However, even if we concede to previous exegetes the possibility that Paul alluded in 11:19 to a Jesus logion preserved by Justin, there would be no pay off;

---

[15] See David C. Sim, *Apocalyptic Eschatology in the Gospel of Matthew* (Cambridge: Cambridge University, 1996), 160–9.

[16] See also the very late Syriac *Didascalia* 6.5.2, and Ps. Clement, *Hom.* 16:21.4.

[17] Timothy A. Brookins, 'The Supposed Election of Officers in 1 Cor 11.19: A Response to Richard Last', *NTS* 60 (2014), 423–32 (425).

interpreters have yet to explain the mechanics of the sentence in 11:19 (i.e., how do *factions* clarify who is genuine in an association?) with or without Justin.

The most serious problem with the 'factions' translation is not that it makes 11:19 obscure. Rather, the primary difficulty is explaining why Paul would tell the Corinthians that 'factions are necessary' anywhere in the Corinthian correspondence – and especially in 11:17–34 where he combats the problem of divisions that have, in Paul's stated perspective, destroyed the Lord's Supper. To date there is no satisfying explanation.[18] Gordon Fee, like many others who translate αἱρέσεις as 'factions', is astounded by the verse. For him, 1 Cor 11:19 is 'one of the true puzzles in the letter. How can he who earlier argued so strongly against "divisions among you" (1:10–17; 3:1–23) now affirm a kind of divine necessity to "divisions"?'[19] Dale Martin observes that 'Throughout the section, Paul emphasizes that the Lord's Supper is supposed to be the common meal of the church and hence that it is the worst time to have divisions surface.'[20] James Dunn agrees that factional strife was a serious source of disorder in the congregation: Paul speaks of quarrels (1:11), jealousy (3:3), arrogant members (4:19), boastfulness (5:6), legal proceedings between two affiliates (6:1) and disorder (14:33).[21] To this list we might add divisions at the Lord's Supper (11:18) and drunkenness (11:21). In 1 Cor 11:17–34, Paul attempts to provide solutions for divisions, not reasons for the Corinthians to accept them as necessary. The precarious economic situation of a new Christ group devoted to a Galilean hero that is otherwise unknown in Corinth, and which consists of nine or ten members, all but precludes the likelihood that the group's founder would insist that in-group factions are necessary. Where would the Christ group be if one-third or one-half of its nine or ten members cancelled their membership upon realising that they were not genuine, or after becoming agitated that Paul implied as much?

---

[18] Hans Lietzmann argued that 'v.19 ist entweder resigniert oder ironisch gemeint' in *An die Korinther I/II*, 5th ed. (HNT 9; Tübingen: Mohr Siebeck, 1969), 56. Anthony Thiselton, *First Epistle*, 858–9, alternatively, suggests that Paul quoted a Corinthian saying. This possibility has no implications for how the phrase should be translated. For my engagement with Lietzmann's proposal, see Appendix.

[19] Fee, *First Epistle*, 538.

[20] Dale B. Martin, *The Corinthian Body* (New Haven: Yale University Press, 1995), 74. Martin's quote is from a brief summary of Theissen's work. While the context is a review of scholarship, Martin does support Theissen's conclusions.

[21] See James D. G. Dunn, *1 Corinthians* (Sheffield: Sheffield Academic, 1995), 27; cf. Chester, *Conversion*, 218.

From σχίσματα in 1 Cor 11:18 to the αἱρέσεις in 11:19

A better strategy for interpreting 1 Cor 11:19 is to follow the lead of scholarship on 11:18. In this verse, Paul describes divisions at the Lord's Supper with the word σχίσματα. Colin Roberts, Theodore Skeat, and Arthur Nock's showed in 1926 that an Egyptian Zeus association used this word[22] to refer to its own divisions (*P. Lond.* VII 2193.13 = *AGRW* 295, Philadelphia, Egypt; 69–58 BCE).[23] The association's legal regulations clarify that any divisions (l.13) would be the fault of elected or appointed leaders. The leader (ἡγούμενος) and his assistant (ὑπηρέτης) carried responsibility over the behaviour of members during the feast: 'all are to obey' the officers in all matters pertaining to the association (ll.10–11).[24] When factions (σχίσματα) occur, they signal poor leadership – either the president and assistant pushed ahead with unpopular policies regarding banquet proceedings, or they were unable to fulfill the duties of their offices by preventing σχίσματα in the first place. This papyrus illuminates how talk of σχίσματα in 1 Cor 11:18 would lead rather naturally to a consideration of a leadership change (αἱρέσεις) in 11:19.

In a second association source (*IG* XII, 3 330, Col. C. 260 = *AGRW* 243; Thera, Aegean; 210–195 BCE), elected (αἱρεῖσθαι) leaders are again deemed responsible for proliferation of divisions (διαιρεῖν). This domestic-based association stipulates in its regulations that if the majority voted to do something that would create divisions in the group, a pre-elected supervisory committee had the authority and obligation to seize all decision-making power, and to veto the divisive decision (Col. C. 254–67). As with the Egyptian group, the rise of divisions in this group would signal weak or irresponsible leaders in the elected supervisory committee.

One more example will suffice to establish a connection between divisions (11:18) and poor leadership (11:19). The Athenian Iobacchoi went so far as to threaten leaders with temporary expulsion if they allowed divisive behaviour to go unchecked:

> The penalty ... for the officer in charge of order (εὔκοσμος) if he does not expel those who fight [is temporary expulsion and a

---

[22] The guild misspelt the word as σχίματα.

[23] Colin Roberts, Thodore C. Skeat, and Arthur Darby Nock, 'The Gild of Zeus Hypsistos', *HTR* 29 (1936), 39–88.

[24] The Greek reads: ὑπακούσειν δὲ πάντας τοῦ τε ἡγουμένου κạὶ τ[οῦ] τούτου ὑπηρέτου ἔν τε τοῖς ἀγήκουσι τῶι κοινῶι.

fine up to 25 silver denarii] (*IG* II² 1368.94–5 = *GRA* I 51; Athens, 164/5 CE [Kloppenborg and Harland]).

If needed, the εὔκοσμος officer could request the group's bouncers to help with the physical responsibilities of his office, such as throwing out brawlers who would not leave voluntarily. So, physical restrictions could not be cited as a reason for the officer's allowance of divisions to persist (ll.136–46) – perseverance of divisions (in the form of brawling) was purely a consequence of the εὔκοσμος officer's incompetence.

Paul's prior knowledge that the *ekklēsia*'s leadership was incompetent (1 Cor 6:1–8), combined with new information about divisions (σχίσματα), which tend to be the fault of club leadership, leads rather logically to his suggestion that changes in leadership (i.e., elections, αἱρέσεις) 'were necessary' in order for problems in the jurisdiction of the Christ group's leadership (e.g., management of internal disputes, administration of the banquet) to be resolved.

Elections among the Corinthians

Αἱρέσις is a technical term that, along with its cognates, is commonly used in civic and association sources to describe the election of a magistrate. The noun derives from αἱρεῖν, which, when in middle and passive forms, refers to elections of officers. For example, the Iobacchoi of Athens elected a new treasurer every two years: ταμίαν δὲ αἱρείσθωσαν οἱ ἰόβακχοι ψήφῳ εἰς διετίαν.²⁵ An association of θιασῶται mentions that one of their honourees was an 'elected' official: 'Demetrios, who was elected (αἱρεῖσθαι) secretary by the θιασῶται ... took care of all of the affairs of the association honorably and justly.'²⁶ In another Greek association, a certain Menis was elected (αἱρεῖσθαι) to become the group's treasurer.²⁷ Sometimes members were elected to complete special tasks. The θιασῶται of Bendis in Salamis (Attica) elected a writing team:

> (The association resolves) to elect [αἱρεῖσθαι] three men who, after receiving the money that has been set aside for this purpose, shall set up a stele in the temple and shall inscribe it with this decree and with the names of each of those who have

---

²⁵ 'The Iobakchoi shall elect a treasurer by vote every two years' (*IG* II² 1368.146–7 = *GRA* I 51; Athens, Attica 164/5 CE). This is a slight adaptation of the *GRA* I translation.
²⁶ *IG* II² 1263.5–10 = *GRA* I 11 (Piraeus, Attica; 300/299 BCE).
²⁷ *IG* II² 1271 = *GRA* I 13 (Attica; 299/8 BCE).

been thus crowned; and those elected [αἱρεθέντες] (to do this) shall render an account of the money that was set aside for the votive plaque. The following were elected [αἱρεῖσθαι]: Batrachos, Dokimos and Krates (*SEG* 2:9.8–13 = *GRA* I 21; Salamis, Attica; 243/2 BCE [Kloppenborg and Ascough with slight adaptations]).

We also hear of ones 'additionally elected' such as in *IG* II² 1282 (Athens, Attica; 262/1 BCE), where an unstated number of members were elected to help the supervisor perform a building task: 'the ones elected with (οἱ προσαιρεθέντες) the supervisor Aphrodisios for the building additions to the temple of Ammon' (ll.5–7).²⁸ Classicists commonly draw attention to the frequency with which αἱρεῖσθαι denotes the act of electing a magistrate.²⁹

While the verb, αἱρεῖσθαι, refers to the act of electing, the cognate noun Paul employs refers to the actual election itself. Liddell and Scott list '*choice* or *election* of magistrates' as one signification of αἵρεσις.³⁰ We encounter this meaning well before Paul's first letter to the Corinthians. In the fifth century, Thucydides writes about a difference between being defeated in a democracy and being denied promotion in an oligarchy: ἐκ δὲ δημοκρατίας αἱρέσεως γιγνομένης ῥᾷον τὰ ἀποβαίνοντα ὡς οὐκ ἀπὸ τῶν ὁμοίων ἐλασσούμενός τις φέρει (8.89).³¹ Pseudo-Aristotle speaks frequently about the αἱρέσεις of various officials in Athens' democratic institutions.³² In one instance he discusses the social-economic elites (elected archons) who were members of the

---

²⁸ See also *IG* II² 1258.12–13 where three men are elected (αἱρεῖσθαι) to assist a certain Polyxenos in a legal matter.

²⁹ For example, Ilias N. Arnaoutoglou, *Thusias Heneka Kai Sunousias: Private Religious Associations in Hellenistic Athens* (Yearbook of the Research Centre for the History of Greek Law 37/4; Athens: Academy of Athens, 2003), 104; and Arnold Hugh Martin Jones, 'The Election of the Metropolitan Magistrates in Egypt', *JEA* 24 (1938), 65–72 (71).

³⁰ Henry Stuart Liddell and Robert Scott, *A Greek-English Lexicon*, revised ed. (Oxford: Clarendon Press, 1940), 41.

³¹ 'whereas under a democracy an election is held and every man acquiesces more readily in the result because he feels that those to whom he owes his defeat are not his equals' (Loeb translation [Charles Forster Smith]). The accompanying LCL note clarifies how Thucydides could speak of democratic election candidates as 'unequal': 'in an oligarchy all are of the same class, and the promotion of one is a slight upon the rest; but in a democracy the defeated candidate may claim that the electors were ignorant or prejudiced, that he was not beaten on his merits, and so pass the matter over' (352).

³² For example, *Ath. Pol.* 26.14 (ἀρχόντων αἵρεσιν), 31.9–10, 44.4 (αἵρεσιν/ἀρχαιρεσίας τῶν στρατηγῶν).

Areopagus: ἡ γὰρ αἵρεσις τῶν ἀρχόντων ἀριστίνδην καὶ πλουτίνδην
ἦν, ἐξ ὧν οἱ ᾿Αρεοπαγῖται καθίσταντο (*Ath. Pol.* 3.37).³³ The word
continued to be used in such a manner in the initial centuries of the
Common Era. A third-century report of proceedings of the senate from
Egypt demonstrates this quite well (*P.Oxy.* 1414; 270–5 CE). In this text
αἱρεῖσθαι and αἵρεσις are used interchangeably to refer to the act of
electing a civil servant, and the election itself (ll.17–23).
Sometimes Greeks employed the synonymous verb χειροτονεῖν to
refer to elections or appointments.³⁴ Demosthenes, who quite consistently prefers χειροτονεῖν over αἱρεῖσθαι, actually also employs a phrase
that is analogous to Paul's 'elections among you' (αἱρέσεις ἐν ὑμῖν)
construction: 'But have you not been electing from among yourselves
ten brigadiers and ten generals and ten squadron-leaders and a couple of
cavalry-commanders?' (Demosthenes, *1–4 Philippic* 1.26 (Loeb translation [J. H. Vince]).³⁵ The usage of χειροτονεῖν by early Christ believers
indicates that standard Greek and Roman ordination practices were
known and used within the earliest Christ groups.³⁶
Election is not the sole manner of ordination in Greco-Roman associations. Often, clubs appointed (καθιστάναι) members to their office.³⁷
Other times, an affiliate achieved office through allotment (λαχάνειν), a
method generally reserved for sacerdotal positions.³⁸ In still other cases,
inscriptions remain vague concerning the method of ordination. Many
magistrates simply 'become' (γενέσθαι) officers in the extant sources,
with no further details about the process.³⁹ Paul uses this verb in 11:19
to describe the transformation from regular member to officer,

---

³³ 'For there was an election of archons according to birth and wealth, from which the
ones of the Areopagus were appointed.'

³⁴ Associations: *IRhamnous* II 59 = *GRA* I 27 (Rhamnous, Attica; after 216/15 BCE).
Literary works: Ps.-Aristotle, *Ath. Pol.* 54.5; 61. 4, 5, 7; Demosthenes, *Against Meidias* 15;
and Demosthenes, *Against Boeotus* II, 34.

³⁵ οὐκ ἐχειροτονεῖτε δ᾿ ἐξ ὑμῶν αὐτῶν δέκα ταξιάρχους καὶ στρατηγοὺς καὶ φυλάρχους
καὶ ἱππάρχους δύο.

³⁶ 2 Cor 8:19; Acts 14:23; *Did.* 15:1. For more, see Edwin Hatch, 'Ordination', in
*Dictionary of Christian Antiquities. Comparising the History, Institutions, and Antiquities
of the Christian Church from the Time of the Apostles to the Age of Charlemagne*, 2 vols.,
ed. W. Smith and S. Cheetham (London: J. Murray, 1908), 2.1501–20 (1501).

³⁷ *IG* II² 1278.6 = *GRA* I 17 (Attica; 272/1 BCE); *IG* II² 1277.5 = *GRA* I 15 (Athens,
Attica; 278/7 BCE); *SEG* 2:10.4 (Salamis, Attica; mid III BCE); Acts 6:4; Eusebius, *Hist.
eccl.*, 2.1; cf. Ps.-Aristotle, *Ath. Pol.* 3.37.

³⁸ *IG* II² 1263.39 = *GRA* I 11 (Piraeus, Attica; 300/299 BCE); *IG* II² 1273A.13 = *GRA* I
18 (Piraeus, Attica; 265/4 BCE); *SEG* 2.9.5 = *GRA* I 29 (Piraeus, Attica; 211/0 BCE).

³⁹ *IG* II² 1261A.4 = *GRA* I 9 (Piraeus, Attica; 302/1 BCE); *IG* II² 1297.12 = *GRA* I 24
(Athens, Attica; 236/5 BCE); *IG* II² 1298.14 = *GRA* I 20 (Athens, Attica; 248/7 BCE).

acknowledging that it is through elections (αἱρέσεις) that the ordination process happens in the Christ group.[40] Most cryptic, though, are the sources that simply mention club magistrates without a word on the selection process.[41]

The Approval of Electees

A second term from 1 Cor 11:19 that resembles formulaic election terminology is οἱ δόκιμοι. Interpreters often take the substantive to signify divine eschatological testing,[42] however, that reading drags us into a translation of 11:19 that is unexplained by commentators (i.e., how do eschatological *factions* make known the δόκιμοι in a Christ group?) and fails to fit within Paul's broader take on divisions throughout the letter. The adjective more likely describes a formal scrutiny process to which Corinthians were subjected after being elected to office but before the beginning of their tenure. Civic institutions used a related term to denote a 'scrutiny' (δοκιμασία) of elected or appointed officers of the βουλῆ and other public officials.[43] This procedure occurred between the time when an officer was appointed (through election or sortition) and the time of their actual assumption of the office. The scrutiny consisted of an examination of the electee's full life to determine if he was a 'good and patriotic citizen'.[44] Gabriel Adeleye summarises, 'It was a comprehensive examination which took into consideration a

---

[40] For usage of the term in the context of association elections, see *IG* II² 1261A.4 = *GRA* I 9 (Piraeus, Attica; 302/1 BCE); *IG* II² 1297.12 = *GRA* I 24 (Athens, Attica; 236/5 BCE); *IG* II² 1298.14 = *GRA* I 20 (Athens, Attica; 248/7 BCE). This is a very common verb appearing in a range of contexts. Paul uses it (γένωνται) in 11:19 to describe the transformation from regular member to officer, acknowledging that it is through elections (αἱρέσεις) that this process happens in the Christ group.

[41] For example, see *IG* II² 1291= *GRA* I19 (Piraeus? Attica; mid III BCE) and *IG* II² 1298 = *GRA* I 20 (Athens, Attica; 248/7 BCE).

[42] See, e.g., Johannes Munck, 'The Church without Factions: Studies in 1 Corinthians', in *Paul and the Salvation of Mankind* (London: SCM, 1959), 135–67; Schrage, *Der erste Brief*, 3:21–2; Friedrich Lang, *Die Briefe an die Korinther* (NTD 7; Göttingen and Zürich: Vandenhoeck & Ruprecht, 1994), 148; Thiselton, *First Epistle*, 858–9; Barrett, *First Epistle*, 261–2; Héring, *First Epistle*, 113; Witherington, *Conflict and Community*, 248.

[43] Gabriel Adeleye, 'The Purpose of the *Dokimasia*', *GRBS* 24 (1983), 295–306 (295).

[44] Douglas Maurice MacDowell, *The Law in Classical Athens* (Ithaca: Cornell University, 1978), 168; quoted from Adeleye, 'Purpose', 295. Cf. John S. Kloppenborg, 'The Moralizing of Discourse in Graeco-Roman Associations', in *'The One Who Sows Bountifully': Essays in Honor of Stanley K. Stowers*, ed. Caroline Johnson Hodge, Saul M. Olyan, Daniel Ullucci, and Emma Wasserman (Brown Judaic Studies 356; Providence, Rhode Island: Brown Judaic Studies, 2013), 217–19.

194   *The Election and Crowning of Officers*

candidate's legal qualifications, both as a citizen and for the office in question, and the probity of his life and past political activities.'[45] Civic institutions and associations employed several cognate terms, all of which implied a scrutiny of the officer, when describing elections. For example, δοκιμάζειν is very frequently found to mean 'to approve after scrutiny as fit for a civic office'.[46] Here is an example of the word appearing together with αἱρεῖσθαι in reference to civic elections:

ταμίας δὲ δὴ τῶν τε ἱερῶν χρημάτων ἑκάστοις τοῖς ἱεροῖς καὶ τεμενῶν καὶ καρπῶν τούτων καὶ μισθώσεων κυρίους αἱρεῖσθαι μὲν ἐκ τῶν μεγίστων τιμημάτων τρεῖς εἰς τὰ μέγιστα ἱερά, δύο δ' εἰς τὰ σμικρότερα, πρὸς δὲ τὰ ἐμμελέστατα ἕνα· τὴν δὲ αἵρεσιν τούτων καὶ τὴν δοκιμασίαν γίγνεσθαι καθάπερ ἡ τῶν στρατηγῶν ἐγίγνετο.   (Plato, Laws 6.759–760a)

As treasurers to control the sacred funds in each of the temples, and the sacred glebes, with their produce and their rents, we must elect (αἱρεῖσθαι) from the highest property-classes three men for the largest temples, two for the smaller, and one for the least extensive; and the method of election (αἵρεσις) and testing (δοκιμασίαν) these shall be the same as that adopted in the case of the commanders.
(Translation by Bury [LCL] with my amendments)[47]

Paul's reference to 'the approved ones' (οἱ δόκιμοι) probably betrays a vetting practice adopted by the Corinthians in the manner of the civic institution. After a Corinthian is selected for office, they must undergo scrutiny before taking their new promotion. A Hellenistic association records the procedure as follows in their rule for how a supervisor becomes 'approved' after an election:

ὅπως δὲ ἐπίσσοφός τε ἀπο-
δειχθῇ, καὶ ὁ αἱρεθεὶς ἐγγράφει πάντα τὰ
κατὰ τὸν νόμον, συναχθήτω σύλλογος
ἐπὶ ἐφόρων τῶν σὺν Ἱμέρτωι μηνὸς Διοσ-   270
θύου δεκάται καὶ αἱρεθήτω ἐπίσσοφος·

[45] Gabriel, 'Purpose', 305.
[46] Lysias, *For Mantitheus*, 15.6; Plato, *Laws* 759d; Ps.-Aristotle, *Ath. Pol.* 45.3. Acts records an election process that includes all the components of standard elections: the seven were elected by the general assembly and then 'appointed', and therefore approved, by the apostles thereafter (Acts 6:3–5).
[47] Robert Gregg Bury, *Plato* (LCL 36; vol. 10; Cambridge and London: Harvard University Press, 1926).

In order that the supervisor should be approved . . . let a meeting
be held by the ephorate (leadership) who are with Himertos,
on the tenth of Diosthyos, and (at this time) let the supervisor
be elected. (*IG* XII, 3 330 C = *AGRW* 343; Thera, Aegean;
210–195 BCE [Ascough, Harland, and Kloppenborg]).[48]

In this association, a supervisor (ἐπίσσοφός) is elected (αἱρεῖσθαι, C
1.202) and, later, 'approved' (ἀποδέχεσθαι) by a leadership cohort
headed by a certain Himertos. After receiving approval, the supervisor
would formally begin the office's tenure. It is due to the approval process
('scrutiny') out of which civic and association officers successfully
emerged that they could be called οἱ δόκιμοι, as evidenced not just
from Paul but also from Philo, who describes elected civic officials
this way: συνεξιστιῶντο δὲ καὶ ἄλλοι τῶν παρ' Αἰγυπτίοις δοκίμων
(*Joseph* 201).[49]

Vetting procedures were rather standard in associations. John
Kloppenborg shows that some associations even scrutinised recruits
before allowing them to become members.[50] In their description of the
entrance of new members, the Athenian Iobacchoi association documents a procedure not entirely different from the election and scrutiny
of officers. The club states that prospective members must be approved
(δοκιμάζεσθαι) through a vote (i.e., elected) in order to join the group: 'If
a brother of an Iobakchoi should join, having been approved by a vote, he
shall pay fifty denarii' (ll. 53–5).[51] In this variant of the approval procedure, a vote in favour of accepting a new member produces an 'approved
one'. Associations' mimicry of civic voting procedures and terminology
represents part of a broader practice of adopting civic nomenclature and
activities, reaching far beyond formal scrutiny procedures and elections.

Corinthian Officers as φανεροί

Given the social capital of holding an association office,[52] Paul's identification of the approved (δόκιμοι) *ekklēsia* officers as φανεροί is rather

---

[48] This translation is slightly adapted from *AGRW*'s version.

[49] 'Other Egyptian dignitaries feasted with them' (Colson [LCL]); cf. Campbell,
'Acquiesce', 68. See also *IG* II² 1361.24 = *GRA* I 4 (Piraeus, Attica; 330–4/3).

[50] Kloppenborg, 'Moralizing of Discourse', 216–23.

[51] Translation by Kloppenborg. The Greek reads: ἐὰν δὲ ἰοβάκχου ἀδελφὸς ἰσέρχηται
ψήφῳ δοκιμασθείς, διδότω δηνάριον ν´.

[52] Halsey L. Royden, *The Magistrates of the Roman Professional Collegia in Italy:
From the First to the Third Century A.D.* (Bibliotheca di studi antichi 61; Pisa, Giardini,
1988); Sandra R. Joshel, *Work, Identity, and Legal Status at Rome: A Study of the*

expected. The term simply denotes 'distinctive persons' or the 'worthy'.
Paul's point in labelling *future* electees as 'worthy' could be to distinguish them from the current leaders and, thereby, to imply what we already know from 1 Cor 6:5: Paul does not regard the present leadership to be 'worthy'.

Rendering φανεροί as 'worthy' or 'persons of distinction' fits well within the adjective's range of meanings in antiquity.[53] We find the cognate adjective, ἐπιφανής, in superlative form in our earliest association price declaration to describe Constantine and Maximus as ἐπιφανέστατοι Καίσαρες ('distinguished' or 'notable' Augusti).[54] Several Pauline authors use this word elsewhere as a marker for a notable object or person. Luke speaks of a 'notable sign' (σημεῖον φανερόν) in Acts 4:16; while Paul speaks of his imprisonment as something 'notable' (Phil 1:13).[55]

The notion that approved Corinthians would become φανεροί ('worthy ones') after a vote and scrutiny (δοκιμασία) in their favour is what we should expect in an *ekklēsia* setting. The Athenian Iobacchoi describe a similar procedure in their club, employing typical election language that is also found in 11:19:

μηδενὶ ἐξέστω ἰόβακχον εἶναι, ἐὰν μὴ
πρῶτον ἀπογράψηται παρὰ τῷ ἱερεῖ
τὴν νενομισμένην ἀπογραφὴν καὶ
δοκιμασθῇ ὑπὸ τῶν ἰοβάκχων ψή-   35
φῳ, εἰ ἄξιος φαίνοιτο καὶ ἐπιτήδειος
τῷ Βακχείῳ.

It is not allowed for anyone to become an Iobakchos unless he first registers with the priest the customary notice and is vetted by a vote (δοκιμασθῇ ὑπὸ ... ψήφῳ) of the Iobakchoi (to determine) if he appears to be worthy and

Occupational Inscriptions (Norman, OK: University of Oklahoma Press, 1992), 114–18; Ilias Arnaoutoglou, '*Between* Koinon *and* Idion: Legal and Social Dimensions of Religious Associations in Ancient Athens', in *Kosmos. Essays in Order, Conflict and Community in Classical Athens*, ed. Paul Cartledge, Paul Millett, and Sitta von Reden (Cambridge: Cambridge University Press, 1998), 63–83 (80–1).
    [53] See, e.g., Thucydides (*War* 1.17) who speaks of 'being held back from achieving something notable' (κατείχετο ... φανερὸν ... κατεργάζεσθαι); and Philostratos (*Apollonios*, 2.20) who comments on persons with social capital, or 'persons of distinction' (οἱ φανερώτεροι).
    [54] *P.Ant.* I 38.25 (Antinoopolis, Egypt; 301 CE).
    [55] The word carries similar implications in Matt 12:16; Mark 3:12, and 6:14.

suitable (ἄξιος φαίνοιτο καὶ ἐπιτήδειος) for the Bakcheion (translation by Kloppenborg with slight adaptation).[56] In this passage, the outcome of a vote in someone's favour is their appearance of worthiness, just as in 1 Cor 11:19. Designating office holders as worthy and distinguished affirms the rather obvious reality that incumbency provided the officer with social enhancement (as long as they performed their role honourably). Language of being 'shown' as legitimated appears not only in the Iobacchoi's description of electing new members but also in another association's articulation of the elected (αἴρεσθαι) officers as 'being shown as approved' (ἀποδέχεσθαι) (*IG* XII, 3 330 = *AGRW* 243, Col. C. 267–8; Thera, Aegean; 210–195 BCE). If οἱ δόκιμοι were elected magistrates, then 'notable', 'distinguished', or 'worthy' are appropriate translations of φανεροί. The long-standing alternative that 'becoming manifest' (φανερὸς γίγνεσθαι) holds eschatological meaning seems forced. These are, individually, very common words that need to be interpreted on a case-by-case basis. Amphilochios Papathomas recently observed that they were commonly placed together without eschatological significance in first-century papyri.[57]

The Continuity of 1 Cor 11:18–20

In Timothy Brookins's response to an earlier version of my reading of 11:19, he helpfully questioned the continuity of 11:18–20 on the elections theory. Brookins claimed that by translating αἱρέσεις as 'elections', the continuity within this sequence is disrupted and, on the whole, that my 'interpretation makes 11.19, as it were, an island'.[58]

As a preliminary concern with Brookins's assessment of the passage, he fails to consider questions related to the practices of participants at club banquets, which is the topic of 11:18–34. How does food distribution work in the private cultic groups? What would the word αἱρέσεις signify to members of an association? Who are the typical parties of σχίσματα in cultic groups? What role do banquet leaders play in

---

[56] Kloppenborg, 'Moralizing of Discourse', 218.

[57] 'Man sollte jedoch den Umstand nicht außer Acht lassen, dass der Ausdruck im I. Jh. N. Chr. Auch eine ausgeprägte juristische Konnotation hatte, da er um diese Zeit vorwiegend als Klauselteil in Ammenverträgen und in Eingaben an die Behörden verwendet wurde.' Arzt-Grabner, et al., *1. Korinther* (Papyrologische Kommentare zum Neuen Testament 2; Göttingen: Vandenhoeck & Ruprecht, 2006), 152.

[58] Brookins, 'Supposed Election', 432.

disorderly conduct at club meals? Previous interpreters have realised that both Paul's theology as well as Corinthian social behaviour shaped the discourse in 11:18–20 and, therefore, both need to be part of the interpreter's consideration.[59] Brookins's reading of the verses shows no concern for any of these questions.

Since Paul had no need to describe for the Corinthians the details of their own routine social activities, clues must be sought elsewhere concerning ancient dining practices in clubs, specifically the epigraphy and papyri of other private groups who met regularly for dinner. The range of activities attested in these sources help to control speculation about how meals, leadership, and conflicts worked in a Christ group. After considering these data, Paul's language in 1 Cor 11:18–20 can then be fitted into spectrums of ancient Mediterranean cult group practices, placed within broader motifs found in 1 Corinthians, and protected against anachronistic assumptions about the Corinthians. By analysing 1 Cor 11:18–20 – a mere three verses – in isolation from a massive body of analogous evidence on the meal practices and leadership activities that Paul describes in 1 Cor 11:18–20, it is impossible for Brookins to analyse the continuity of the verses on either theory, especially since Paul's Greek allows for various workable translations.[60]

In describing my explanation for the transition between 11:18–19, Brookins argues that it necessitates the following translation of the second half of v.18 and the first part of v.19: 'I believe the report *because* (γάρ) elections are necessary.'[61] He correctly observes that this would be an odd reason for Paul to believe the report. What do elections have to do with the trustworthiness of a report about misbehaviour at the Corinthian banquet? This is where attention to associative practices becomes crucial. But, first, it would be helpful to offer a complete translation of vv.18–19:

> I hear there are divisions [σχίσματα] among you, and I believe the report in part because [γάρ] elections are necessary in order for *the approved ones* (as opposed to the irresponsible current leaders) to become the leaders/persons of distinction [φανεροί].

Paul believes the report, in my reading, because he already had reason to evaluate the current φανεροί (persons of distinction; officers) as

[59] See, e.g., Theissen, *Social Setting*, 164; and Campbell, 'Does Paul Acquiesce', 61, and throughout.

[60] See Campbell's alternative reading and analysis of the Greek in 11.19, in 'Does Paul Acquiesce?', 61–70.

[61] Brookins, 'Supposed Elections', 9 (emphasis original).

irresponsible. This is an ordinary reason for someone to believe that divisions might be happening in a club; poor officers tended to be blamed for divisiveness in associations. By this point in the letter, Paul had already written off the Corinthians' leaders as incompetent (6:1–8). Paul now believes the report about divisiveness because divisiveness is just one natural outcome of electing irresponsible leaders. Elections are necessary to fix the problem since the root problem is poor leadership, not divisions. The phrase 'elections are necessary' is equivalent to an expression of disapproval for the current leadership. To paraphrase Paul: 'I believe the report about divisions because your current leaders are irresponsible and you need to elect new ones of whom you now approve.'

We know from 6:1–8 that Paul, by the time he gets to 11:19, does not approve of the way the leaders have handled themselves with regards to conflict resolution. In 6:1–8, the *ekklēsia* is lambasted for not enforcing (or having in place) mechanisms to resolve internal disputes outside of public courts. Paul does not say who is at fault for the internal disputes in 6:1–8 (leaders? everyone?), but the association data consistently indicate that a club's officers had charge over enforcing proper behaviour.[62] We even have data showing that officials held the responsibility of ensuring that members did not seek public courts for conflict resolution – the very problem in 6:1–8. Here is a particularly descriptive example of this phenomenon:

> If someone comes to blows, the one who struck shall file a report with the priest or the vice priest, who shall without fail convene a meeting and the Iobakchoi shall judge by a vote with the priest presiding. The offender shall be penalized by not being permitted to enter for a time – as long as it seems appropriate – and (by paying) a fine up to twenty-five silver denarii. The same penalty shall also be applied to the one who is beaten and does not go to the priest or the archibakchos but (instead) brings a charge with the public courts. The penalty shall be the same for the officer in charge of order (*eukosmos*) if he does not expel those who fight. (*IG* II² 1368.84–95 = *GRA* I 51; Athens, Attica; 164/5 CE [Kloppenborg and Ascough]).

---

[62] Some of the many examples of officers being responsible for the enforcement of their clubs' bylaws include *P.Mich.* V 244.18–20 = *AGRW* 301 (Tebtynis, Egypt; 43 CE); *P.Mich.* V 245.37–42 = *AGRW* 302 (Tebtynis, Egypt; 47 CE); *IG* II² 1368.99–100, 102–7 = *GRA* I 51 (Athens, Attica; 164/5 CE); *IG* II² 1292 = *GRA* I 26 (Athens or Piraeus, Attica; 215/4 BCE); *IDelos* 1520.66–8, 88–9 = *AGRW* 224 (Delos, Asia Minor; after 153/2 CE).

In this regulation, it is the responsibility of an officer (i.e., the priest or vice priest) to call an internal court meeting upon being approached by a member who was struck by another member. This internal procedure was meant to replace the need for members to seek justice at public courts. After the association made a decision on the case, the officer (i.e., priest or vice priest) must then expel the guilty party for a period of time that seems best to them.[63] Several additional association sources also forbid usage of public courts.[64] When Paul criticises the Corinthians for not having (or enforcing) an internal club justice system like this, the current leaders would likely endure most of the blame if the Corinthians were typical in this respect since it was commonplace for ancient associations to give their magistrates charge of maintaining good order and proper conduct. In summary of my transition from vv.18–19, news from Chloe's people (1:11)[65] about the leadership's failure to properly manage *ekklēsia* banquets is believable to Paul (and is just further indication of what Paul already knows) *for* it affirms that 'elections are necessary in order that approved ones become persons of distinction [i.e. officers]'.

The specific banquet problem that 'elections' would fix is the club's current food-distribution policy (11:20), as I argue in the second part of this chapter. New officers bring the hope that food-distribution problems might be resolved adequately.[66] Indeed, if the *ekklēsia* would prefer that a perceived food-distribution problem be solved, then the new officers should better implement it, otherwise they might not be voted customary honours, an attested punishment for irresponsible officers in other associations.[67] The key to understanding the continuity in vv.18–20 on the elections theory is engagement with the way that ancient cult groups organised their meals (the primary topic in

---

[63] The quoted passage does not specify that the priest or vice-priest unilaterally makes this decision, but elsewhere in the inscription the group leaves decisions such as this to the priest (ll.102–7).

[64] For example, *P.Mich.* V 243.7–8 = *AGRW* 300 (Tebtynis, Egypt; 14–37 CE); and *P.Lond.* VII 2193.6–17 = *AGRW* 295 (Philadelphia, Egypt; 69–58 BCE).

[65] Alternatively, the report could be from Stephanas and company (16:17–18).

[66] For a club banquet where only officers are guaranteed shares of food, see *IG* II² 1368.117–25 = *GRA* I 51 (Athens, Attica; 164/5 CE).

[67] One association blatantly forbids commendations for irresponsible officers (*IG* II² 1328.14–15 = *GRA* I 34; Piraeus, Attica; 183/2 or 175/4 BCE). Others stipulated that officers could be fined for misbehaviour. An officer slapped with a fine might also have trouble passing the scrutiny at the end of their tenure and, therefore, risked being denied of formal commendation. See *IDelos* 1520.66–8, 88–9 = *AGRW* 224 (Delos, Asia Minor; after 153/2 CE); *CIL* XIV 2112, II.8–9 = *AGRW* 310 (Lanuvium, Italy; 136 CE).

11:17–34) and familiarity with the lines along which divisions tended to be drawn in club disputes and banquets.

The language in 1 Cor 11:19 is what we should expect when reading about real elections within an ancient Greek institution. Paul does not spend more than a few words on the topic, which suggests that the Corinthians did not require lessons on how to elect their officers. Greeks had been electing magistrates into civic and associative orders for hundreds of years before Paul wrote 1 Corinthians, so we should not suspect that Paul would need to convince them to adopt the practice, either. We can also be relatively sure that the Corinthians valued the process of electing and scrutinising *ekklēsia* functionaries since Paul tells them in 2 Cor 8:16–24, in an attempt to garner their trust, that the transfer of the Jerusalem collection will be done by elected and scrutinised dignitaries. One of the emissaries was elected (χειροτονεῖν) by the congregations for completion of administrative duties, and the other was selected somehow and then scrutinised (δοκιμάζειν).[68]

In 1 Cor 11:18–19 Paul is suggesting to the Corinthians that the real answer to their banquet problems (i.e., σχίσματα) is elections when the time is right. In other words, he explicitly lays responsibility for the banquet issues on the shoulders of the current magistrates responsible for banquet accommodations, food distribution, and the overall structure of the meal.[69] Elections are necessary because elected and scrutinised officers (not social elites) ran the banquet, as was typical in associations throughout the ancient Mediterranean.

Strengthening the Weak at the Corinthian Banquet

For the past four decades, the majority of interpreters have contended that the authority figures at the Corinthian banquet were fixed leaders – namely, the socially strong. Moreover, it is assumed, no mechanisms existed to democratise leadership through annual elections or other

[68] Edwin Hatch ('Ordination', 1501–20) has assembled a vast amount of data showing consistency between civic modes of ordination and those found within the early Christian literature. His article throws light on data from the first century; however, it unfortunately neglects the usage of αἵρεσις / αἱρεῖσθαι in civic ordinations. Hatch's overall proposal that Christ believers ordinated leaders the same way as Greeks and Romans is very effectively supported with much data.

[69] This conclusion directly opposes Schweizer's (*Church Order*, 187): 'This ministry [of the Lord's Supper] never appears as a special gift of grace, nor as an office. In I Cor 11.17ff. Paul cannot appeal to anyone who is responsible for the proper conduct of the Lord's Supper.'

means of choosing rotating leaders. Gerd Theissen famously suggested, 'the *wealthy Christians* not only ate by themselves and began before the regular Lord's Supper, but also had more to eat.'[70] Anthony Thiselton recently posited that the divisions were mostly between 'first-class and second-class guests at dinner';[71] Gordon Fee contended that the divisions result from the wealthy 'acting merely as the rich would always act with poorer guests in their homes';[72] and Jerome Murphy O'Connor proposed:

> It became imperative for the host to divide his guests into two categories: the first-class believers were invited into the triclinium while the rest stayed outside. Even a slight knowledge of human nature indicates the criterion used. The host must have been a wealthy member of the community and so he invited into the triclinium his closest friends among the believers, who would have been of the same social class. The rest could take their places in the atrium, where conditions were greatly inferior.[73]

In such a system, the same few Corinthians would derive social benefits from the structure of the meal, and the Corinthian banquet would offer no opportunity for the apparently economically weak members to earn status achievements.

There is little direct evidence that divisions and hostilities happened in associations between subgroups of socially strong and socially weak members.[74] Conversely, associations seem particularly concerned with

---

[70] Theissen, *Social Status*, 155 (emphasis added).

[71] Thiselton, *First Epistle*, 858.

[72] Fee, *First Epistle*, 539.

[73] Jerome Murphy O'Connor, *St. Paul's Corinth. Texts and Archaeology* (Good News Studies 6; Wilmington, DE: Michael Glazier, 1983), 159. While Murphy-O'Connor's thesis remains influential, Horrell provides a robust alternative in his investigation of domestic architecture used by the lower socio-economic strata of Corinthian society ('Domestic Space', 349–69). Horrell's overall contribution stands even though there are difficulties in his analysis of the buildings 1 and 3 on East Theatre Street. For these, see Daniel N. Schowalter, 'Seeking Shelter in Roman Corinth: Archaeology and the Placement of Paul's Communities', in *Corinth in Context: Comparative Studies on Religion and Society*, ed. Steven J. Friesen, Daniel N. Schowalter, and James Walters (Supplements to Novum Testamentum 134; Leiden: Brill, 2010), 327–41 (333–4).

[74] Two rather lengthy and famous inscriptions come from clubs whose members were both slaves and of free status. Since both contained legal regulations, we might expect that conflict between the socially strong and socially weak would be anticipated by the groups, and that the inscriptions would include a few preventative bylaws, if they were typical problems in associations. It is striking that such regulations are absent from these inscriptions and, indeed, absent from other socially heterogeneous clubs, as well. See

fights between officers and regular members. This is to be expected. Officers tended to recline on better couches than those reserved for regular members, and they were given extra portions of food. We can imagine how an irresponsible officer would attract hostility from a regular member who ate half the portion size as that of the magistrate and reclined in a less honourable couch.[75]

Association bylaws show that some clubs attempted to prevent hostilities between officers and regular members. In a papyrus from Tebtynis (*P. PragueDem.* 1; 137 BCE), it is agreed that fines will result for officers who strike members, for members who hit officers, for officers who threaten members, for anybody who threatens officers, and for anybody who insults officers. The fee for striking an officer is twice as high (100 deben) as the fee for striking a regular member (50 deben).[76] The Lanuvium inscription (*CIL* XIV 2112 = *AGRW* 310; 136 CE) also attempts to prevent hostilities between officers and regular members. As in the Egyptian association, the Lanuvium group's leaders performed administrative duties at the banquet, and its *quinquennalis* received a double portion at the meal (II.17–19, 29–31). This group specified that 'any member who uses any abusive or insolent language to a president (*quinquennalis*) at a banquet shall be fined twenty sesterces' (ll.2.27–8) – a bylaw possibly attesting to officers' tendencies to become obnoxious and involved in factitiousness.

A second-century association from Liopesi (Attica) provides a concrete example of why a regular member might hurl an insult at an officer:

> Those who agree to pick up the pork and the wine[77] who do not
> hand them over during the year that they are providing the

---

*SIG*³ 985 = *AGRW* 121 (Philadelphia, Lydia, Asia Minor; late II–early I BCE); *CIL* XIV 2112 = *AGRW* 310 (Lanuvium, Italy; 136 CE).

[75] It was very common for officers to enjoy control over cult banquet proceedings and receive more food than regular members. See, e.g., *SEG* 31:122 = *GRA* I 50 (Attica; early II CE); *P.Lond.* VII 2193.8, 11–12 = *AGRW* 295 (Philadelphia, Egypt; 69–58 BCE); *P.Mich.* VIII 511 (unknown provenance; early III CE); *IG* II² 1368 = *GRA* I 51 (Athens, Attica; 165/4 CE).

[76] See Andrew Monson, 'The Ethics and Economics of Ptolemaic Religious Associations', *Ancient Society* 36 (2006), 221–36. For another association bylaw that explicitly distinguishes between offence against officers and offences against regular members, see *P. LilleDem.* 29 (Qus, Egypt; 223 BCE).

[77] An analogy to this practice can be observed from a first-century beer account. Here, we find the record of an association officer picking up beer for his club (*P.Tebt.* II 401.23; Tebtynis, Egypt; after 14 CE).

dinners shall be fined a double portion (*SEG* 31:122.20–2 = *GRA* I 50; early II CE [Kloppenborg and Ascough]).[78]

It is imaginable that if an incompetent functionary was responsible for procuring pork and wine, conflict might result between the functionary and the club's regular members at banquets when the functionary failed to bring the appropriate amount of food. If the incompetent functionary reclined in a better couch than disgruntled regular members and also was awarded more food than regular members – and in addition to all this, behaved haughtily – they were as vulnerable to a verbal or physical attack from a regular member: a situation that associations attempted to curtail time and again by writing bylaws prohibiting regular members from attacking officers.

That club officers would be targets and perpetrators of ill-will in Egypt, Italy, and Greece is partially a manifestation of heightened status concerns that accompany association common meals. At these events, participants were visibly ranked, and officers enjoyed status distinctions in the form of bigger food portions, better couches on *triclinia*, and honourable roles in presiding over the evening's proceedings.[79] Given the authority and, perhaps, pretension, of some officers, it is not surprising to find them participating in, and sometimes even to blame for, factitious behaviour.[80]

Food Distribution at the Corinthian Banquet

Paul mentions in passing that he received a report (1 Cor 1:11; 11:18) suggesting that only some members were in control of food distribution

---

[78] Slightly adapted from Kloppenborg and Ascough's translation.

[79] Koenraad Verboven, 'The Associative Order, Status and Ethos of Roman Businessmen in Late Republic and Early Empire', *Athenaeum* 95 (2007), 861–93 (885).

[80] Officers were not only at the centre of banquet factions, but also could foster controversies during award ceremonies. Disgruntled members sometimes tried to prevent voted honours (e.g., olive wreaths, honorific inscriptions) from being rewarded to magistrates. In response, some associations felt it necessary to assume officers that their voted honours would be announced in front of their peers even if their enemies plotted against them. See *AM* 66 228 no. 4.18–20 = *GRA* I 39 (Athens, Attica; 138/7 BCE); *IG* II² 1273AB.22–3 = *GRA* I 18 (Piraeus, Attica; 265/4 BCE); *IG* II² 1292.16–17= *GRA* I 26 (Attica; 215/4 BCE); *IG* II² 1297.17–18 = *GRA* I 24 (Athens, Attica; 236/5 BCE); cf. Kloppenborg, 'Greco-Roman *Thiasoi*', 209–13. See also the fines threatened to prevent disgruntled members from snubbing officers by means of intentional absenteeism when magistrates were awarded gifts of honour or displayed status in other ways. *IG* II² 1339.7–8 = *GRA* I 46 (Athens, Attica; 57/6 BCE); *IG* II² 1368.96–9 = *GRA* I 51 (Athens, Attica; 164/5 CE); *IG* IX/1² 670.13–15 = *GRA* I 61 (Physkos, Central Greece; mid II CE); cf. Kloppenborg, 'Membership Practices'.

(11:21–2), and that they distributed food unevenly. Indeed, some banquet participants 'had nothing' (οἱ μὴ ἔχοντες, 1 Cor 11:22). While scholars generally assume that these 'have-nots' were destitute members in the *ekklēsia* (i.e., the weak),[81] this is now untenable in light of the data presented in Chapter 3: membership in a Christ group is an economic indicator, which explains why Wayne Meeks could correctly observe that the Pauline epistles do not evidence people 'having nothing' in their life or, in other words, people living in the lowest social strata.[82] It is most likely, I would suggest, that 'those with nothing' (οἱ μὴ ἔχοντες) were members who had nothing at the Corinthian Christ group's recent banquets rather than those who had nothing to their name in their whole life. They lacked food portions at recent banquets because after each of the officers 'took first' (προλαμβάνειν, 11:21) their unregulated portion, nothing was left for ordinary members. This unfortunate situation (in the estimation of some Corinthians; 1:11) resulted in Paul's call for the group to elect competent (δόκιμος) officers. First Corinthians 11:17–22 is about the banquet, after all, not the overall economic status of members. This is a more tenable reading than what has been offered previously because it is grounded in an understanding of economic trends in associations.

Our new reading of 11:17–22 allows us to examine food procurement practices in associations in order to further understand the routine banquet practices of the Corinthian group to which Paul only alludes. The mechanisms for bringing food to club banquets and then dividing portions among participants varied from club to club. But, generally, the officers held the responsibility of bringing food to common meals. The host (ἑστιάτωρ) in an Athenian association of ὀργεῶνες is described as having accepted the responsibility to do the following:

> He must render an account of whatever he has expended and must not spend more than the income. Let him distribute (shares of) the meat to the *orgeōnes* who are present – and up to a half-share to their sons – and to the women of *orgeōnes*, giving to free women the same share and up to a half share to their

---

[81] Horrell (*Social Ethos*, 95) argues, '1 Cor 11.17–34 clearly shows that some in the community could afford lavish amounts of food and drink, in a way which contrasted them with other community members who are described as τοὺς μὴ ἔχοντας, 'the have-nots' (1 Cor 11.22).' See also Barrett, *First Epistle*, 263; Theissen, *First Epistle*, 150, 865; Murphy-O'Connor, *St. Paul's Corinth*, 161; Bruce Winter, 'The Lord's Supper at Corinth: An Alternative Reconstruction', *RTR* 37 (1978), 73–82; Raymond F. Collins, *First Corinthians* (Collegeville, MN: Liturgical Press, 1999), 418.

[82] Meeks, *First Urban*, 73.

daughters and up to a half-share for one attendant. Let him hand
over the woman's share to the man (*Agora* 16:161.16–23 = *GRA*
1:14; Athens; III BCE [Kloppenborg and Ascough]).

This association specifies that the ἑστιάτωρ must purchase the food – not
spending more money than he is given from the treasury (ll.16–17) – and
also distribute food portions to members at the banquet on the basis of
the club's distribution policy. The rotating *magistri cenarum* of the
Lanuvium association funded and supplied food for six of the club's
meals each year (*CIL* XIV 2112.II.14–16). An association of hymn
signers in Pergamon delegates to its officers (εὔκοσμος, ἱερεύς,
γραμματεύς) the responsibility to procure bread, crowns, incense, table
settings, and sacrifices without reimbursement (*IPergamon* II 274 B-D =
AGRW 117; 129–138 CE). In an association of ἐρανισταί from second-
century Attica, mention is made of οἱ ἐργολαβήσαντες ('the ones who
work for hire' or 'the ones who contract for the execution of work').[83]
They 'contract' to obtain pork and wine for a year. Ilias Arnaoutoglou
observes that hosts (ἑστιάτορες) and sacrifice makers (ἱεροποιοί) commonly shared responsibilities such as these.[84] In light of the broader
pattern of magistrates bringing food to club banquets, I would suggest
that responsibilities of food procurement in the Corinthian group fell to
their officers rather than to the so-called socially strong.

Unregulated Portions at the Corinthian Meal

There is one immediate issue with reading οἱ μὴ ἔχοντες as members
who brought nothing to the banquet (i.e., as non-officers rather than as
socially weak members): namely, associations' distribution policies
often ensured that each participant would receive a portion even if they
brought nothing.[85] Why, then, did some Corinthian ordinary members
'have nothing' at recent Corinthian banquets?

It was not always the case that ordinary members were promised food
at banquets. In some instances, associations allowed magistrates to take
unregulated shares of food before regular members had an opportunity to

---

[83] *SEG* 31:122 = *GRA* I 50 (Liopesi, Attica; early II CE).

[84] Arnaoutoglou, *Thusias*, 107–8.

[85] For example, the Lanuvium inscription attests to all members receiving portions, even
though larger portions were taken by the *quinquennalis* and messenger (*CIL* XIV
2112.17–19 = *AGRW* 310; 136 CE). The ἐρανισταί mentioned earlier specify that the priest
will receive a double portion but everyone else will be guaranteed regular allotments (*SEG*
31:122.16–20 = *GRA* I 50; Liopesi, Attica; early II CE).

take whatever size portion was left for them (e.g., *IG* II² 1368.117–25 = *GRA* I 51 [Athens, Attica; 164/5 CE]). Paul provides some indication of a similar situation at the Corinthian meal. The *ekklēsia* magistrates were able to προλαμβάνειν 'take first', and apparently did so with the following result:

> ἕκαστος γὰρ τὸ ἴδιον δεῖπνον προλαμβάνει ἐν τῷ φαγεῖν, καὶ ὃς μὲν πεινᾷ, ὃς δὲ μεθύει. μὴ γὰρ οἰκίας οὐκ ἔχετε εἰς τὸ ἐσθίειν καὶ πίνειν; ἢ τῆς ἐκκλησίας τοῦ θεοῦ καταφρονεῖτε, καὶ καταισχύνετε τοὺς μὴ ἔχοντας; τί εἴπω ὑμῖν; ἐπαινέσω ὑμᾶς; ἐν τούτῳ οὐκ ἐπαινῶ.

> For each (leader) takes their own dinner first when it comes time to eat, and someone is hungry, and someone becomes drunk. Do you not have homes where you are able to eat and drink or do you despise the *ekklēsia* of God and dishonour the ones who have nothing? What should I say to you? Should I commend you? For this, I do not commend you.

Since some members had no food and were hungry, Paul's detail that ἕκαστος 'takes their own food' (11:21) cannot denote each banquet participant. It needs to reference only those who actually took food. The next verse makes it probable that the Corinthians who took food were the ones in charge of food distribution (i.e., *ekklēsia* officers). Here, Paul refuses to ἐπαινεῖν the ones who προλαμβάνειν (11:22). Ἔπαινος in this context would be expected only by officers in charge of food procurement and distribution, not all participants. Paul, then, informs us that the act of 'taking first' (προλαμβάνειν) was performed by the current leaders with the result that some regular members received no portions. The problem was not *that* they 'took first', but, rather, it was the way that these leaders προλαμβάνειν. In other words, the issue was that they took unregulated shares of food, greedily leaving nothing for regular members.

The food distribution policy at the Iobacchoi's winter feast on the 10th day of Elaphebolion provides an instructive analogy. This group met on several occasions throughout the year (ll.43–4, 120), but the inscription contains information concerning food distribution only at the Elaphebolion meal. The relevant lines read as follows:

> The *archibakchos* shall sacrifice the victim to the god and make a libation on the tenth day of Elaphebolion. When the parts (of the sacrificial victims) are distributed, let them go to the priest, the vice-priest, the *archibakchos*, the treasurer, the

one playing the cowherd (*boukolikos*), 'Dionysos', 'Kore', 'Palaimon', 'Aphrodite', 'Proteurythmos'. Let these roles be apportioned among all by lot. (*IG* II² 1368.117–27 = *GRA* I 51; [Kloppenborg and Harland])

Here, only the officers and specified role players are guaranteed shares of food. Dennis Smith is probably right that the other members took what was left after the officers selected their own portions.[86] One can imagine how problems might occur if the officers 'took first' in such a way as to leave others 'having nothing'. Behaviour such as this might lead to the very types of divisions between officers and regular members that many association bylaws sought to prevent.

Unregulated food portions also seem to be permitted in the Egyptian association of Zeus Hypsistos, where the president (ἡγούμενος) is responsible for making (ποιεῖσθαι) a monthly banquet for 'all the contributors' (συνεισφόροις δὲ πᾶσι) (*P. Lond.* VII 2193.8 = *AGRW* 295; Philadelphia, Egypt; 69–58 BCE). The papyrus provides no information concerning shares of food but, notably, the club's two officers, the president and the attendant, have the authority to make all decisions concerning food distribution at the banquet and therefore could take as much as they thought fit since 'All are to obey the president and his servant in matters pertaining to the corporation' (ll.11–12).

Many associations foresaw the very problem that Paul references in 11:21 (i.e., officers taking all the food before the ordinary members have a turn). Association bylaws pertaining to officers' shares both promise the officers an honourably large share and, crucially, also limit the portion of the officers' share so that there is enough food and wine for other members. In an inscription from Attica, we come across a club's bylaw limiting its leading officer (ἀρχερανιστής) to a 'double portion, except for the wine' at the association's banquets (*SEG* 31:122.19–20 = *GRA* I 50; Liopesi, Attica; early II CE). In the regulations of a salt merchants guild (*P.Mich.* V 245 = *AGRW* 302; Tebtynis, Egypt; 47 CE), there is attestation to two officers, the supervisor (ἐπιμελητής) and the leader (ἡγούμενος). These magistrates do not have the authority to drink all the beer at the banquets because one bylaw stipulates that 'It is agreed that they [i.e., the association] shall drink always on the twenty-fifth of each month with each member having a liquid measure of beer' (ll.34–5; [Kloppenborg]). This clause is equally about securing and limiting an amount of beer for each member – a measure cannot be

---

[86] Smith, *From Symposium*, 116.

secured for each member unless everyone is limited to a measure each. In another Athenian club, various regulations limit the portions of banquet participants: for example, some participants are restricted to 'up to (εἰς) half a share' (*Agora* 16:161.19–22 = *GRA* I 14; Athens, Attica; early III BCE). These inscriptions demonstrate how the specification of officers' extra food shares functioned to achieve a balance where magistrates would receive appropriate levels of status affirmation through their portions while regular members would be guaranteed that there would be enough food to go around even after officers take first.

The Iobacchoi and the Zeus Hypsistos associations, like the Corinthians, did not include such a safeguard against food depletion at their banquets. This probably indicates that good order could be maintained even at club banquets without restrictions on officers' food portions as long as the officers were not so concerned with status affirmation that they would be willing to humiliate (καταισχυνεῖν, 1 Cor 11:22) their peers by leaving them with no food.

Summary of 1 Cor 11:18–22

A coherent reconstruction of the food distribution issue in 1 Cor 11:18–22, one which avoids the problems of previous exegeses, is now possible. The *ekklēsia* did not limit officials' food portions at Christ group banquets. This, coupled with the emergence of greedy (in Paul's description) magistrates, led to hostilities between officers and regular members over food portions. Each Corinthian officer took first (προλαμβάνειν) their unregulated share, failing to show restraint, according to Chloe or Stephanas.[87] This left subscription-paying regular

---

[87] Interpreters remain almost unanimous in the opinion that Paul learnt of the banquet problems through an oral report rather than from the Corinthians' letter. There are a few reasons for this. For one, Barrett has observed that the divisive banquet situation would have been an embarrassment for the Corinthians and therefore left out of their letter to Paul (*First Epistle*, 261). A second reason to suppose an oral report is that when Paul begins his instructions about the common meal, he tells the Corinthians that he 'hears (ἀκούειν) that there are divisions among you' (1 Cor 11:18). This gives the impression that some of his audience was unaware that Paul knew this information. Thiselton supposes, 'Paul's redescription of *what he understands* to be taking place at the Lord's Supper . . . indicates that he is not responding to a question first raised by the addressees, but initiates the raising of an urgent matter for censure and re-education. This is prompted by oral reports of occurrences and practices at Corinth' in *First Epistle*, 849, emphasis added). Two emissary teams reached Paul prior to the composition of 1 Cor 11:17–34: Chloe's people (1:11), and the group of Stephanas, Fortunatus, and Achaicus (16:17). It is impossible to determine which travellers made the report.

members without food, a problem that some other associations anticipated and prevented by specifying in their bylaws that officers must
take no more than a certain amount of (extra) food so that there would
be enough for everyone else. Some other associations were like the
Corinthian group in allowing their magistrates to take unregulated
portions of food, which illustrates that even the Corinthians' policy
could work in practice under responsible leaders.[88] Paul advised the
Corinthians to elect a new leadership because the present leaders –
not the group's unregulated food distribution policy – were the root
problems behind *ekklēsia* divisions. A motion to change the club's
food distribution policy might be forwarded by the new magistrates if
they deemed it to be in the long-term interest of the *ekklēsia*.

In the short term, Paul encouraged the magistrates to restrain themselves, even though the Christ group's bylaws did not require them to
do so – they should eat at home if that would make it easier for them to
leave more food for the others (11:22). If Paul were familiar with the
ethos of association life,[89] he would know that this short-term solution
would never work, and hence, it would explain why he also suggested
elections as a resolution to the group's food-distribution problems. It
would not matter if the current leadership ate at home prior to the club
banquet since the point of taking large food portions at an *ekklēsia*
banquet was to be seen doing so: these meals functioned as public displays of status, not as subsistence meals.[90]

[88] The Iobacchoi, who left officers' portions unregulated for their Elaphebolion meal,
diplomatically included in their bylaw direct mention of the temporary tenure of these
offices and, thereby, highlighted the reality that all members would eventually be in the
position to take unregulated portions: τὰ δὲ ὀνόματα αὐτῶν συνκληρούσθω πᾶσι
(ll.125–7) ... ταμίαν δὲ αἱρείσθωσαν οἱ ἰόβακχοι ψήφῳ εἰς διετίαν (ll.146–7).

[89] Peter Arzt-Grabner recently suggested that Paul, as a craft worker, would have been
familiar with practices in occupational guilds. This is discernible to Arzt-Grabner particularly in Paul's framing of the *ekklēsia*'s sombre response to a member's misbehaviour in 2
Cor 7:9–11. Following Andrew Monson, Arzt-Grabner suggests that membership in
associations functioned in part to convey to outside society that these individuals were
honest and upstanding people who could abide by associations' behaviour ethics and who
would make good business partners and social colleagues. As a result, associations needed
to threaten misbehaviours that endangered trustworthiness, and the reputation of the club as
a 'trust network', particularly harshly – not unlike what we find Paul describing rather
accurately in this passage. See Peter Arzt-Grabner, *2. Korinther* (Papyrologische
Kommentare zum Neuen Testament 4. Göttingen: Vandenhoeck & Ruprecht, 2014),
376–81.

[90] Katherine M. D. Dunbabin, *The Roman Banquet: Images of Conviviality* (New York:
Cambridge University Press, 2004), 72–102; Ernest Will, 'Banquets et salles de banquet
dans les cultes de la Grèce et de l'Empire romain', in *Mélanges d'histoire ancienne et*

The deprivation suffered by the so-called have nots (whose overall economic status is unknown) lasted only temporarily, and it was felt exclusively within the context of *ekklēsia* meals as far as Paul lets on. Paul provides no information concerning their economic positions relative to the group's current leaders, but they cannot be imagined as especially weak economically in outside society given the one financial activity of theirs of which we are aware: joining a Christ group. Moreover, their ranks were not statically weak even within the context of the *ekklēsia*. Upon the end of the current *ekklēsia* magistrates' tenures, new elections would dismantle the current order and potentially result in promotion for some among the weak.

Honours for Banquet Administrators

With this new understanding of social dynamics and leadership fluidity at the Corinthian banquet, it is apparent that the group's common meal provided opportunities to generate strength even for members who were slightly less wealthy than some others in the group: upon election to an office, a so-called weak member would obtain whatever honours the group customarily provided its magistrates. These could have included honourable couches (τόποι, 1 Cor 14:16) at the *triclinium*, larger than ordinary portions of food, and perhaps other commendation if they performed their duties responsibly.

Obviously, customs for reciprocating banquet benefactions were known in first-century Corinth. One particularly relevant piece of evidence for this is an honorific inscription for the public benefactor, Lucius Castricius Regulus, who organised a public feast for everyone in Corinth (*ICorinth* III 153; 22/23 CE). Given the inclusiveness and date of Regulus's feast, it is possible that an *ekklēsia* member, now in their 40s or 50s, attended the public banquet as a youth or young adult.

In addition to the presence of honours in wider Roman Corinthian banquet practices, there is also evidence of the Christ group's own honorific customs at their common meals. When scrutinising the *ekklēsia*'s current leaders' quality of service (1 Cor 11:22), Paul asks them,

> Do you show contempt for the church of God and humiliate those who have nothing? What should I say to you? Should

d'archéologie offerts à Paul Collart, ed. Pierre Ducrey (Cahiers d'archéologie romande de la Bibliothèque historique vaudoise 5; Lausanne: Bibliothèque historique vaudoise, 1976), 353–62.

I commend (ἐπαινεῖν) you? In this matter I do not commend
(ἐπαινεῖν) you! (NRSV)

By highlighting that the leaders' poor quality of service prevented them
from earning ἔπαινος, Paul indirectly reveals that ἔπαινος would
normally be available for responsible magistrates. Paul's usage of
ἔπαινος in a letter to an association should not be overlooked. The
term, ἐπαινεῖν, is stereotypical of Greek honorific epigraphy, where it
denotes normative forms of commendation such as crowns, proclamations, and honorific inscriptions.[91]

Conclusions

In 1 Cor 11:18–34, Paul speaks in passing about some of the most routine
experiences of associations: selections of leaders, displays of equality
and inequality at banquets, and conflict between officers and regular
members. So much scholarship on the Corinthian *ekklēsia* has assumed
an absence of Corinthian officers on the basis of passages that do not
even treat the topic of Corinthian behaviour (1 Cor 12:4–30) when all
along the interesting data on this topic appear just a few verses earlier
(11:18–19) where Paul employs formulaic election terminology to
describe the group's ordination practices. Categorising this language as
apocalyptic discourse creates hitherto unsolvable difficulties that tend to
be acknowledged but ultimately dismissed in the major commentaries on
the letter. Paul's attestation to a fluid hierarchy of temporary, elected,
officers in the group is one more example of how the Corinthians'
structural organisation would have prevented the rise of a perpetually
strong subgroup in the *ekklēsia*.

---

[91] John S. Kloppenborg, 'Greco-Roman *Thiasoi*, The *Ekklēsia* at Corinth, and Conflict
Management', in *Redescribing Paul and the Corinthians*, ed. Ron Cameron and Merrill
P. Miller (Early Christianity and Its Literature 5; Atlanta: Society of Biblical Literature,
2011), 187–218 (213); cf. McRae, 'Eating with Honor', 213–14. For examples of associations' usage of the term, see: *SEG* 2:10.8 (Salamis, Attica; 248 BCE); *IG* II² 1291.11, 16,
21, 27 = *GRA* I 19 (Piraeus? Attica; mid III BCE); *IG* II² 1337.11–12 = *GRA* I 44 (Piraeus,
Attica; 97/6 BCE); *IG* II² 1334.14 = *GRA* I 45 (Piraeus, Attica; after 71/70 BCE).

CONCLUSION

Summary of Findings

This book's analysis of the Corinthian *ekklēsia*'s organisational structure produced several new findings in addition to broader conclusions about the group's need to collect subscription dues, select magistrates, and honour service providers with formal commendation. I summarise below ten new proposals that were developed over the course of the book:

1 The social groups that previous scholarship labels as synagogues and Judean groups are better described as 'Yahweh groups' and are classified on individual bases according to a fivefold, membership-based, taxonomy of associations. It makes no better sense to compare or identify Christ groups exclusively with Yahweh groups than it would to study Christ groups in comparison with Herakles associations alone.

2 Identifying the Corinthian group as a collection of family networks, and situating the group's meetings exclusively in domestic architecture, fails to account for the non-domestic social connections within the Christ group's membership profile, and overlooks the possibility that their meeting space was rented. Occasionally, previous scholarship's emphasis on the domestic and familial setting of Christian origins has served apologetic goals.

3 Membership numbers in the Corinthian group fluctuated. At minimum, there were nine or ten members in the *ekklēsia*, plus the occasional guest. The maximum number of members might have been limited to twelve in order to not crowd the places/couches (τόποι, 1 Cor 14:16) of the *triclinium*.

4 Gaius (Rom 16:23) was a fee-paying guest (ξένος), not a host. The group possessed no known stable meeting place.

5   Members were economically modest but not without the
     surplus resources requisite for club membership. Wayne
     Meeks's description of the social level of members in
     Pauline groups tends to be more tenable than recent
     critiques of the new consensus' position.
6   The Corinthians established a common fund where income
     was stored.
7   Activities, including meals, were funded by all members
     through subscription fees and any other income they could
     generate (e.g., from guests, from voluntary accounts).
8   The Christ group's leaders were elected officials whose
     leadership positions were temporary.
9   Formal honorifics and office-holding were available to all
     members. No one was perpetually strong in the group's
     social or ecclesiastical hierarchy. *Ekklēsia* hierarchies
     were fluid, not fixed according to social status in outside
     society.
10   Conflict in the Christ group tended to divide members
     according to their current social position in the *ekklēsia*
     (e.g., officers and regular members) and not on the basis of
     their status outside the Christ groups (e.g., strong and
     weak).

It would be methodologically flawed or irrelevant to take from this
summary that the Corinthian group was an association. Such a statement
would imply that there was some alternative model for organising a
private cult group in the ancient Mediterranean, such as the synagogue
or philosophical cult, when these supposedly categorically different
models actually belong within the association *genus*. It might also generate the notion that associations were homogeneous and, therefore, that
the Corinthians were either similar to or different from all of them. It is
better to conclude that in various individual comparators (i.e., membership size and financial policies) the Christ group was similar to hundreds
of associations and different from hundreds more. Only *some* associations elected their officers; others used sortition and appointment processes. Only *some* associations rewarded service providers with cheap
crowns; others provided honorific inscriptions and proclamations. Only
some associations failed to regulate the portion size of officer's take at
banquets; others inscribed bylaws that limited officer's portions in order
to ensure that there would be enough food for all participants. We could
go on. Simply identifying the Corinthian group as similar to associations

tells us little about them; even worse, identifying the Corinthian group as unique from associations necessarily results in transporting modern church behaviour or Pauline idealisation onto the ground level of first-century Corinth when nothing of the sort was actually happening.

In light of Richard Ascough's cautions against the usage of the Corinthian *ekklēsia* as a model for first-century Christ groups, I hesitate to suggest that other Pauline groups possessed features in common with the Corinthians.[1] Any attempt to imagine coherence between Pauline groups, or to list definitive features of Pauline groups, would be grounded in a highly problematic assumption about a coherence in beliefs and practices in so-called Pauline Christianity.[2] Nonetheless, the Macedonian, West Asian, and Roman groups to which Paul wrote would have faced some of the same challenges experienced by the Corinthians, such as the need to keep debt at a controllable level and the requirement to secure recruits. To meet these challenges, all of the Pauline groups likely shared the three features that most associations more generally had in common: collection of membership dues, selection of officers, and delivery of formal recognition to magistrates.

Finances in Other Pauline Groups

The epistolary nature of Pauline evidence nearly precludes the possibility of finding direct evidence of subscription dues in Pauline groups. Some indication exists from 1 Cor 16:2 for the presence of a common fund from which donations to the Jerusalem collections were kept separate, but in other letters Paul devotes little space to mundane financial activities practised by Christ groups. One striking passage, though, is 2 Thess 3:6–15, which was composed by either Paul or a later writer but presumably addressed to the same group to whom First Thessalonians was delivered.[3] The text describes members of that *ekklēsia* having free

---

[1] Richard S. Ascough, 'Of Memories and Meals: Greco-Roman Associations and the Early Jesus-Group at Thessalonikē', in *From Roman to Early Christian Thessalonikē. Studies in Religion and Archaeology*, ed. Laura Nasrallah, Charalambos Bakirtzis, and Steven J. Friesen (Harvard Theological Studies 64; Cambridge, MA: Harvard University Press, 2010), 49–72 (58).

[2] Stanley K. Stowers, 'The Concept of "Community" in the History of Early Christianity', *MTSR* 23 (2011), 238–56 (252–3).

[3] For standard arguments in favour of pseudepigraphic authorship of 2 Thessalonians, see Karl P. Donfried, '2 Thessalonians and the Church at Thessalonica', in *Origins and Method: Towards a New Understanding of Judaism and Christianity. Essays in Honour of John C. Hurd*, ed. B. H. McLean (JSNTSup 86; Sheffield: JSOT Press, 1993), 128–44. For a

Christ group meals.⁴ Most interpreters contend that these members were 'busybodies' (περιεργαζόμενοι) to whom the Christ group gave free meals out of brotherly love. Περιεργάζεσθαι carries a wide semantic range and must be translated according to the context in which a writer places it.⁵ The context in which Paul uses it in 2 Thess 3:11 makes 'busybodies' an unlikely translation: meddlesome behaviour was part of associative life, not prohibited misbehaviour as in 2 Thess 3:6–15; the causative linkage between meddlesomeness and eating free meals as in 2 Thess 3:6–15 in the dominant reading seems strained in analogous material; and busybodies tended not to be described as disorderly (ἀτάκτως, 3:11) in comparative material. A better rendering of the word, one which we find in other sources concerned with money and property, is 'haggling'. In this new rendering, the freeloaders ate free meals because they bargained deals with the ekklēsia to do so temporarily.⁶ Paul contrasts the bargainers with members who 'worked' (ἐργάζεσθαι). I take the 'work' concept here to carry the same signification it holds in 1 Thess 5:12–13 where Paul uses it to designate financial contributions to the ekklēsia.⁷ Paul, now, asks the Christ group to end their leniency towards the freeloaders and to make a list of debtors, which

recent suggestion of Pauline authorship, see Paul Foster, 'Who Wrote 2 Thessalonians: A Fresh Look at an Old Problem', JSNT 35 (2014), 150–75.

⁴ Paul's instruction in 2 Thess 3:10 makes no sense if he were speaking about everyday meals for subsistence: a Christ group would not be able to enforce starvation in private settings. Since an association would actually have the authority to restrict access to food at their own meals, scholars correctly identify the meals described in 2 Thess 3:6–15 as ekklēsia banquets, not private dinners. For this argument, see Robert Jewett, 'Tenement Churches and Communal Meals in the Early Church: The Implications of a Form-Critical Analysis of 2 Thessalonians 3:10', BR 38 (1993), 23–43 (38); and Ascough, 'Of Memories and Meals', 61–7. Other interpreters have argued that the meal was a Christ group banquet for other reasons. See, e.g., Ronald Russell, 'The Idle in 2 Thess 3.6–12: An Eschatological or a Social Problem?', NTS 34 (1988), 101–19 (107–8); and Ernest Best, The First and Second Epistles to the Thessalonians (London: Black, 1972), 333–4.

⁵ This point is made by Christina M. Kreinecker, 2. Thessaloniker (Papyrologische Kommentare zum Neuen Testament 3; Göttingen: Vandenhoeck & Ruprecht, 2010), 206.

⁶ For the practice of temporary leniency towards debtors see IG II² 1339.5–15 = GRA I 46 (Athens, Attica; 57/56 BCE); P.Tebt. III/2 894, Frag.9 recto, II.36–8 (Tebtynis, Egypt; 114 BCE). For the possibility of gradual repayment, see IG II² 1368.102–7 = GRA I 51 (Athens, Attica; 164/5 CE). For other examples of temporary financial assistance, see P.Mich. V 243.8–9 = AGRW 300 (Arsinoites, Egypt; 14–37 CE); P.Mich. V 244.9–10 = AGRW 301 (Tebtynis, Egypt; 43 CE); P.Ryl. II. 94 = Sel. Pap. II 255 (Euhemeria, Arisinoites, Egypt; 14–37 CE).

⁷ The work (τὸ ἔργον) of the κοπιῶντες in 1 Thess 5:13 earns them esteem (ἡγεῖσθαι αὐτοὺς ὑπερεκπερισσοῦ). The κοπιῶντες are also denoted as προϊστάμενοι (v.12), that is, leaders in the ekklēsia, not manual labourers in private life (See Ascough, Macedonian

would serve as a shaming mechanism (2 Thess 3:14).[8] A full exploration of this interpretative framework, and its implications for the financial structure of the Thessalonian group, cannot be offered here.[9] The special monetary collections completed by the Macedonian groups raise questions about these groups' more ordinary financial collections. We know that the Philippian affiliates were wealthy enough to sponsor Paul's travels by means of patronage (Phil 4:15–17), and that their donations, along with the Thessalonians' contributions, to the Jerusalem fund apparently impressed Paul (2 Cor 8:3). Given the Macedonian associations' practice of collecting money for external projects, we can be sure, at the very least, that they had the apparatuses in place to collect money for their own needs.

Paul asked the Galatians to contribute to the Jerusalem collection (1 Cor 16:1–2) but received no money from them (Rom 15:26). It is possible that theological differences between Paul and the Galatians – and resulting social hostilities – are to explain for the Galatians' lack of participation in the project. But the Tebtynis papyrus (*P.Tebt.* III/2 894; 114 BCE) generates another possibility for understanding the Galatians' lack of participation in the extraordinary Jerusalem collection – namely, a lack of surplus economic resources among members to do so. In the Tebtynis group, only the more financially stable members were able to contribute to their extraordinary collections. Perhaps the financial demands of *ekklēsia* membership clarify why these individuals failed to offer benefaction to the Jerusalem group. The idea here is that the members of these *ekklēsiai* did not possess the level of surplus economic resources necessary to keep their own groups out of debt as well as to finance the activities of the Jerusalem group. Part of the issue would have been the Galatians' required payments of subscription to their own Christ groups – the arguments made in Chapter 4 concerning the presence of a common fund in the Corinthian group apply also to the

Associations, 176–7). The kind of 'work' that earned leaders (προϊστάμενοι) esteem in cultic groups was financial contributions, or proper handling of leadership duties. For the former, see *AM* 66:228 no. 4 = *GRA* I 39 (Athens, Attica; 138/7 BCE) *IBeroia* 22 = *AGRW* 35 (Beroea, Macedonia; 7 BCE); *IG* X/2.1 58 = *AGRW* 47 (Thessalonica, Macedonia; I BCE–I CE); *IJO* 1, *Ach67* = *ASSB* 101 (Delos, Asia Minor; 150–50 BCE). For the latter, see *IG* II² 1298 = *GRA* I 20 (Athens, Attica; 248/7 BCE); *IG* II² 1334 = *GRA* I 45 (Piraeus, Attica; after 71/70 BCE); *IG* II² 1343 = *GRA* I 48 (Athens, Attica; 37/6 or 36/5 BCE); *IJO* II 168 = *ASSB* 103 (Acmonia, Phrygia, Asia Minor; 50–100 CE).

[8] For an association that makes a list of its debtors as a shaming mechanism, see *Agora* 16:161.2–8 = *GRA* I 14 (Athens, Attica; early III BCE).

[9] Richard Last, 'The Myth of Free Membership in Pauline Groups' (forthcoming in an edited volume).

Galatian groups since Paul's instructions in 1 Cor 16:1–2 were delivered to both.

Officers and Honours in Other Pauline Groups

Evidence of magistrates and of the delivery of symbolic capital to service providers could be expected from Pauline groups' financial accounts, written regulations, and inscriptions. Since we lack these types of materials from Paul's groups, and are left only with epistles that focus on these groups' extraordinary activities and conflicts as opposed to their routine practices, there will not be much extant information concerning magistrates in the *ekklēsiai*. But there are pieces of information scattered throughout Paul's letters indicating the presence of officers and honorific rewards. Three small indications can be highlighted here. First, in 1 Thess 5:12, Paul speaks of προϊστάμενοι. These are, literally, 'appointed leaders'. While it is possible to assume that their leadership was informal (e.g., they were leaders because they possessed houses and offered hospitality),[10] this would be special pleading. The Thessalonian *ekklēsia* most likely originated as a professional guild[11] and so there is little reason to describe its hierarchy according to Pauline idealisation (from 1 Corinthians, at that) rather than to place it within the range of typical hierarchical practices in occupational associations. According to Paul, these appointed magistrates deserved to be acknowledged (εἰδέναι, 5:12) and esteemed (ἡγεῖσθαι, 5:13). Paul takes no time to teach the Thessalonian guild how to do this properly, which suggests that these groups knew how to honour their service providers fittingly.

In Paul's letter to the Philippians, we finally find evidence of actual office titles, ἐπίσκοποι and διάκονοι (Phil 1:1). These titles fall within the range of titles used by associations for their magistrates.[12] The fact that Paul fails to address the specific holders of these offices suggests that Paul did not know the names of the current incumbents. If Paul knew their names, then he would have mentioned them like he did in Rom 16:1 when commending the διάκονος of the *ekklēsia* at Cenchrea, Phoebe.

---

[10] Recently, Roger W. Gehring, *House Church and Mission. The Importance of Household Structures in Early Christianity* (Peabody, MA: Hendrickson, 2004), 198–9.

[11] For this argument, see Richard S. Ascough, 'The Thessalonian Christian Community as a Professional Voluntary Association', *JBL* 119 (2000), 311–28.

[12] For ἐπίσκοποι, see Franz Poland, *Geschichte des griechischen* Vereinswesens (Leipzig: Teubner, 1909), 377; for διάκονοι, see Poland, *Geschichte*, 391–2.

Moving beyond the Periodised Approach to Christ Groups

The way forward in social historical investigations of the Pauline groups begins with a rejection of the 'strongly periodized perception of ancient Christianity'.[13] Kim Bowes has shown that the periodised approach takes Constantine's legalisation of Christianity in 313 CE to mark a monumental shift in the organisation of the Jesus movement and views everything in the post-313 CE period as fundamentally (d)evolved from what came before. Key reconstructions of ancient Christ groups adhere to this periodised approach by imagining the 50s CE as too early of a period in the history of the Jesus movement for officers, subscription dues, inscriptions, honorific rewards, possession of space beyond the domestic quarters in which members dwelled, and more.

There were, of course, developments between the 50s and the 300s CE. But Bowes's new model opens the possibility of exploring later sources as a way for generating new questions about the practices of the earliest Christ groups. Some of this later evidence includes an ἐργασία (association) of Christian workers in Egypt who handed out loans to its members;[14] *ekklēsiai* that collected fees from members to fund their group activities (Justin, *1 Apology* 67); Christian groups that threatened fines for improper behaviour (*IPerinthos* 167–8 [Thrace, after 212 CE); Christ groups that selected leaders (*Did.* 15:1–2); and Christian churches that delivered honorific inscriptions to service providers (e.g., *SEG* 29: 1610; Palestine, mid VI CE). Indeed, Paul's description of the Corinthians' financial and leadership activities in the 50s CE confirm that, in these practices, the behaviours of Christ groups were far more static and much less dynamic than is often imagined.

---

[13] Kim Bowes, *Private Worship, Public Values, and Religious Change in Late Antiquity* (Cambridge: Cambridge University Press, 2008), 9.

[14] *P.Stras.* IV 287 (Hermopolis, Egypt; VI CE). For an earlier example of a Christ craft guild, see Edward L. Hicks, 'Inscriptions from Eastern Cilicia', *JHS* 11 (1890), 236–54 (no. 1) = *GRA* II 153 (Flaviopolis?, Cilicia; before 300 CE).

Appendix

A REPLY TO TIMOTHY BROOKINS

Reasserting the 'Factions' Reading of 1 Cor 11:19

In the July 2014 issue of *NTS*, Timothy Brookins offered a thoughtful defence of the traditional reading of 1 Cor 11:18–19 in light of some of its difficulties that I observed in an earlier and abbreviated version of this book's Chapter 7.[1] Parts of my response to Brookins have been addressed in Chapter 7. Here, I reply to the sections with which I did not have occasion to engage in that chapter.

Towards the end of Brookins's article, he provides a fresh translation of 1 Cor 11:18–20 on the traditional theory:

> To begin with, I hear that when you come together to assembly, there are divisions among you, and I believe it in part – indeed, it is quite natural that such divisions should exist, for it is necessary that there be 'factions' among you, in order that there might come to light those among you who are, as you say, 'approved' – accordingly, when you come together to the same place, it is not to eat a '*Lord's*' Supper . . .[2]

R. Alastair Campbell spoke of the 'enormous psychological difficulty' that (now) Brookins's translation causes.[3] The two main 'psychological difficulties' generated by the traditional reading are: how do factions make 'the approved ones' come to light in antiquity? And, how do we reconcile Paul's statement that 'αἱρέσεις are necessary' (11:19) with his opposition to Christ group divisions everywhere else? Brookins believes

---

[1] Timothy A. Brookins, 'The Supposed Election of Officers in 1 Cor 11.19: A Response to Richard Last', *NTS* 60 (2014), 423–32; cf. Richard Last, 'The Election of Officers in the Corinthian Christ-Group', *NTS* 59 (2013), 365–82. Throughout this reply, I refer to my original article rather than Chapter 7 in the present book.

[2] Brookins, 'Supposed Election', 432 (emphasis original).

[3] R. Alastair Campbell, 'Does Paul Acquiesce in Divisions at the Lord's Supper', *NovT* 33 (1991), 61–70 (62–3).

that these problems 'are not as great as [Last] makes them out to be'.[4] In the following section of this rejoinder, Brookins's treatment of exegetical problems associated with the 'factions' translation is evaluated. The section on Brookins's Contribution to the Debate addresses Brookins's original challenges to my new reading of 11:19.

Old Problems with Translating αἱρέσεις as Factions

The first major issue with 11:19 on the 'factions' theory (i.e., explaining how 'factions' make known 'the approved Corinthians' in an *ekklēsia* setting) is neglected in Brookins's treatment of 11:18–20. It is difficult to properly evaluate Brookins's exegesis since in the end it leaves us with an incomprehensible 11:19.

In my reading of the passage, I produced data showing how αἱρέσεις ('elections') can lead to δόκιμοι ('the approved ones') in antiquity, including in private cultic groups, such as the one with which Paul is communicating in 11:18–20. Neither Brookins nor other proponents of the traditional theory have done the equivalent.[5] The danger in not specifying the mechanics of this social process in their theory, and supporting it with actual data – and showing how it makes sense in an *ekklēsia* setting – is that it will allow untested assumptions about Paul and the Corinthians to occupy the dominant role in exegesis of 11:19. Believing, as Brookins does, that Justin's logion (ἔσονται σχίσματα καὶ αἱρέσεις; *Dial.* 35) is early and most probably an authentic Jesus saying[6] does not solve the problem since Paul's key logistical moves in 11:19 are absent from Justin: in Justin, αἱρέσεις are neither necessary nor causative of (or related at all to) οἱ δόκιμοι.

Not only is 11:19 problematic as a contained verse on the 'factions' theory, but it also has Paul treat 'divisions' in a unique way when placed within the context of 1 Corinthians. Brookins admits that there is a problem here. My solution is to propose a new translation for αἱρέσεις

---

[4] Brookins, 'Supposed Election', 424.

[5] This is not to say that older defences of the traditional theory are silent on the matter. C. K. Barrett understands the mechanism by which factions produce 'genuine ones' in light of 1 Cor 3.13, 15.25, 53, 2 Cor 5.10 and quotes W. G. Kümmel in concluding that 'the appearance of divisions contributes to the making of a clear decision at the judgement' (*First Epistle*, 262). The group of texts Barrett cites does not provide grounds for this interpretation of 11:19. For a response to Barrett's model, see Campbell, 'Does Paul Acquiesce?', 62–3.

[6] 'As it is, verbal evidence gives us ample warrant to suppose that Justin and 1 Cor 11.18–19 commonly preserve an authentic, if otherwise unattested, saying of Jesus, eschatological in orientation' (Brookins, 'Supposed Election', 425).

that, Brookins will agree, keeps 11:19 harmonious with Paul's arguments against divisions prior, and is consistent with terminology in the verse that appears in civic and private election contexts. Brookins's solution is to adopt Hans Lietzmann's argument that Paul's supposed change of approach to 'dissensions' in 11:19 was intentional and delivered with a hint of irony or 'eschatological resignation'.[7] This theory is articulated by Brookins as follows:[8]

> Undoubtedly, Paul's arguments were capable of shifting with his rhetorical purposes. Such as he was, it should come as no surprise if he momentarily shifted into his audience's own frame of mind in order to score a point. In this regard, I find it quite likely that we have here simply a further instance of Paul's penchant for 'redefinition': Paul turns the self-attribution of those high-status Corinthians as 'approved' (δόκιμοι) over on its head, agreeing that 'divisions' among them serve to mark out those who are 'distinguished', only *not* in the way they fancy. In effect: 'Well, I suppose divisions are necessary after all, for only then will it become evident who is *truly* 'approved'.' It would seem to me to be entirely within his character for him to have spoken in such a way.[9]

Brookins points to another instance of Pauline irony to show that Paul sometimes wrote in this manner. The analogy (6:5) is explained by Brookins as follows:

> after spending four chapters trying to convince them that there [*sic*] were *not* acting as wise men at all, he presumes in 6.5 to ask them whether there is not some 'wise man' (σοφός) among them who is able to judge among his brothers, the introductory οὐκ indicating clearly that his question *now wants the answer 'Yes'*.[10]

This reading of 1 Cor 6:5 will hold up as long as it is agreed that some Corinthians self-identified as σοφοί (1 Cor 1:19–20), which is less

---

[7] Hans Lietzmann, with W. G. Kummel, *An die Korinther I/II*, 5th ed. (Handbuch zum Neuen Testament 9; Tübingen: Mohr Siebeck, 1969), 56; cf. Last, 'Election of Officers', 370–1 n.16.

[8] Brookins seems unaware that I entertained this possibility in Last, 'Election of Officers', 370–1, n.16. I repeat here my reasoning for rejecting it.

[9] Brookins, 'Supposed Election', 427.

[10] Brookins, 'Supposed Election', 426 (emphasis original).

certain than is sometimes assumed.[11] But it has little significance for 11:19.

When Brookins moves to 11:19, he suggests that Paul employs here the same rhetorical strategy as in 6:5: consistent with his ironic designation of some Corinthians as σοφοί in 6:5, Paul employs δόκιμος ironically in 11:19, effectively 'turn[ing] the self-attribution of those high-status Corinthians as "approved" (δόκιμοι) over on its head' and 'agreeing that "divisions" among them serve to mark out those who are "distinguished", only not in the way they fancy'.[12] Brookins moves too fast here and without providing the necessary support for such a theory. For Brookins's reading of 11:19 to work, he will need to show that some Corinthians called themselves δόκιμοι, and that some Corinthians thought αἱρέσεις would make clear the δόκιμοι among them. There is no evidence of this in 1–2 Corinthians and, therefore, no evidence of irony in 11:19 analogous to what he claims Paul was doing in 6:5.[13]

A second issue with Brookins's analysis of 11:19 is its basis in an anachronism. Little quibbles between church members may carry small consequences in contemporary church organisations, but misbehaviours causing disorderliness in an ancient cultic group were not tolerated and absolutely not treated ironically or with resignation by honourable members. Rather, disorderliness at the banquet of associations was punishable by fines or even expulsion.[14] In *P. Lond.* VII 2193.13 = *AGRW* 295 (Philadelphia, Egypt; 69–58 BCE) σχίσματα are explicitly outlawed given their potential danger to the group. Associations needed to come down hard on disorderly members since disorderly actions could jeopardise the honour of members[15] and even cause a club to dissolve (*CIL* III 1 Alburnus Major, Dacia; 167 CE).[16] We know from papyrological evidence, moreover, that the fines threatened in association bylaws were not just preventative; they were actually extracted from

---

[11] For recent caution about the identity of the wise in 1:20, see Wolfgang Schrage, *Der erste Brief an die Korinther* (4 vols.; Evangelisch-katholischer Kommentar zum Neuen Testament 7; Neukirchen-Vluyn: Neukirchener Verlag, 1991–2001), 1:176.

[12] Brookins, 'Supposed Election', 427.

[13] Campbell entertains the possibility that this might be a Corinthian self-designation but is unable to find support after analysing δόκιμος (and cognates) in Pauline literature. See 'Does Paul Acquiesce?', 67–9.

[14] See the finable offenses in the inscriptions cited in Last, 'Election of Officers', 371–2. See also John S. Kloppenborg, 'Disaffiliation in Associations and the ἀποσυναγωγός of John', *HTS* 67 (2011), 1–16.

[15] Such as taking the seat of another member, absenteeism during award ceremonies, and failure to inscribe or announce honours.

[16] In this club, the issue of disorderliness was failure to pay fees.

misbehaving members (*P.Tebt.* III/2 894, *Frag.3* verso, I.12–13; Tebtynis, Egypt; 114 BCE). To quote Campbell, 'This is no time to be offering the Corinthians ... mild irony.'[17]

Brookins's Contribution to the Debate

Brookins presents a few new arguments in favour of the 'factions' theory.[18] The first comes in a section where he searches for words from 11:19 (ἐν ὑμῖν, αἵρεσις, δόκιμος, φανερός) that are also found in passages of 1 Corinthians that are clearly eschatological in content.[19] His focus ultimately turns to Paul's usage of the prepositional phrase ἐν ὑμῖν in 1:10–11 (σχίσματα ἐν ὑμῖν) and 3:3 (ἐν ὑμῖν ζῆλος καὶ ἔρις), which, confusingly, are not clearly eschatological in content. Nonetheless, his point is that since Paul uses ἐν ὑμῖν in 11:18–19 ('σχίσματα ἐν ὑμῖν; αἱρέσεις ἐν ὑμῖν) and in 1:10–11 and 3:3 all where 'dissentions' are at issue, we have here 'a varied semantic cluster centered around "dissensions", including four different terms of similar meaning, each occurring with ἐν ὑμῖν'.[20]

This is an interesting observation; however, it is based on an incomplete set of data and circular reasoning. If Brookins wishes to analyse Paul's usage of ἐν ὑμῖν in 1 Corinthians, then he has to consider all the ἐν ὑμῖν passages in the epistle. Paul uses this common phrase eighteen times in 1 Corinthians and not just with 'four different terms of similar meaning'.[21] In fact, the phrase more often does not revolve around discussions of 'dissensions' (to use Brookins's category). Why should we categorise the ἐν ὑμῖν phrase in 11:19 – and note that there are two in 11:19 with only one falling into Brookins's manufactured category – with the ones Brookins selects (1:10–11, 3:3, 11:18), rather than categorise it with the ἐν ὑμῖν phrases revolving around phenomena that might protect against

---

[17] Campbell, 'Does Paul Acquiesce?', 65.

[18] I have omitted discussion of Brookins's linguistic analysis ('Supposed Election', 429–31) because it is based on a misunderstanding of my proposal. See my discussion of the continuity between vv.18–19 in Chapter 7.

[19] 'We need not go far ... to find striking thematic clustering, and with more abundant resonances in the letter, in proof that the context here [i.e., 11.19] is eschatological' ('Supposed Election', 427).

[20] Brookins, 'Supposed Election', 428.

[21] The full list is here: 1 Cor 1:6, 10, 11; 2:2; 3:3, 16, 18; 5:1; 6:2, 5, 19; 11:13, 18, 19 (2), 30; 14:25; 15:12.

'dissensions'?[22] The ἐν ὑμῖν inquiry, once completed, does not stand as a proper defence of the 'factions' theory.

Brookins frames a second contribution as new; however, it had already been articulated by many other interpreters. He argues that 'the literature hereto has not adverted attention to' the eschatological context in which φανερός (and cognates) sometimes appear.[23] In fact, it is well known that 'becoming manifest' (φανερὸς γίγνεσθαι) can hold eschatological significance, but more recently Amphilochios Papathomas has shown that these terms are often placed together without eschatological connotation, particularly in papyri from the first century.[24]

Equipped with two terms from 11:19 that sometimes appear in eschatological discourse (δόκιμος and φανερός), Brookins suggests that the 'clinching text' in determining whether 11:19 pertains to Pauline eschatology or to Corinthian elections is a passage where these two words (δοκιμάζειν and φανερός) appear together in an eschatological context (3:13). This holds significance for Brookins because, he states, 'as far as I can tell [Last] does not locate a single text where any two of these terms [i.e. from 11.19] appear together in the same [election] context.'[25] Since Paul uses δόκιμος and φανερός (or cognates) in both non-eschatological and eschatological settings, it is unclear to me why 3:13 should be decisive evidence for how 11:19 is to be read, even if the two words are used together in that verse. Brookins might have attributed less significance to his observation about 3:13 if he had considered more broadly Paul's usage of δόκιμος (and cognates). In 1991, Campbell investigated this wider set of Paul's usages of δόκιμος and concluded that 'we should notice that in none of these passages is there anything about eschatological testing.'[26] Brookins was only able to employ 3:13 in defence of the traditional theory because he cherry-picked instances where Paul used these two words in ways that he believed supported his reading of 11:19 rather than analyse Paul's discourse more systematically.

[22] For example, 'testimony of Christ ἐβεβαιώθη ἐν ὑμῖν' (1 Cor 1:6); 'the δόκιμοι ... ἐν ὑμῖν' (11:19b); 'God is ἐν ὑμῖν' (14:25); 'God's spirit dwells ἐν ὑμῖν' (3:16); and 'temple of the holy spirit ἐν ὑμῖν' (6:19).
[23] Brookins, 'Supposed Election', 428.
[24] See Papathomas's examples in Peter Arzt-Grabner Ruth Elisabeth Kritzer, Amphilochios Papathomas, and Franz Winter, *1 Korinther* (Papyrologische Kommentare zum Neuen Testament 2; Göttingen: Vandenhoeck & Ruprecht, 2006), 152.
[25] Brookins, 'Supposed Election', 427.
[26] Campbell discusses 1 Cor 11:28; 2 Cor 10:18, 13:7; Rom 14:18, 16:10.

With regard to Brookins's point that there is 'not ... a single text' to
his knowledge where formulaic election terms appear together in my
original article, this is mistaken.[27] Beyond the examples that I cited in
the original article (and, now, in Chapter 7) it should be remembered that
it is rather common for ancient authors to speak about civic and associative elections using the language from 11:19.[28] The Iobacchoi example
cited in the original article and now quoted in Chapter 7 (*IG* II²
1368.32–27 = *GRA* I 51; Athens, 164/165 CE) is exactly the type of
data that Brookins's theory lacks. We have here a private cultic group
mimicking civic voting practices and clarifying how αἱρέσεις actually
lead to δόκιμοι in antiquity. For individuals explicitly becoming
'approved ones' (οἱ δοκιμασθέντες) after being vetted, see *IG* II²
1361.24 = *GRA* I 4 (Piraeus, Attica; 330–324/3 BCE).[29]

First Corinthians 3:13, as Brookins notes, shows that two words from
11:19 can appear together in eschatological discourse. This does not
resolve the matter at hand and, indeed, does not even assist in the process
of deciding whether we should interpret 11:18–19 as eschatological or
non-eschatological discourse. It was already clear at the outset that
eschatological discourse was one possible framework for understanding
11:19, and I also admitted that this traditional theory was one possibility
in my original discussion of δόκιμος.[30] The question is this: why should
we maintain an eschatological reading of αἱρέσεις in 11:19 when it
causes so many problems and especially when a viable alternative is
available?

Conclusions

The major objections to the 'elections' theory are overcome when the
ekklēsia's practices are understood in light of the wide spectrum of
typical banqueting, leadership, and conflict-resolution customs in

[27] Last, 'Election of Officers', 372 n.22; 373 n.24; 376, n.38. Plato, *Laws* 6.759–760a,
which was referenced in the original article, is quoted in this book's Chapter 7.

[28] Gabriel Adeleye and John Kloppenborg have published detailed studies on the
pervasiveness of approval processes (δοκιμασία and cognates) in ancient literary and
epigraphic material pertaining to elections and voting. See Gabriel Adeleye, 'The
Purpose of "*Dokimasia*"', *GRBS* 24 (1983), 295–306; and John S. Kloppenborg, 'The
Moralizing of Discourse in Graeco-Roman Associations', in *'The One Who Sows
Bountifully': Essays in Honor of Stanley K. Stowers*, ed. Caroline Johnson Hodge, Saul
M. Olyan, Daniel Ullucci, and Emma Wasserman (Brown Judaic Studies 356; Providence,
Rhode Island: Brown Judaic Studies, 2013), 215–28.

[29] See Kloppenborg, 'Moralizing of Discourse', 217.

[30] Last, 'Election of Officers', 377.

associations. Neglecting the spectrum of practices attested in the association data brings with it the danger of uncontrolled speculations about how a Christ group *must* have held banquets, and often results in depictions of Pauline *ekklēsiai* as mirror-images of Paul.

Brookins kindly regards my reading of 11:19 in light of associations as 'innovative'. I think that further comparative research on the practices of Pauline *ekklēsia* might make reading αἱρέσεις as 'elections' seem ordinary in comparison to the traditional theory. It is in Brookins's defence of the traditional theory, after all, where Justin's logion is claimed as an authentic Jesus saying,[31] where Paul must have used irony or eschatological resignation in 11:19 in order for the verse to make half sense,[32] where Paul and the Corinthians are the only people in antiquity who know how factions could create 'the approved ones', and where a small minority of Paul's eighteen ἐν ὑμῖν phrases are said to constitute their own category. The 'elections' alternative offers an explanation for how αἱρέσεις lead to δόκιμοι in social formations similar to the Corinthian *ekklēsia* and is backed up with actual data that illustrates the movement from one to the other. An additional benefit to the 'elections' reading is that it allows Paul's position on divisiveness in the Christ group to remain consistent throughout the epistle.

---

[31] Brookins, 'Supposed Election', 425. Since even the authenticity of some of the most frequently attested and early Jesus sayings are debated, it seems preferable to interpret 11:19 without having to assume Justin's logion existed 100 years before it is first attested.
[32] Brookins, 'Supposed Election', 426–7.

BIBLIOGRAPHY

Adams, Edward. *The Earliest Christian Meeting Places. Almost Exclusively Houses?* Library of New Testament Studies 450. London and New York: Bloomsbury T&T Clark, 2013.

Adams, Edward. 'Placing the Corinthian Common Meal'. Pages 22–35 in *Text, Image, and Christians in the Graeco-Roman World. A Festschrift in Honor of David Lee Balch*. Edited by Aliou Cissé and Carolyn Osiek. Princeton Theological Monograph Series. Eugene, OR: Pickwick, 2012.

Adeleye, Gabriel. 'The Purpose of "*Dokimasia*"'. *Greek, Roman, and Byzantine Studies* 24 (1983): 295–306.

Althaus, Paul. *Der Brief an die Römer übersetzt und erklärt.* Neue Testament Deutsch 6. Göttingen: Vandenhoeck & Ruprecht, 1966.

Ameiling, Walter. *Kleinasien.* Volume 2 of *Inscriptiones Judaicae Orientis.* Texte und Studien zum antiken Judentum 99. Tübingen: Mohr Siebeck, 2004.

Applebaum, Shimon. 'The Organization of the Jewish Communities in the Diaspora'. Pages 464–503 in *The Jewish People in the First Century: Historical Geography, Political History, Social, Cultural and Religious Life and Institutions.* Edited by Shemuel Safrai and Menahem Stern. Compendia rerum Iudaicarum ad Novum Testamentum 1/1. Assen: Van Gorcum; Philadelphia: Fortress, 1974.

Arnaoutoglou, Ilias N. 'ΑΡΧΕΡΑΝΙΣΤΗΣ and Its Meaning in Inscriptions'. *Zeithschrift für Papyrologie und Epigraphik* 104 (1994): 107–10.

Arnaoutoglou, Ilias N. 'Between *Koinon* and *Idion*: Legal and Social Dimensions of Religious Associations in Ancient Athens'. Pages 63–83 in *Kosmos. Essays in Order, Conflict and Community in Classical Athens.* Edited by Paul Cartledge, Paul Millett, and Sitta von Reden. Cambridge: Cambridge University Press, 1998.

Arnaoutoglou, Ilias N. *Thusias Heneka Kai Sunousias: Private Religious Associations in Hellenistic Athens.* Yearbook of the Research Centre for the History of Greek Law 37/4. Athens: Academy of Athens, 2003.

Arterbury, Andrew. *Entertaining Angels. Early Christian Hospitality in Its Mediterranean Setting.* New Testament Monographs 8. Sheffield: Sheffield Phoenix Press, 2005.

Arzt-Grabner, Peter. *2. Korinther.* Papyrologische Kommentare zum Neuen Testament 4. Göttingen: Vandenhoeck & Ruprecht, 2014.

Arzt-Grabner, Peter, Ruth Elisabeth Kritzer, Amphilochios Papathomas, and Franz Winter. *1. Korinther.* Papyrologische Kommentare zum Neuen Testament 2. Göttingen: Vandenhoeck & Ruprecht, 2006.

Ascough, Richard S. 'Apples-to-Apples: Reframing the Question of Models for Pauline Christ Groups'. Paper presented at the annual meeting of the SBL, San Diego, CA, 24 November 2014.

Ascough, Richard S. 'The Completion of a Religious Duty: The Background of 2 Cor 8.1–15'. *New Testament Studies* 42 (1996): 584–99.

Ascough, Richard S. 'Implications of Association Meeting Places for Imagining the Size of Pauline Christ Groups'. Paper presented at the annual meeting of the SNTS, Szeged, Hungary, 8 August 2014.

Ascough, Richard S. 'Of Memories and Meals: Greco-Roman Associations and the Early Jesus-Group at Thessalonikē'. Pages 49–72 in *From Roman to Early Christian Thessalonikē. Studies in Religion and Archaeology.* Edited by Laura Nasrallah, Charalambos Bakirtzis, and Steven J. Friesen. Harvard Theological Studies 64. Cambridge, MA: Harvard University Press, 2010.

Ascough, Richard S. *Paul's Macedonian Associations: The Social Context of Philippians and 1 Thessalonians.* Wissenschaftliche Untersuchungen zum Neuen Testament II/161. Tübingen: Mohr Siebeck, 2003.

Ascough, Richard S. 'Sensing Space: Association Buildings and Socio-Rhetorical Interpretations of Christ-Group Texts'. Paper presented at 2013 annual meeting of the Society of Biblical Literature, Baltimore, MD, 25 November 2013.

Ascough, Richard S. 'The Thessalonian Christian Community as a Professional Voluntary Association'. *Journal of Biblical Literature* 119 (2000): 311–28.

Ascough, Richard S. 'Voluntary Associations and the Formation of Pauline Churches: Addressing the Objections'. Pages 149–83 in *Vereine, Synagogen und Gemeinden im kaiserzeitlichen Kleinasien.* Edited by Andreas Gutsfeld and Dietrich-Alex Koch. Studien und Texte zu Antike und Christentum 25. Tübingen: Mohr Siebeck, 2006.

Ascough, Richard S. *What Are They Saying about the Formation of Pauline Churches?* New York: Paulist Press, 1998.

Ascough, Richard S., Philip A. Harland, and John S. Kloppenborg, eds. *Associations in the Greco-Roman World. A Sourcebook.* Waco, TX: Baylor University Press, 2012.

Ausbüttel, Frank. *Untersuchungen zu den Vereinen im Westen des römischen Reiches.* Frankfurter Althistorische Studien 11. Kallmünz: Michael Laßleben, 1982.

Bagnall, Roger S. *The Oxford Handbook of Papyrology.* New York: Oxford University Press, 2011.

Bailey, Kenneth E. *Paul through Mediterranean Eyes. Cultural Studies in 1 Corinthians.* Madison: InterVarsity, 2011.

Balch, David L. *Roman Domestic Art and Early House Churches.* Wissenschaftliche Untersuchungen zum Neuen Testament I/228. Tübingen: Mohr Siebeck, 2008.

Bandy, Anastasius C. 'Early Christian Inscriptions of Crete'. *Hesperia* 32 (1963): 227–47.

Banks, Robert. *Paul's Idea of Community: The Early House Churches in Their Historical Setting.* Revised edition. Peabody, MA: Hendrickson, 1994.

Barclay, John M. G. 'Money and Meetings: Group Formation among Diaspora Jews and Early Christians'. Pages 113–27 in *Vereine, Synagogen und Gemeinden in kaiserzeitlichen Kleinasien.* Edited by Andreas Gutsfeld and

Dietrich-Alex Koch. Studien und Texte zu Antike und Christentum 25. Tübingen: Mohr Siebeck, 2006.

Barclay, John M. G. 'Poverty in Pauline Studies: A Response to Steven Friesen'. *Journal for the Study of the New Testament* 26 (2004): 363–6.

Barclay, John M. G. 'Thessalonica and Corinth: Social Contrasts in Pauline Christianity'. *Journal for the Study of the New Testament* 15 (1992): 49–74.

Barrett, Charles Kingsley. *The First Epistle to the Corinthians*. London: Hendrickson, 1968.

Barton, S. C., and G. H. R. Horsley. 'A Hellenistic Cult Group and the New Testament Churches'. *Jahrbuch für Antike und Christentum* 24 (1981): 7–41.

Ben Zeev, Miriam Pucci. *Jewish Rights in the Roman World: The Greek and Roman Documents Quoted by Josephus Flavius*. Texte und Studien zum antiken Judentum 74. Tübingen: Mohr Siebeck, 1998.

Bendlin, Andreas. 'Associations, Funerals, Sociality, and Roman Law: The *collegium* of Diana and Antinous in Lanuvium (CIL 14.2112) Reconsidered'. Pages 207–96 in *Das Aposteldekret und das antike Vereinswesen*. Edited by Markus Öhler and Hermut Löhr. Wissenschaftliche Untersuchungen zum Neuen Testament I/280. Tübingen: Mohr Siebeck, 2011.

Bendlin, Andreas. 'Gemeinschaft, Öffentlichkeit und Identität: Forschungsgeschichtliche Anmerkungen zu den Mustern sozialer Ordnung in Rom'. Pages 9–40 in *Religiöse Vereine in der römischen Antike: Unversuchungen zu Organisation, Ritual und Raumordnung*. Edited by Ulrike Egelhaaf-Gaiser and Alfred Schäfer. Studien und Texte zu Antike und Christentum 13. Tübingen: Mohr Siebeck, 2002.

Best, Ernest. *The First and Second Epistles to the Thessalonians*. London: Black's, 1972.

Blue, Bradley B. 'Acts and the House Church'. Pages 119–222 in *The Book of Acts in Its Graeco-Roman Setting*. Volume 2 of *The Book of Acts in Its First Century Setting*. Edited by D. W. J. Gill and C. Gempf. Grand Rapids, MI: Eerdmans, 1994.

Bodel, John. 'Cicero's Minerva, *Penates*, and the Mother of the *Lares*: An Outline of Roman Domestic Religion'. Pages 248–75 in *Household and Family Religion in Antiquity*. Edited by John Bodel and Saul M. Olyan. Malden, MA: Blackwell, 2008.

Bowes, Kim. *Private Worship, Public Values, and Religious Change in Late Antiquity*. Cambridge: Cambridge University Press, 2008.

Branick, Vincent. *The House Church in the Writings of Paul*. Wilmington, DE: Glazier, 1989.

Bremmer, Jan N. 'The Social and Religious Capital of Early Christians'. *Hephaistos* 24 (2006): 269–78.

Bricault, Laurent. 'Les cultes isiaques en Grèce centrale et occidentale'. *Zeithschrift für Papyrologie und Epigraphik* 119 (1997): 118–19.

Brock, Sebastian. 'Regulations for an Association of Artisans from the Late Sasanian or Early Arab Period'. Pages 51–62 in *Transformations of Late Antiquity: Essays for Peter Brown*. Edited by Philip Rousseau and Manolis Papoutsakis. Surrey, England and Burlington, Vermont: Ashgate, 2009.

Brookins, Timothy A. 'The Supposed Election of Officers in 1 Cor 11.19: A Response to Richard Last'. *New Testament Studies* 60 (2014): 423–32.

Bruneau, Philippe. *Recherches sur les cultes de Délos à l'époque hellénistique et à l'époque impériale.* Bibliothèques de l'Ecole française d'Athènes et de Rome 217. Paris: de Boccard, 1970.

Burtchaell, James Tunstead. *From Synagogue to Church: Public Services and Offices in the Earliest Christian Communities.* Cambridge and New York: Cambridge University Press, 1992.

Bury, Robert. Gregg *Plato.* Loeb Classical Library 36. Volume 10. Cambridge and London: Harvard University Press, 1926.

Campbell, R. Alastair. 'Does Paul Acquiesce in Divisions at the Lord's Supper'. *Novum Testamentum* 33 (1991): 61–70.

Campenhausen, Hans. *Ecclesiastical Authority and Spiritual Power in the Church of the First Three Centuries.* London: Adam and Charles Black, 1969.

Chester, Stephen J. *Conversion at Corinth. Perspectives on Conversion in Paul's Theology and the Corinthian Church.* London and New York: T&T Clark, 2003.

Chester, Stephen J. 'Divine Madness? Speaking in Tongues in 1 Corinthians 14:23'. *Journal for the Study of the New Testament* 27 (2005): 417–46.

Chow, John K. *Patronage and Power: A Study of Social Networks in Corinth.* Sheffield: JSOT Press, 1992.

Clark, Gillian. *Christianity and Roman Society.* Cambridge: Cambridge University Press, 2004.

Clarke, Andrew D. *Secular and Christian Leadership in Corinth. A Socio-Historical and Exegetical Study of 1 Corinthians 1–6.* Arbeiten zur Geschichte des antiken Judentums und des Urchristentums 18. Leiden, NY, and Köln: Brill, 1993.

Clarke, Andrew D. *Serve the Community of the Church. Christians as Leaders and Ministers.* Grand Rapids, MI: Eerdmans, 2000.

Clarke, Elizabeth A. 'Early Christian Asceticism and Nineteenth-Century Polemics'. *Journal of Early Christian Studies* 17 (2009): 281–307.

Clay, Diskin. *Paradosis and Survival: Three Chapters in the History of Epicurean Philosophy.* Ann Arbor, MI: University of Michigan Press, 1998.

Collins, Raymond F. *First Corinthians.* Collegeville, MN: Liturgical Press, 1999.

Conzelmann, Hans. *An Outline of the Theology of the New Testament.* 2nd edition. New York: Harper & Row, 1969.

Conzelmann, Hans. *1 Corinthians. A Commentary on the First Epistle to the Corinthians* Hermeneia; Philadelphia: Fortress Press, 1975.

Countryman, William L. 'Patrons and Officers in Club and Church'. Pages 135–43 in *Society of Biblical Literature 1977 Seminar Papers.* Edited by Paul J. Achtemeier. Society of Biblical Literature Seminar Ppapers 11. Missoula, MT: Scholars Press, 1977.

Coxe, Arthur Cleveland, ed. *Ante-Nicene Fathers.* 9 Volumes. Buffalo, NY: Christian Literature Company, 1887–1896.

Coxe, Arthur Cleveland. *The Criterion: A Means of Distinguishing Truth from Error, In Questions of the Times. With Four Letters on the Eirenicon of Dr. Pusey.* New York: H.B. Burand; Buffalo, NY: Martin Taylor, 1866.

Coxe, Arthur Cleveland. *Moral Reforms Suggested in a Pastoral Letter with Remarks on Practical Religion.* Philadelphia, PA: J.B. Lippincott and Co., 1869.

Coxe, Arthur Cleveland. *The Vatican Council. A Letter to Pius the Ninth, Bishop of Rome*. London: James Parker and Co., 1870.

Cranfield, C. E. B. *A Critical and Exegetical Commentary on the Epistle to the Romans*. 2 Volumes. ICC. Edinburgh: T&T Clark, 1975–1979.

Creaghan, John S., and A. E. Raubitschek. 'Early Christian Epitaphs from Athens'. *Hesperia* 16 (1947): 1–51.

Crook, Zeba A. *Reconceptualising Conversion: Patronage, Loyalty, and Conversion in the Religions of he Ancient Mediterranean*. Berlin and New York: De Gruyter, 2004.

Cullmann, Oscar. 'The Early Church and the Ecumenical Problem'. *Anglican Theological Review* 40 (1958): 181–9, 294–301.

Cumont, Franz. *Hypsistos*. Supplément à la *Revue de l'instruction publique en Belgique*. Brussels: Polleunis & Ceuterik, 1897.

Danker, Frederick W. *Benefactor: Epigraphic Study of a Graeco-Roman and New Testament Semantic Field*. St. Louis, MO: Clayton, 1982.

Davies, W. D., and D. C. Allison. *The Gospel According to Matthew*. 3 Volumes. ICC. London and New York: T&T Clark, 1988–2004.

De Rossi, Giovanni Battista. *Inscriptiones Christianae urbis Romae septimo saeculo antiquiores*. Rome: Libaria Pontificia, 1822–1894.

De Vos, Craig. *Church and Community Conflicts: The Relationships of the Thessalonian, Corinthian, and Philippian Churches with Their Wider Civic Communities*. Atlanta, GA: Scholars Press, 1999.

Deissmann, Adolf. *Light from the Ancient East: The New Testament illustrated by Recently Discovered Texts of the Greco-Roman World*. Revised edition. London: Hodder and Stoughton, 1927.

Dix, Gregory. *The Shape of the Liturgy*. 2nd edition. London: Dacre Press, 1945.

Donahue, John. *The Roman Community at Table During the Principate*. Ann Arbor: University of Michigan Press, 2004.

Donfried, Karl P. '2 Thessalonians and the Church at Thessalonica'. Pages 128–44 in *Origins and Method: Towards a New Understanding of Judaism and Christianity: Essays in Honour of John C. Hurd*. Edited by Bradley H. McLean. Journal for the Student of the New Testament Supplement Series 86. Sheffield: JSOT Press, 1993.

Downs, David J. *The Offering of the Gentiles. Paul's Collection for Jerusalem in Its Chronological, Cultural, and Cultic Contexts*. Wissenschaftliche Untersuchungen zum Neuen Testament II/248. Tübingen: Mohr Siebeck, 2008.

Drexhage, Hans-Joachim. *Preise, Mieten/Pachten, Kosten und Löhne im römischen Ägypten*. St. Katharinen: Scripta Mercaturae, 1991.

Dunbabin, Katherine M. D. *The Roman Banquet: Images of Conviviality*. New York: Cambridge University Press, 2004.

Duncan-Jones, Richard P. *Structure and Scale in the Roman Economy*. Cambridge: Cambridge University Press, 1990.

Dunn, James D. G. *1 Corinthians*. Sheffield: Sheffield Academic, 1995.

Dunn, James D. G. *Romans*. 2 Volumes. Word Biblical Commentary 38. Dallas: Word, 1988.

Ebel, Eva. *Die Attraktivität früher christlicher Gemeinden: Die Gemeinde von Korinth im Spiegel grichisch-römischer Vereine*. Wissenschaftliche Untersuchungen zum Neuen Testament II/178. Tübingen: J. C. B. Mohr Siebeck, 2004.

234   *Bibliography*

Edgar, C. C. 'Records of a Village Club'. Pages 369–76 in *Raccolta di scritti in onore di Giacomo Lumbroso (1844–1925)*. Pubblicazioni di 'Aegyptus'. Serie scientifica 3. Milan: Aegyptus, 1925.

Eitrem, Samson, and Leiv Amundsen, eds. *Papyri osloenses*. Oslo: J. Dybwad, 1925–.

Engels, Donald. *Roman Corinth: An Alternative Model for the Classical City*. Chicago: University of Chicago, 1990.

Falls, Thomas B. *St. Justin Martyr. Dialogue with Trypho*. Volume 3 of *Selections from the Fathers of the Church*. Washington, DC: Catholic University of America, 2003. 54.

Fee, Gordon D. *The First Epistle to the Corinthians*. New International Commentary on the New Testament. Grand Rapids, MI: Eerdmans, 1987.

Feissel, Denis. 'Notes d'e épigraphie chétienne (II)'. *Bulletin de correspondance hellénique* 101 (1977): 209–28.

Fellmann, Rudolf. 'Der Sabazios-Kult'. Pages 316–40 in *Die orientalischen Religionen im Römerreich*. Edited by Maarten J. Vermaseren. Etudes préliminaires aux religions orientales dans l'Empire romain 93. Leiden: Brill, 1981.

Ferguson, William Scott. 'The Attic Orgeones'. *Harvard Thelogical Review* 37 (1944): 61–140.

Filson, Floyd V. 'The Significance of the Early House Churches'. *Journal of Biblical Literature* 58 (1939): 105–12.

Fitzmyer, Joseph A. *First Corinthians*. Anchor Bible Commentary 32. New Haven and London: Yale University, 2008.

Foucart, Paul. *Des associations religeuses chez les Grecs: thiases, éranes, orgéons, avec le texte des inscriptions rélative à ces associations*. Paris: Klingksieck, 1873.

Forbes, Clarence A. 'Ancient Athletic Guilds'. *Classical Philology* 50 (1955): 238–52.

Foster, Paul. 'Who Wrote 2 Thessalonians: A Fresh Look at an Old Problem'. *Journal for the Study of the New Testament* 35 (2014): 150–75.

Friesen, Steven J. 'Paul and Economics: The Jerusalem Collection as an Alternative to Patronage'. Pages 27–54 in *Paul Unbound: Other Perspectives on the Apostle*. Edited by Mark D. Given. Peabody, MA: Hendrickson, 2010.

Friesen, Steven J. 'Poverty in Pauline Studies: Beyond the So-called New Consensus'. *Journal for the Study of the New Testament* 26 (2004): 323–61.

Friesen, Steven J. 'The Wrong Erastus: Ideology, Archaeology, and Exegesis'. Pages 231–56 in *Corinth in Context: Comparative Studies on Religion and Society*. Edited by Steven J. Friesen, Daniel N. Schowalter, and James C. Walters. Leiden and Boston: Brill, 2010.

Furnish, Victor. *II Corinthians: Translated with Introduction, Notes, and Commentary*. Anchor Bible 32A. Garden City: Doubleday, 1984.

Gäckle, Volker. *Die Starken und die Schwachen in Korinth und in Rom: zu Herkunft und Funktion der Antithese in 1 Kor 8,1–11,1 und in Rom 14,1–15,13*. Tübingen: Mohr Siebeck, 2005.

Garnsey, Peter. *Cities, Peasants, and Food in Classical Antiquity: Essays in Social and Economic History*. Cambridge and New York: Cambridge University Press, 1998.

Garnsey, Peter. *Food and Society in Classical Antiquity*. Cambridge: Cambridge University Press, 1999.

Garnsey, Peter, and Greg Woolf. 'Patronage of the Rural Poor in the Roman World'. Pages 153–70 in *Patronage in Ancient Society*. Edited by Andrew Wallace-Hadrill. London: Routledge, 1989.

Gehring, Roger W. *House Church and Mission. The Importance of Household Structures in Early Christianity*. Peabody, MA: Hendrickson, 2004.

Gielen, Marlis. 'Zur Interpretation der paulinischen Formel ἡ κατ᾽ οἶκον ἐκκλησία'. *Zeitschrift für die neutestamentliche Wissenschaft* 77 (1986): 109–25.

Goodrich, John. 'Erastus, Quaestor of Corinth: The Administrative Rank of ὁ οἰκονόμος τῆς πόλεως (Rom 16.23) in an Achaean Colony'. *New Testament Studies* 56 (2010): 90–115.

Goodrich, John Kenneth. *Paul, the Oikonomos of God: Paul's Apostolic Metaphor in 1 Corinthians and Its Greco-Roman Context*. PhD Diss., Durham University, 2010.

Grenfell, Bernard P., Arthur S. Hunt, and J. Gilbart Smyly, eds. *Tebtunis Papyri*. Cambridge: Cambridge University Press, 1902–1938.

Gutsfeld, Andreas, and Dietrich-Alex Koch, eds. *Vereine, Synagogen und Gemeinden in kaiserzeitlichen Kleinasien*. Studien und Texte zu Antike und Christentum 25. Tübingen: Mohr Siebeck, 2006.

Hanges, James C. '1 Corinthians 4:6 and the Possibility of Written Bylaws in the Corinthian Church'. *Journal of Biblical Literature* 117 (1998): 275–98.

Hansen, Mogens Herman, and Thomas Heine Nielsen. *An Inventory of Archaic and Classical Poleis*. Oxford and New York: Oxford University Press, 2004.

Harl, Kenneth W. *Coinage in the Roman Economy, 300 B.C. to A.D. 700*. Baltimore: Johns Hopkins University Press, 1996.

Harland, Philip A. *Associations, Synagogues, and Congregations. Claiming a Place in Ancient Mediterranean Society*. Minneapolis, MN: Fortress, 2003.

Harland, Philip A. *Dynamics of Identity in the World of the Early Christians. Associations, Judeans, and Cultural Minorities*. New York and London: T&T Clark, 2009.

Harnack, Adolf. *The Expansion of Christianity in the First Three Centuries*. 2 Volumes. New York: Putnam's Sons, 1904–1905.

Harrison, James R. 'The Brothers as the "Glory of Christ" (2 Cor 8:23) Paul's *Doxa* Terminology in Its Ancient Benefaction Context.' *Novum Testamentum* 52 (2010): 156–88.

Harrison, James R. *Paul's Language of Grace in Its Graeco-Roman Context*. Wissenschaftliche Untersuchungen zum Neuen Testament II/172. Tübingen: Mohr Siebeck, 2003.

Hatch, Edwin. 'Ordination'. Pages 1501–20 in *Dictionary of Christian Antiquities Comprising the History, Institutions, and Antiquities of the Christian Church from the Time of the Apostles to the Age of Charlemagne*. Edited by W. Smith and S. Cheetham. 2 Volumes. London: J. Murray, 1908.

Hatch, Edwin. *The Organization of the Early Christian Churches: Eight Lectures Delivered before the University of Oxford in the Year 1880 on the Foundation of the Late John Bampton*. London: Rivingtons, 1881.

Heinrici, Georg. 'Die Christengemeinden Korinths und die religiösen Genossenschaften der Griechen'. *Zeitschrift für wissenschaftliche Theologie* 19 (1876): 465–526.

Héring, Jean. *The First Epistle of St. Paul to the Corinthians*. London: Epworth, 1962.

Hicks, Edward L. 'Inscriptions from Eastern Cilicia'. *The Journal of Hellenic Studies* 11 (1890): 236–54.

Hodges, Charles. *1 Corinthians*.Wheaton: Crossway Books, 1995.

Holl, Karl. *Gesammelte Aufsätze zur Kirchengeschichte*. 2 Volumes. Tübingen: J. C. B. Mohr, 1928–1932.

Holmberg, Bengt. *Paul and Power: The Structure of Authority in the Primitive Church as Reflected in the Pauline Epistles*. Philadelphia: Fortress, 1980.

Horsley, Richard A. *1 Corinthians*. Nashville: Abingdon, 1998.

Horsley, Richard A. '1 Corinthians: A Case Study of Paul's Assembly as an Alternative Society'. Pages 371–95 in *Urban Religion in Roman Corinth. Interdisciplinary Approaches*. Edited by Daniel N. Schowalter and Steven J. Friesen. Harvard Theological Studies 53. Cambridge: Harvard University Press, 2005.

Horsley, Richard A. *Paul and Empire. Religion and Power in Roman Imperial Society*. Harrisburg, PA: Trinity Press International, 1997.

Horrell, David. 'Domestic Space and Christian Meetings at Corinth: Imagining New Contexts and the Buildings East of the Theatre'. *New Testament Studies* 50 (2004): 349–69.

Horrell, David. 'Paul's Collection: Resources for a Materialist Theology'. *Epworth Review* 22 (1995): 74–83.

Horrell, David. *The Social Ethos of the Corinthian Correspondence: Interests and Ideology from 1 Corinthains to 1 Clement*. Edinburgh: T&T Clark, 1996.

Hughes, Dennis D. 'Hero Cult, Heroic Honors, Heroic Dead: Some Developments in the Hellenistic and Roman Periods'. Pages 167–75 in *Ancient Greek Hero Cult: Proceedings of the Fifth International Seminar on Ancient Greek Cult, Organized by the Department of Classical Archaeology and Ancient History, Göteborg University, 21–23 April 1995*. Edited by Robin Hägg. Stockholm: Svenska Institutet i Athen, 1999.

Jeremias, Joachim. *Unknown Sayings of Jesus*. 2nd edition. London: SCM, 1964.

Jewett, Robert. *Romans: A Commentary*. Hermeneia; Minneapolis, MN: Fortress Press, 2007.

Jewett, Robert. 'Tenement Churches and Communal Meals in the Early Church: The Implications of a Form-Critical Analysis of 2 Thessalonians 3:10'. *Revue Biblique* 38 (1993): 23–43.

Johnson, Allan Chester. *Roman Egypt to the Reign of Diocletian*. Volume 2 of *An Economic Survey of Ancient Rome*. Baltimore: The Johns Hopkins Press, 1936.

Johnson Hodge, Caroline. 'Married to an Unbeliever: Households, Hierarchies, and Holiness in 1 Corinthians 7:12–16'. *Harvard Theological Review* 103 (2010): 1–25.

Jones, Arnold Hugh Martin. 'The Election of the Metropolitan Magistrates in Egypt'. *Journal of Egyptian Archaeology* 24 (1938): 65–72.

Joshel, Sandra R. *Work, Identity, and Legal Status at Rome: A Study of the Occupational Inscriptions*. Norman, OK: University of Oklahoma Press, 1992.

Joubert, Stephen. *Paul as Benefactor: Reciprocity, Strategy, and Theological Reflection in Paul's Collection*. Wissenschaftliche Untersuchungen zum Neuen Testament II/124. Tübingen: Mohr Siebeck, 2000.

Judge, Edwin A. 'Did the Churches Compete with Cult Groups?' Pages 501–24 in *Early Christianity and Classical Culture: Comparative Studies in Honor of Abraham J. Malherbe*. Edited by John T. Fitzgerald, Thomas H. Olbricht, and L. Michael White. Supplements to Novum Testamentum 110. Leiden: Brill, 2003.

Judge, Edwin A. The *Social Pattern of the Christian Groups in the First Century: Some Prolegomena to the Study of New Testament Ideas of Social Obligation*. London: Tyndale Press, 1960.

Judge, Edwin A. 'What Makes a Philosophical School?' Pages 1–5 in *New Documents Illustrating Early Christianity 10*. Edited by Stephen R. Llewelyn and Jim R. Harrison. Grand Rapids, MI: Eerdmans, 2012.

Jülicher, Adolf. *Der Brief an die Römer*.Die Schriften des Neuen Testaments 2. Göttingen: Vandenhoeck und Ruprecht, 1917. Pages 223–335.

Kautsky, Karl. *Der Ursprung des Christentus*. Hannover: J.H.W. Dietz, 1910.

Kayser, François. *Recueil des inscriptions grecques et latines, non funéraires, d'Alexandrie imperial: Ier-IIIe s, apr. J.-C.* Cairo: Institut français d'archéologie orientale du Caire, 1994.

Kent, John Harvey. *Corinth: Results of Excavations. The Inscriptions 1926–1950*. Volume 8/3. American School of Classical Studies at Athens. Cambridge, MA: Harvard University Press, 1966.

Klauck, Hans Josef. *Hausgemeinde und Hauskirche im frühen Christentum*. Stuttgarter Bibelstudien 103. Stuttgart: Katholisches Bibelwerk, 1981.

Klinghardt, Matthias. *Gemeinschaftsmahl und Mahlgemeinschaft. Soziologie und Liturgie frühchristlicher Mahlfeiern*. Texte und Arbeiten zum neutestamentlichen Zeitalter 13. Tübingen: Franke, 1996.

Klinghardt, Matthias. 'The Manual of Discipline in the Light of Statues of Hellenistic Associations'. Pages 251–70 in *Methods of Investigation of the Dead Sea Scrolls and the Khirbet Qumran Site: Present Realities and Future Prospects*. Edited by Michael O. Wise, Norman Golb, John J. Colllins, and Dennis G. Pardee. Annals of the New York Academy of Sciences 722. New York: New York Academy of Sciences, 1994.

Kloppenborg, John S. 'Associations and their Meals'. Paper presented at the annual meeting of the SBL. Chicago, IL, 18 November 2012.

Kloppenborg, John S. 'Collegia and *Thiasoi*: Issues in Function, Taxonomy and Membership'. Pages 16–30 in *Voluntary Associations in the Graeco-Roman World*. Edited by John S. Kloppenborg and Steven G. Wilson. London and New York: Routledge, 1996.

Kloppenborg, John S. 'Disaffiliation in Associations and the ἀποσυναγωγός of John'. *HTS Teologiese Studies/Theological Studies* 67 (2011): 1–16.

Kloppenborg, John S. 'Edwin Hatch, Churches and *Collegia*'. Pages 212–38 in *Origins and Method: Towards a New Understanding of Judaism and Christianity. Essays in Honour of John C. Hurd*. Edited by Bradley H. McLean. Journal for the Study of the New Testament: Supplement Series 86. Sheffield: JSOT Press, 1993.

Kloppenborg, John S. 'Egalitarianism in the Myth and Rhetoric of Pauline Churches'. Pages 247–63 in *Reimagining Christian Origins: A Colloquium Honouring Burton L. Mack*. Edited by Elizabeth A. Castelli and Hal Taussig. Valley Forge, PA.: Trinity Press International, 1996.

238   *Bibliography*

Kloppenborg, John S. 'Greco-Roman *Thiasoi*, The *Ekklēsia* at Corinth, and Conflict Management'. Pages 187–218 in *Redescribing Paul and the Corinthians*. Early Christianity and Its Literature 5. Edited by Ron Cameron and Merrill P. Miller. Atlanta: Society of Biblical Literature, 2011.

Kloppenborg, John S. 'Membership Practices in Pauline Christ Groups'. *Early Christianity* 4 (2013): 183–215.

Kloppenborg, John S. 'The Moralizing of Discourse in Graeco-Roman Associations'. Pages 215–28 in *'The One Who Sows Bountifully': Essays in Honor of Stanley K. Stowers*. Edited by Caroline Johnson Hodge, Saul M. Olyan, Daniel Ullucci, and Emma Wasserman. Brown Judaic Studies 356. Providence, Rhode Island: Brown Judaic Studies, 2013.

Kloppenborg, John S. 'Pneumatic Democracy and the Conflict in *1 Clement*'. Pages 61–81 in *Early Christian Communities Between Ideal and Reality*. Edited by Mark Grundeken and Joseph Verheyden. Wissenschaftliche Untersuchungen zum Neuen Testament I/342. Tübingen: Mohr Siebeck, 2015.

Kloppenborg, John S. 'Precedence at the Communal Meal in Corinth'. Paper presented at the annual meeting of the SNTS. Seged, Hungard, 2014.

Kloppenborg, John S., and Richard S. Ascough, eds. *Attica, Central Greece, Macedonia, Thrace*. Volume 1 of *Greco-Roman Associations: Texts, Translations, and Commentary*. Berlin and New York: W. de Gruyter, 2011.

Kloppenborg, John S., and Stephen G. Wilson, eds. *Voluntary Associations in the Graeco-Roman World*. London and New York: Routledge, 1996.

Knudtzon, Erik Johan. *Bakchiastexte und andere Papyri der Lunder Papyrussammlung*. 4th *volume of Aus der Papyrussammlung der Universitätsbibliothek in Lund*. Lund: Hakan Ohlssons Boktryckeri, 1946.

Kornemann, Ernst. 'Collegium', *Paulys Realencyclopädie der classischen Altertumswissenschaft* 4 (1901): 380–479.

Kraabel, A.Thomas. 'Paganism and Judaism: The Sardis Evidence'. Pages 13–33 in *Paganisme, Judaïsme, Christianisme. Influences et affrontements dans le monde antique. Mélanges offerts à Marcel Simon*. Edited by André Benoit, Marc Philonenko, and Cyrille Vogel. Paris: Boccard, 1978.

Kraus, Thomas. '"Uneducated", "Ignorant", or even 'Illiterate'? Aspects and Background for an Understanding of ΑΓΡΑΜΜΑΤΟΙ (and ΙΔΙΩΤΑΙ) in Acts 4.13'. *New Testament Studies* 45 (1999): 434–49.

Kreinecker, Christina M. *2. Thessaloniker*. Papyrologische Kommentare zum Neuen Testament 3. Göttingen: Vandenhoeck & Ruprecht, 2010.

Kümmel, Werner Georg. *The New Testament: The History of the Investigation of Its Problems*. Nashville, TN: Abingdon, 1972.

Lampe, Peter. 'The Corinthian Eucharistic Dinner Party: Exegesis of a Cultural Context (1 Cor 11:17–34)'. *Affirmation* 4 (1991): 1–15.

Lampe, Peter. 'Das korinthinische Herrenmahl im Schnittpunkt hellenistisch-römischer Mahlpraxis und paulinischer Theologia Crucis (1 Kor 11,17–34)'. *Zeitschrift für die neutestamentliche Wissenschaft* 82 (1991): 183–212.

Lampe, Peter. *From Paul to Valentinus: Christians at Rome in the First Two Centuries*. Minneapolis, MN: Fortress, 2003.

Lane, Eugene N. 'Sabazius and the Jews in Valerius Maximus: A Re-examination'. *Journal of Roman Studies* 69 (1979): 35–8.

Lang, Friedrich. *Die Briefe an die Korinther*. Neue Testament deutsch 7. Göttingen and Züruck: Vandenhoeck & Ruprecht, 1994.

La Piana, George. 'Foreign Groups in Rome during the First Centuries of the Empire'. *Harvard Thelogical Review* 20 (1927): 183–403.

Last, Richard. 'The Election of Officers in the Corinthian Christ-Group'. *New Testament Studies* 59 (2013): 365–81.

Last, Richard. 'The Myth of Free Membership in Pauline Groups' (forthcoming).

Last, Richard, and Sarah E. Rollens. 'Accounting Practices in *P.Tebt.* III/2 894 and Pauline Groups'. *Early Christianity* 5 (2014): 441–74.

Le Guen, Brigitte. 'L'association des technites d'Athènes ou les resorts d'une cohabitation réussie'. Pages 339–64 in *Individus, groups et politique à Athènes de Solon à Mithridate*. Edited by Jean-Christophe Couvenhes. Perspectives Historiques 15. Tours: Presses Universitairres François Rabelais, 2007.

Leiwo, Martti. 'Religion, or Other Reasons? Private Associations in Athens'. Pages 103–17 in *Early Hellenistic Athens: Symptoms of a Change*. Edited by Jaakko Frösén. Papers and Monographs of the Finnish Institute at Athens. Helsinki: Finnish Institute at Athens, 1997.

Levine, Lee I. *The Ancient Synagogue: The First Thousand Years*. New Haven: Yale University Press, 2000.

Levinskaya, Irina. *The Book of Acts in Its Diaspora Setting*. Volume 5 of *The Book of Acts in Its First Century Setting*. Grand Rapids, MI: Eerdmans, 1996.

Lewis, Naphteli, and Meyer Reinhold. *Roman Civilization*. 2 volumes. New York: Harper and Row, 1966.

Liddell, Henry Stuart, and Robert Scott. *A Greek-English Lexicon*. Revised edition. Oxford: Clarendon Press, 1940.

Lietzmann, Hans. *An die Römer*. Handbuch zum Neuen Testament 8. Tübingen: Mohr Siebeck, 1928.

Lietzmann, Hans, with W. G. Kummel. *An die Korinther I/II*. 5th edition. Handbuch zum Neuen Testament 9. Tübingen: Mohr Siebeck, 1969.

Lieu, Judith. 'Charity in Early Christian Thought and Practice'. Pages 13–20 in *The Kindness of Strangers: Charity in the Pre-Modern Mediterranean*. Edited by Dionysios Stathakopoulos. CHS Occasional Publications. London: King's College London, 2007.

Lifshitz, B. *Donateurs et fondateurs dans les synagogues juives*. Paris: Gabalda, 1967.

Lincoln, Bruce. *Gods and Demons, Priests and Scholars: Critical Explorations in the History of Religions*. Chicago: University of Chicago Press, 2012.

Lindemann, Andreas. *Der Erste Korintherbrief*. Handbuch zum Neuen Testament 9/1. Tübingen: Mohr, 2000 [1945–1947].

Liu, Jinyu. *Collegia Centonariorum. The Guilds of Textile Dealers in the Roman West*. Columbia Studies in the Classical Tradition 34. Leiden and Boston: Brill, 2009.

Liu, Jinyu. 'The Economy of Endowments: the case of Roman associations'. Pages 231–56 in *'Pistoi dia tèn technèn'. Bankers, loans and archives in the Ancient World. Studies in honour of Raymond Bogaert*. Edited by Koenraad Verboven, Katelijn Vandorpe, and Véronique Chankowski-Sable. Studia Hellenistica 44. Leuven: Peeters, 2008.

Liu, Jinyu. *Occupation, Social Organization, and Public Service in the Collegia Centonariorum in the Roman Empire (First Century BC-Fourth Century AD)*. PhD Diss.; Columbia University, 2004.

Liu, Jinyu. 'Pompeii and *collegia*: A New Appraisal of the Evidence'. *Ancient History Bulletin* 22 (2008): 53–69.

Llewelyn, Stephen R. 'The Use of Sunday for Meetings of Believers in the New Testament'. *Novum Testamentum* 43 (2001): 205–23.

Llewelyn, Stephen R., and Jim R. Harrison, *New Documents Illustrating Early Christianity.* Volume 10 of *New Documents Illustrating Early Christianity. Grand Rapids.* Michigan: Eerdmans, 2012.

Lohmeyer, Ernst. *Der Brief an die Philipper.* Göttingen: Vandenhoeck, 1928.

Longenecker, Bruce W. *Remember the Poor: Paul, Poverty, and the Greco-Roman World.* Grand Rapids, MI and Cambridge: Eerdmans, 2010.

MacDonald, Margaret Y. *The Pauline Churches: A Socio-Historical Study of Institutionalization in the Pauline and Deutero-Pauline Writings.* Society for New Testament Studies Monograph Series 60. Cambridge and New York: Cambridge University Press, 1988.

MacDowell, Douglas Maurice. *The Law in Classical Athens.* Ithaca: Cornell University, 1978.

Mack, Burton L. 'On Redescribing Christian origins'. *Method and Theory in the Study of Religion* 8 (1996): 247–69.

Malherbe, Abraham J. *Social Aspects of Early Christianity.* 2nd edition. Philadelphia: Fortress Press, 1983.

Malina, Bruce J. *The New Testament World: Insights from Cultural Anthropology.* Atlanta, GA: John Knox Press, 1981.

Marshall Fraser, Peter. *Ptolemaic Alexandria.* Oxford: Clarendon Press, 1972.

Martin, Dale B. *The Corinthian Body.* New Haven: Yale University Press, 1995.

Mason, Steve N. '*Philosophiai*: Greco-Roman, Jewish, and Christian'. Pages 31–58 in *Voluntary Associations in the Graeco-Roman World.* Edited by John S. Kloppenborg and Steven G. Wilson. London and New York: Routledge, 1996.

Mayerson, Philip. 'The Monochoron and Dichoron: Standard Measures of Wine Based on the Oxyrhynchition'. *Zeithschrift für Papyrologie und Epigraphik* 131 (2000): 169–72.

McLean, Bradley H. 'The Agrippinilla Inscription: Religious Associations and Early Church Formation'. Pages 239–70 in *Origins and Method: Towards a New Understanding of Judaism and Christianity. Essays in Honour of John C. Hurd.* Edited by Bradley H. McLean. Journal for the Study of the New Testament: Supplement Series 86. Sheffield: JSOT Press, 1993.

McLean, Bradley H. *An Introduction to Greek Epigraphy of the Hellenistic and Roman Periods from Alexander the Great down to the Reign of Constantine (323 B.C.–A.D. 337).* Ann Arbor, MI: University of Michigan Press, 2002.

McRae, Rachel M. 'Eating with Honor: The Corinthian Lord's Supper in Light of Voluntary Association Meal Practices'. *Journal of Biblical Literature* 130 (2011): 165–81.

Meeks, Wayne A. *The First Urban Christians: The Social World of the Apostle Paul.* 2nd edition. New Haven: Yale University Press, 2003 [1983].

Meggitt, Justin J. *Paul, Poverty and Survival.* Edinburgh: T&T Clark, 1998.

Meritt, Benjamin Dean. *Corinth: Results of Excavations. Greek Inscriptions 1896–1927.* Volume 8/1. American School of Classical Studies at Athens. Cambridge, MA: Harvard University Press, 1931.

Mitchell, Alan C. 'Rich and Poor in the Courts of Corinth: Litigiousness and Status in 1 Corinthians 6:1–11'. *New Testament Studies* 39 (1993): 562–86.

Mitchell, Margaret M. *Paul and the Rhetoric of Reconciliation. An Exegetical Investigation of the Language and Composition of 1 Corinthians.* Louisville: Westminster/John Knox, 1992.

Mommsen, Theodor. *De Collegis et sodaliciis romanorum.* Kiliae: Libraria Schwersiana, 1843.

Monson, Andrew. 'The Ethics and Economics of Ptolemaic Religious Associations'. *Ancient Society* 36 (2006): 221–36.

Moo, Douglas J. *The Epistle to the Romans.* New International Commentary on the New Testament. Grand Rapids, MI: Eerdmans, 1996.

Munck, Johannes. *Paul and the Salvation of Mankind.* Atlanta: John Knox, 1959.

Murphy-O'Connor, Jerome. 'Lots of God-Fearers? Theosebeis in the Aphrodisias Inscription'. *Biblique Revue* 99 (1992): 418–24.

Murphy-O'Connor, Jerome. *St. Paul's Corinth. Texts and Archaeology.* Good News Studies 6. Wilmington, DE: Michael Glazier, 1983.

Nielsen, Thomas Heine, et al. 'Athenian Grave Monuments and Social Class'. *Greek, Roman, and Byzantine Studies* 30 (1989): 411–20.

Nock, Arthur Darby. *Conversion. The Old and the New in Religion from Alexander the Great to Augustine of Hippo.* Oxford: Clarendon Press, 1933.

Nolan, Brian T. 'Inscribing Costs at Athens in the Fourth Century B.C'. Ph.D. Diss., Ohio State University, 1981.

Noy, David. *Foreigners at Rome: Citizens and Strangers.* London: Gerald Duckworth, 2000.

Noy, David, Alexander Panayotov, and Hanswulf Bloedhorn, eds. *Inscriptiones Judaicae Orientis I: Eastern Europe.* Texts and Studies in Ancient Judaism 101. Tübingen: J. C. B. Mohr [Paul Siebeck], 2004.

Oakes, Peter. 'Methodological Issues in Using Economic Evidence in Interpretation of Early Christian Texts'. Pages 9–34 in *Engaging Economics: New Testament Scenarios and Early Christian Reception.* Edited by Bruce W. Longenecker and Kelly D. Liebengood. Grand Rapids, MI: Eerdmans, 2009.

Oakes, Peter. *Reading Romans in Pompeii: Paul's Letter at Ground Level.* Minneapolis, MN: Fortress; London: SPCK, 2009.

Ogereau, Julien M. *Paul's Koinonia with the Philippians: A Socio-historical Investigation of a Pauline Economic Partnership.* Wissenschaftliche Untersuchungen zum Neuen Testament II/377. Tübingen: Mohr Siebeck, 2014.

Öhler, Markus. 'Antikes Vereinswesen'. Pages 79–86 in *Neues Testament und antike Kultur II: Familie, Gesellschaft, Wirtschaft.* Edited by Kurt Scherberich. Neukirchen-Vluyn: Neukirchener, 2005.

Öhler, Markus. 'Das ganze Haus. Antike Alltagsreligiosität und die Apostelgeschichte'. *Zeitschrift für die neutestamentliche Wissenschaft* 102 (2011): 201–34.

Öhler, Markus. 'Iobakchen und Christusverehrer: Das Christentum im Rahmen des antiken Vereinswesens'. Pages 63–86 in *Inkulturation: Historische Beispiele und theologische Reflexionen zur Flexibilität und Widerständigkeit des Christlichen.* Edited by Rupert Klieber and Martin Stowasser. Theologie Forschung und Wissenschaft 10. Vienna: LIT, 2004.

Økland, Jorunn. *Women in Their Place: Paul and the Corinthian Discourse of Gender and Sanctuary Space*. Journal for the Study of the New Testament: Supplement Series 269. London: T&T Clark, 2004.

Origen, *Commentary on the Epistle to the Romans*. 2 Volumes. The Fathers of the Church 104. Translated by Thomas P. Scheck. Washington, DC: The Catholic University of America Press, 2002.

Osiek, Carolyn, and Margaret Y. MacDonald, with Janet H. Tulloch. *A Woman's Place: House Churches in Earliest Christianity*. Minneapolis, MN: Augsburg Fortress, 2006.

Otto, Walter. *Priester und Tempel im hellenistischen Ägypten: Ein Beitrag zur Kulturgeschichte des Hellenismus*. 2 Volumes. Leipzig and Berlin: Teubner, 1905.

Parker, Robert. *Athenian religion. A History*. Oxford: Clarendon, 1996.

Patterson, John R. *Landscapes and Cities: Rural Settlement and Civic Transformation in Early Imperial Italy*. Oxford: Oxford University Press, 2006.

Paulsen, Henning. 'Schisma und Häresie. Untersuchungen zu 1 Kor 11:18, 19'. *Zeitschrift für Theologie und Kirche* 79 (1982): 180–211.

Perkins, Pheme. *First Corinthians*. Paideia Commentaries on the New Testament. Grand Rapids, MI: BakerAcademic, 2012.

Pilhofer, Peter. *Die frühen Christen und ihre Welt: Greifswalder Aufsätze 1996–2001*. Wissenschaftliche Untersuchungen zum Neuen Testament II/145. Tübingen: Mohr Siebeck, 2002.

Pilhofer, Peter. *Philippi. Der erste christliche Gemeinde Europas*. Wissenschaftliche Untersuchungen zum Neuen Testament I/87. Tübingen: Mohr Siebeck, 1995.

Pleket, Henry W. 'Some Aspects of the History of Athletic Guilds'. *Zeitschrift für Papyrologie und Epigraphik* 10 (1973): 197–227.

Poland, Franz. *Geschichte des griechischen Vereinswesens*. Leipzig: Teubner, 1909.

Pollock, Sheldon. 'Comparison without Hegemony'. Pages 185–204 in *The Benefit of Broad Horizons. Intellectual and Institutional Preconditions for a Global Social Science. Festschrift for Björn Wittrock on the Occasion of his 65th Birthday*. Edited by Hans Joas and Barbro Klein. Leiden and Boston: Brill, 2010.

Pucci Ben Zeev, Miriam. *Jewish Rights in the Roman World: The Greek and Roman Documents Quoted by Josephus Flavius*. Texte und Studien zum antiken Judentum 74. Tübingen: Mohr Siebeck, 1998.

Radt, Wolfgang. *Pergamon: Geschichte und Bauten einer antiken Metropole*. Darmstadt: Primus, 1999.

Rajak, Tessa. 'Synagogue and Community in the Graeco-Roman Diaspora'. Pages 22–39 in *Jews in the Hellenistic and Roman Cities*. Edited by John R. Bartlett. London and New York: Routledge, 2002.

Rajak, Tessa. 'Was There a Roman Charter for the Jews?' *Journal of Roman Studies* 74 (1984): 107–23.

Rathbone, Dominic. *Economic Rationalism and Rural Society in Third-Century AD Egypt: The Heroninos Archive and the Appianus Estate*. Cambridge and New York: Cambridge University Press, 1991.

Reekmans, Tony. 'Monetary History and the Dating of Ptolemaic Papyri'. *Studia Hellenistica* 5 (1948): 15–43.

Reekmans, Tony. 'The Ptolemaic Copper Inflation'. Pages 61–118 in *Ptolemaica*. Edited by E. van 'T Dack and Tony Reekmans. Studia Hellenistica 7. Leiden: Brill, 1951.

Reynolds, Joyce Maire and Robert Tannenbaum. *Jews and Godfearers at Aphrodisias. Greek Inscriptions with Commentary: Texts from the Excavations at Aphrodisas*. Cambridge: Cambridge Philological Society, 1987.

Richardson, Peter G. 'An Architectural Case for Synagogues as Associations'. Pages 90–117 in *The Ancient Synagogue from Its Origins Until 200 C.E.: Papers Presented at an International Conference at Lund University October 14–17, 2001*. Edited by Birger Olson and Magnus Zetterholm. Coniectanea biblica New Testament series 39. Stockholm: Almqvist and Wiksell, 2003.

Richardson, Peter G. 'Early Synagogues as Collegia in the Diaspora and Palestine'. Pages 90–109 in *Voluntary Associations in the Graeco-Roman World*. Edited by John S. Kloppenborg and Stephen G. Wilson. London and New York: Routledge, 1996.

Roberts, Colin, Thodore C. Skeat, and Arthur Darby Nock, 'The Gild of Zeus Hypsistos'. *Harvard Theological Review* 29 (1936): 39–88.

Robertson, Archibald, and Alfred Plummer. *1 Corinthians*. Edinburgh: T&T Clark, 1911.

Rordorf, Willy. *Sunday, The History of the Day of Rest and Worship in the Earliest Centuries of the Christian Church*. London: SCM Press, 1968.

Rossi, Giovanni Battista de. *Inscriptiones Christianae urbis Romae septimo saeculo antiquiores*. Rome: Libaria Pontificia, 1822–1894.

Royden, Halsey L. *The Magistrates of the Roman Professional Collegia in Italy: From the First to the Third Century A.D. Bibliotheca di studi antichi 61*. Pisa: Giardini, 1988.

Ruggini, Lelia. 'Ebrei e orientali nell'Italia settentrionale fra il IV e il VI secolo'. *Studia et documenta historiae et iuris* 25 (1959): 186–308.

Runesson, Anders. *Origins of the Synagogue: A Socio-Historical Study*. Coniectanea biblica New Testament series 37. Stockholm: Almqvist & Wiksell, 2001.

Runesson, Anders. 'The Origins of the Synagogue in Past and Present Research – Some Comments on Definitions, Theories, and Sources'. *Studia Theologica* 57 (2003) 60–76.

Runesson, Anders, Donald D. Binder, and Birger Olsson. *The Ancient Synagogue from Its Origins to 200 C.E. A Source Book*. Arbeiten zur Geschichte des antiken Judentums und des Urchristentums 72. Leiden and Boston: Brill, 2008.

Russell, Ronald. 'The Idle in 2 Thess 3.6–12: An Eschatological or a Social Problem?' *New Testament Studies* 34 (1988): 101–19.

Sanday, William. *A Critical and Exegetical Commentary on the Epistle to the Romans*. New York: C. Scribner's Sons, 1923.

Sandnes, Karl Olav. 'The Role of the Congregation as a Family within the Context of Recruitment and Conflict in the Early Church'. Pages 333–45 in *Recruitment, Conquest, and Conflict: Strategies in Judaism, Early Christianity, and the Greco-Roman World*. Edited by Peder Borgen, Vernon K. Robbins, and David B. Gowler. Atlanta, GA: Scholars Press, 1998.

Sanday, William. 'The Origin of the Christian Ministry II'. *The Expositor* 3.5 (1887): 97–114.

Sanders, Guy R. D. 'Landlords and Tenants: Sharecroppers and Subsistence Farming in Corinthian Historical Context'. Pages 103–26 in *Corinth in Contrast: Studies in Inequality*. Edited by Steven J. Friesen, Sarah A. James, and Daniel N. Schowalter. Supplements to Novum Testamentum 155. Leiden: Brill, 2014.

San Nicolò, Mariano. *Ägyptisches Vereinswesen zur Zeit der Ptolemäer und Römer*. 2 Volumes. Münchener Beiträge zur Papyrusforschung und antiken Rechtsgeschichte 2. Munich: Berk, 1972.

Scheidel, Walter, and Steven J. Friesen. 'The Size of the Economy and the Distribution of Income in the Roman Empire'. *Journal of Roman Studies* 99 (2009): 61–91.

Schmeller, Thomas. *Hierarchie und Egalität: eine sozialgeschichtliche Untersuchung paulinischer Gemeinden und griechisch-römischer Vereine*. Stuttgart: Verlag Katholisches Bibelwerk, 1995.

Schnabel, Eckhard J. *Der erste Brief des Paulus an die Korinther*. Wuppertal: R. Brockhaus, 2006.

Schöllgen, Georg. 'Was wissen wir über die Sozialstruktur der paulinischen Gemeinden?' *New Testament Studies* 34 (1988): 71–82.

Schowalter, Daniel N. 'Seeking Shelter in Roman Corinth: Archaeology and the Placement of Paul's Communities'. Pages 327–41 in *Corinth in Context: Comparative Studies on Religion and Society*. Edited by Steven J. Friesen, Daniel N. Schowalter, and James Walters. Supplements to Novum Testamentum 134. Leiden: Brill, 2010.

Schrage, Wolfgang. *Der erste Brief an die Korinther*. 4 Volumes. Evangelisch-katholischer Kommentar zum Neuen Testament 7. Neukirchen-Vluyn: Neukirchener Verlag, 1991–2001.

Schuman, Verne B. 'The Seven-Obol Drachma of Roman Egypt', *Classical Philology* 47 (1952): 214–18.

Schüssler Fiorenza, Elizabeth. *In Memory of Her: A Feminist Theological Reconstruction of Christian Origins*. New York: Crossroad, 1983.

Schweizer, Eduard. *Church Order in the New Testament*. London: SCM, 1961.

Sim, David C. *Apocalyptic Eschatology in the Gospel of Matthew*. Cambridge: Cambridge University, 1996.

Smith, Dennis E. *From Symposium to Eucharist: The Banquet in the Early Christian World*. Minneapolis, MN: Fortress Press, 2003.

Smith, Dennis E. 'The House Church as Social Environment'. Pages 3–21 in *Text, Image, and Christians in the Graeco-Roman World. A Festschrift in Honor of David Lee Balch*. Edited by Aliou Cissé and Carolyn Osiek. Princeton Theological Monograph Series. Eugene, OR: Pickwick, 2012.

Smith, Dennis E., and Hal E. Taussig. *Many Tables. The Eucharist in the New Testament and Liturgy Today*. Philadelphia: Trinity, 1990.

Smith, Jonathan Z. *Drudgery Divine: On the Comparison of Early Christianities and the Religions of Late Antiquity*. Jordan Lectures in Comparative Religion 14. London: The School of Oriental and African Studies. Chicago: University of Chicago Press, 1990.

Smith, Kendall K. 'Greek Inscriptions from Corinth II'. *American Journal of Archaeology* 23 (1919): 331–94.

Sohm, Rudolf. *Outlines of Church History*. London and New York: MacMillan and Co., 1895.

Solin, Heikki. *Die griechischen Personennamen in Rom: Ein Namenbuch.* 3 volumes. Berlin: W. de Gruyter, 1982.

Solin, Heikki. *Die stadtrömischen Sklavennamen: Ein Namenbuch.* 3 Volumes. Forschungen zur antiken Sklaverei 2. Stuttgart: Franz Steiner, 1996.

Stählin, Gustav. 'ξένος κτλ.', *TDNT* 5 (1967): 1–36.

Stegemann, Ekkehard W., and Wolfgang Stegemann. *The Jesus Movement: A Social History of Its First Century.* Minneapolis, MN: Fortress Press, 1999.

Still, Todd D., and David G. Horrell, eds. *After the First Urban Christians. The Social-Scientific Study of Pauline Christianity Twenty-Five Years Later.* London: T&T Clark, 2009.

Stock, St. George. 'Hospitality (Greek and Roman)'. Pages 808–12 in Volume 6 of *Encyclopedia of Religion and Ethics.* 12 Volumes. New York: Charles Scribner's Sons, 1908–1922.

Stowers, Stanley K. 'The Concept of 'Community' in the History of Early Christianity'. *Method and Theory in the Study of Religion* 23 (2011): 238–56.

Stowers, Stanley K. 'Does Pauline Christainity Resemble a Hellenistic Philosophy?' Pages 219–43 in *Redescribing Paul and the Corinthians.* Edited by Ron Cameron and Merrill P. Miller. Early Christianity and Its Literature 5. Atlanta: Society of Biblical Literature, 2011.

Stowers, Stanley K. 'Kinds of Myth, Meals, and Power: Paul and the Corinthians'. Pages 105–49 in *Redescribing Paul and the Corinthians.* Early Christianity and Its Literature 5. Atlanta: Society of Biblical Literature, 2011.

Theissen, Gerd. *The Social Setting of Pauline Christianity.* Philadelphia: Fortress, 1982.

Theissen, Gerd. 'The Social Structure of Pauline Communities: Some Critical Remarks on J.J. Meggitt, *Paul, Poverty and Survival*'. *Journal for the Study of the New Testament* 84 (2001): 65–84.

Thiselton, Anthony. *The First Epistle to the Corinthians.* New International Greek Testament Commentary. Grand Rapids: Eerdmans, 2000.

Tran, Nicholas. *Les membres des associations romaines. Le rang social des collegiate en Italie et en Gaules, sous le Haut-Empire.* Rome: École française de Rome, 2006.

Trebilco, Paul R. *Jewish Communities in Asia Minor.* Society for New Testament Studies Monograph Series 69. Cambridge: Cambridge University Press, 1991.

Trümper, Monika. 'Negotiating Religious and Ethnic Identity: The Case of Clubhouses in Late Hellenistic Delos'. *Hephaistos* 24 (2006): 113–40.

Ullucci, Daniel. 'Towards a Typology of Religious Experts in the Ancient Mediterranean'. Pages 89–103 in *'The One Who Sows Bountifully': Essays in Honor of Stanley K. Stowers.* Edited by Caroline Johnson Hodge, Saul M. Olyan, Daniel Ullucci, and Emma Wasserman. Brown Judaic Studies 356. Providence, RI: Brown Judaic Studies, 2013.

Van Nijf, Onno M. *The Civic World of Professional Associations in the Roman East.* Amsterdam: J.C. Gieben, 1997.

Van Nijf, Onno M. '*Collegia* and Civic Guards. Two Chapters in the History of Sociability'. Pages 305–40 in *After the Past: Essays in Ancient History in Honour of H.W. Pleket.* Edited by Willem Jongman and Marc Kleijwegt. Mnemosyne Supplement 233. Leiden: Brill, 2002.

Venticinque, Philip. 'Family Affairs: Guild Regulations and Family Relationships in Roman Egypt'. *Greek, Roman, and Byzantine Studies* 50 (2010): 273–94.

Verboven, Koenraad. 'The Associative Order, Status and Ethos of Roman Businessmen in Late Republic and Early Empire'. *Athenaeum* 95 (2007): 861–93.

Verboven, Koenraad. 'Magistrates, Patrons and Benefactors of Collegia: Status Building and Romanisation in the Spanish, Gallic and German Provinces'. Pages 159–67 in *Transforming Historical Landscapes in the Ancient Empires. Proceedings of the First Workshop Area of Research in Studies from Antiquity, Barcelona 2007*. Edited by I. B. Antela-Bernárdez and T. Ñaco del Hoyo. British Archaeological Reports; International Series 1986. Oxford: John and Erica Hedge, 2009.

Veyne, Paul. *Bread and Circuses: Historical Sociology and Political Pluralism*. London: Penguin, 1990.

Von Reden, Sitta. *Money in Ptolemaic Egypt. From the Macedonian Conquest to the End of the Third Century BC*. Cambridge and New York: Cambridge University Press, 2007.

Von Wilamowitz-Moellendorff, Ulrich. 'Excurs 2: Die rechtliche Stellung der Philosophenschulen'. Pages 263–91 in *Antigonos von Karystos*. Philologische Untersuchungen 4. Berlin: Weidmann, 1881.

Walters, James C. 'Paul and the Politics of Meals in Roman Corinth'. Pages 343–64 in *Corinth in Context: Comparative Studies on Religion and Society*. Edited by Steven J. Friesen, Daniel N. Schowalter, and James C. Walters. Leiden and Boston: Brill, 2010.

Waltzing, Jean-Pierre. *Étude historique sur les corporations professionelles chez les Romains depuis les origines jusqu'à la chute de l'empire d'Occident*. 4 Volumes. Mémoires Couronnés et Autres Mémoires Publié par l'Académie Royale des Sciences, des Lettres et des Beaux-Arts de Belgique 50. Bruxelles: F. Hayez, 1895–1900.

Watts Henderson, Suzanne. '"If Anyone Hungers . . . ": An Integrated Reading of 1 Cor 11.17-34'. *NTS* 48 (2002): 195–208.

Weiss, Alexander. 'Keine Quästoren in Korinth: Zu Goodrichs (und Theißens) These über das Amt des Erastos (Röm 16.23)'. *New Testament Studies* 56 (2010): 576–81.

Weiss, Johannes. *Der Erste Korintherbrief*. Göttingen: Vandenhoeck & Ruprecht, 1910.

Welborn, L. L. *An End to Enmity: Paul and the 'Wrongdoer' of Second Corinthians*. Beihefte zur Zeitschrift für neutestamentliche 185. Berlin: Walter de Gruyter, 2011.

Wendt, Heidi. 'At the Temple Gates: The Religion of Freelance Experts in Early Imperial Rome. Ph.D. Diss., Brown University, 2013.

Wendt, Heidi. '*Iudaica Romana*: A Rereading of Evidence for Judean Expulsions from Rome', *Journal of Ancient Judaism* 6 (forthcoming).

White, L. Michael. *Building God's House in the Roman World: Architectural Adaptation among Pagans, Jews, and Christians*. Volume 1 of *The Social Origins of Christian Architecture*. Harvard Theological Studies 42. Valley Forge, PA: Trinity Press, 1996.

Whitehead, David. 'Cardinal Virtues: The Language of Public Approbation in Democratic Athens'. *Classica et Mediaevelia* 44 (1993): 37–75.

Wilcken, Robert L. 'Collegia, Philosophical Schools, and Theology'. Pages 268–91 in *The Catacombs and the Colosseum: The Roman Empire as the Setting of Primitive Christianity*. Edited by Stephen Benko and John J. O'Rourke. Valley Forge: Judson, 1971.

Will, Ernest. 'Banquets et salles de banquet dans les cultes de la Grèce et de l'Empire romain'. Pages 353–62 in *Mélanges d'histoire ancienne et d'archéologie offerts à Paul Collart*. Edited by Pierre Ducrey. Cahiers d'archéologie romande de la Bibliothèque historique vaudoise 5. Lausanne: Bibliothèque historique vaudoise, 1976.

Winter, Bruce W. *After Paul Left Corinth: The Influence of Secular Ethics and Social Change*. Grand Rapids, MI: Eerdmans, 2001.

Witherington III, Ben. *Conflict and Community in Corinth: A Socio-Rhetorical Commentary on 1 and 2 Corinthians*. Grand Rapids, MI: Eerdmans, 1995.

Woodhead, Geoffrey A. *Inscriptions: The Decrees*. Volume 16 of *The Athenian Agora*. Athens: American School of Classical Studies at Athens, 1997.

Woodthorpe Tarn, William. *Hellenistic Civilization*. New York: Plume, 1974.

Yavetz, Zvi. *Julius Caesar and His Public Image*. Ithaca, NY: Cornell University Press, 1983.

Zahn, Theodor. *Der Brief des Paulus an die Römer*. Kommentar zum Neuen Testament 6. Leipzig: Deichert, 1910.

Ziebarth, Erich. *Das griechische Vereinswesen*. Stuttgart: S. Hirzel, 1969.

INDEX OF ANCIENT SOURCES

Josephus (cont.)
  Ant. 5.243, 69 n. 101
  Ant. 14.110, 36
  Ant. 14.213–16, 27, 34 n. 35
  Ant. 14. 214–15, 31
  Ant. 14.216, 25
  Ant. 14.235, 28
  Ant. 16.164, 29
Justin
  1 Apol. 65–67, 139 n. 78
  1 Apol. 67, 123 n. 37, 219
  Dial. 35.3 187, 222
Juvenal
  1.134, 106 n. 89
  3.283, 106 n. 89
  5.87, 106 n. 89
Lucian
  Lex. 13, 119 n. 22
Lysias
  For Mantitheus 15.6, 194 n. 46
Martial
  13.13.1, 106 n. 89
Origen
  Cels. 3.23, 19
  Comm. Rom. 10.41, 63
Pausanias
  *Descr.*10.12.9, 30
Persius
  Sat. 3.114, 106 n. 89
Philo
  Cherubim 48, 138 n. 76
  Embassy 155, 35
  Embassy 157, 35
  Embassy 271, 138 n. 75
  Good Person 2.13–15, 39 n. 55
  Joseph 201, 195
  Moses 1.58, 69 n. 101
  Moses 1.275, 69 n. 101
  Spec. 1.324–5, 25 n. 8
  Unchangeable 111, 25 n. 8
  Virtues 1.173, 69
Philostratus
  Vit. Apoll. 2.20, 196 n. 53
  Vit. Soph. 524, 41
  Vit. Soph. 533, 41
Plato
  Laws 6.759–760a, 194, 227 n. 27
  Laws 6.759d, 194 n. 46
Plautus
  Poen. 1314, 106 n. 89
  Quaest. Conv. 2.10.1–2, 120
Pliny the Younger
  Ep. 10.96, 19
  Ep. 10.97, 139 n. 78

Plutarch
  Adv. Col. 117d-e, 41 n. 62
Pseudo-Aristotle
  Ath. pol. 3.37, 192, 192 n. 37
  Ath. pol. 26.14, 191 n. 32
  Ath. pol. 31.9–10, 191 n. 32
  Ath. pol. 44.4, 191 n. 32
  Ath. pol. 45.3, 194 n. 46
  Ath. pol. 54.5, 192 n. 34
  Ath. pol. 61.4, 192 n. 34
  Ath. pol. 61.5, 192 n. 34
  Ath. pol. 61.7, 192 n. 34
Pseudo Clement
  Hom. 16.21.4, 187 n. 16
Strabo
  Geography 10.3.10, 39 n. 55
  Geography 17.1.8, 40
Thucydides
  1.17, 196
  8.89, 191
Xenophon
  Anab. 68, 66 n. 95
  Mem. 3.13.2, 138 n. 76
  Mem. 3.14.1, 119 n. 22

Papyri and Ostraka
BGU III 993, 59 n. 67
BGU IV 1074, 171 n. 34
BGU IV 1137, 30 n. 19, 58
BGU VII 1501, 106, 122 n. 35
BGU VII 1506, 106, 122 n. 35
BGU VII 1545, 106, 122 n. 35
CPJ I 138 = *ASSB* 170, 33
CPJ I 139, 31, 112 n. 118
CPJ II 432, 31
CPJ III 456, 31
O.Mich. II 712, 66 n. 99
O.Theb. 142, 95 n. 64
P.Ant. I 38, 196 n. 54
P.Athen. 41, 129, 145, 146 n. 96, 173, 174 n. 44
P.Cair.Dem. 30606 = *AGRW* 299, 174 n. 44
P.Cair.Zen. I 59059, 101 n. 79
P.Cair.Zen. II 59218, 138 n. 75
P.Cair.Zen. IV 59659, 59 n. 67
P.Cair.Zen. IV 59753, 138 n. 75
P.Corn. 22, 66 n. 99
P.Enteux. 32, 138 n. 75
P.Fay. 44, 128 n. 49
P.Fay. 101, 128 n. 49
P.Giss. I 99, 68
P.Hamb. I 114, 101 n. 79
P.Hib. I 51, 95 n. 64

INDEX OF SUBJECTS

Printed in the United States
By Bookmasters